THE ETHNIC MYTH

Books by Stephen Steinberg

WRITING AND THINKING IN THE
SOCIAL SCIENCES   1989
(*with Sharon Friedman*)

THE ETHNIC MYTH   1981

THE ACADEMIC MELTING POT   1974

THE TENACITY OF PREJUDICE   1969
(*with Gertrude Jaeger Selznick*)

STEPHEN STEINBERG

THE ETHNIC MYTH

Race, Ethnicity, and Class in America

Updated and Expanded Edition
with a New Epilogue by the Author

Beacon Press   *Boston*

Beacon Press
25 Beacon Street
Boston, Massachusetts 02108-2800

Beacon Press books
are published under the auspices of
the Unitarian Univeralist Association of Congregations.

96   9 8 7

The table on p. 41 from Richard M. Burkey, *Ethnic and Racial Groups,*
© 1978, is reprinted by permission of The Benjamin/Cummings Publishing Company. Excerpts from the A. Lawrence Lowell presidential
papers are reprinted by permission of Harvard University. A portion
of figure 116 (p. 142) in *Historical Atlas of Religion in America,* rev.
ed. by Edwin Scott Gaustad, is reprinted in p. 19 by permission of
Harper & Row, Publishers, Inc. Chapter 2 of this book is a revision
of an article published in the *International Journal of Group Tensions*
7 (1977):3–4. Parts of Chapters 3, 5, and 9 are adapted from *The
Academic Melting Pot* (McGraw-Hill, 1974; paperback ed. 1977 by
Transaction Books). A shorter version of Chapter 9 also appeared in
Commentary (September 1971).

Library of Congress Cataloging-in-Publication Data
Steinberg, Stephen.
   The ethnic myth : race, ethnicity, and class in America / Stephen
Steinberg. — Updated and expanded ed.
       p.   cm.
   Includes bibliographical references and index.
   ISBN 0-8070-4151-3
   1. United States—Ethnic relations.   2. United States—Race
relations.   3. Minorities—United States—Social conditions.
4. Afro-Americans—Social conditions.   5. Social classes—United
States.   I. Title.
E184.A1S794 1989
305.8'00973—dc20   89-42587

TO SHARON

Acknowledgments

THIS BOOK is a product of fifteen years of teaching and research which have compelled me to reexamine my original assumptions concerning race and ethnicity in American society. A great many colleagues and students have contributed to this reassessment. Especially memorable are the spirited conversations with Joseph Bensman, Sharon Friedman, Gertrude Jaeger, and Benjamin Ringer.

Over these years I have also had the benefit of research grants from the Anti-Defamation League, the Carnegie Commission on Higher Education, the PSC/CUNY Research Award Program, and in 1977, a National Endowment for the Humanities Fellowship for Independent Study and Research. I am grateful to these organizations for their support. Needless to say, responsibility for the views expressed in this book is mine alone.

Judith Greissman helped to bring this book to fruition, and several friends and colleagues—Milton Mankoff, Jon Peterson, and Mary Ryan—read various chapters and gave me valuable criticism. I owe special thanks to my editors at Atheneum—to Tom Stewart for his unflagging support, and to Ileene Smith for editing the manuscript with extraordinary skill and perseverance.

Thanks also to Connie Grover for her expert typing and to Sylvia and Joseph Friedman for their many kindnesses.

Contents

Preface to the Updated Edition   ix
Preface: The Demystification of Ethnicity   xiii
Acknowledgments   xv

PART ONE   THE SIMMERING MELTING POT

Introduction: The New Ethnicity in Historical Perspective   3
Chapter 1.   The Ignominious Origins of Ethnic Pluralism
  in America   5
Chapter 2.   The Ethnic Crisis in American Society   44

PART TWO   SOCIAL CLASS AND ETHNIC MYTHS

Introduction: The New Darwinism   77
Chapter 3.   The Myth of Ethnic Success: The Jewish Horatio
  Alger Story   82
Chapter 4.   The Culture of Poverty Reconsidered   106
Chapter 5.   Education and Ethnic Mobility: The Myth of
  Jewish Intellectualism and Catholic Anti-Intellectualism   128
Chapter 6.   Why Irish Became Domestics and Italians and
  Jews Did Not   151

PART THREE   THE CLASS CHARACTER OF RACIAL
AND ETHNIC CONFLICT

Introduction: The "Iron Law of Ethnicity" Revised   169
Chapter 7.   The Reconstruction of Black Servitude after the
  Civil War   173
Chapter 8.   Racial and Ethnic Conflict in the Twentieth
  Century   201
Chapter 9.   The "Jewish Problem" in American Higher
  Education   222

Chapter 10.   Dilemmas and Contradictions of Ethnic
      Pluralism in America   253

EPILOGUE
Ethnic Heroes and Racial Villains in American
      Social Science   263
Index   303

Preface to the Updated Edition

AUTHORS OF second editions easily fall prey to vanity. It is all too tempting to take stock of the intervening years since the original publication, to marvel at how one's analysis has been sustained by events, and to congratulate oneself on one's prescience and insight. I shall avoid this temptation. If anything, the years since the publication of *The Ethnic Myth* have demonstrated the book's utter failure. Myths and misconceptions about race and ethnicity are no less prevalent now than they were eight years ago. It will take more than an academic treatise—even a score of scholarly works—before this nation is prepared to discard its ethnic heroes and racial villains.

Not even social science is easily jogged from its lamentable proclivity for giving scientific legitimacy to crude popular notions about race, ethnicity, and class. Indeed, in recent years new heroes have been discovered, and a new jargon has been concocted that, when properly decoded, ends up blaming racial victims for their own plight. To oppose these ideological currents is like swimming upstream—one starts out with a burst of energy, makes some headway, but eventually succumbs to the unrelenting downstream force. To think that social science can reverse these powerful ideological

currents would not only be self-deluding, but would also contradict
the central tenet of this book—that ideas have little "life of their
own" independent of the social structures in which they are embedded. It will be possible to dispel myths about race and ethnicity
only when the conditions that produce and nourish these myths are
changed.

Fortunately, we do not need to wait for the millennium to liberate
the mind. So long as we have the capacity to think, and to think
critically, we can experience the transcendental power of ideas. In
this sense, debunking the racial and ethnic myths that pervade our
society can be a liberating experience. At least this is how I hope
readers will respond to this book.

A new edition also provides an opportunity to correct an over-
sight. I neglected to acknowledge a person who had no direct in-
volvement in the book, but who nonetheless had a profound
influence on it. Robert Blauner provided my initiation into the field
of race and ethnic relations during my graduate years at Berkeley
in the 1960s. As a scholar and teacher, Bob developed an eclectic
approach that challenged many of the orthodoxies and assumptions
in the field. He also realized that the Third World groups, active
on the Berkeley campus, represented an important viewpoint previously excluded from mainstream sociology. His book *Racial
Oppression in America* gave serious exposition to many of the ideas
that were emanating from "the movement," within the context of
a sweeping and lucid reappraisal of race history. In my opinion his
work marks the seminal beginning of a revisionist literature with
which I associate this book.

Several individuals contributed to the epilogue for this volume.
Donal Malone assisted in the research and provided valuable feed-
back. Neil McLaughlin and I were not always in agreement, but I
benefited from our spirited debates. Other friends and colleagues—
particularly those in the irascible "Monday lunch group" at Queens
College—also provided both support and criticism. As always, I
have relied on Sharon Friedman for her unique blend of intelligence
and intuition.

It is a pleasure to acknowledge my debt to my students, both at
Queens College and the CUNY Graduate Center. I have benefited
from the rich and diverse experiences that they bring to the classroom, and from the access they give me to spheres far removed

from my personal orbit. Needless to say, we often clashed, but the task of challenging some of their most cherished assumptions has forced me to think through and clarify my own point of view.

Finally, my thanks to my editors at Beacon Press—Joanne Wyckoff and Thomas Fischer—for their enthusiastic support and their editorial judgment.

Preface

———◆———

The Demystification of Ethnicity

I T I S commonplace to think of ethnicity as a phenomenon that belongs to the cultural domain. By its very nature, ethnicity involves ways of thinking, feeling, and acting that constitute the essence of culture. That ethnic groups have unique cultural character can hardly be denied. The problem, however, is that culture does not exist in a vacuum; nor is it fixed or unchanging. On the contrary, culture is in constant flux and is integrally a part of a larger social process. The mandate for social inquiry, therefore, is that ethnic patterns should not be taken at face value, but must be related to the larger social matrix in which they are embedded. Though this principle itself is anything but controversial, its scrupulous application challenges many cherished ideas concerning ethnic phenomena, as will become clear in the pages that follow.

The theoretical perspective that governs this study insists on establishing the social origins of ethnic values and trends. There is nothing in this approach that denies that ethnicity can be a determinant in its own right. Without doubt, ethnicity informs consciousness and influences behavior. But what informs ethnicity and influences *its* character? The tendency in modern social thought has been to treat ethnicity as a given and to explore its consequences. The present study does not deny that ethnic factors can have causal significance, but its main purpose is to explore their historical and structural foundations.

Thus, the title of this book is not meant to convey that ethnicity itself is mythical. Issue arises only when ethnicity is taken out of historical context and assumed to have independent explanatory power. The problem is fundamentally one involving the reification of culture. Reification occurs whenever culture is treated as though it is a thing unto itself, independent of other spheres of life. The reification of ethnic values has made a mystique of ethnicity, creating the illusion that there is something ineffable about ethnic phenomena that does not lend itself to rational explanation. This is especially the case when ethnic groups are assumed to be endowed with a given set of cultural values, and no attempt is made to understand these values in terms of their material sources. Thus, to demystify ethnicity requires an exploration of how social forces influence the form and content of ethnicity; and an examination of the specific relationships between ethnic factors on the one hand, and a broad array of historical, economic, political, and social factors on the other.

This approach is applied to three sets of problems, corresponding to the three parts of the book: (1) the origins of ethnic pluralism in the United States, and the viability of ethnic identities now and in the future; (2) the rates of mobility and success experienced by different ethnic groups; and (3) the social class character of racial and ethnic conflict. In each instance, the thrust of the analysis is to challenge the cultural explanations that have been commonly advanced, by establishing the historical and material bases of the ethnic patterns in question.

PART ONE

THE SIMMERING MELTING POT

Introduction

———◆———

The New Ethnicity in Historical Perspective

T H E L A T E 1960s witnessed an outbreak of what might be called "ethnic fever." One after another, the nation's racial and ethnic minorities sought to rediscover their waning ethnicity and to reaffirm their ties to the cultural past. Ethnic fever had its origins in the black community, where black nationalism, after a long period of quiescence, emerged with renewed force. The contagion rapidly spread to other racial minorities—Chicanos, Puerto Ricans, Asians, Native Americans—who formed a loosely organized coalition under the banner of the Third World. Eventually ethnic fever reached the "white ethnics"—Jews, Irish, Italians, Poles, and others of European ancestry. For decades the dominant tendency among the nation's ethnic and racial minorities had been toward integration into the economic, political, and cultural mainstream. Now the pendulum seemed to be swinging back, as these groups repudiated their assimilationist tendencies. Through art, literature, and politics, they sought to promote ethnic pride and solidarity, and to affirm their right to a separate identity within the framework of a pluralist nation.

Moreover, pluralism, both as a political concept and as a national symbol, has been granted a belated legitimacy. Groups that in recent history were considered pariahs and intruders have been accorded an unprecedented respectability, and in its determination to exorcise the ghosts of nativism, the nation seems to have forsaken notions of Anglo-Saxon supremacy, conceiving of itself instead as a "nation of nations." Exulting in this new climate of tolerance, a number of leading writers both within and outside the university proclaimed that ethnic groups have survived the legendary melting pot, predicting a future in which ethnicity can again flourish.

The trouble with this current celebration of ethnicity is that it ignores the essentially negative basis on which pluralism developed historically. In doing so, it fails to recognize the fragility of ethnic institutions, and it misconstrues the significance of the recent ethnic upsurge.

The chapters that follow attempt to reassess the status of ethnicity in American life. In tracing the "ignominious origins" of ethnic diversity in the United States, Chapter 1 seeks to develop a more realistic, if less sanguine, perspective on ethnic pluralism in America. Chapter 2 then undertakes a broad assessment of contemporary patterns of ethnic life, and on the basis of this assessment, takes a decidedly skeptical view of the so-called ethnic revival of the 1970s. Together these chapters pose the ultimate question: Did the ethnic past establish an adequate basis for ethnic preservation? Or is the melting pot—the obliteration of ethnic groups as distinctive social and cultural entities—an impending reality?

———◆———

Chapter 1

The Ignominious Origins of Ethnic
Pluralism in America

*"If there are sordid, servile, and laborious offices to be
performed, is it not better that there should be sordid,
servile, and laborious beings to fill them?"*

CHANCELLOR WILLIAM HARPER,
A Memoir on Slavery, 1837

ETHNIC PLURALISM in America has its origins in conquest,
slavery, and exploitation of foreign labor. Conquest, first, in the case of
native Americans who were systematically uprooted, decimated and
finally banished to reservation wastelands; and second, in the case
of Mexicans in the Southwest who were conquered and annexed by
an expansionist nation. Slavery, in the case of the millions of Africans who were abducted from their homelands and forced into perpetual servitude on another continent. Exploitation of foreign labor,
in the case of the tens of millions of immigrants who were initially
imported to populate the nation's land mass, and later to provide
cheap labor for industrial development.

To say that ethnic pluralism in America had its origins in conquest, slavery, and exploitation is not to deny that in the course of
American history ethnic diversity has come to assume positive value.
Nor is it to deny that minorities have often reaped the benefits of an
affluent society, notwithstanding the circumstances of their origins.

Nevertheless, it is imperative to come to terms with the essentially negative basis on which pluralism developed. Only in this way is it possible to begin to understand why virtually all the nation's racial and ethnic minorities have confronted intense and virulent bigotry, why all have had to struggle to preserve their ethnic identities and institutions, and why the history of race and ethnicity has been fraught with tension, rivalry, and conflict.

It might be said of the United States that it is a nation without a people. With the notable exception of the American Indian, the American people are not ethnically rooted on American soil. When the first colonial settlements were established in the seventeenth century, the Indian population amounted to roughly 800,000 people. Here was a vast expanse of virginal land—nearly three million square miles—that was virtually unpopulated, a remarkable circumstance that would profoundly influence the course of ethnic history in America.

In contrast to the European colonization of Asia and Africa, there was no large indigenous population that could be exploited by the colonial power. This dearth of population had different implications for the nation at different points in its economic development, and concomitantly, different expediencies were employed to secure the necessary population and labor. It was in this process of aggregating population that the nation came to acquire the racial and ethnic diversity that is characteristic of American society today.

For the purpose of this analysis, it is useful to distinguish four stages of national development: (1) settlement, (2) expansion, (3) agricultural development, and (4) industrial development. Each stage brought about major changes in the ethnic profile of the American people; each introduced new racial and ethnic stocks into the national population; and each defined new sets of relationships between the society at large and its constituent minorities.

Settlement

Franklin Roosevelt once began a speech to the Daughters of the American Revolution by addressing them as "fellow immigrants." Though one might applaud the equalitarian sentiment behind this gesture, it is not really correct to refer to the colonial settlers as "immigrants." They came not as migrants entering an alien society, forced to acquire a new national identity, but as a colonial vanguard that would create a new England in the image of the one they had left behind. Colonists even referred to themselves as "emigrants" rather than "immigrants," and it was not until the late 1780s that newcomers began to be identified with the country they entered rather than the one they had left behind.[1]

In their quest for legitimacy, various minority groups have made much of the fact that one or another of their forebears was present in the colonies or crossed the Potomac with Washington's army. Whatever validity these claims may have, the truth of the matter is that the colonial population was predominantly British. As one historian writes of the seventeenth century:

> For despite the Dutch on the Hudson, and small groups of Swiss, Swedes, Finns, and French Huguenots pocketed along the coast, the small vessels which set out on the American voyage were chiefly English built and English manned. Their cargoes, moreover, consisted largely of Englishmen and, later and in smaller numbers, Englishwomen. Even the Scots and Irish, who in the next century would crowd the harbors of the New World, were a minority in the first century.[2]

When the colonies won their independence from Britain, the population was still homogeneous. According to the best available estimates, 61 percent of the white population of the United States in 1790 were of English descent, and another 17 percent were Scotch or Irish. Thus, over three-quarters of the population had their origins in the English-speaking states of the British Isles. Of the remainder, 9 percent were German, 3 percent Dutch, 2 percent Irish, 1 percent Swedish; various other nationalities were represented, but only in minute proportions.[3]

1. John Higham, *Send These to Me* (New York: Atheneum, 1975), pp. 5-6; Marcus Lee Hansen, *The Immigrant in American History* (New York: Harper, 1948), p. 11.
2. Mildred Campbell, "Social Origins of Some Early Americans," in James Smith, ed., *Seventeenth-Century America* (Chapel Hill: University of North Carolina Press, 1959), p. 63.
3. *Historical Statistics of the United States* (Washington, D.C.: Government Printing Office, 1975), p. 1168.

Even these non-British settlers had important cultural affinities to the English majority. Most had their origins in northern or western Europe, though this was barely noticed until there was an influx of groups from more diverse backgrounds a century later. Of greater and more immediate significance was the fact that as many as 99 percent of the colonists were Protestant.[4] Of course, Catholics and Jews were present, but not in significant numbers, and their freedoms were often severely restricted. In short, at its inception, the United States had a population that was remarkably homogeneous in terms of both ethnicity and religion. Devoid of its invidious implications, the claim that the nation was founded by white Anglo-Saxon Protestants is reasonably accurate.

To be sure, there was some ethnic differentiation in terms of both population and patterns of settlement. New York still reflected its Dutch origins, and had a far greater ethnic mix than did New England. Pennsylvania had sizable concentrations of Germans and Scotch-Irish, and the Southern states, which a century later would become the last bastion of "ethnic purity," were characterized by a high degree of ethnic heterogeneity, at least in comparison to New England. But it would be a mistake to construe this as evidence of a rudimentary pluralism, at least in a political sense. Not only were the English predominant numerically, but they enjoyed a political and cultural hegemony over the life of the fledgling nation. Non-English colonials were typically regarded as aliens who were obliged to adapt to English rule in terms of both politics and culture. As John Higham has written:

> Like the Dutch in New York, the English in all of the colonies before the Revolution conceived of themselves as founders, settlers, or planters—the formative population of those colonial societies—not as immigrants. Theirs was the polity, the language, the pattern of work and settlement, and many of the mental habits to which the immigrants would have to adjust.[5]

4. Charles Anderson, *White Protestant Americans* (Englewood Cliffs, N.J.: Prentice-Hall, 1970), p. 2. Of course, denominational differences among Protestants were a source of great division. Nevertheless, by the time of the influx of Irish Catholics in the mid-nineteenth century, these differences had waned in importance and Protestants found themselves united in reaction to the Papist threat.

5. Higham, op. cit., p. 6.

Though the English tolerated non-English in their midst, there was no question as to their exclusive claim on the state. Determined to avoid the cleavages that engendered wars in Europe, the founding fathers placed high value on the homogeneous origins of the American people, as reflected in the *Federalist Papers:*

> Providence [had] been pleased to give this one connected country to one united people—a people descended from the same ancestors, speaking the same language, professing the same religion, attached to the same principles of government, very similar in their manners and customs. . . .[6]

The most obvious sign of the cultural preeminence of the English was the establishment of the English language as the lingua franca. In 1814 De Witt Clinton, soon to become the governor of New York, commented with undisguised pleasure: "The triumph and adoption of the English language have been the principal means of melting us down into one people, and of extinguishing those stubborn prejudices and violent animosities which formed a wall of partition between the inhabitants of the same land."[7] The early history of the United States seems to bear out Clinton's contention that the establishment of the English language was a critical first step in the gradual assimilation of the various ethnic stocks of the colonial period. Even before the Revolution, French and Swedish were in decline, and gradually Dutch and German gave way to English also.

After the Revolution the pace of assimilation gained momentum. Aside from the rising nationalism engendered by the War for Independence, the lull in immigration, according to Marcus Hansen, "not only allowed the melting pot to simmer gently, but also hastened the Americanization of those non-British groups which had not yet lost their distinctive identity."[8]

Given the ethnocentrism and xenophobia that reigned during the colonial period, one might ask why the British admitted non-British settlers in the first place. Obviously, had they been guided by their prejudices alone, they would have restricted entry to their own

6. Quoted in Maldwyn Allen Jones, *American Immigration* (Chicago: University of Chicago Press, 1960), p. 39.

7. Ibid., p. 76.

8. Marcus Lee Hansen, *The Atlantic Migration* (New York: Harper & Row, 1961), p. 70.

countrymen. The simple truth is that English were not coming in sufficient numbers to populate the colonies. Aside from the high costs of travel and the hardships of colonial life, the economy was not sufficiently developed to sustain large-scale immigration. Except for a small class of artisans, traders, and skilled workers, most settlers eked out their livelihoods as subsistence farmers. Of course, pariah religious groups had non-economic reasons for subjecting themselves to the perils of the New World, and this is why they figured prominently among the earliest settlers.

Because so few Englishmen spontaneously set out for British America, a number of inducements were devised to encourage immigration. Of special importance was the development of a system of indentured servitude, whereby a settler was provided transportation in exchange for seven years of labor. This system of voluntary servitude became a major source of population and labor. Historians estimate that as many as one-half to two-thirds of whites who emigrated during the colonial period came as indentured servants.[9]

Retaining colonials as permanent settlers was also problematic. From the time of the first settlements in Virginia and New England until the War of Independence, settlers generally regarded themselves as Englishmen in temporary exile, and so many sailed back to England that colonial authorities periodically became alarmed about the depletion of the colonial population.[10]

If there were no compelling "pull" factors luring Englishmen to America, neither were there potent "push" factors. In fact, after 1718 labor shortages at home induced the British government to place restrictions on emigration, especially of skilled artisans and other laborers needed in Britain's nascent industries. It was this scarcity of emigrants from Britain that induced colonial authorities to permit the immigration of non-English nationalities. From a British perspective, this arrangement was ideal: "While Englishmen labored in the home islands, the Protestant masses of Europe and

9. Campbell, op. cit., p. 66; Abbott Smith, *Colonists in Bondage* (Chapel Hill: University of North Carolina Press, 1947), p. 34.

10. Wilbur S. Shepperson, *Emigration and Disenchantment* (Norman: University of Oklahoma Press, 1965), pp. 3–4.

Ireland were invited to people the British colonies and thereby strengthen the British Empire."[11]

The one push factor that did operate, however, assumed a rather explicit form: throughout the eighteenth century England routinely dumped paupers, vagrants, and convicts onto American soil. It has been estimated that as many as 30,000 English and 7,500 Irish had this unceremonious initiation to the New World.[12] Not without reason, Samuel Johnson once described Americans as a "race of convicts."

Thus, it was out of economic necessity rather than a principled commitment to the idea of America as an asylum that the United States imposed no nationality restrictions on immigration, either before or after Independence. Indeed, foreigners were generally regarded with suspicion, if not outright hostility. As one historian writes of the colonial period: "At one time or another, immigrants of practically every non-English stock incurred the open hostility of earlier comers."[13] Furthermore, xenophobia pervaded all levels of colonial society. When Madison Grant sought to legitimize nativist opposition to immigration in the early part of the twentieth century, he published a compendium entitled *The Founders of the Republic on Immigration, Naturalization, and Aliens,* in which the founding fathers eloquently warned of the dangers that foreigners posed for the new republic.[14] For example:

> Why should the Palatine boors be suffered to swarm into our settlements, and, by herding together, establish their language and manners, to the exclusion of ours? Why should Pennsylvania, founded by the English, become a colony of aliens, who will shortly be so numerous as to Germanize us, instead of our Anglifying them . . . ?
>
> Benjamin Franklin, 1751

11. John Miller, *This New Man* (New York: McGraw-Hill, 1974), p. 373.

12. Ibid., p. 330; Jones, op. cit., p. 9; Roy Garis, *Immigration Restriction* (New York: Macmillan, 1928), p. 12. Garis estimates that between 1750 and 1770 some 20,000 convicts were sent to Maryland alone.

13. Jones, op. cit., p. 44.

14. Madison Grant, *The Founders of the Republic on Immigration, Naturalization, and Aliens* (New York: Scribner, 1928). Excerpts come from pp. 26, 59–60, 90, and 51, respectively.

But are there no inconveniences to be thrown into the scale against the advantage expected from a multiplication of numbers by the importation of foreigners? . . . They will bring with them the principles of the governments they leave, imbibed in their early youth; or, if able to throw them off, it will be in exchange for an unbounded licentiousness, passing, as is usual, from one extreme to another. . . . In proportion to their numbers, they will share with us the legislation. They will infuse into it their spirit, warp and bias its directions, and render it a heterogeneous, incoherent, distracted mass.

Thomas Jefferson, 1782

My opinion, with respect to immigration, is that except of useful mechanics and some particular descriptions of men or professions, there is no need of encouragement, while the policy or advantage of its taking place in a body (I mean the settling of them in a body) may be much questioned; for, by so doing, they retain the language, habits, and principles (good or bad) which they bring with them.

George Washington, 1794

To admit foreigners indiscriminately to the rights of citizens, the moment they put foot in our country, as recommended in the message, would be nothing less than to admit the Grecian horse into the citadel of our liberty and sovereignty.

Alexander Hamilton, 1802

It is especially noteworthy that these sentiments flourished at a time when the population was relatively homogeneous and the level of immigration rather low. Predictably, as immigration grew in volume and complexity, xenophobia developed into a full-fledged ideology and political movement.

A distrust for foreigners was reflected in the protracted debates that the founding fathers had over the issue of naturalization. During the Constitutional Convention there was some movement to declare naturalized citizens as ineligible for Congress, but it was feared that such a restriction would discourage immigration, which was considered crucial to the nation's prosperity. As a result the Constitution required seven years of residence before a naturalized citizen became eligible for the House, and nine years for the Senate. During the First Congress the same division of opinion occurred on the naturalization question, and again the "liberal" position, providing for easy naturalization, prevailed. The Naturalization Act of 1790 required only two years of residence before citizenship could be claimed; but in 1795 the Naturalization Act was revised, increasing the residency period from two to five years, and again in 1798, as the nation found itself on the brink of a war with France, the residency period was increased to fourteen years. However, in 1802 it was reduced to five years, where it has remained ever since.

Although the young nation imposed no restrictions on immigration, it vacillated in the restrictions imposed on naturalization. Despite the seeming contradiction, these two policies actually resolved the national dilemma with respect to immigration, in that the nation was assured of population and labor without having to absorb foreigners too rapidly into the body politic.

Thus, long before the onset of mass immigration, there was a deeply rooted consciousness of the nation's Anglo-Saxon and Protestant origins. From the beginning, the nation's political institutions, culture, and people all had an unmistakably English cast, and despite denominational differences, Protestantism was the near-universal creed. The early stirrings of nativism clearly signaled the fact that however much the nation might tolerate foreigners in its midst, it was determined to protect its Anglo-Saxon and Protestant legacy.

Expansion

The fact that the United States originated as a British colony affected no group more profoundly than the American Indian. Even the claim that "Columbus discovered America" is symptomatic of an enduring colonialist mentality that denies the very existence of Native Americans, whose ancestors had migrated from Asia and "discovered" America some 15,000 years earlier.

An inveterate disregard for the Indian's humanity was in evidence from the earliest contact with white men. Columbus himself had abducted six Indians in full regalia and decorated them with war paint to display to Queen Isabella. Four centuries later, when the Indian had been vanquished and reduced to utter dependency,

Buffalo Bill carried his Wild West Show to Europe, replete with stone-faced Indians in headdress. These two events bracket an epoch of almost unrelenting violence and inhumanity to Native Americans, the dimensions of which have yet to penetrate the American conscience.

Many factors contributed to the endless series of Indian wars, but the overriding issue was land. By issuing generous land grants to colonial settlers, European monarchs unleashed forces that resulted in several centuries of internecine warfare with the indigenous populations of the New World. Each step in the extension of American dominion precipitated renewed conflict, which invariably ended with the forced cession of Indian land. The advancing frontier, so celebrated in American folklore, inevitably meant the dispossession of Indian land and the elimination of the Indians themselves.

The dispossession of Indian land and the displacement of the Indian population occurred gradually over several centuries, though it is possible to discern several stages. During the early colonial period, the settlers were obliged to recognize Indian nations as independent powers because of their relative strength. As Indian historian Wilcomb Washburn writes:

> The period of Indian-white equality . . . was based first of all upon the power of the Indian to maintain that equality. . . . The Iroquois Confederacy possessed the requisite power and political organization to command respect from all interested European governments.[15]

In addition, early settlers were dependent upon Indians for protection and trade, not to mention tutelage in agricultural techniques suitable to the New World. Consequently, settlers were temporarily compelled to negotiate with Indians for the purchase of land. Even where this theoretical "equality" prevailed, however, it was qualified by images of the Indian as savage and beastlike—images that served to justify land grabs by whites. The utter contempt for Indians and their land rights is manifested in one early-seventeenth-century document which held that "savages have no particular propertie

15. Wilcomb E. Washburn, *The Indian in America* (New York: Harper & Row, 1975), p. 85.

in any part or parcell of that country, but only a generall residencie there, as wild beasts have in the forests."[16]

As the balance of power shifted in their favor—thanks to their superior technology and weapons—settlers were even less inclined to recognize Indian land rights. From the seventeenth century on, Europeans claimed for themselves the right of "dominion," acknowledging only "possessory rights" of Indians to the lands actually occupied by them.[17] Furthermore, occupancy came to be defined in terms of agricultural settlement, thus denying Indian ownership of land used for hunting or fishing. A series of Indian wars during the colonial period effectively secured English rule over the entire eastern seaboard, thereby establishing a beachhead for further penetration of the mainland.

As conflict between whites and Indians intensified, there was a corresponding transformation in the ideological characterization of the Indian. Indians had always been regarded as semihuman and uncivilized, but as long as whites were dependent upon them, this image was tempered by a romantic image of the Indian as "noble red man." Gradually this gave way to an image of the Indian as bloodthirsty savage and a menace to white civilization. This new image not only reflected the increasingly violent relationship between whites and Indians, but also set the ideological stage for wars of extermination that would eliminate the Indian "menace."

After the Revolution the nation was seized with a land fever that reached far beyond the original thirteen colonies. With the acquiescence if not outright complicity of state governments, white settlers wantonly intruded on Indian lands protected by past treaties. Eventually the encroachment on their lands provoked Indians to attack settlers, and invariably this "violence" was ruthlessly suppressed. Each Indian war ended with treaties whereby Indians ceded enormous parcels of land in exchange for promises that their remaining land would be inviolate of white settlement. But it was only a matter of time before the cycle of white encroachment, warfare, and land cession repeated itself, with the result that Indians were pushed farther and farther behind the advancing frontier. By

16. Quoted in Miller, op. cit., p. 171.

17. Washburn, op. cit., p. 82; also, Wilcomb Washburn, *Red Man's Land/ White Man's Law* (New York: Scribner, 1971), pp. 27–46.

the 1830s a large region west of the Mississippi, consisting mostly of arid land deemed unsuitable for white settlement, was put aside as "Indian Territory," and used as the repository for the displaced tribes east of the Mississippi.

The prevailing justification for the dispossession of Indian land was that the soil was destined to be tilled, and despite the fact that most tribes subsisted on agriculture as well as hunting, the belief was propagated that Indians were nomadic hunters who had no rightful claim to the land. As Theodore Roosevelt later wrote in *The Winning of the West*, "the settler and pioneer have at bottom had justice on their side; this great continent could not have been kept as nothing but a game preserve for squalid savages."[18] That this was merely a rationalization for land hunger is clear from the events surrounding the forced removal of the Cherokee Indians from the Southeast to Indian Territory in the 1830s.

The Cherokee homeland was in the mountainous area where Georgia, Tennessee, and North Carolina meet. Previous treaties both before and after the Revolution had already whittled down the original Cherokee nation by millions of acres, but the remaining territory was supposedly protected by a 1791 treaty that recognized the sovereignty of the Cherokee nation and stipulated that "the United States solemnly guarantee to the Cherokee nation, all their lands not hereby ceded."[19]

The Cherokee contradicted the prevailing stereotypes of Indians as nomadic hunters and uncivilized savages. They had assimilated a great deal of white culture, and lived in cultivated settlements replete with mills, schools, and churches. The Cherokee were also unique in that they had their own written language, and in 1827 drafted a constitution modeled after that of the surrounding white society. Despite the fact that the Cherokee had fought courageously on the American side during the War of 1812, their land was coveted for white settlement, especially after gold was discovered in the heart of the Cherokee nation in 1829.

It is noteworthy that the ultimate removal of the Cherokee from

18. Quoted in Wilcomb E. Washburn, "The Moral and Legal Justifications for Dispossessing the Indians," in James Morton Smith, ed., *Seventeenth Century America* (Chapel Hill: University of North Carolina Press, 1959), p. 23.

19. Samuel Carter, *Cherokee Sunset* (Garden City, N.Y.: Doubleday, 1976), p. 13.

their ancestral homeland did not occur by dint of force alone, but was legitimized through the nation's highest political and judicial institutions. The legal groundwork was laid in an 1823 Supreme Court decision in which Chief Justice John Marshall effectively nullified all previous treaties by declaring that Indians did not have unqualified sovereignty over their territories. Marshall reasoned that discovery gave exclusive title to those who made it, and in effect, placed a stamp of legitimacy on the conquest of the Indian by the colonists. On the basis of this decision, the State of Georgia proceeded to invalidate all statutes adopted by the Indians, including those that restricted the sale of land. When the Cherokee appealed to the federal government for protection of their treaty rights, Jackson replied that "the President of the United States has no power to protect them against the laws of Georgia."[20] The coup de grâce was delivered by Chief Justice Marshall in *The Cherokee Nation* v. *The State of Georgia*. Marshall ruled that the Cherokee Nation, though a "state," was not a "foreign state" but a "domestic dependent nation," and disavowed any jurisdiction in the case. In 1830 Congress passed a Removal Act that empowered the President to deport Indians east of the Mississippi to Indian Territory. Finally, in 1838 some 12,000 Cherokee were rounded up at bayonet point, interned in stockades, and finally forced on a grueling midwinter march to Kansas. An estimated 2,500 died during the roundup and incarceration, and another 1,500 died on what the Cherokee called the Trail of Tears.

The eviction of the Cherokee from their ancestral homeland not only was a turning point in the development of the reservation system, but it also demonstrated that it was not the Indian way of life, but the Indians themselves who were the obstacle to the nation's territorial ambitions. Some historians still puzzle over "the unnecessary brutality and lack of compassion" on the part of whites, but a Cherokee chief once provided a succinct explanation: "The truth is if we had no lands, we should have [had] no enemies."[21]

The history of white-Indian conflict in the East presaged a still more violent course of events in the West. One historian summed it up this way:

20. Washburn, *Red Man's Land/White Man's Law*, op. cit., p. 66.
21. Quoted in Carter, op. cit., p. 9.

The plight of the Indian west of the Mississippi River was only a sad, monotonous duplication of what had happened east of it—warfare, broken treaties, expropriation of land, rebellion, and ultimately defeat. No sooner were the eastern Indians dropped down on the plains than the United States discovered the natural resources of the West. Miners and settlers were on the move, emigrant trains rumbled across the plains, and once again the aim of the frontiersman was to get the Indian out of the way.[22]

By 1880 the last of the Indian wars had been fought, and the surviving Indian population was isolated on reservations.

The combined effect of a century of warfare, the destruction of the Indian way of life, and devastating epidemics, which were welcomed as acts of Providence, was the decimation of the Indian population. Between 1800 and 1850 the Indian population was actually cut in half (see Table 1). When the nation celebrated its bicentennial a few years ago, the Indian population was not much larger than it had been two centuries earlier.

Though the Indian was now out of the way, the reservation system systematically attacked the residues of Indian culture and self-sufficiency. With the political and economic affairs of the reservation empowered to the Bureau of Indian Affairs, the Indian had effectively been reduced to colonial status, as is suggested by the following description of the reservation system:

Ultimately, white officials determined who would live upon a reserve, where, and how. Depending upon the time, they also decided upon the sale and leasing of tribal lands and other resources, the overall economic development of the reserves, the nature of educational facilities, and even at times the churches and religions, as well as whether or not to recognize tribal governments. The line of command stretched from officials and politicians in Washington to the BIA agents on the reservations who were expected to put these policies in effect and so were given power to call out the military to enforce their powers, to exercise judicial authority at times, to control rations and trust funds, to lease and sell lands, water rights,

22. Peter Farb, *Man's Rise to Civilization* (New York: Dutton, 1978), p. 242.

Table 1

THE SIZE OF THE INDIAN POPULATION, 1800–1950

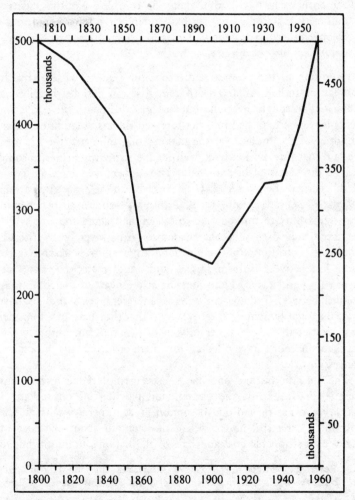

SOURCE: Portion of Figure 116 (p. 142) in *Historical Atlas of Religion in America,* revised edition by Edwin Scott Gaustad. Copyright © 1962, 1976 by Edwin Scott Gaustad. Reprinted by permission of Harper & Row Publishers, Inc.

minerals, and forests, to remove children from their parents in order to send them to school, and to recognize or to sidestep traditional tribal political systems—all to further decisions made in the capital. Thus Indians became at best clients patronized by the agents sent to rule over them. So complete was the agents' authority that some analysts have likened the reservation to a colony; others have gone so far as to depict the reserves as the equivalent of concentration camps.[23]

In addition to the political and economic powers wielded by the Bureau of Indian Affairs, a program that can best be described as deracination sought to stamp out Indian culture and life-styles, and schools were established in order to speed the assimilation of Indian children. If the Indian was the nation's first minority, then it must be said that this did not bode well for the many minorities to come.

The dispossession of Indian land continued well into the twentieth century. Between 1887—the year of the Dawes Act, which chopped reservations into small farmsteads—and 1934, tribal holdings fell from 138 million acres to 56 million acres, most of which has been judged by soil conservationists to be severely or critically eroded.[24] According to Congressional figures, over 800,000 acres were lost between 1948 and 1952, and another 1,800,000 acres between 1953 and 1957.[25] Land remains at the heart of the continuing conflict between Indians and whites. In recent years Indians have waged a legal campaign to recover land that they held title to under past treaties that were either broken or ignored, but with few exceptions the courts have ruled against them or have made only token concessions.

The most significant land battle is occurring on the reservations themselves. Ironically, the barren land pawned off on Indians a century ago has turned out to contain great mineral wealth.[26] The 50 million acres still under Indian title contain about one-third of the West's strippable coal and half of the nation's uranium, not to

23. Robert F. Berkhofer, Jr., "Native Americans," in John Higham, ed., *Ethnic Leadership in America* (Baltimore: Johns Hopkins University Press, 1978), p. 124.

24. *New York Times Magazine*, February 11, 1979, p. 32. Farb, op. cit., p. 257.

25. *New York Times Magazine*, February 11, 1979, p. 21.

26. Ibid.

mention enormous quantities of oil, a circumstance that has resulted in a modern version of the Indian wars of previous centuries. The cast of characters has changed, however. Instead of hordes of settlers intruding on their land with horse and plow, Indians confront giant corporations armed with the formidable weapons of modern industrial technology. And in the place of the United States cavalry are white-collar bureaucrats of the Bureau of Indian Affairs, who have a record of negotiating leases that cheat the Indians of their fair share of the royalties—for example, by neglecting to put escalation or termination clauses in leases negotiated when coal was cheap. And even as the land is raped of its wealth, the majority of reservation Indians are still destitute, and in fact constitute one of the most impoverished groups in the nation. As two civil rights activists wrote in *The New York Times:* "We are still killing the Indians. Not with bullets but with more shameful and crippling weapons of destruction—poverty, hunger, disease, and neglect."[27]

Finally, increasing numbers of Indians—at least a third today—live not on reservations, but in the red ghettos of cities like Minneapolis, Chicago and Los Angeles. Here the cycle of Indian-white conflict has gone full circle, and it is the Indians who find themselves, like immigrants, on strange terrain, forced to adapt to the imperatives of an alien society.

Indians were not the only group to be engulfed by a land-hungry nation. In 1803 the United States doubled its national domain by prevailing upon Napoleon to sell Louisiana. Mexico was less accommodating, and its territories were conquered and annexed in 1848 under a treaty ending the Mexican-American War.

The conquest of Mexican territory and the treatment of Mexican nationals were foreshadowed by the Indian experience. The seeds of territorial conquest had been planted long before the nation arrogantly pronounced that it was its "manifest destiny" to extend its dominion from coast to coast. Furthermore, the moral and ideological justifications for conquest that had been perfected with respect to the Indian were now tailored to fit the Mexican. In essence, it

27. Melvin Friedman and Marian Viviano, Op-Ed Page, *New York Times,* May 21, 1977, p. 23.

was argued that the Mexicans were a degenerate and backward people who wasted land and resources. The land was destined to be tilled, and as one politician expounded in 1859, "no nation has the right to hold soil, virgin and rich, yet unproducing. . . ."[28] Did not the dispossession of Indian land demonstrate that land previously uncultivated could, under American dominion, produce great bounty?

As the nation cast a predatory eye on Mexican territories, the Indian was commonly cited as precedent and justification for conquest. On the eve of the Mexican-American War in 1848, Sam Houston reasoned that since Americans had always cheated Indians, and since Mexicans were no better than Indians, "I see no reason why we should not go on the same course now and take their land."[29] An editorial in the *New York Evening Post* also stressed the similarity between Indians and Mexicans:

The Mexicans are *Indians*—Aboriginal Indians. . . . They do not possess the elements of an *independent* national existence. The Aborigines of this country have not attempted and cannot attempt to exist *independently* along side of us. Providence has so ordained it, and it is folly not to recognize the fact. The Mexicans are Aboriginal Indians, and they must share the destiny of their race.[30]

In 1846 the United States deliberately provoked a war with Mexico, and after seizing Mexico City itself, forced Mexico to cede one-half her national territory, an area corresponding to Germany and France combined, and today encompassing Arizona, California, Nevada,

28. Quoted in Albert Katz Weinberg, *Manifest Destiny* (Baltimore: Johns Hopkins Press, 1935), p. 90. In a similar vein, the *New York Morning News* editorialized in 1845: "With the valleys of the Rocky Mountains converted into pastures and sheep-folds, we may with propriety then turn to the world and ask, whom have we injured?" As the question itself implies, Mexicans, like the Indians before them, simply did not count in the moral calculus of expansionism. Quoted in Frederick Merk, *Manifest Destiny and Mission in American History* (New York: Knopf, 1963), p. 25.

29. Quoted in Weinberg, op. cit., p. 90.

30. Reprinted in Melvin Steinfield, ed., *Cracks in the Melting Pot* (Beverly Hills, Calif.: Glencoe Press, 1970), p. 74.

New Mexico, Utah, half of Colorado, and the part of Texas that had not been annexed a decade earlier.[31]

Nearly 80,000 Mexican citizens lived in the ceded territory, most of whom elected to become citizens of the United States under the terms of the peace treaty. The treaty also guaranteed that their property rights would be protected, but as in the case of the Indians, the Mexicans were gradually dispossessed of their land through a combination of legal chicanery and outright violence. When gold was discovered in California in 1848, Spanish-speaking miners were driven from the mines by vigilante groups.

Unlike Indians who were isolated on reservations, Mexicans of the Southwest—augmented by a steady migration of Mexican nationals—became an integral part of the regional economy, providing the cheap labor that was necessary for the growth of agriculture, ranching, mining, and industry. Since the 1880s special interest groups have actively recruited Mexican nationals whenever labor has been in short supply, as it was during the two world wars. Immigration policy has also been manipulated according to need, and under the bracero program, which operated between 1942 and 1964, over four million Mexican workers were admitted for limited periods, usually coinciding with the seasonal harvest of crops.

In the 1830s and 1840s it was Mexico's inability to control the "illegal immigration" of Americans that ultimately led to her loss of these territories. Today, of course, it is the Mexicans who are defined as illegal immigrants and threatened with deportation. Denied citizenship, unable to form unions, ineligible for welfare or unemployment compensation, lacking roots in the community, the "illegals" are at the mercy of their employers. Forced to work for substandard wages, they continue in their historic role as a cheap-labor reserve for agriculture and industry. This is the principal reason why state and local officials commonly welcome the influx of illegals, even as the federal government wages a halfhearted campaign to close the borders.[32]

As in the case of the Indians, the fact that Mexicans originated

31. Matt S. Meier and Feliciano Rivera, *The Chicanos* (New York: Hill & Wang, 1972), p. 70.

32. Wayne A. Cornelius, "Mexican Migration to the United States," in Jerome Skolnick and Elliot Currie, eds., *Crisis in American Institutions* (Boston: Little, Brown, 1979), pp. 134–48.

as a "conquered minority" continues to define their relationship to what one Chicano writer has dubbed "occupied America." Another writer summed up the Mexican experience as a conquered minority in these terms:

> As the only minority, apart from the Indians, ever acquired by conquest, the Mexican Americans have been subjected to economic, social, and political discrimination, as well as a good deal of violence at the hands of their Anglo conquerors. . . . But the worst violence has been the unrelenting discrimination against the cultural heritage—the language and customs—of the Mexican Americans, coupled with the economic exploitation of the entire group. Property rights were guaranteed, but not protected, by either the federal or state governments. Equal protection under law has consistently been a mockery in the Mexican-American communities.[33]

As in the case of the Indian, conquest was only a devastating first step in a long history of expropriation. Paradoxically, the fact that Indians and Mexicans have ancestral claims to the land and its resources has not mitigated their oppression, but on the contrary, has given rise to a more extreme form of exploitation and control.

Agricultural Development

Unlike European nations, the United States in the seventeenth and eighteenth centuries had no surplus population, and in particular, no class of serfs to provide cheap agricultural labor. Attempts were made in colonial times to enslave the Indian, but these generally proved unsuccessful, in part because the supply of Indian slaves was never adequate, in part because the presence of Indian slaves posed danger to the colonies, and in part because Indians did not adapt well to agricultural labor and escape was relatively easy.[34]

33. Wayne Moquin, ed., *A Documentary History of the Mexican Americans* (New York: Praeger, 1971), p. 181.

34. Almon Wheeler Lauber, *Indian Slavery in Colonial Times within the Present Limits of the United States* (New York: Columbia University, 1913), pp. 296–98; Winthrop Jordan, *White over Black* (Baltimore: Penguin Books, 1969), pp. 89–90.

Long before chattel slavery was introduced, southern planters had experimented with a system of white servitude by importing indentured servants from Europe. However, indentured servants were both scarce and expensive. Furthermore, as contract laborers they could bargain for acceptable terms, and once their contracts expired, they entered the ranks of free labor. In the end, a system of chattel slavery, which reduced blacks to perpetual servitude, was more expedient and more profitable. In his book on *Capitalism and Slavery*, Eric Williams put it well:

> The servant expected land at the end of his contract; the Negro, in a strange environment, conspicuous by his color and features, and ignorant of the white man's language and ways, could be kept permanently divorced from the land. Racial differences made it easier to justify and rationalize Negro slavery, to exact the mechanical obedience of a plough-ox or a cart-horse, to demand that resignation and that complete moral and intellectual subjection which alone make slave labor possible. Finally, and this was the decisive factor, the Negro slave was cheaper. The money which procured a white man's services for ten years could buy a Negro for life.[35]

Yet slavery also had its disadvantages, which planters weighed as they experimented with different labor systems. In the first place, the purchase of a slave involved a large capital outlay, thereby limiting slave ownership to the wealthy planters. In addition, slaves had to be fed, clothed, and maintained even during periods of their life cycle when their productivity was low. An elaborate and costly system of controls was also necessary in order to deal with recalcitrant and runaway slaves, and to protect the larger community

35. Eric Williams, *Capitalism and Slavery* (New York: Capricorn Books, 1966), p. 19. In 1844 one writer's calculations led him to conclude: "Where the free man or laborer would require one hundred dollars a year for food and clothing alone, the slave can be supported for twenty dollars a year, and often is. This makes the wages of one forty cents a day, of the other six cents only." Nathaniel A. Ware, *Notes on Political Economy* (New York: Augustus M. Kelley, 1967; orig. 1844), p. 201.

For other secondary sources on the relative costs of slave labor, see Jordan, op. cit., pp. 76–77; Lewis Gray, *History of Agriculture*, vol. 1 (Gloucester, Mass.: Peter Smith, 1958), pp. 361–71; M. B. Hammond, *The Cotton Industry*, Publications of the American Economic Association, new series, no. 1 (December 1897), pp. 36–37.

from the constant danger of slave revolts. Self-interest alone might have led planters to avoid the reprehensible trade in human flesh, if other sources of cheap labor had been available.

The point, however, is that other sources of cheap labor were not available. Not only was there a paucity of native laborers, but European peasants were hardly inclined to uproot themselves only to become serfs in America. Immigrants who entered farming did so because they could buy land. Those who lacked capital to become independent farmers typically found employment in towns or rural settlements. In short, slaves were not merely the cheapest labor for southern agriculture, they were the *only* labor. Since the United States lacked an indigenous class of serfs, it had to create one, and this it did through the forced importation and enslavement of over half a million Africans.[36]

Initially slaves were employed in tobacco and indigo production, but it was cotton that would eventually create the greatest demand for slaves. Cotton production was uniquely adapted to slavery. Unlike seasonal crops, cotton's 200-day growing season required continuous employment of labor for most of the year. After the cotton was harvested, the ginning, hauling to shipping points, and other farm operations continued so that one year's growing cycle actually overlapped that of the next. Planters gradually discovered that economies could be achieved by employing a large number of laborers who could work in teams and shift from one field to another. The result was a plantation system. Though a few slaves acquired skills as craftsmen and others worked as domestic servants, the overwhelming majority were employed in agriculture, and by 1850 about two-thirds of these were employed in cotton production.[37]

36. According to one authoritative source, the United States imported about 400,000 slaves between 1619 and 1808, and another 270,000 after the slave trade became officially illegal in 1808. These figures, however, do not convey the full magnitude of the slave trade. The same source estimates that 2.7 million Africans were sent to the New World in the seventeenth century, 7 million in the eighteenth, and 4 million in the nineteenth—a total of nearly 14 million. *The American Negro Reference Book* (Englewood Cliffs, N.J.: Prentice-Hall, 1966), pp. 6 and 100. These estimates square with those provided by Philip Curtin, *The Atlantic Slave Trade* (Madison: University of Wisconsin Press, 1969).

37. It is estimated that only 5 percent of the total slave population worked in industry. See Robert Starobin, *Industrial Slavery in the Old South* (New

All farm labor involves dirty, arduous, and menial work, but cotton is worse than most. As one writer describes it: "Cotton picking is one of the most disliked of farm jobs. It is tiresome and backbreaking, and with hoeing and chopping included, the enterprise is first-class drudgery."[38] Given this, together with the option of more lucrative employment in other sectors of the national economy, southern planters could not hope to attract European immigrants to the cotton fields, something that they attempted to do without success after slavery was abolished.

Yet slavery was more than an expedient for southern agriculture. Though the vast majority of slaves did work in the cotton fields of the South, the benefits of slavery redounded to the entire nation. It is not possible to comprehend the significance of slavery either as an economic institution or as an abomination of American ideals without understanding the role that cotton played in the economic development of the North as well as the South.

In 1790 the United States faced the same obstacles to economic development that beset underdeveloped countries today. The most formidable obstacle, according to Douglass North, was the development of an export market that would attract foreign capital and stimulate internal growth.[39] But America's export market was in deep trouble in the late eighteenth century. Since there was no domestic industry to speak of, the chief exports consisted of raw materials and agricultural products. Aside from the high transportation costs to European markets, international trade was hampered by the fact that after Independence, the United States lost its trade privileges as a British colony. Between 1768 and 1790 the nation's foreign trade actually declined, and according to North, there was little prospect of rapid growth on the horizon.

It was cotton that eventually provided the United States with an export staple that could sustain an expansive export market. The invention of spinning machinery and the power loom in the late nineteenth century revolutionized the manufacture of

York: Oxford University Press, 1970), p. 11. Richard Wade estimates that of 3,200,000 slaves in 1850, about 2,800,000 worked on farms and plantations. Cited in *The American Negro Reference Book*, op. cit., p. 29.

38. John Leonard Fulmer, *Agricultural Progress in the Cotton Belt Since 1920* (Chapel Hill: University of North Carolina Press, 1950), p. 82.

39. Douglass C. North, *The Economic Growth of the United States, 1790–1860* (New York: W. W. Norton, 1966), p. 2.

cloth, leading to the first textile factories and generating an almost unlimited demand for raw cotton. At first the technological capacity to use raw cotton exceeded the capacity to produce it, but this was remedied with the invention of the cotton gin in 1793. By automatically separating the cotton fibers from the husk and seed—a laborious operation so long as it was done by hand—Whitney's cotton gin accomplished in one hour what had previously required ten, thereby allowing for the mass production of raw cotton. The result was a cotton boom in the southern states, where the climate and soil were ideally suited to the cotton culture.

Both slavery and the plantation system had their origins prior to the development of the cotton culture, but neither reached its apex until the cotton gin transformed southern agriculture around the turn of the nineteenth century. The slave labor force grew from 530,000 in 1800 to 1,180,000 in 1830, to 2,340,000 in 1860.[40] As cotton production became more profitable, the South gradually made the transformation from a diversified agriculture to a single crop and, in fact, became one of the most specialized agricultural regions in the world. After 1790 cotton exports increased dramatically. Whereas only 12,000 pounds of cotton were exported in 1790, by 1860 the figure had grown to 1.7 billion pounds. It is especially noteworthy that the largest increase occurred between 1850 and 1860, which indicates that slavery was far from a dying institution at the outset of the Civil War.

Cotton gradually emerged as king, not only of the southern economy, but of the American export market as well. By 1860 cotton constituted 60 percent of American exports; by contrast, its nearest rivals, flour and tobacco, together accounted for less than 20 percent. Virtually all of America's vast cotton export went to Britain, which in turn relied on the United States for 80 percent of its raw cotton. This cotton went into the production of a wide range of textiles both for domestic use and for export, and in 1860 British-produced textiles constituted about a third of American imports. Clearly, cotton was at the center of Anglo-American trade in the nineteenth century. As one economic historian notes: "The key to American

---

40. *Historical Statistics of the United States,* op. cit., p. 139. For figures on cotton production and cotton exports, see Stuart Bruchey, *Cotton and the Growth of the American Economy, 1790–1860* (New York: Harcourt, 1967), pp. 14–17.

growth before the Civil War must be sought in European and largely British, markets, European and again largely British, capital resources; in other words, in the dynamics of an Atlantic economy. . . . Cotton was the most important stimulus to growth in both countries."[41]

Not only was the United States the major supplier of cotton for Britain's expanding textile industry, but it rapidly developed its own thriving domestic industry. The number of textile mills increased from 15 in 1808 to 105 in 1809; the number of spindles increased from 31,000 in 1809 to 80,000 in 1811.

Growth in the textile industry set off a chain reaction in manufacturing that ramified throughout the economy. To quote North again:

Forward linkages with a vast array of final consumer goods industries to meet the needs of the northeastern urban dweller, the southern slave and planter, and the western farmer made the complex of industries which grew up around cotton and wool the most important in pre-Civil War America.[42]

The backward linkages went into textile machinery, machine tools, and iron products. In addition, the textile industry supported the development of an interregional transportation network, shipping and port facilities, and a distribution system, not to speak of banking, insurance, and other such ancillary industries. Thus, it can be said without exaggeration that cotton was the sine qua non of early industrial development in both the United States and Britain. Marx summed up the relationship between slavery, cotton, and industrial development in a single epigrammatic statement: "Without slavery there is no cotton; without cotton there is no modern industry."[43]

41. Frank Thistlethwaite, *The Anglo-American Connection in the Early Nineteenth Century* (Philadelphia: University of Pennsylvania Press, 1959), pp. 10–11.

42. North, op. cit., p. 171.

43. Karl Marx, *The Philosophy of Poverty* (Chicago: Charles H. Kerr, 1934), p. 121. Marx makes his point with characteristic hyperbole. However, essentially the same point is made in more sobering language by Douglass C. North in his book on *The Economic Growth of the United States, 1790–1860:* "Without cotton the development in the size of the [export] market would have been a much more lengthy process since there was no alternative

The enslavement of the African, like the earlier conquest of the Indian, required a rationalizing ideology. It is facile to think that blacks were enslaved because they were seen as inferior; it would be closer to the truth to say that they were defined as inferior so that they might be enslaved. This is not a matter of theoretical induction alone. As Winthrop Jordan has shown, negative conceptions of blacks date back to the earliest contacts between Europeans and Africans, but racist ideology as we know it today evolved in tandem with slavery, and in every epoch was modified and adapted to prevailing concepts of rational knowledge.[44] Consider the following characterization of "the Negro," which appeared in the 1910 *Encyclopaedia Britannica:*

> . . . the negro would appear to stand on a lower evolutionary plane than the white man. . . . Mentally the negro is inferior to the white. . . . [T]he remark of F. Manetta, made after a long study of the negro in America, may be taken as generally true of the whole race: "the negro children were sharp, intelligent and full of vivacity, but on approaching the adult period a gradual change set in. The intellect seemed to become clouded, animation giving place to a sort of lethargy, briskness yielding to indolence. . . ." On the other hand negroes far surpass white men in acuteness of vision, hearing, sense of direction and topography. . . . For the rest, the mental condition is very similar to that of a child, normally good-natured and cheerful, but subject to sudden fits of emotion and passion during which he is capable of performing acts of singular atrocity. . . .[45]

---

way to expand the domestic market rapidly without recourse to external demand. In short, cotton was the most proximate cause of expansion. . . ." (p. 68).

Some economic historians have challenged North's suggestion that cotton was *the* major expansive force in the antebellum economy. While there is room for disagreement over precisely what weight to assign to this single factor, it is clear that cotton was *a* major factor in nineteenth-century economic development, and that, from an economic standpoint, the North had a large stake in slavery.

44. Jordan, op. cit., chap. 1.

45. *Encyclopaedia Britannica* (1911), vol. 19, pp. 344–45.

It is not difficult to see how these characterizations were originally tailored to a slave system. To assert that Negroes occupy a lower plane in the evolutionary scale is to "explain" their inferior position in society. To claim that they lapse into indolence as they reach adulthood is to justify the whip. To allow that Negroes have sharp sense and primitive impulses is to suggest that they are constitutionally akin to beasts of burden suited for labor in the fields. To portray them as childlike, good-natured, and cheerful is to create the illusion of the contented slave, and to sanction the patriarchal elements inherent in slavery. And finally, to warn that the Negro is given to fits of passion and acts of singular atrocity is to account for the slaves' rebelliousness and rage without acknowledging them as such, and hence also to justify a system of controls to keep Negroes in their assigned place. In all these ways, racist allegations functioned as an ideological smoke screen designed to give moral legitimacy to a brutal and inhumane system of labor exploitation.

Such was the inauspicious beginning of the nation's first minority whose roots were outside the Western Hemisphere. If the benefits of slavery had been limited to a small class of slaveholders, or even to the regional economy of the South, it is hardly conceivable that the "peculiar institution" would have persisted for so long. But the benefits redounded to the nation as a whole, which helps to explain why blacks were kept in quasi-servitude even after slavery itself was abolished. In these various forms of racial domination and exploitation, the nation, under the guise of a racist mythology, had established a precedent not only for tolerating extremes of inequality, but for imparting them with political and moral legitimacy as well. This would have fateful consequences for other racial and ethnic outsiders, even if they entered the country under more favorable circumstances.

Industrial Development

The relationship between southern cotton and northern industry was only one element in a complex pattern of regional specialization and interdependence that facilitated the nation's economic development. As Louis Schmidt described it in 1920:

The rise of internal commerce after 1815 made possible a territorial division of labor between the three great sections of the Union—the West, the South, and the East. . . . The South was thereby enabled to devote itself in particular to the production of a few plantation staples contributing a large and growing surplus for the foreign markets and depending on the West for a large part of its food supply and on the East for the bulk of its manufactured goods and very largely for the conduct of its commerce and banking. The East was devoted chiefly to manufacturing and commerce, supplying the products of its industries as well as the imports and much of the capital for the West and the South while it became to an increasing extent dependent on the food and the fibers of these two sections. The West became a surplus grain- and livestock-producing kingdom, supplying the growing deficits of the South and East.[46]

Corresponding to this pattern of regional specialization was a distinctive pattern of ethnic concentration. All three regions were confronted with an acute deficit of population and labor, and all three were compelled to import settlers and workers. Just as the South came to depend primarily on slave labor, at least in the critical area of cotton production, the North, and to a lesser extent the West, came to depend heavily on foreign labor imported primarily from Europe.

Immigration began as a trickle, gradually gained momentum during the nineteenth century, and finally assumed the dimensions of a flood by the beginning of the twentieth century. A few figures will help to convey the immensity of this movement.[47] As late as

46. Quoted in North, op. cit., p. 103. It should be noted that North's sectional trade hypothesis has been criticized by economic historians who argue that, notwithstanding the tendency toward sectional specialization, each region had a diversified economy that resulted in a significant degree of regional independence and self-sufficiency. For example, see Diane Lindstrom, *Economic Development in the Philadelphia Region, 1810–1850* (New York: Columbia University Press, 1978), chap. 1. This is a valid qualification, and the complexity of regional economies should not be minimized, but it is still true that there was an overall pattern of regional specialization that spurred economic development. Of paramount importance here is the fact that the unique economic character of each region required different solutions to the labor deficit that hampered growth in all regions.

47. *Historical Statistics of the United States,* op. cit., pp. 105–6.

1820, when the first official immigration statistics became available, only about 8,000 immigrants entered the country annually. In the six decades between Independence and 1840, total immigration was only three quarters of a million people. After 1840, however, there were two great waves of immigration that provided the necessary manpower for sustained economic growth. Between 1840 and 1880 over eight million Europeans entered the country. Between 1880 and 1930 the figure rose to over 23 million. This extraordinary population movement—the largest in recorded history—was fundamentally the result of an extraordinary economic expansion—also the largest and most concentrated in history.

Demographers and historians have identified a host of push and pull factors that operated on different groups, and much effort has gone into assessing the relative importance of each. However, the push and pull factor that was of overriding significance was one and the same: the process of industrialization which, paradoxically, had contrary effects on opposite sides of the Atlantic.

In Europe, industrialization resulted in a series of economic dislocations that affected both the rural and urban populations, and provided the major stimulus for emigration. In the countryside, improved farm technology not only reduced the need for labor, but also transformed the organization of rural economies, leading to a consolidation of small farms into larger and more productive estates. The impact of these changes was exacerbated by the fact that falling mortality rates resulted in a population explosion. Even this was indirectly a function of the industrial age, inasmuch as famine and epidemics were virtually eliminated by increased farm productivity on the one hand, and advances in medicine on the other. Occurring at a time when the demand for farm labor was shrinking, the population explosion triggered a mass migration of peasants to European cities where the labor markets were also overcrowded. As a consequence, millions of these displaced peasants continued their journey to the underpopulated countries of the New World.

The agrarian crisis was further compounded by increased competition from cheap grain produced outside Western Europe. As Maldwyn Jones points out:

> Thanks to the railroad and the cargo steamer the cost of transporting grain fell dramatically, with the result that the wheat farmers of the United States, Russia, India, and other distant

countries could for the first time compete successfully in the European market.[48]

The impact of foreign competition on European farming was often catastrophic. Periodic agricultural depressions and poor harvests, furthermore, prompted landowners to convert their land from grain production to pasturage, especially in England and Ireland where wool was in demand from the nascent textile industry. The end result, once again, was a massive displacement of the peasant population.

Of course, the urban and industrial sectors of these societies were expanding, but not nearly fast enough to absorb all of the surplus rural population. Indeed, industrialization was playing havoc with the urban labor markets as well. The introduction of the factory system, and the increasing use of machinery for work that was previously done by hand, meant the displacement of large numbers of craftsmen and artisans from their traditional occupations. Industrial workers were also at the mercy of economic vicissitudes and periodic depressions, which provided a further spur to emigration. Confronted with a population surplus in both rural and urban sectors, most European societies came to regard emigration as a useful safety valve and relaxed earlier restrictions on emigration. The final barrier to mass immigration was removed with the advent of the steamship, which reduced the transatlantic voyage from several weeks to just ten days. The steamship changed the character as well as the volume of emigration, inasmuch as it now became practical for migrants to return to their countries of origin once they had accumulated some savings. By the end of the nineteenth century, the immigrant pool increasingly consisted of migrant laborers who left their wives and children behind, and shuttled back and forth across the Atlantic, though in the end many settled permanently in America.

In short, the economic dislocations associated with the industrialization of European societies provided the major stimulus for mass immigration.[49] Eastern European Jews are a notable exception to

48. Jones, op. cit., p. 193.

49. Simon Kuznets, "Long-Term Changes in the National Income of the United States of America since 1870," in Kuznets, ed., *Income and Wealth of the United States: Trends and Structure* (Cambridge: Bowes & Bowes, 1952), pp. 198–99.

this pattern, in that religious persecution and political oppression provided the chief motivation for emigrating. Although some immigrants, especially among the Jews, British, and Germans, were industrial workers or skilled craftsmen, the overwhelming number of European immigrants were peasants or farm laborers.

Virtually all of the eight million immigrants who came to America between 1840 and 1880 had their origins in northwestern Europe. Most came from Germany, Britain, Ireland, and Scandinavia, in that order. In contrast, the 24 million immigrants who constituted the second wave between 1880 and 1930 largely had their origins in eastern and southern Europe. Italians, Poles, and Russian Jews were by far the largest groups, but numerous other nationalities had significant representation: Slavs, Slovaks, Croatians, Serbs, Czechs, Bulgarians, Hungarians, Lithuanians, Romanians, Spanish, Portuguese, and others. Even though eastern and southern Europeans constituted the bulk of the "new immigration," especially after 1890, this second wave included substantial numbers of "old" immigrants from northwestern Europe. For example, Germany, Ireland, and England each contributed more than one million immigrants between 1891 and 1930.

At the same time that industrialization uprooted millions of Europeans it generated an almost unsatiable demand for labor in the United States. In the first place, improvements in farm technology, together with increasing demand for farm products, contributed to an expansive rural economy throughout the nineteenth century. Nor were cities saddled with surplus population, and during these early stages of industrialization, it was unskilled labor that was most in demand. Brute strength, rather than technical skills, was the main "qualification" for the armies of workers engaged in mining, construction, and manufacturing.

Even those industries that traditionally employed skilled workers were undergoing a process of skill diminution as machines were substituted for manual skills. As Gabriel Kolko has written of the 1880s: "Mechanization was quite generally the rule, and it could incorporate a polyglot labor force with minimal talents into the operation of an industrialism that required skilled labor less and less."[50] Consequently, the fact that the bulk of immigrants were

50. Gabriel Kolko, *Main Currents in Modern American History* (New York: Harper & Row, 1976), p. 73.

peasants in background was not an obstacle to their entry into the industrial work force.

It would be difficult to overestimate the critical role that immigrant labor played in the industrialization of America. The volume of immigration itself closely followed the vagaries of the economy, as Harry Jerome has shown in his book on *Migration and the Business Cycle*. [51] With every peak and trough in the business cycle, immigration tended to rise and fall accordingly. Despite occasional recessions, however, the overall direction was one of dramatic growth, and the expanding labor force became increasingly dependent on immigrant labor. By 1910, the foreign-born made up a quarter of the nation's work force, and in many of the industries closest to the industrial center, the foreign-born were a clear majority. In 1910 the Dillingham Commission conducted a survey of twenty principal mining and manufacturing industries, and found that 58 percent of workers were foreign-born. In coal mines the figure was 48 percent; in iron mines 67 percent; in clothing factories 76 percent; in slaughter- and packing-houses 46 percent; in car and railroad shops 46 percent; in tanneries 53 percent; in steel mills 51 percent; in rubber factories 41 percent; in textile mills 49 percent; in road construction 46 percent.[52] Despite its nativist inclinations, the Dillingham Commission was forced to concede that the economic expansion of the previous two decades would not have been possible without the "immigrant hordes." Indeed, if slavery is to be credited with laying the foundation for the nation's industrial development, then it was foreign labor that finally erected the industrial edifice itself.

What overall judgment is to be made with respect to the mass immigration of the late nineteenth and early twentieth centuries? Did immigration represent opportunity to the "huddled masses" of Europe, as has been proclaimed in American folklore? Or would it be more accurate to say that immigration involved the exploitation of foreign labor on a colossal scale? This question cannot be an-

51. Harry Jerome, *Migration and the Business Cycle* (New York: National Bureau of Economic Research, 1926).

52. United States Immigration Commission, *Immigrants in Industries* (Washington, 1911), vol. VIII. Gerald Rosenblum, *Immigrant Workers* (New York: Basic Books, 1973), pp. 70–81.

swered simply. Unlike the millions of Africans who were imported against their will, and unlike Indians and Mexicans who were conquered by force, European immigrants came as a matter of choice. Clearly, no matter how dire their circumstances were in America, conditions were still worse in their countries of origin, which is why they wrenched themselves away from their homes and families, and why they so frequently sent for relatives and friends after they arrived. Contrary to legend, few immigrants came with illusions of streets paved with gold; most were lured primarily by industrial wages and had fairly realistic expectations of a better life. If the moral calculus depends on such a comparison between the lives of immigrants before and after their arrival in America, then the question of whether immigration was exploitation or opportunity must be decided in favor of the latter.

But can the question be so easily dismissed? Can the injustices visited upon immigrants be dismissed because most of them would have been still worse off in Europe? Apologists for slavery had also contended that blacks had been rescued from "barbarism and paganism," but not only is such an argument based on a false assumption—Africans lived in stable and highly developed agricultural settlements—the circumstances of blacks in Africa can hardly mitigate the inhumane aspects of slavery. Whatever benefits eventually came to immigrants, it must be remembered that immigration was anything but a work relief program for Europe's masses. If America did not desperately need immigrant labor, then tens of millions of immigrants would never have been permitted to come in the first place. To put it simply, America needed the immigrant at least as much as the immigrant needed America.

In effect, Europe functioned as an immense labor reserve for America's burgeoning industries. Immigrant labor was especially desirable because it was so malleable. Uprooted from their families and communities, immigrants could be deployed to remote areas of the country, and specifically to such low-wage industries as mining and railroad construction that could not attract native workers in sufficient numbers. As indigents from abroad, lacking alternatives and living on the edge of survival, they were ripe for exploitation. Forced by their circumstances to accept the dirty, backbreaking, and menial work that native workers were unwilling to do, immigrants constituted a cheap and highly mobile labor force for the most exploitative jobs at a time when American capitalism was in its most rapacious phase.

But if immigrants were so easily exploited and so valuable to the nation's economic growth, why were they so maligned? How are we to explain the pervasive bigotry and systematic abuse that were the experience of virtually every immigrant group? Was nativism a simple expression of xenophobia on the part of native-born Americans, or was it fundamentally a result of a conflict of interest between immigrant and native workers?

To be sure, the nation's expanding industries needed labor, but even more than that, they needed cheap labor. For labor to be cheap, it had to exceed demand even at a time when demand was accelerating rapidly. A tight labor market not only would have constricted economic growth, but also would have resulted in an upward pressure on wages as industries competed for scarce labor. The existence of a labor surplus had the opposite effect. It exerted pressure on workers to accept long hours, poor conditions, and low wages. The real function of the liberal immigration policies of the period, therefore, was to flood the labor market in order to keep labor abundant and cheap. Without this contrived surplus of immigrant labor, the costs of economic growth would have been immeasurably greater, thereby shrinking the capital base that was essential for economic growth.

In addition, mass immigration had adverse effects on organized labor in at least two respects. The abundance of cheap labor provided incentive to industrialists to introduce new technology which substituted unskilled machine operators for skilled workers, triggering a nativist reaction among craft workers. Secondly, so long as there was a surfeit of labor, industrial unions were practically doomed to failure, which in turn helped to keep wages low. Thus, immigrants were not only exploited themselves, but they were also used as an instrument for the more effective exploitation of others, whether native or immigrant. For this reason, immigrant workers were sometimes compelled to put aside their ethnic loyalties and to join the chorus agitating for immigration restriction. For example, after losing a strike in 1905, a union composed primarily of Jewish garment workers passed the following resolution:

Resolved: That the unprecedented movement of the very poor into America from Europe in the last three years has resulted in wholly changing the previous social, political, and economic aspects of the immigration question. . . . The overstocking of the labor market has become a menace to many trade-unions, especially those of the lesser skilled workers. . . . The fate of the majority of the foreign wage-workers now here has served to demonstrate on the largest possible scale that immigration is no solution for the world-wide problem of poverty.[53]

In his 1912 study of *Immigration and Labor,* Isaac Hourwich argued that by spurring economic growth, immigration actually created opportunities for native workers, a view that is widely held among contemporary historians as well.[54] Nevertheless, the immediate effects were not always favorable, especially for workers who were in direct competition with immigrants. For example, between 1880 and 1914 there was little or no improvement in the real wages of workers, despite a rising level of affluence generally.[55] Thus, there was more than xenophobia and irrationality behind the nativist backlash among rank-and-file workers.[56]

Despite over half a century of nativist agitation and repeated efforts to restrict immigration by introducing a literacy test or some other device, the floodgates of immigration remained open so long as cheap foreign labor was in demand. By the 1920s, however, the rate of capital growth declined from its previous heights, and the ap-

53. Quoted in John R. Commons, *Races and Immigrants in America* (New York: Augustus M. Kelley, 1967; orig. edition 1907), pp. 115–16. This was not an anomalous event; see Zosa Szajkowski, "The Attitude of American Jews to East European Jewish Immigration (1881–1893)," *Publications of the American Jewish Historical Society* (March 1951), pp. 221–80.

54. Isaac Hourwich, *Immigration and Labor* (New York: Putnam, 1912).

55. Economic historians disagree on whether there was an absolute increase in the real wages of manufacturing workers during the quarter century prior to the First World War. However, as Gabriel Kolko (op. cit., p. 169) has written: "Whatever the exact truth, America's growth was below known European rates, and all agree that 1900–1914 saw the lowest expansion of real income during the past century, and this was largely due to immigration."

56. See John Higham, "Another Look at Nativism," in *Send These to Me,* op. cit., pp. 102–15.

plication of new labor-saving technology further reduced the demand for labor. Besides, nearly a century of mass immigration, consisting largely of adults in their childbearing ages, had swelled the population to a point where the nation was assured of an adequate labor supply in the future without depending on massive infusions of foreign labor. With the passage of the Immigration Acts of 1921 and 1924, the door was rudely shut on the "huddled masses of Europe."

At last the nation had resolved its population deficit. In the process of aggregating population, however, the ethnic profile of the American people had been drastically and irreversibly changed. Roughly 32 million Europeans immigrated between 1820 and 1930. As Table 2 shows, Germans had the largest representation, with nearly six million immigrant arrivals. Next are the Italians and Irish, with about four and a half million each, followed by the Poles, Canadians, Jews, and English. Together these seven groups account for about 80 percent of all immigration from Europe between 1820 and 1930, though numerous other nationalities are represented in smaller but substantial numbers. For a nation that once prided itself on its ethnic homogeneity, the United States had become the most polyglot nation in history.

Conclusion

The historical circumstances under which groups entered American society—whether they were overpowered by a nation bent on territorial conquest, whether they were shackled to slave galleys, or whether they came over on immigrant vessels in search of a better life—is of obvious importance. But related to this, and of more enduring significance, is the fact that these groups played vastly different roles in the development of American capitalism. Robert Blauner has addressed this issue with unusual insight and clarity:

Like European overseas colonialism, America has used African, Asian, Mexican and, to a lesser degree, Indian workers for the cheapest labor, concentrating people of color in the most unskilled jobs, the least advanced sectors of the economy, and the most industrially backward regions of the nation. In an his-

Table 2

NET IMMIGRATION OF VARIOUS EUROPEAN NATIONALITIES, 1820–1930

Ethnic Group	Estimated Total
1. Germans	5,900,000
2. Italians	4,600,000
3. Irish	4,500,000
4. Poles	3,000,000
5. Canadians	2,800,000
6. Jews*	2,500,000
7. English	2,500,000
8. Swedes	1,200,000
9. Scots and Scots-Irish	1,000,000
10. Norwegians	770,000
11. Slavs	750,000
12. French	580,000
13. Hungarians	500,000
14. Greeks	400,000
15. Danes	300,000
16. Finns	275,000
17. Portuguese	250,000

* Approximate

SOURCE: Adapted from Richard M. Burkey, *Ethnic and Racial Groups,* copyright © 1978, The Benjamin Cummings Publishing Co., pp. 200–201.

torical sense, people of color provided much of the hard labor (and the technical skills) that built up the agricultural base and the mineral-transport-communication infrastructure necessary for industrialization and modernization, whereas the European worked primarily within the industrialized, modern sectors. The initial position of European ethnics, while low, was therefore strategic for movement up the economic and social pyramid. The placement of nonwhite groups, however, imposed barrier upon barrier on such mobility, freezing them for long periods of time in the least favorable segments of the economy.[57]

Although their labor was exploited, at least immigrants were employed mostly in industry, and as Blauner notes, "had a foot in the most dynamic centers of the economy and could, with time, rise to semiskilled and skilled positions."[58] In contrast, racial minorities were for the most part relegated to the preindustrial sectors of the national economy and, until the flow of immigration was cut off by the First World War, were denied access to the industrial jobs that lured tens of millions of immigrants. All groups started at the bottom, but as Blauner points out, " 'the bottom' has by no means been the same for all groups."

Related to this difference in labor deployment and economic function was a difference in the prevailing ideologies regarding racial and immigrant minorities. Although the prejudice against immigrants was greater than is generally realized, it still was not as virulent, as pervasive, or as enduring as that experienced by racial minorities; nor was it given official sanction. But the qualitative differences are even more important. Immigrants were disparaged for their cultural peculiarities, and the implied message was, "You will become like us whether you want to or not." When it came to racial minorities, however, the unspoken dictum was, "No matter how much like us you are, you will remain apart." Thus, at the same time that the nation pursued a policy aimed at the rapid assimilation of recent arrivals from Europe, it segregated the racial minorities who, by virtue of their much longer history in American society, had already come to share much of the dominant culture.

Yet each system of prejudice was perfectly tailored to fit the respective functions that the different groups played in the national economy. It required a much more oppressive system of controls to keep blacks, for example, in a position of quasi-servitude in southern agriculture, than to regulate immigrant workers who, for all the hardships they endured, at least were wage laborers. The prejudice directed against immigrants was rooted in the fact that

57. Robert Blauner, *Racial Oppression in America* (New York: Harper & Row, 1972), p. 62.
58. Ibid., p. 63.

they were both alien and poor, and gradually declined as these groups became more assimilated and achieved middle-class respectability.

Thus, the different origins of America's minorities were fateful for their respective destinies in American society. From a larger perspective, however, neither racial nor immigrant minorities had origins that were conducive to their long-term survival as distinct social and cultural entities. Unlike some plural societies that were formed out of a fusion of neighboring territories with distinct ethnic populations, pluralism in the United States evolved out of the displacement of masses of individuals. As transplanted minorities, ripped from their cultural moorings and lacking a territorial base, cultural survival would have been problematic under the best of circumstances.

In actuality, the native cultures of Indians and blacks were ruthlessly stamped out, though paradoxically, the extreme segregation of these groups allowed for an evolution of distinctive ethnic subcultures built upon vestiges of their original cultures. In comparison, immigrant minorities had greater freedom to promote their special identities, which they did in the communities that developed around ethnic populations. Nevertheless, given their position at or near the bottom of the class system, and dependent economically on the surrounding society, immigrants were compelled to relinquish much of their European heritage in order to achieve their aspirations for social and economic mobility.

In short, American society provided only a weak structural basis for ethnic preservation. The very circumstances under which ethnic groups entered American society virtually predestined them to a gradual but inexorable decline. There is room for debate concerning the future of ethnic pluralism in America, especially in light of the recent influx of new groups from Latin America and Asia. However, the arrival of these groups may serve only to highlight the cultural affinities that have developed among ethnic groups that by now have historic roots in this country.

Chapter 2

The Ethnic Crisis in American Society

*"There she lies, the great melting pot—listen! Can't you
hear the roaring and the bubbling?"*

ISRAEL ZANGWILL, *The Melting Pot*, 1909

A NEW ethnic generation is coming of age—a fourth generation:
the great-grandchildren of immigrants who were part of the last
great wave of immigration that ended with the imposition of quotas
in 1924. What makes this generation unique is that its members
have no direct ancestral memories that reach back to their countries
of origin. Their parents and grandparents were rooted in the immigrant generation and had this as a point of cultural reference,
even as they jettisoned much of the cultural baggage that their immigrant forebears carried over with them from Europe. But the
fourth generation, whose grandparents were also American-born,
lack this personal anchor in the cultural past, even as they attempt
to recover and reaffirm aspects of their waning ethnicity. In this
sense the fourth generation represents a watershed in American
ethnic history, and the ethnic future is more clouded than ever
before.

For over half a century the number of Americans who were born
in Europe has been on a steady decline. In the case of most European nationalities—including Irish, Germans, Scandinavians, Poles,
Eastern European Jews—the number of foreign-born persons has

been cut by half or even two-thirds from its high point earlier in the century. Furthermore, the foreign-born are an aging population: their median age in 1970 was 55 years, twice that of the overall population.[1] It is clear that the nation's European-born population is rapidly vanishing.

Of course, by itself this does not signify a decline of ethnicity. Any such conclusion must obviously be based on an assessment of the strength of ethnic identity among more recent generations. Nevertheless, the passing immigrant generation constitutes an irreparable loss to groups striving to preserve their unique cultures and identities. Immigrants, after all, were the purveyors of the authentic culture. So long as the stream of European immigration continued, it replenished the ranks of ethnic groups with individuals who personified their ethnicity in the purest form. By their presence alone, immigrants represented a cultural point of reference even for the more assimilated members of the groups involved. Though second- and third-generation Americans strayed far from immigrant culture, they did so with a deeply personal knowledge of their roots acquired through their immigrant parents and grandparents, and this undoubtedly kept them from straying even farther. It remains to be seen how the fourth generation will fare without this living symbol of the ethnic past.

With the passing of the immigrant generation, there has been a precipitous decline in the number of Americans who speak the native tongue of their ethnic group. Studies conducted by Joshua Fishman indicate an almost complete breakdown in the transmission of non-English languages between the second and third generations. For example, when Fishman collected his data in 1960, there were 2,300,000 second-generation Italians who spoke Italian, but among the third generation, the figure plummeted to 147,000. Similarly, between the second and third generations, the number speaking Yiddish dropped from 422,000 to 39,000. For Poles, the comparable figures are 1,516,000 and 87,000; for Swedes, 187,000 and 17,000. Even in the case of Germans, where commitment to language runs strong, the number speaking German dropped from 1,279,000 in the second generation to 588,000 in the third. Notwithstanding the title

1. *Historical Statistics of the United States* (Washington, D.C.: Government Printing Office, 1975), pp. 116–17. The age figures are based on foreign-born whites (p. 19).

of his study—*Language Loyalty in the United States*—Fishman was forced to conclude that "these figures clearly indicate a serious erosion of the manpower base upon which language maintenance may well depend."[2]

Language is important not only in itself, but also because it shapes cultural perceptions and attitudes. To be sure, ethnic distinctiveness can and does endure after the mother tongue is lost, but it is equally clear that a vital link to the cultural past has been severed. The almost complete break in language transmission between the second and third generations marks a decisive stage in the assimilation process, and it means that the fourth generation is the first generation to be reared by parents who, except in rare instances, cannot speak the native tongue of their ethnic group.

The adoption of English as the exclusive language is only one symptom of a larger transformation in the nature and content of ethnicity. Studies conducted over several decades have documented the far-reaching changes over ethnic generations, especially as these groups have overcome the economic disabilities associated with the immigrant generation and achieved middle-class respectability. No one denies that the ethnicity of groups today is profoundly different from the ethnicity that immigrants carried over with them from Europe. What is argued is that people still identify powerfully with their ethnic groups, and through a proliferation of voluntary organizations and an elaborate network of interpersonal relationships, have been able to rebuild ethnic communities in a way that is compatible with American life. Issue arises, however, over whether the accommodations of earlier generations constitute a new basis for a lasting ethnicity, or whether they signal the demise of ethnic groups.

Two Views of the Melting Pot

On this issue there has been a striking shift in the prevailing view among ethnic specialists in the various social sciences. Generally speaking, the battle lines have been drawn between an earlier generation of sociologists who emphasized the assimilating tenden-

2. Joshua Fishman et al., *Language Loyalty in the United States* (The Hague: Mouton & Company, 1966), pp. 42–44.

cies among immigrant minorities, and a more recent group of writers who insist that ethnicity is a powerful and enduring factor in American life. Let us refer to the former as "melting pot theorists," and the latter as "ethnic pluralists."

The melting pot theorists were based at the University of Chicago, with Robert Park as the leading theorist. Though their writing spanned several decades, Park and his followers began their research in the 1910s, when over one million immigrants were entering the United States each year. According to the 1910 census, nearly 70 percent of Chicago's population was made up of immigrants and their children, and over twenty nationalities were represented in substantial numbers. Against this backdrop, the Chicago sociologists turned to the question of what happens "when people of divergent cultures come into contact and conflict."[3]

In response to this question, Park posited a "race relations cycle," drawing upon the ecological perspective that was the hallmark of the Chicago school. The three stages of this cycle—contact, accommodation, and assimilation—involve different degrees of absorption of the dominant culture. By "assimilation," Park meant something less than a total obliteration of ethnic difference. Rather, the term referred to a "superficial uniformity" between the minority and dominant groups that could conceal differences in "opinion, sentiments, and belief."[4] However, Park believed that this stage in the assimilation process would lead inexorably to a final stage—amalgamation—which occurred through interbreeding and intermarriage.*

For Park the race relations cycle was "progressive and irreversible," but contrary to the claims of his modern critics, he did not predict an abrupt and complete "melting" of ethnic groups. On the contrary, he was careful to point out that "the process of ac-

---

3. Robert Park, *Race and Culture* (Glencoe, Ill.: Free Press, 1950), p. 5.
4. Robert Park, "Racial Assimilation in Secondary Groups," *American Journal of Sociology*, 1914, p. 607.

*Throughout this chapter "assimilation" is used in a way consistent with Park—to indicate a stage in an assimilation process that involves the adoption of significant aspects of the dominant culture, but that does not preclude subtle differences in values and outlook among ethnic groups. Whether assimilation in this sense leads to amalgamation is an empirical question that can be addressed only by examining trends in intermarriage, as is done at the end of the chapter.

culturation and assimilation and the accompanying amalgamation of racial [i.e., ethnic] stocks does not proceed with the same ease and the same speed in all cases."[5] Park was never so rash as to project a specific timetable for assimilation, recognizing that "assimilation is not a simple process, and above all else, takes time."[6] Since his attention was riveted on long-term historical trends, he was not distracted by the complexities and nuances of the moment. From an evolutionary standpoint it was evident that the race relations cycle was a universal phenomenon, and Park found evidence for this principle in the fact that all modern nationalities were "a composite of the broken fragments of several different groups."[7] Did it not follow that a new nationality would evolve out of the melange of racial and ethnic groups that were coming together in America?

Paradoxically, the melting pot theorists wrote at a time when ethnic groups were more entrenched and distinct than at any other time in American history. Yet Park and his followers were struck by the rapidity with which immigrant groups adopted at least the "outward forms" of the dominant culture, and subjectively as well as objectively were becoming Americanized. On the other hand, today's "ethnic pluralists" write at a time when the cultures of ethnic groups have been radically transformed after several generations of accommodation and change, and the lines of ethnic distinctiveness are more blurred than ever. Yet the ethnic pluralists insist that ethnic groups are holding their own, and they scoff at the very idea of a melting pot. Unfortunately, much of their polemic against the melting pot theorists is based on two false assumptions: first, that the melting pot theorists predicted an imminent dissolution of ethnic groups into the American mainstream; and second, that because they saw assimilation as inevitable in the long run, they gave it moral sanction. These assumptions have allowed the ethnic pluralists to present themselves as stalwart defenders of ethnicity, protecting it from the heresies of usually unnamed antagonists who are scored as having little sympathy or understanding of

5. Robert Park, "Human Migration and the Marginal Man," *American Journal of Sociology*, 1914, p. 890.

6. Robert Park, *Race and Culture*, op. cit., p. 169.

7. Ibid., p. 611.

the richness of ethnic life, and would reduce ethnics to "jellyfish Americans," or "plastic Americans," lacking in cultural integrity.[8]

Such polemics are obviously of little enduring value, however much they may bolster the spirits of individuals and groups struggling to preserve their ethnicity. Actually, once the position of the ethnic pluralists is stripped of its rhetorical excess, it is not altogether at odds with the position of the melting pot theorists, at least on questions concerning the ethnic past. Much of the controversy between the two schools boils down to a different conception and definition of ethnicity. Writing at a time when immigration was in full sway, the Chicago sociologists gauged ethnic trends in terms of the transformations that they observed in immigrant culture. Apprehending the ethnic scene a half-century later, when immigrant culture is on the wane, the ethnic pluralists are basing their assessment of ethnic trends on the modes of identity and cohesion that they observe among the second and third generations. As already suggested, however, the key question is whether these new forms of ethnicity only amount to stages in an ineluctable process of assimilation, or whether they form a basis for a lasting ethnicity, and this question the ethnic pluralists have chosen to ignore.

Writing in the early 1970s, the ethnic pluralists not only sought to interpret the ethnic fever of the moment, but they also became unabashed spokesmen for the "new ethnicity." In a real sense they became part of the phenomenon they were writing about, especially since their ideas were given wide currency in popular journals and books. Their books had titles that looked *Beyond the Melting Pot,* and that reveled in *The Decline of the WASP* and *The Rise of the Unmeltable Ethnics.*[9] The ethnic writers celebrated what they viewed as the triumph of ethnicity over the forces of assimilation. Their overall position was encapsulated in the title of an article in

8. Richard Gambino, *Blood of My Blood* (Garden City, N.Y.: Anchor, 1975), p. 357; Peter Schrag, *The Decline of the WASP* (New York: Simon and Schuster, 1971), pp. 185–225.

9. Nathan Glazer and Daniel Patrick Moynihan, *Beyond the Melting Pot* (Cambridge: MIT Press, 1970); Peter Schrag, *The Decline of the WASP,* op. cit.; Michael Novak, *The Rise of the Unmeltable Ethnics* (New York: Macmillan, 1971).

The New York Times Magazine: "America is NOT a Melting Pot."[10]

Interestingly enough, it was a renowned Swedish critic of American society, Gunnar Myrdal, who was among the first to attack the unsubstantiated claims of the ethnic writers. As he wrote in 1974:

Ethnic writers have concentrated on an abstract craving for historical identity, but they have not clarified by intensive study what cultural traits are implied, who wants this identity, who should want it, and why, and how it should and could come about. I am afraid, therefore, one must characterize this movement as an upper-class intellectual romanticism.[11]

That same year, Herbert Gans wrote in a similar vein that:

. . . even the raw materials for an ethnic cultural revival in America are unavailable, and despite the claim of some ethnic intellectuals, so is the interest for such a revival.[12]

Comparing the ethnic revival to the religious revival of the 1950s, Gans predicted that "in a few years the revival of ethnicity will also be forgotten."

Now that some years have lapsed since the ethnic upsurge, the time is right to ask why it occurred and whether it will have lasting impact. In any such inquiry, it is necessary to distinguish between racial minorities and white ethnics. Although both groups expressed a common impulse to raise ethnic consciousness and strengthen group bonds, there was a fundamental difference between them, rooted in the fact that racial minorities are generally poorer and must cope with a more intense and pervasive bigotry based on indelible marks of race. That the ethnic resurgence involved more than nostalgia became clear as racial minorities and white ethnics became polarized on a series of issues relating to schools, housing, local government, and control over federal programs. Given the different economic and political dimensions of ethnicity in the two

10. W. H. Auden, *New York Times Magazine,* March 18, 1972.

11. Gunnar Myrdal, "The Case against Romantic Ethnicity," *Center Magazine,* 1974, p. 30.

12. Herbert Gans, in his introduction to Neil C. Sandberg, *Ethnic Identity and Assimilation: The Polish-American Community* (New York: Praeger, 1974), p. vii.

instances, it would not be correct to treat the ethnicity of racial minorities and immigrant white minorities as variants of the same phenomenon; the analysis that follows deals exclusively with the ethnicity of white immigrant minorities.

Although the ethnic upsurge of the 1960s was in part a response to the racial polarization and conflict of that turbulent decade, in important respects it was the outgrowth of long-range historical trends unrelated to the racial issue. The thesis advanced here is that the ethnic revival was a "dying gasp" on the part of ethnic groups descended from the great waves of immigration of the nineteenth and early twentieth centuries. That is to say, the revival did not signify a genuine revitalization of ethnicity, but rather was symptomatic of the atrophy of ethnic cultures and the decline of ethnic communities. Placed in historical perspective, the revival appears to have been doomed from the outset, inasmuch as it could not possibly reverse trends that have been in the making for several generations and that are firmly rooted in the larger society.

Problematic Origins

The first point to be considered is that the circumstances under which European immigrants began life in America were hardly conducive to a genuine and lasting pluralism. As transplanted minorities, separated by long distances from their homelands and lacking historical roots in their adopted country, immigrants were plunged into a crisis of identity upon their arrival in America. In an autobiographical book entitled *An American in the Making,* Marcus Ravage articulated the sense of cultural vertigo that was endemic to the immigrant experience:

· Cut adrift suddenly from their ancient moorings, they were floundering in a sort of moral void. Good manners and good conduct, reverence and religion, had all gone by the boards, and the reason was that these things were not American.[13]

The theme of immigrants "cut adrift suddenly from their ancient moorings" runs through most early ethnographic studies of im-

13. Marcus Ravage, *An American in the Making* (New York: Harper, 1917), p. 79.

migrants, as well as through a large body of literary accounts of the immigrant experience. For example, in their pioneering study of *The Polish Peasant in Poland and America,* Thomas and Znaniecki found evidence of a great cultural chasm that separated immigrant parents from their American-born children, and recognized the accompanying strains on the family system.[14] The second generation was characterized by what the Chicago sociologists termed "marginality"—the experience of living in two worlds and not fully belonging to either.

On a social level marginality often expressed itself as a creative release from traditional authority, and was associated with an outpouring of innovative art and literature, as well as new approaches to society and politics. But on a personal level, marginality was often experienced as a painful split, involving feelings of insecurity, alienation, and ambivalence toward both the ethnic subculture and the dominant society. The impulse to embrace American culture stemmed less from a strain of self-hatred, as is often suggested, than out of a need on the part of immigrants and their children to feel a part of their adopted society.

This conflict was explored in Abraham Cahan's novella *Yekl,* on which the film *Hester Street* was based. Cahan's protagonist, Jake, is torn between his past, represented by his Old World wife, and his hopes for the future; at a climactic moment he explodes: "Once I live in America, I want to know that I live in America." It is noteworthy that this passage was excluded from the screenplay which was too bent on condemning Jake's assimilationist tendencies to explore the facets of the immigrant experience that made assimilation inevitable.[15]

It might thus be said that the sheer act of immigration—of leaving one country and entering another—precipitated a crisis of values among immigrant groups, and set in motion a process of cultural accommodation and change. However, ordinary problems of adjustment were exacerbated by factors associated with the position of immigrants in the class system. Admitted to the United States because of a demand for cheap unskilled labor, immigrants found

14. W. I. Thomas and Florian Znaniecki, *The Polish Peasant in Poland and America* (New York: Knopf, 1923), vol. II.

15. Sharon Friedman and Stephen Steinberg, " 'Hester Street' and the Politics of Culture," *Jumpcut,* Fall 1976.

themselves at or near the bottom of the social and economic ladder. Their immediate economic survival, not to speak of their hopes for the future, required that they become Americanized. The fact that immigrant status was virtually equated with poverty and disadvantage inevitably played havoc with ethnic self-conceptions. All immigrant groups developed a disdain for the "greenhorn," and as one writer recalls, the word "carried with it a stigma, and it was meant to hurt."[16] But the word also carried with it a powerful message from the larger society, which was that the "greener" was destined to remain on the periphery of the society and its system of rewards. To pursue the American Dream, to escape from grinding poverty, immigrants realized they would have to shed at least the more obvious marks of their immigrant background. "In behalf of its sons," Irving Howe writes, "the East Side was prepared to commit suicide; perhaps it did."[17]

Indeed, throughout American history ethnicity has been preserved most authentically by those groups who, for one reason or another, have remained economically marginal. Even among groups that have experienced wide-scale mobility, the lower-class strata continue to function as a cultural anchor for their more affluent relatives.

The Structural Limits on Ethnic Communities

The ethnic literature abounds with community studies that explore the uniqueness and complexities of ethnic life. As a rule, however, these studies go too far in treating ethnic communities as "worlds unto themselves," and tend to gloss over the extent to which these communities are integrated into and dependent upon the institutions of the surrounding society. It would be more accurate to refer to them as "colonies," which in fact was the popular nomenclature early in the century.

In the first place, immigrant communities generally lacked a significant economic base. Although there was the semblance of

16. Quoted in Elinor Hanna, "Attitudes toward the United States as Revealed in Published Writings of Immigrants from Europe, 1900 to 1944," unpublished dissertation, New York University, 1946, p. 368.

17. Irving Howe, *World of Our Fathers* (New York: Harcourt Brace Jovanovich, 1976), p. 253.

a flourishing economy that catered to the special needs of its residents, the ghetto economy generally consisted of retail stores and small businesses that, at best, provided an adequate livelihood for a small entrepreneurial class. Most immigrants were forced to go outside the ethnic community for employment, and this was even more true of the children of immigrants whose mobility depended on their gaining access to the occupational structures of the larger society.

A second aspect of ethnic communities that militated against ethnic preservation was their lack of control over the public schools in the immigrant quarter. In other multiethnic societies—Canada is the most proximate example—schools are organized on a pluralistic basis, thus allowing minorities to promote their special heritages in publicly subsidized schools under their own control. But in the United States, educators and policymakers were unyielding in their determination to maintain a centralized school system. Indeed, the "common school" was consciously designed to function as the chief instrument for assimilating the children of immigrants, and for producing a common culture out of the melange of immigrant groups that were pouring into the country. More than any other single factor, the public school undermined the capacity of immigrant groups to transmit their native cultures to their American-born children.

In an effort to offset the assimilating influences of the public schools, most ethnic communities sponsored their own language schools designed to promote ethnicity. In the case of Catholics, parochial schools often functioned as a surrogate for language schools, and served ethnic as well as religious purposes. However, language and religious schools are obviously a poor substitute for a truly pluralistic system of public education, if only because they reach only a small segment of the ethnic population. Ethnicity in the United States would be an altogether different phenomenon had Germans, Irish, Italians, Poles, Jews, Latins, Asians, and others been permitted to use tax revenues to develop their own schools. There were, perhaps, overriding ideological and social reasons for rejecting such a balkanization of the public school system, and certainly the common school served the nation in its determination to minimize ethnic division and mold a unified and harmonious people out of the tens of millions of immigrants that were being absorbed. Nevertheless, as a point of simple historical fact, it is clear that the state, through its educational institutions, dealt a devastating blow to ethnic pluralism by refusing to organize the schools on a pluralistic basis. It is only now when "the destruction of memories" is largely an accomplished fact that schools have been willing to introduce bilingual education and innocuous programs of "ethnic heritage" into their curricula.

This is not to say that ethnics were hapless victims of assimilationist policies. Indeed, it is not at all certain that ethnic groups would have opted for a school system organized along ethnic lines even if such an alternative had been available—not because they were eager to assimilate, but because they viewed the public school as their most promising chance for a better life. But this is only to say, once again, that the options were so defined as to induce ethnic groups to make "choices" that were antithetical to the long-term preservation of their special cultures and identities.

The Decline of Prejudice: A Mixed Blessing?

Much of the stigma once attached to ethnicity has disappeared, but this has had a paradoxical result. In the past ethnic groups gained internal strength from the prejudices and exclusionary practices of the surrounding society. To the common refrain, "How have Jews survived thousands of years of persecution?" one might respond that they have survived precisely because they have been persecuted. All groups tend to experience a heightened group consciousness and to close ranks when threatened from the outside, and thus the removal of this threat also eliminates one of the major obstacles to assimilation.

Of course, part of the reason for the decline in ethnic prejudice is that after several decades of accommodation and change, ethnic groups have blended in culturally with the rest of American society. For example, one national survey asked whether Jews had changed in recent years and a third of those interviewed responded in the affirmative.[18] When asked *how* Jews had changed, almost everyone suggested that they were becoming more assimilated and considered

18. Gertrude Jaeger Selznick and Stephen Steinberg, *The Tenacity of Prejudice* (New York: Harper & Row, 1968), pp. 34–36.

that a change for the better. Just as they were once penalized for their differences, ethnic groups have been "rewarded" with a greater degree of acceptance as they assume the cultural trappings of the society at large.

Other factors must also be cited in explaining the decline of ethnic antagonisms. With the passage of time, the distinction between "natives" and "foreigners" has lost its salience. As immigrants and their children have entered the occupational mainstream, the class basis for ethnic rivalry and conflict has been greatly reduced, especially for those groups that have achieved middle-class status. Nor are ethnic groups any longer suspected of having dual loyalties. A major turning point in establishing the patriotism of the nation's ethnic minorities occurred during the Second World War. As Andrew Hacker has commented: "That half-decade did a work of assimilation that would otherwise have taken two generations."[19] The irony of all this, however, is that as ethnic groups experience less rejection from the society at large, the possibilities and temptations of assimilation are that much greater.

Homogenizing Tendencies of Modern Mass Society

From a larger perspective, the crisis of identity and community that besets ethnic groups in America may be seen as only a particular manifestation of a condition that afflicts modern man generally. As Robert Nisbet points out in *Quest for Community,* no theme is more central to modern thought and writing than "the theme of the individual uprooted, without status, struggling for revelation, seeking fellowship in some kind of moral community."[20] Clearly, the act of leaving one country and settling in another is a case of uprootedness in the most literal sense. Yet, such a condition is virtually endemic to all modern societies where, in the process of modernization, traditional forms of social organization have been torn asunder, leaving individuals with a diminished sense of identity

19. Andrew Hacker, *The End of the American Era* (New York: Atheneum, 1970), p. 14.

20. Robert Nisbet, *Community & Power* (originally published as *The Quest for Community,* 1953) (New York: Oxford University Press, 1962), p. 11.

and belonging. Specifically, the three institutions that served as the pillars of traditional society, and of the ethnic community in particular—the family, the church, and the local community—have all been weakened in terms of their authority over the lives of individuals. Thus, ethnic groups are struggling to reconstruct and maintain identity and community in a society where these facets of social life are increasingly unstable.

If a single factor can be cited for the weakening of traditional institutions of family, church, and community, it is that they have been divested of many of the functions that once justified their existence and bound individuals to them. Nisbet sums up the problem in these terms:

> Our present crisis lies in the fact that whereas the small traditional associations, founded upon kinship, faith, or locality, are still expected to communicate to individuals the primary moral ends and psychological gratifications of society, they have manifestly become detached from positions of functional relevance to the larger economic and political decisions of our society. Family, local community, church, and the whole network of informal interpersonal relationships have ceased to play a determining role in our institutional systems of mutual aid, welfare, education, recreation, and economic production and distribution. Yet despite the loss of these manifest institutional functions, and the failure of most of these groups to develop any new institutional functions, we continue to expect them to perform adequately the implicit psychological or symbolic functions in the life of the individual.[21]

This statement applies with equal force to ethnic groups, to whom we continue to look for psychological and symbolic functions despite the fact that they have lost many of their manifest institutional functions. In their countries of origin, the ethnic group constituted a total nexus for individual and group life, and provided a design for living that regulated social behavior from the cradle to the grave. In instances where migrating groups enter a society organized along traditional lines, it has sometimes been possible to reconstruct and maintain such an organic existence. European immigrants to the United States, however, entered a society in the process of

21. Ibid., p. 54.

modernization where family, church, and community—the institutional cement for ethnic existence—are all in retreat.

"People do not live together merely to be together," Ortega y Gasset has written. "They live together to do something together."[22] And the simple fact is that in contemporary American society members of ethnic groups do very little together. No longer does the ethnic group provide the context for work and economic advancement, except in rare instances. Increasingly, cultural values and life-styles are shaped by influences alien to the ethnic milieu—the mass media and popular culture, on the one hand, and educational institutions committed to universal values, on the other. Even activities involving charity and recreation, which are still central to ethnic communities, have been substantially coopted by the larger society. Ethnic groups in America, it must be remembered, all have their origins in other countries. Certainly if they had to be created anew, the functional imperatives would not be found in present-day American society.

This is not to deny that ethnic groups continue to perform valuable psychological and symbolic functions for their members, even though they have lost many of their original material functions. Indeed, a number of writers have suggested that in a society where individuals are increasingly atomized and lack a clear sense of identity and belonging, there is a special urgency to preserving the ethnic bond. The problem, however, is that the separation between the material and symbolic functions of ethnicity necessarily renders it precarious. Again, Nisbet's analysis of the problem of community in mass society is apropos:

No amount of veneration for the psychological functions of a social group, for the capacity of the group to gratify cravings for security and recognition, will offset the fact that, however important these functions may be in any given individual's life, he does not join the group essentially for them. He joins the group if and when its larger institutional or intellectual functions have relevance both to his own life organization and to what he can see of the group's relation to the larger society. The individual may indeed derive vast psychic support and integration from the pure fact of group membership, but he will

22. Quoted in Nisbet, op. cit., p. 61.

not long derive this when he becomes in some way aware of the gulf between the moral claims of a group and its actual institutional importance in the social order.[23]

"In hard fact," Nisbet declares, "no social group will long survive the disappearance of its chief reasons for being."

The Atrophy of Ethnic Cultures

Yet questions of group survival are not so easily resolved. Groups can and do survive the loss of their chief reasons for being by changing and adapting to new sets of circumstances, as the ethnic pluralists have argued. This position was first advanced by Glazer and Moynihan in *Beyond the Melting Pot:*

> As the old culture fell away—and it did rapidly enough—a new one, shaped by the distinctive experience of life in America, was formed and a new identity was created. Italian-Americans. might share precious little with Italians in Italy, but in America they were a distinctive group that maintained itself, was identifiable, and gave something to those who were identified with it.[24]

According to this view, new forms of identity have evolved to replace older ones, and even economically mobile ethnics have been able to reconstruct ethnic communities in their middle-class suburbs. Proponents of this view like to point out that the culture immigrants carried over with them was itself a product of earlier cycles of adaptation and change. Their overall assessment is that there is nothing unique or foreboding about contemporary ethnic trends in America.

The dogmatic assertions of the ethnic pluralists that the melting pot is a "myth" should perhaps be regarded with a degree of skepticism. As John Higham has observed, "loud assertions of pluralism almost invariably betray fears of assimilation."[25] Some of the writers who have argued most forcefully that ethnic groups have adapted successfully to their new circumstances still express

23. Ibid.
24. Glazer and Moynihan, op. cit., p. xxxiii.
25. John Higham, *Send These to Me* (New York: Atheneum, 1975), p. 234.

disquiet about the future. For example, in his book on *Conservative Judaism,* Marshall Sklare advanced the thesis that Conservatism arose to "reduce the incongruity between a Western, Protestant, secular environment and the Eastern, Orthodox, Jewish system," and also "brought into harmony newly-achieved status with patterns of Jewish worship." Yet Sklare concludes that: "While the adjustments that various types of intellectuals and secularists make may be personally acceptable to them, the question of how satisfactory they are in terms of their transmissive power to the next generation remains *the* crucial question."[26]

Indeed, this *is* the crucial question. Has the "transmissive power" of ethnicity been impaired by the accommodations of previous generations? As commented earlier, the second and third generations were clear in their ethnic self-conceptions even as they modified traditional institutions to conform to their new circumstances. But can the same be said of the new generation which has known only the Americanized versions of the original culture? The ethnic pluralists skirt this issue by dwelling on the self-evident fact that the melting pot has not happened. But it is perhaps premature to celebrate the survival of Old World cultures in the New World because we do not yet know to what extent ethnic groups are sacrificing their authenticity in the interest of adaptation, and whether their "reconstructed ethnicity" constitutes an adequate basis for cultural continuity for generations to come.

Unfortunately, a rigid adherence to the doctrine of cultural relativism has deterred social scientists from asking critical questions about the *quality* and *depth* of reconstructed ethnicity. According to this doctrine, the social scientist may observe cultural differences among groups, but must eschew making judgments as to their relative superiority or inferiority. However, it is one thing to treat different expressions of ethnicity as morally equivalent, and another thing to treat them as socially equivalent. Cultural relativism has been carried to the point where students of ethnicity are fearful of making any statement concerning the validity or social significance of ethnic patterns, lest they be accused of contaminating their research with personal bias. Differences between generations, though measured with scientific precision by survey researchers, are ac-

26. Marshall Sklare, *Conservative Judaism* (Glencoe, Ill.: Free Press, 1955), pp. 246, 251.

cepted at face value, and no attempt is made to assess their larger implications.

Herbert Gans is one of the few writers who has ventured to comment critically on the qualitative aspects of ethnic life. In a 1956 article on American Jews, published in *Commentary* magazine, Gans went so far as to say that "traditional Judaism has ceased to be a living culture for the second-generation Jew."[27] In his view, traditional Judaism is rapidly being replaced by a "symbolic Judaism"—symbolic because it lacks real substance and organic unity. Specifically, Gans characterizes symbolic Judaism in terms of three barely related themes. The first is an "objects culture," which objectifies Judaism in "doilies and tablecloths with the Star of David, pictures, books, and records depicting Jews (usually conspicuously pious ones), and *dreidls* whose faces are crammed with Jewish history." The second is a "popular culture" consisting of Jewish food, comedians, music, and such rarefied adaptations as Jewish bacon and Jewish Mother Goose rhymes. Finally, there is a "problems culture," which is preoccupied with anti-Semitism, Jewish cultural preservation, and more recently, support of Israel. For Gans, symbolic Judaism is a highly tenuous culture, pieced together out of fragments of the abandoned culture that do not conflict with middle-class American cultural patterns.

Gans's critique is a valuable description of the cultural atrophy that afflicts all ethnic groups in America. Atrophy occurs when cultural symbols lose their evocative power, and when the remaining culture has little intellectual or spiritual depth and is not integrated into the material circumstances of people's lives. Symbols that once inspired passionate loyalty and provided moral and spiritual guidelines for living have been reduced to convenient appurtenances, serving only as superficial reminders of the cultural past.

The culture that is being preserved, furthermore, consists of residues of a culture that immigrants carried over with them generations earlier, and often does not exist any longer even in the home countries, which have also undergone processes of modernization and cultural change. After the 1956 Hungarian revolution, for

27. Herbert Gans, "American Jewry: Present and Future," *Commentary*, 1956, p. 425. Also, "Symbolic Ethnicity: The Future of Ethnic Groups and Cultures in America," *Ethnic and Racial Studies* 2 (January 1979), pp. 1–18.

example, thousands of refugees settled in one of New York City's Hungarian neighborhoods. However, the refugees were mostly young and educated, had little in common with the ethnic old-timers, and moved to the suburbs as soon as they acquired the means to do so, much to the disappointment of the older residents.[28]

The incongruity between the culture of the home country and that of hyphenated Americans is also pointed up by the experience of a group of affluent Americans of Scottish descent who returned to Scotland in 1977 for the International Gathering of the Clans. Replete with kilts and bagpipes, they spent two weeks searching the countryside for their roots. According to *The New York Times,* the Americans were met with ridicule, not only for making a spectacle of themselves, but also for fraternizing with the wealthy clan chiefs whose ancestors had driven their ancestors out of Scotland.[29]

Thus, one part of the ethnic dilemma is that the cultural symbols of ethnic groups exist in limbo, without structural roots either in the home country or in American society. The other part of the ethnic dilemma, however, is that attempts to update ethnic traditions, and to tailor them to the realities of American life, all too often prove to be frivolous or even pathetic. Consider, for example, the following *New York Times* account of one "modernized" Bar Mitzvah celebration:

> Nearly sixty years ago, Robert Cohen's bar mitzvah party was held in a noisy and crowded tenement flat on Manhattan's Lower East Side. Last night, Mr. Cohen stood on the 50-yard line of the Orange Bowl at the lavish bar mitzvah party of his grandson Harvey. "It doesn't matter, I guess, where a bar mitzvah party is held so long as there is love and family and joy," Mr. Cohen said after a 64-piece band, cheerleaders, and pompom girls from a local high school stormed onto the field blasting football marches and "Happy Birthday, **Harvey**."[30]

Though admittedly an extreme case, the above example nevertheless typifies a process of cultural atrophy that assumes more subtle and more pervasive forms. Indeed, it is not uncommon for ethnic insiders to decry what they see as a lack of spiritual vitality in updated

28. *East Side Express,* November 11, 1979, p. 5.
29. *New York Times,* May 16, 1977, p. 2.
30. *New York Times,* May 15, 1978, p. D10.

versions of traditional culture. As the Jewish theologian and educator Abraham Joshua Herschel once wrote: "Our services are conducted with pomp and precision. The rendition of the liturgy is smooth. Everything is present: decorum, voice, ceremony. But one thing is missing: Life."[31]

Notwithstanding their genuine desire to preserve their special identities, ethnic groups in America are in deep crisis. The ethnic crisis only begins with the fact that core elements of traditional culture have been modified, diluted, compromised, and finally relinquished. The additional problem is that those elements of traditional culture that have been preserved are removed from the social and cultural matrix in which they once belonged. It is fundamentally a crisis of authenticity. Cultural patterns that were once rooted in the exigencies of life are increasingly found to be either irrelevant or dysfunctional in the society to which they have been transplanted. It is difficult to avoid the conclusion that ethnicity in American society has become culturally thin. It consists mainly of vestiges of decaying cultures that have been so tailored to middle-class patterns that they have all but lost their distinctive qualities.

Indeed, it is precisely because the real and objective basis for ethnic culture is rapidly disappearing that identity has been elevated to a "symbolic" plane, and a premium is placed on the subjective dimensions of ethnicity. People desperately wish to "feel" ethnic precisely because they have all but lost the prerequisites for "being" ethnic.

Ethnic Food: The Last Bastion

Many who have severed all other attachments to their ethnic background still retain a passion for their native cuisine. It would be wrong automatically to dismiss this as trivial. As one writer put it: "Cooking is a language through which a society expresses itself. For man knows that the food he ingests in order to live will become assimilated into his being, will become himself. There must be, therefore, a relationship between the idea he has formed of specific items of food and the image he has of himself and his place in the

31. Quoted in Lucy Dawidowicz, *The Jewish Presence* (New York: Holt, Rinehart & Winston, 1977), p. 73.

universe."[32] But it is one thing when food is integrated into a larger cultural matrix, another when food is valued for itself, rather than as a symbol of something larger. Furthermore, most Americans have developed a palate for the food of ethnic outsiders, thereby denying them exclusive claim to their own cuisine and reducing its symbolic value. As one advertisement goes: "You don't have to be Jewish to like Levy's bread." Indeed, ethnic food has become symbolic not of ethnic pluralism, but of the melting pot itself. Each year, for example, New York City sponsors an International Food Festival, attended by as many as a quarter-of-a-million people a day, which features every imaginable ethnic cuisine at over a hundred street food stalls.[33] It is apparent that for many people ethnicity has been reduced to a culinary event.

The relationship of ethnic food to the larger society is also worth noting. In *Eating in America,* Waverley Root and Richard de Rochement reached the conclusion that, notwithstanding the proliferation of ethnic restaurants, ethnic food has not significantly altered native American cuisine. As they write: "Despite all the foreign contributions which have been offered to it, American cooking remains as uncompromisingly Anglo-Saxon as it has been from the beginning, at least in spirit."[34] If ethnic food has had little influence on American cooking, the opposite claim cannot be made. Most ethnic cuisine has been adapted to prevailing taste—or some would say, tastelessness. For example, a recent *New York Times* article on the best pastrami in town reported on interviews with owners of delicatessens whose pastrami comes closest to Old World authenticity:

> Owners of those delicatessens were most enlightening about the changing public tastes to which they feel they must adapt. Among the most frequent complaints are that pastrami is too spicy and corned beef too salty (as a result, seasonings are toned down in the direction of blandness), or too fatty (result-

32. Jean Soler, "The Dietary Prohibitions of the Hebrews," *New York Review of Books,* June 14, 1979, p. 24.

33. *New York Times,* May 16, 1977, p. 32.

34. Waverley Root and Richard de Rochement, *Eating in America* (New York: Morrow, 1976), p. 312.

ing in dry, lean meat with little flavor), or that sandwiches are not neat enough (by which is meant that strips of meat hang over bread edges, or that slices are not wide, thin and uniform).[35]

These humble epicureans leave no doubt that the pastrami sandwich is gradually becoming Anglo-Saxonized. If ethnic food is the last bastion of ethnicity, then it, too, is losing ground.

Ethnicity as Structure

Though most social scientists would agree that the cultural integrity of ethnic groups has been strained by several generations of cultural adaptation and change, some writers have sought to minimize this fact by shifting the analytical focus away from the cultural dimensions of ethnicity toward the social dimensions. This was certainly the thrust of Milton Gordon's influential book on *Assimilation in American Life,* and especially of his distinction between cultural and structural pluralism.

According to Gordon, ethnic groups are not just cultural entities with a distinctive cultural heritage, but also "subsocieties" consisting of a proliferation of voluntary organizations and friendship networks which allow their members to live out their lives within an ethnic milieu. As Gordon writes:

From the cradle in the sectarian hospital, to the child's play group, to the social clique in high school, the fraternity and religious centers in college, the dating group within which he searches for a spouse, the marriage partner, the neighborhood of residence, the church affiliation and the church clubs, the men's and the women's social and service clubs, the adult clique of "marrieds," the vacation resort, and then as the age-cycle nears completion, the rest home for the elderly and, finally, the sectarian cemetery—in all of these activities and relationships which are close to the core of personality and selfhood—the member of the ethnic group may, if he wishes . . . follow a

35. *New York Times,* March 2, 1979, p. C16.

path which never takes him across the boundaries of his sub-
societal network.[36]

For Gordon, the ethnic subsociety can exist even after it has lost
most of its distinctive cultural attributes:

> . . . here a crucial theoretical point must be recognized. While
> it is not possible for cultural pluralism to exist without the
> existence of separate subsocieties, the reverse is not the case.
> It *is* possible for separate subsocieties to continue their existence
> even while the cultural differences between them become pro-
> gressively reduced and even in greater part eliminated.[37]

Thus, on the one hand Gordon acknowledges "a massive trend
toward acculturation of all groups—particularly the native-born—
to American cultural patterns," while on the other hand, he sees a
persistence of "structurally separate subsocieties of the three major
religious and the racial and quasi-racial groups, and even vestiges
of nationality groupings." In Gordon's view, these trends are so
advanced that "a more accurate term for the American situation
is structural rather than cultural pluralism, although some of the
latter remains also."[38]

What are the implications of having "structural pluralism rather
than cultural pluralism"? In plain language, it means that family,
neighborhoods, and community may continue to be organized
along ethnic lines, but are increasingly devoid of distinctive ethnic
content. Supporting evidence for this view can be found in a
number of surveys that despite assiduous effort to turn up cultural
differences between ethnic groups, have generally failed to do so.
For example, a 1974 study by Andrew Greeley tested people from
Irish, Italian, and British backgrounds with respect to an array of
personality attributes, as well as attitudes toward sex, alcohol, and
politics.[39] The differences he found are small and inconsistent, and
since Greeley does not report any breakdowns by age, there is no

36. Milton M. Gordon, *Assimilation in American Life* (New York: Oxford
University Press, 1964), p. 34.

37. Ibid., p. 158.

38. Ibid., p. 159.

39. Andrew Greeley, *Ethnicity in the United States* (New York: Wiley,
1974), pp. 91–109.

indication of whether even these small differences are persisting or whether they are on the decline. Furthermore, many cultural attributes commonly associated with ethnicity are not rooted in ethnicity as such, but are artifacts of social class or geographical differences between ethnic groups. Some critics of the survey method have suggested that there are important differences in cultural idiom and style which defy scientific measurement, and this is unquestionably the case. However, unless ethnic idiom and style are rooted in ethnic institutions, it is doubtful that they can long survive on their own, despite their hold on the present generation.

Although the existence of ethnic subsocieties is self-evident, it remains to be seen whether Gordon is correct in his assumption that it is possible for these subsocieties to continue even after they lose their cultural distinctiveness. That they have done so, with more or less success, is obvious. The question is whether they will continue to do so, and for how long? Can ethnic communities maintain their boundaries at the same time that their cultures are eroding from within? Or is structural pluralism only another stage in the assimilation process—another line of defense—that does indeed presage the eventual collapse of ethnic communities?

In the view of the melting pot theorists of an earlier generation, the ethnic subsociety is not a last bastion against assimilation, but an unwitting agent in the assimilation process. As Warner and Srole wrote on the basis of their classic study of Newburyport, Massachusetts:

> We have seen in the Yankee City study how these cultural groups . . . groom their own social world to nurse their members through a period of transition until these members "unlearn" what they have been taught and successfully learn the new way of life necessary for full acceptance into the host society.[40]

Indeed, the ethnic subsocieties have acquired so many of the cultural trappings of the society at large that it is not always clear whether they function to preserve ethnicity or to facilitate assimilation. What is especially problematic for ethnic survival is that both of these processes occur simultaneously. In attempting to preserve ethnicity

40. W. Lloyd Warner and Leo Srole, *The Social Systems of American Ethnic Groups* (New Haven: Yale University Press, 1945), p. 28.

and curtail the loss of more assimilated members, the ethnic sub-societies must adapt to the prevailing culture, but in doing so, they inevitably promote the assimilation of the less assimilated members of the community. This is the bind in which all ethnic groups in America find themselves: they are practically forced to give up their cultures in order to save them.

Trends in Ethnic Intermarriage

Speculation on the ethnic future leads ultimately to the question of intermarriage. The significance of intermarriage goes beyond the loss of some members from the ethnic group; it is also an un-mistakable sign of social and cultural disintegration. As Julius Drachsler wrote in his pioneering study of intermarriage:

> Individuals who freely pass in marriage from one ethnic circle into another are not under the spell of an intense cultural or social consciousness. Consequently, the greater number of mixed marriages, the weaker, broadly speaking, the group solidarity.[41]

Studies over several decades have found that rates of intermar-riage across ethnic lines have been on the upswing. The most recent data are reported in a 1976 study by Richard Alba, based on a 1963 national sample of the Catholic population.[42] Alba found gigantean leaps in the rate of intermarriage between the first and fourth generations of all six European groups in his sample—Irish, Germans, French, Poles, Italians, and Eastern Europeans. In each instance, by the third generation a substantial majority were marry-ing outside their group, and in the case of the Irish over three-quarters were doing so. These figures raise serious questions con-cerning the future of these groups as distinct biological and social entities.

Historically the level of ethnic intermarriage has been con-siderably higher than that of religious intermarriage, a fact that

41. Julius Drachsler, *Democracy and Assimilation: The Blending of Immi-grant Heritages in America* (New York: Macmillan, 1920), p. 87.

42. Richard Alba, "Social Assimilation among American Catholic National-Origin Groups," *American Sociological Review* 41 (1976), pp. 1030–46.

gave rise to the thesis of a "triple melting pot," which referred to the tendency of Protestants, Catholics, and Jews to marry across ethnic lines but within religious categories. In recent decades, however, religious intermarriage has also been on the upswing. Estimates of the rate of mixed marriage among Catholics range between 22 and 30 percent.[43] Though Jews historically have maintained a low level of intermarriage, this also appears to be changing dramatically, as indicated by a 1973 study based on a national sample of over 7,000 Jewish households. The overall rate of intermarriage for Jews was not unusually high—about 9 percent. But among the youngest generation studied—those marrying between 1966 and 1972—the rate of intermarriage climbed to 32 percent.[44]

The discovery that one out of every three Jews was choosing a non-Jewish spouse has sent shock waves through the Jewish community. Even before these latest data became available, two demographers at the Harvard Center for Population Studies predicted that by 2076, the present Jewish population of over five million will have dwindled to no more than 944,000 persons, and perhaps as few as 10,420.[45] These doomsday figures were based not only on a high rate of intermarriage, but also on the comparatively low fertility rate among the Jewish population. In 1977 the Jewish magazine *Midstream* published an article on "The American Jewish Population Erosion," in which the author attributed the population crisis to a failure on the part of the Jewish community "to establish the sort of roots that would sustain it as a viable community."[46] A year later *Midstream* published a somewhat less pessimistic analysis of the same data, but the authors also projected "slow growth for the Jewish population until early in the next century, when a sustained decline is likely to set in."[47]

So prevalent is intermarriage that, as Marshall Sklare has pointed

43. Gordon, op. cit., p. 215.

44. Fred Massarik and Alvin Cherkin, "The United States National Jewish Population Study: A First Report," *American Jewish Yearbook*, 1973, p. 292.

45. Harvey Leibenstein and Samuel Lieberman, Harvard Center for Population Studies, 1975, unpublished, cited in Elihu Bergman, "The American Jewish Population Erosion," *Midstream*, October 1977, p. 13.

46. Ibid.

47. Samuel S. Lieberman and Morton Weinfeld, "Demographic Trends and Jewish Survival," *Midstream*, November 1978, p. 11.

out, "it is becoming impossible to view intermarriage as an indication either of personal aberrations or of social persecution."[48] Not only are youth of different ethnic backgrounds coming into more frequent contact in colleges and on the job, but since they increasingly share the same basic values and life-styles, they easily develop the kind of intimacy that leads to wedlock. In a word, the social and cultural constraints that once kept intermarriage at a minimum have all but dissolved.

A number of writers have sought to underplay the significance of the soaring rate of intermarriage by arguing that the intermarried couple typically settle upon a single ethnic identity for their children.[49] This is a facile argument, however, that suggests that ethnicity increasingly has become what Robert Merton calls "a matter of purely technical definition."[50] Even if the parents "convert" in some manner of speaking, can the children of such marriages be counted upon to develop and maintain stable ethnic identities? If so many children of endogamous couples are intermarrying, what can be expected of the children of mixed marriages? Indeed, a recent study of intermarried couples in which one of the partners was Jewish reached the following conclusion: "In most mixed marriages the born-Jewish spouse affirms a Jewish identity, but does little to act on this affirmation. Only a minority, when they become parents, provide formal Jewish education for their children, and in general, the transmission of Jewish knowledge, skills and experience is minimal."[51]

It is also noteworthy that the soaring rate of intermarriage has been accompanied by changes in popular attitudes, as indicated by two Gallup polls conducted a decade apart. When asked in 1968 if they approved of marriages between Catholics and Protestants, 63 percent of the national sample indicated approval. By

48. Marshall Sklare, "Intermarriage and the Jewish Future," *Commentary* 37 (1964), p. 51.

49. Andrew Greeley, *Why Can't They Be Like Us?* (New York: Dutton, 1971), p. 93. William Newman, *American Pluralism* (New York: Harper & Row, 1973), pp. 162–64: National Jewish Population Study, op. cit., p. 298.

50. Robert Merton, "Intermarriage and the Social Structure: Fact and Theory," *Psychiatry* 4 (1941), p. 364.

51. Egon Mayer and Carl Sheingold, *Intermarriage and the Jewish Future* (New York: American Jewish Committee, 1979), p. 29.

1978 the figure had increased to 73 percent in the sample as a whole, and to 80 percent among Catholics. A similar trend was revealed with respect to marriages between Jews and non-Jews. In 1968, 59 percent of those interviewed approved of such marriages, but by 1978 the figure had increased to 69 percent.[52] The survey also found that approval of interreligious marriage increased with greater education. While the shift of popular opinion in favor of intermarriage may well reflect a greater tolerance for religious and ethnic minorities, it can also be construed as signifying a weakening commitment to a pluralistic society.

Traditionally, the taboo against intermarriage was so powerful that Jewish parents actually disowned children who married non-Jews. Today, however, intermarriage has become so commonplace that the organized Jewish community had been forced to relax its stringent objections. As a professor of Jewish studies at Brandeis University told members of the Union of American Hebrew Congregations: "Our continued rejection of the intermarried does not seem to affect the popularity of intermarriage very much. A redirection of our efforts, a welcoming of intermarried couples into our midst rather than a shunning of them, may become a more useful response than outrage or despair."[53] Increasing numbers of Reform rabbis are willing to perform intermarriages, and, according to a study conducted by the American Jewish Committee, the efforts of the organized Jewish community have been redirected toward converting non-Jewish marriage partners to Judaism. "From a cold-blooded point of view," confesses the director of the American Jewish Committee, "it is a way of minimizing losses."[54] Such an attitude clearly signifies a last line of defense for a group whose very existence is threatened by assimilation.

Conclusion

Despite a mounting body of evidence indicating that the assimilation process is entering an advanced stage for many of the nation's ethnic minorities, social scientists have steadfastly resisted such a

52. *New York Times,* November 23, 1978, p. A18.
53. *New York Times,* January 24, 1979, p. B3.
54. *New York Times,* May 16, 1976, p. 29 and January 15, 1979, p. A15.

conclusion. The pattern of sociological reasoning over the decades has been to acknowledge grudgingly the most recent step in the assimilation process, but to deny that the process will go any further. Thus the overarching theme of one generation of scholars was that ethnic groups in America were accommodating without assimilating.

A next generation conceded that cultural assimilation was indeed advanced, but insisted that social assimilation was not, on the assumption that while ethnic groups were converging culturally they nevertheless maintained separate subsocieties. Now that there is incontrovertible evidence that the ultimate form of social assimilation—intermarriage—is occurring at high rates, sociologists undertake painstaking research to show that intermarriage does not always lead to a loss of membership from the ethnic community. The flaw running through much of the recent literature on ethnicity is a failure to view contemporary patterns of ethnicity in the context of long-range historical trends.

A considerable body of evidence now points to the conclusion that, at least in the case of ethnic groups with European origins, amalgamation can no longer be dismissed as apocalyptic nonsense. History seems to bear out the contention of the melting pot theorists that amalgamation is an inevitable last step in the assimilation process. From a global perspective, this should come as no surprise. As Robert Park once wrote: "Every nation, upon examination, turns out to have been a more or less successful melting pot."[55]

This is not to say that the disappearance of ethnicity is imminent. Ethnic subsocieties are firmly established in American society and, for large segments of the population, continue to function as focal points for identity and community. Threatened as they have been by powerful assimilating forces, ethnic communities have resourcefully tried to compensate for the breakdown of traditional channels of cultural transmission. Certainly, the ethnic subsociety has been effective in slowing the pace of assimilation.

Of course, for those ethnics who have not experienced significant mobility, problems of assimilation are less severe and traditional value systems are relatively intact. To some extent the racial polarization of the society has also heightened ethnic consciousness and stimulated ethnic responses on the part of communities threatened

55. Robert Park, "Human Migration and the Marginal Man," op. cit., p. 883.

by racial integration. For all these reasons, ethnicity is certain to remain a viable force in American society for the foreseeable future, though for declining segments of the national population.

None of this, however, should obscure the larger historical picture. When one considers the profound changes that have occurred among American ethnic groups over the past century—the loss of the mother tongue and most other core elements of immigrant culture, the dispersion of immigrant communities, the considerable economic and occupational mobility over several generations, the erosion and atrophy of ethnic cultures, the decline of religion which once buttressed ethnicity, the cultural convergence of the various ethnic subsocieties, and the accelerating rates of ethnic and religious intermarriage—it is difficult to avoid the conclusion that what we have been witnessing for several decades is the melting pot in the making.

What, then, can be said of the ethnic resurgence that began in the late 1960s? At a time when between a third and a half of the current generation is marrying across ethnic lines, surely it would be a mistake to take the ethnic resurgence at face value. Indeed, the impulse to recapture the ethnic past is itself symptomatic of the ethnic crisis, and a belated realization that ethnicity is rapidly diminishing as a significant factor in American life. Irving Howe is probably right when he suggests that much of the romantic lure of the ethnic past rests on the fact that it is irretrievable. As he writes with blunt eloquence:

> These ethnic groups now turn back—and as they nervously insist, "with pride"—to look for fragments of a racial or national or religious identity that moves them to the extent that it is no longer available. Perhaps, also, *because* it is no longer available.[56]

The history of ethnic groups in America is a history of institutional resistance to assimilating forces, and the ethnic revival is only the latest chapter. For all of its energy and passion, however, it cannot even begin to reverse trends that are deeply rooted in the structure of American society. There are inherent limitations on movements that strive to revitalize ethnicity. If they go too far in forging a new identity, the link to the cultural past is strained to the break-

56. Irving Howe, "The Limits of Ethnicity," *New Republic*, June 25, 1977, p. 18.

ing point. On the other hand, the more they restore the original culture, the less compatible they are with American society and culture, and the less their ability to attract a large following. This is the dilemma of revivalism among groups in the process of assimilation.

There is good reason to lament the passing of the rich heritages and the cultural vitality of the nation's ethnic minorities, and it has not been easy for these groups to reconcile themselves to the whittling away of their collective existence. However, ethnicity cannot long survive the erosion of the material and institutional underpinnings which was precipitated by the immigrant experience. The harsh reality is that even if we assume a tolerance for ethnic diversity that did not exist in American society, the conditions were never promising for a genuine and lasting pluralism.

PART TWO

SOCIAL CLASS AND ETHNIC MYTHS

Introduction

———

The New Darwinism

FEW IDEAS were better established in nineteenth-century social thought than the idea that the races that achieved preeminence were superior, while those that occupied the lowest echelons of the social order were inferior. Though notions of racial superiority and inferiority had always been invoked to justify slavery, this argument received a considerable boost after the publication of Darwin's *Origin of Species* in 1859. Darwin, of course, had offered a theory of evolution that pertained to the natural order, but the Social Darwinists, as they came to be called, sought to apply his theory to the social order as well. In the concept of natural selection, the Social Darwinists found a basis for postulating that individuals and races alike are engaged in a struggle for existence that leads inexorably to the survival of the fittest. In this popularized form, Darwinism provided a pseudoscientific rationale for domination and hierarchy in society. Theories that imputed racial superiority to groups on the top of the social heap and inferiority to those on the bottom could now be asserted with the force of natural law.

Eventually Darwinism was used to give scientific legitimacy to nativism as well as slavery, despite the fact that there was nothing in Darwinism that was inherently antagonistic to the interbreeding of racial and ethnic stocks. Indeed, Darwin viewed migration as a vehicle of natural selection, and consistent with the prevailing attitude of the first half of the nineteenth century, he believed that the United States was drawing the best specimens of European stock and would produce a new and superior race. By the end of the nineteenth century, however, immigration had come to be equated in the popular mind with congested urban slums, pauperism, crime, and all the other festering problems related to the rapid expansion of capitalism in America. All attention focused on the racial traits of the newcomers, who, in contrast to earlier waves of immigrants, came mostly from eastern and southern Europe. Now Darwinian theory was molded to fit the nativist reaction against foreigners, and immigration came to be viewed not as a progressive force in human evolution but as a catalyst to racial mongrelization and biological defeat.

The hallmark of Social Darwinism was its hereditary determinism. There was hardly any attribute statistically associated with race or nationality that was not traced to the genes. Even poverty and crime, which previously had been regarded as moral defects, were now assumed to be manifestations of inherited tendencies. Accordingly, the high incidence of poverty, crime, and other pathologies among immigrant populations was seen as symptomatic of an innate perversity, and the causes were to be found in the germ plasms of whole races. By collecting data on the relative incidence of these pathologies among different groups, social scientists believed they could ascertain grades of races. Unsurprisingly they came to the same conclusion that nativists reached by other avenues —namely, that restrictions should be placed on the immigration of all nationalities that were not of the northern and western European stock that originally settled America.

The Social Darwinists also held that the acquired mental and emotional states of one generation were passed down to the next. This seemed to explain the fact that different races and nationalities exhibited different personality dispositions, corresponding to what are today recognized as common stereotypes. If Italians were impulsive, Jews mercenary, Germans bellicose, Asians treacherous, and so on, it was because these traits were inbred and part of a hereditary process. Thus it was feared that the massive immigration of these groups would overwhelm and irrevocably distort the more temperate, moral, and democratic qualities of native-born Americans.

Needless to say, modern social science has come to reject these biological theories. Though there is an occasional recrudescence of biological determinism, especially on the issue of intelligence, the thrust of modern social thought has been to establish the essentially social character of race and nationality, and the overriding importance of environmental factors in the shaping of personality and behavior. The concept of race has itself undergone revision, so that the various European nationalities are not generally perceived as belonging to different races, and even in the case of groups still regarded as constituting distinctive races, genetic factors are not considered relevant to the social or cultural character of these groups. Though there are still a few antiquarians who look for genetic factors in poverty and crime, most social scientists would regard any such suggestion as patent nonsense. Above all, a consensus seems to have been reached that regards any claims of biological superiority or inferiority as belonging to a class of benighted ideas that have no scientific validity whatsoever.

Yet modern social science has not transcended the logic and values of Social Darwinism as completely as is generally supposed. All too often, notions of biological superiority and inferiority have been replaced with a new set of ideas that amount to claims of *cultural* superiority and inferiority. According to this perspective, differences in social class position among ethnic groups in America are a product of cultural attributes that are endemic to the groups themselves. In a sense, nineteenth-century Social Darwinism has been replaced with a "New Darwinism" that has simply substituted culture for genes.

Though the New Darwinists eschew such value-laden terminology as cultural "superiority" and "inferiority," they nevertheless argue that the relative socioeconomic success of each ethnic group depends upon the extent to which it exemplifies a given set of cultural values. The specific values cited are familiar to anyone who has heard Benjamin Franklin's homilies or read Horatio Alger novels— frugality, industry, foresight, perseverance, ingenuity, and the like. Though masked in pseudoscientific terminology, and obscured by an avalanche of statistics, the underlying premise of the New Darwinism is that "good" things come to those with the "right" cultural values, whereas social dishonor and a host of social problems befall those groups that are culturally aberrant.

The affinity to nineteenth-century Social Darwinism is especially pronounced where culture is treated as fixed—that is, as a relatively permanent and immutable entity that operates as an independent force in history. For the New Darwinists, culture is inherited just as inexorably as if it had been implanted in the genes. Children acquire from their parents cultural traits that either allow them to excel in social competition, or that condemn them to languish behind. The principle of the survival of the fittest still holds, though it is now defined in cultural rather than biological terms.

Of course, the belief that the fittest will prevail is predicated on the assumption that all competitors have more or less equal opportunity. Though lip service is paid to the external obstacles that impede the progress of some groups, especially racial minorities, the overriding emphasis is on the capacity of individuals and groups to triumph if they exhibit the appropriate cultural virtues. In a classic expression of Social Darwinism, the president of Stanford University declared in 1911: "It is not the strength of the strong, but the weakness of the weak which engenders exploitation and tyranny." Stripped of its genetic assumption, this refrain is just as characteristic of the New Darwinists, who attribute the plight of groups on the bottom to cultural weakness—whether of a weak family system, unstable communities, a paucity of ethnic pride, or a defective system of values. As with the Social Darwinists, the focus of blame is shifted away from societal institutions and placed on the victims themselves.

The four chapters that follow deal in different ways with the American tendency in social science to posit cultural factors as the main determinants of class differences between ethnic groups. Chapter 3 attempts to unravel the "mystery" of Jewish success, a mystery that owes itself to the exclusive preoccupation with cultural factors in attempts to explain Jewish success patterns. Chapter 4 challenges the body of thought that holds that lower-class minorities, blacks in particular, are saddled with a "culture of poverty" that perpetuates their social and economic disadvantage. Chapter 5 takes a critical look at the idea that the destiny of ethnic groups in America has depended on the extent to which they have availed themselves of educational opportunities. Finally, Chapter 6 deals with the specific question of why so many Irish immigrants, and so few Italians or Jews, worked as domestics. In each instance, the overarching theoretical issue concerns the relationship between culture and social structure. The thrust of these chapters is to look beyond the simplistic cultural explanations that have been so much a part of both the conventional wisdom and social science, and to explore the interface between cultural values and societal factors.

Chapter 3

The Myth of Ethnic Success:
The Jewish Horatio Alger Story

"The immigrants who had been forced to abandon their homes in Eastern Europe were a hardy lot. With rare exceptions, they arrived penniless and inadequately trained in a profession or handicraft. They did possess, however, indomitable faith in themselves and unflagging courage to face all difficulties. They dug their roots deep into the alien soil until it became home to them. They founded families and raised children and children's children who enriched America with invaluable contributions. This immigrant generation of the post-1881 decades may be called, indeed, the heroic generation."

GILBERT KLAPERMAN, *The Story of Yeshiva*, 1969

IT IS a common observation that the nation's ethnic groups have pursued the American Dream with markedly different results. The relative success of Jews has been singled out for special attention both in popular folklore and in social research, and will serve here as the prototype of ethnic success. Though subject to overgeneralization and distortion, the basic fact of Jewish success, like that of ethnic success generally, can hardly be questioned.

Issue arises not with the fact of ethnic success, but with the theories advanced to explain it. According to the theory that has dominated sociological writing on this question, whether or not ethnic groups rise in the class system depends on their value systems. Implicitly or explicitly, it is assumed that all groups started on the bottom, and those whose values were conducive to individual achievement experienced disproportionate mobility. Thus, it is held that there are ethnic reasons for ethnic success, and the causes are to be found within the groups themselves.

Such an explanation is suspect for several reasons. In the first place, the problem is stated falsely when it is assumed that all immigrant groups started out on the bottom. In point of fact, ethnic groups in the United States come out of very different historical and material circumstances, and therefore different outcomes may only reflect different beginnings. Secondly, depending on the time of their arrival and the patterns of settlement, immigrant groups encountered different opportunities, as well as different external obstacles to their economic advancement. The experiences of the immigrant generation, furthermore, tended to establish a foundation that placed next generations at greater or lesser advantage. Finally, even if it can be shown that ethnic groups differ in values that were instrumental to their mobility and success, this by no means constitutes an adequate explanation. Cultural differences properly mark the beginning, not the end, of sociological analysis, and it is necessary to carry the analysis a step further by investigating their historical and social sources.

The Horatio Alger Theory of Ethnic Success

The classical expression of the American success legend is found in the hundred or so novels that Horatio Alger wrote in the late nineteenth century, a time when immigration was at a historic peak. Alger's heroes typically do not reach great fame or fortune, but in the unraveling of the novel they overcome obstacles placed in their way, correct their errant impulses, and by the final pages are resolutely headed down the road to success. Alger's unmistakable message was that, whatever the obstacles, the individual can triumph by living an exemplary life and piously observing all the middle-class injunctions concerning hard work and moral rectitude.

In their pursuit of the American Dream, immigrants represented an historical enactment of Alger's novels, and like Alger, social scientists have projected the view that success goes to those who exemplify the correct values. Indeed, one prominent sociologist, Milton Gordon, is explicit in describing the Jewish experience as "the greatest collective Horatio Alger story in American immigrant history."[1] Gordon is not referring simply to the fact that as a group Jews have enjoyed disproportionate success. What makes Jewish mobility truly analogous to a Horatio Alger story is Gordon's view that it can be attributed to the distinctive values that Jews carried over with them as part of their cultural baggage from Europe. As Gordon writes:

> Thus the Jews arrived in America with middle-class values of thrift, sobriety, ambition, desire for education, ability to postpone immediate gratifications for the sake of long-range goals, and aversion to violence already internalized. . . . *It is these cultural values which account for the rapid rise of the Jewish group in occupational status and economic affluence.*[2] [Italics added.]

Gordon is not the only adherent of what might be called "the Horatio Alger theory of ethnic success." The supposition that success comes to those groups with the appropriate set of cultural values has been made with respect to every ethnic group that has achieved a notable degree of affluence. For example, social scientists have found in Japanese-Americans another group that, through sheer determination and cultural virtue, has surmounted every obstacle on the road to success. In his book on *Japanese Americans,* William Petersen also alludes to Horatio Alger:

> Every attempt to hamper the progress of Japanese Americans, in short, has resulted only in enhancing their determination to succeed. Even in a country whose patron saint is Horatio Alger's hero, there is no parallel to this success story.[3]

1. Milton M. Gordon, *Assimilation in American Life* (New York: Oxford University Press, 1964), p. 185.

2. Ibid., pp. 186–87.

3. William Petersen, *Japanese Americans* (New York: Random House, 1971), p. 5. Similarly, Richard Gambino writes in *Blood of My Blood:* "However else others have 'made it in America, Italian-Americans have prevailed by their unbreakable amalgam of determination and guts. . . .'" (Garden City, N.Y.: Anchor, 1975, p. 81).

Petersen finds that Japanese are successful because they are blessed with an "admirable" set of cultural attributes. He writes: "As a group, Japanese have all the civic virtues—education, diligence, honesty, competence; and if they apply these admirable qualities to public problems, the whole community gains thereby."[4] According to Petersen, the unusual degree of ethnic pride among the Japanese explains their triumph over adversity: "One important reason that Japanese Americans overcame their extraordinary hardships is that they truly believe (as do Jews) that they are innately superior, that others are inferior."[5] As in Alger's novels, success comes to those who believe in themselves and who doggedly pursue the American Dream.

A similar interpretation runs through another study of Japanese "achievement" by two anthropologists, William Caudill and George DeVos, who conclude that:

> The Japanese Americans provide us, then, with the case of a group who, despite racial visibility and a culture traditionally thought of as alien, achieved a remarkable adjustment to middle class American life because certain compatibilities in the value systems of the immigrant and host cultures operated strongly enough to override the more obvious difficulties.[6]

For groups with the "right" values, the existence of prejudice is not an insurmountable obstacle, and only adds to the heroic dimensions of ethnic success.

Like Jews and Japanese, Chinese-Americans are identified with small businesses and the professions. And once again, social research has reflected the conventional wisdom in attributing Chinese success to various cultural traits—a special value placed upon education, close family ties, disciplined and hardworking children, and sheer fortitude. A study by Betty Lee Sung, entitled *The Story of the Chinese in America,* was severely criticized by Stanford Lyman for its tendency to romanticize ethnic success:

4. Ibid., p. 113.
5. Ibid., p. 225.
6. William Caudill and George DeVos, "Achievement, Culture and Personality: The Case of Japanese Americans," *American Anthropologist* 58 (1956), p. 1117.

Professor Sung's book is a celebration of Chinese success in America. Although it has the superficial trappings of a socio-logical analysis . . . these are but scientistic shibboleths that frame and justify the Chinese American's telling of America's perpetual morality tale about its minorities. With but a few changes in detail, the same fable can be—and has been—told about the Japanese, Irish, Jews, Italians, Greeks, Swedes and many more. Its form is always the same: a people beset by hard-ships and oppression in their own country bravely cross the seas to America, a land which promises freedom and opportunity. Once arrived, however, they encounter prejudice, oppression, and difficult times. However, they never lose faith in the dream that originally compelled them. They work hard, refuse to be discouraged by the abuses that harm their lives and hinder their progress, and eventually—usually in the second, or sometimes the third generation—succeed. . . . History is, thus, nicely en-capsulated within the American Protestant ethic: all the "bad" things happened in the past; sensible courage and patient fortitude were shown in moments of danger; proper diligence and prodigious effort proved the worthiness of a people who were at first sorely tested; ultimately—that is *now*—the rewards for these virtues are granted.[7]

Studies typically have been conducted by ethnic insiders who seem to have a vested interest in trumpeting the achievements of their group. Such an impulse is understandable given the fact that the ethnic groups in question typically have been disparaged and ill-treated by the society at large, and their achievements ignored or minimized by historians. The result, however, is that one myth that belittled ethnic achievements has too often been replaced by an-other myth that, as Lyman suggests, has made a "morality tale" out of ethnic success.

One caveat is in order. No one can deny that ethnic mobility involved a long struggle against difficult odds. The climb up the economic ladder unquestionably required fortitude, self-sacrifice, ingenuity, and all the other virtues claimed by the writers who have been cited. But to posit cultural values as the fulcrum of success is

7. Stanford Morris Lyman, review of Betty Lee Sung, *The Story of the Chinese in America*, in *Journal of Ethnic Studies*, Spring 1973, p. 71.

to engage in an essentially moral interpretation of history. It assumes that society functions as a kind of moral benefactor parceling out its rewards to the most culturally deserving. And it implies that groups that are less successful in the competition are somehow deficient in character or in their cultural values. In these respects, social scientists have essentially adopted the conventional wisdom regarding the prerequisites of success, and have unwittingly advanced the very same theory of mobility that earned Horatio Alger a myth in his own name.

It is time to end this "fabled innocence," to use Stanford Lyman's apt phrase. To understand the determinants of ethnic success it will be necessary, as a first step, to eschew the self-congratulatory sentimentalism that has impaired objective inquiry, and to address some complex questions. What differences in the background and circumstances of ethnic groups allowed some to advance further than others? What was the institutional context in which ethnic mobility occurred, and did it favor certain groups more than others? If it can be shown that groups differed in their cultural values in ways that might have facilitated or impeded mobility, how are these differences to be explained? It is naive to marvel at the "ethnic miracle," as Andrew Greeley has called it,[8] without understanding, concretely, how this success was achieved, what external circumstances made it possible, and why some ethnic groups were better equipped to take advantage of a given set of opportunities. Only by adopting a theoretical approach that explores the interaction between cultural and material factors is it possible to assess the role of values in ethnic mobility without mystifying culture and imputing a cultural superiority to groups that have enjoyed disproportionate success.

The best test of this approach is the example of Jewish success, which is the most widely acclaimed of the various ethnic successes in American history. As Thomas Sowell has written: "The Jews were among the most successful—if not *the* most successful—of American minorities. . . ."[9] In the extensive literature on ethnicity, Jews have served as a prototype of ethnic success, as

8. Andrew Greeley, "The Ethnic Miracle," *Public Interest,* Fall 1976, pp. 20–36.

9. Thomas Sowell, *Race and Economics* (New York: David McKay, 1975), p. 70.

the ideal-typical example of an immigrant group's successful adjustment to American society. Therefore, to explore the mythical aspects of the Jewish success story has implications for theory and research that go far beyond this single case.

Another reason for focusing on Jewish success is that it has often been the basis of invidious comparisons to other groups that have not fared as well, as reflected in the following passage:

> Jews have moved up in American life by utilizing middle-class skills—reason, orderliness, conservation of capital, and a high valuation and use of education. . . . Finding that playing by the "rules of the game"—reward based on merit, training and seniority—has worked for them, many Jews wonder why Negroes do not utilize the same methods for getting ahead.[10]

Indeed, blacks themselves have often held out Jews as an exemplary model to emulate. As early as 1907, Booker T. Washington wrote:

> There is, perhaps, no race that has suffered so much. . . . But these people have clung together. They have had a certain amount of unity, pride, love of race. . . . Unless the Negro learns more and more to imitate the Jew in these matters, he cannot expect to have any high degree of success.[11]

More recently, advocates of black capitalism have also suggested that with the ethnic pride and business enterprise of Jews, blacks could climb the ladder of success too. In a sense, Jews have functioned on a collective level like a Horatio Alger hero, proving that the American Dream is attainable to those groups with the appropriate cultural virtues. The other side of the ethnic coin, however, is that poverty becomes equated with cultural inadequacy, and the focus of blame is shifted away from the societal sources of inequality and placed on the ethnic groups themselves. Against this background, it becomes all the more important to sort out the fact and myth of Jewish success.

10. Murray Friedman, "The Jews," in Peter I. Rose et al., *Through Different Eyes* (New York: Oxford University Press, 1973), pp. 52–53.

11. Booker T. Washington, *The Future of the American Negro* (Boston: Small, Maynard, 1907), pp. 182–83.

The Fact of Jewish Success

Few myths are spun out of thin cloth alone, and there is truth to the claim that Jews in the United States have experienced greater economic mobility than most other immigrant groups. According to one estimate, the median income of Jews in 1971 was nearly $14,000, which was 30 percent higher than that of the average American family.[12]

Data on education and occupation also indicate significant differences between Jews and non-Jews. In 1971 36 percent of the adult Jewish population had graduated from college, as compared with 11 percent of non-Jews. Among those aged 25 to 29, 59 percent of Jews had graduated from college, as compared with 17 percent of non-Jews.[13] The popular identification of Jews with business and the professions also receives confirmation by the data: 70 percent of Jewish males are so employed, compared with about a third of the general male population.[14] Thus, in terms of income, education, and occupation—the usual indices of social class position—there is a clear empirical basis for asserting that Jews have enjoyed relative success.

Yet this conclusion must be qualified in at least three respects:

1. The rediscovery of poverty during the 1960s led to a realization that large numbers of Jews do not share in the prosperity indicated by the overall averages. For example, a 1973 survey of New York's Jewish population found that 272,000 individuals, or 15 percent of the city's Jewish population, are "poor" or "near-poor," according to standards laid down by the Bureau of Labor Statistics.[15]

12. "Characteristics of the Population by Ethnic Origin," 1972 and 1971, United States Bureau of the Census, *Current Population Reports,* P-20, No. 249 (1973), Table 9. Data are reported for "Russians," but this group has been shown to be equivalent to "Jews." See Erich Rosenthal, "The Equivalence of United States Census Data for Persons of Russian Stock or Descent with American Jews: An Evaluation," *Demography,* vol. 12 (May 1975), pp. 275–90.

13. Fred Massarik and Alvin Cherkin, "United States National Jewish Population Study: A Preliminary Report," *American Jewish Yearbook* (New York: American Jewish Committee, 1973), p. 280; *1972 Statistical Abstracts,* p. 111.

14. Massarik and Cherkin, op. cit., p. 284; *1972 Statistical Abstracts,* p. 230.

15. Naomi Levine and Martin Hochbaum, *Poor Jews* (New Brunswick, N.J.: Transaction Books, 1974), p. 2.

Another study estimated that of the nation's six million Jews, between 700,000 and 800,000 are poor.[16] They are mostly elderly people
who never escaped poverty and still inhabit the immigrant neighborhoods abandoned by their upwardly mobile children. That they
exist in such large numbers not only qualifies the image of Jewish
success, but also suggests that being steeped in Jewish culture by
no means guaranteed delivery from poverty.

2. The concentration of Jews in the professions and certain white-
collar occupations also tends to obscure the fact that large numbers
of Jews are still working class. In a review of Nathan Glazer's
American Judaism, Morris Schappes criticized Glazer for his statement that "the movement among Jews toward business and the
professions . . . was to further reduce the Jewish working class to
the point where it forms today no significant part of the Jewish
population."[17] According to Glazer's own data, which pertained to
the mid-1960s, almost a quarter of all employed Jewish males in
New York City were manual workers, and another unspecified
number worked in low-paying white-collar occupations.[18] Clearly,
the popular image of Jews as a middle-class monolith tends to be
overdrawn.

3. The most important qualification of the Jewish success story is
that American Jews by no means constitute an economic elite. The
Jewish middle class has been concentrated mostly in small business
and the professions; Jews are conspicuously absent from the managerial hierarchies of major corporations. This was first established
in 1936, when *Fortune* magazine, in an attempt to refute allegations
of Jewish economic dominance, conducted an extensive survey of
Jewish representation in the national economy.[19] The survey found
that Jews were virtually unrepresented among the executives of
most of the nation's major industries, such as automobiles, steel,

16. Ann G. Wolfe, "The Invisible Jewish Poor," in Levine and Hochbaum, ibid., p. 36.

17. Morris U. Schappes, review of Nathan Glazer, *American Judaism*, in
Journal of Ethnic Studies, Fall 1973, p. 98.

18. Nathan Glazer, *American Judaism* (Chicago: University of Chicago
Press, 1962), p. 167. According to the 1971 National Jewish Population Study,
about 30 percent of adult Jewish males were employed outside business and
the professions.

19. "Jews in America," *Fortune*, February 1936, pp. 130–36.

oil, transportation, utilities, insurance, and finance. Only two industries had significant Jewish representation—the apparel industry and the movie and broadcasting industries. Even today, Jews are still rarely found in the board rooms of major corporations. Despite some progress in combating corporate anti-Semitism, a 1975 study published in the *Harvard Business Review* concluded that as a group executives are more homogeneous than ever.[20]

Notwithstanding these qualifications, the overall record of Jews in America has unquestionably been one of success. In two or three generations, the vast majority of Jews climbed out of poverty and are securely middle class. The crucial question, however, is *why* Jewish mobility was more rapid and widespread than that of other groups, and it is here that fact gives way to myth.

The Myth of Jewish Success

The mystique of Jewish success stems from the assumption that Jewish and non-Jewish immigrants began life in America on an equal footing. The reasoning runs as follows: since all immigrants started out as impoverished aliens, why have the accomplishments of Jews far surpassed all others? Thus, in a college textbook on minority groups, Judith Kramer writes:

> Jewish immigrants, like most immigrants, came with few skills and no money. They started life in American society as workers and peddlers, and they achieved remarkable success.[21]

A 1978 issue of the *American Educator,* published by the American Federation of Teachers, contains a similar synopsis of the Jewish experience:

> Few of the eastern European Jews had skills suitable for an industrial society, and the majority gravitated towards jobs as unskilled laborers in the ready-made clothing industry. . . .

20. Frederick D. Sturdivant and Roy D. Adler, "Executive Origins: Still a Gray Flannel World?" *Harvard Business Review* (November–December 1976), p. 127.

21. Judith Kramer, *The American Minority Community* (New York: Thomas Y. Crowell, 1970), p. 115.

Yet the prevailing atmosphere was one of hope, confidence that the next generation would shake off its immigrant beginnings and succeed in becoming real Americans.[22]

In essence, this statement is consistent with the writing of leading scholars on American Jewish life, who also assume an initial parity between Jewish and non-Jewish immigrants. For example, Nathan Glazer writes that "Jews were scarcely distinguishable from the huge mass of depressed immigrants, illiterate and impoverished"[23] and Marshall Sklare writes that Jews "arrived without capital or marketable skills."[24] If these assumptions are correct, and Jews were barely distinguishable from other immigrants, then how is it that they escaped from poverty so much faster?

As already indicated, the answer most commonly advanced is that Jews possessed the right cultural values and, despite their poverty, were middle class in outlook. Nathan Glazer has been the most notable exponent of this point of view:

> The Jewish immigrants who came from Eastern Europe to the United States during 1881–1924 numbered as many workers, and as many impoverished workers, as any other ethnic group. But they carried with them the values conducive to middle-class success and could, under the proper circumstances, easily return to the pursuit of trade and study, and thus to the ways of their fathers and forefathers.[25]

But how is it that Jews were poor and at the same time exemplified middle-class values? Glazer traces these values to Jewish history and culture, and he is explicit on this point:

> But what is the origin of these values that are associated with success in middle-class pursuits? . . . There is no question that Judaism emphasizes the traits that businessmen and intellectuals require, and has done so at least 1,500 years before

22. Sarah Schmidt, "From Ghetto to University," *American Educator*, Spring 1978, pp. 23–24.

23. Nathan Glazer, "Social Characteristics of American Jews, 1654–1954," *American Jewish Yearbook*, vol. 56, n. 1 (1955), p. 15.

24. Marshall Sklare, *America's Jews* (New York: Random House, 1971), p. 60.

25. Glazer, op. cit., pp. 31–32.

Calvinism. . . . The strong emphasis on learning and study can be traced that far back, too. The Jewish habits of foresight, care, moderation probably arose early during the two thousand years that Jews have lived primarily as strangers among other peoples.[26]

Thus it is in Jewish religion and culture, reaching back through the millennia, that these theorists locate the source of the values that putatively account for the unusually high rate of Jewish mobility.

In at least one detail, the historical scenario that Glazer presents is correct: the majority of Jewish immigrants after 1880 were poor. This is documented by immigration records showing how much money immigrants had in their possession when they entered the country.[27] Over half the English and nearly a third of the Germans reported $50 or more. But in the case of the Jews, the figure is only 12 percent, roughly the same as that for Irish, Scandinavian, Italian, and Polish immigrants arriving after 1880. Thus, in sheer economic terms Jews were generally no better off than other immigrants, most of whom arrived nearly penniless.

In other respects, however, there were important differences between Jewish and non-Jewish immigrants, differences that go back to their European origins and were of fateful significance in shaping their economic destiny in America.

European Origins of Jewish Immigrants

There has been a paucity of social research on the European background of Jewish immigrants, and one book, *Life Is With People,* by two anthropologists, Marc Zborowski and Elizabeth Herzog, has virtually been embraced as a classic.[28]

On the basis of interviews with immigrants in New York City,

26. Nathan Glazer, "The American Jew and the Attainment of Middle-Class Rank: Some Trends and Explanations," in Marshall Sklare, ed. *The Jews* (New York: Free Press, 1958), p. 143.

27. *Reports of the Immigration Commission,* vol. 3 (Washington, D.C.: Government Printing Office, 1911), p. 350; reprinted New York: Arno Press, 1970.

28. Mark Zborowski and Elizabeth Herzog, *Life Is With People* (New York: Schocken Books, 1962).

the authors attempt to piece together a "composite picture" of culture and life in the shtetl, the small-town Jewish community of Eastern Europe. Their book may capture the spirit of shtetl culture, but its historical value is doubtful. Aside from its sentimental excesses, *Life Is With People* deals with only one segment of Eastern European Jews. Though some Jews, especially in Poland, did live in shtetls, by the end of the nineteenth century large and increasing numbers lived in cities.

The urban character of Eastern European Jews is clearly established by an 1897 Russian census which an economist, Israel Rubinow, analyzed in a 1907 report for the United States Bureau of Labor entitled "The Economic Condition of Jews in Russia."[29] According to census figures, in 1897 there were nearly five million Jews in Russia, 94 percent of whom lived in the Pale, the western provinces where most Jews were required to live. As many as three-quarters of the Jews in the Pale lived in urban areas. In the Pale as a whole, Jews were only 12 percent of the total population, but they accounted for over one-third of the urban population. In the northwestern provinces of Lithuania and White Russia, Jews were actually a majority of the urban population, far outnumbering even the native Lithuanians and White Russians.[30]

As is well known, Jews in Eastern Europe were prohibited from owning land, and thus were never rooted to the soil. Nevertheless, they often played an indispensable role in the rural economy, especially as merchants and traders who purchased agricultural products from peasants and sold them to factors in towns and cities. Thus, even when they did not reside in cities, Jews typically occupied the interstitial positions that connected urban and rural economies. During the nineteenth century, however, a series of economic dislocations undermined the role of Jews as middlemen, and legal restrictions were imposed on Jewish commerce. The result was a steady migration from countryside to city, and by the

29. Israel Rubinow, "The Economic Condition of Jews in Russia," *Bulletin of the Bureau of Labor,* no. 72 (Washington, D.C.: Government Printing Office, 1907), pp. 487–583.

30. Ibid., p. 493. The estimate that three-quarters of the Jewish population was urban is based on an 1898 study conducted by the St. Petersburg committee of the Jewish Colonization Society, which Rubinow cites in his report. Using a more stringent definition of "urban," the 1897 census reports that 49 percent of Jews lived in incorporated cities.

end of the century all of the major cities of the Pale—Warsaw, Odessa, Lodz, Reja, Kiev, Vilna, Minsk, etc.—had large Jewish concentrations.[31]

In terms of their eventual adjustment to life in America, what was most significant about the urban background of Eastern European Jews was that they worked in occupations that prepared them for roles in a modern industrial economy. Again, the 1897 Russian census provides indispensable documentation. According to the census (see Table 3 below), 38 percent of Jews were employed in manufacturing or as artisans and another 32 percent in commerce, making a total of 70 percent. In contrast, only 18 percent of Russia's non-Jewish population were so classified. On the other hand, 61 percent of non-Jews, compared with only 3 percent of Jews, were in agriculture.[32] In a word, Eastern European Jews were not peasants. This simple fact would have far-reaching implications for their destiny in the United States.

A still clearer picture of Eastern European Jews emerges from an examination of the particular occupations in which they were concentrated. Among those employed in manufacturing, the greatest number worked in the production of clothing; over 250,000 Jewish workers did so, according to the Russian census, accounting for one-sixth of the Jewish work force. Jewish artisans, on the other hand, covered a wide range of crafts: gold- and silver-smiths, metal workers, carpenters, cabinetmakers, printers, furriers, construction workers, and so on.[33] Many Jews were also found among the ranks of unskilled labor, especially as longshoremen, teamsters, and coachmen. Indeed, there was scarcely a branch of industry in which Jews were not a significant part of the labor force.

Jewish capital, as well as Jewish labor, played an important role in a number of key industries. According to one survey of the role of Jews in the Russian economy in the nineteenth century:

> . . . by 1832 Jews owned 149 [textile] factories and plants out of the total 528 existing at the time in eight provinces in the

31. Ezra Mendelsohn, *Class Struggle in the Pale* (London: Cambridge University Press, 1970), p. 51; I. M. Dijur, "Jews in the Russian Economy," in Jacob Frumkin, Gregor Aronson, and Alexis Goldenweiser, eds., *Russian Jewry, 1860–1917* (New York: Thomas Yoseloff, 1966), pp. 120–43.

32. Rubinow, op. cit., p. 500.

33. Ibid., pp. 498, 503–4.

Table 3

OCCUPATIONS OF JEWS AND NON-JEWS
IN RUSSIA, 1897

	Percent	
Occupations	Jews	Non-Jews
Manufacturing and artisans	38%	15%
Commerce	32	3
Service	19	16
Professions	5	3
Transportation	3	2
Agriculture	3	61
TOTAL	100%	100%

SOURCE: Compiled from the Premier Recensement Général de la Population de l'Empire de Russie, 1897, and printed in Israel Rubinow's "The Economic Condition of Jews in Russia," *Bulletin of the Bureau of Labor*, No. 72 (Washington, D.C.: U.S. Government Printing Office, 1907), p. 500.

northwestern and southwestern territories. . . . [F]rom the 1870s until the First World War, the Jews played a major part in the development of the sugar industry. . . . Flour milling was quite widespread among Jews within the Pale of Settlement. . . . By the early years of the twentieth century, Jews owned or leased 365 mills with an annual business of 20 million rubles. . . . The same can be said of tobacco production, which had long been concentrated in Jewish hands. . . . In the Russian leather industry Jews also played a substantial role. . . . In the woodworking industry, Jews were prominent chiefly in the sawmill business. . . . In the grain and timber trade, Jews obtained enormous success in a relatively short time and may be said to have brought Russia into the world market. . . . A very substantial role was also played by Jews in such leading branches of the Russian national economy as banking, railroad construction, and the extracting industries (coal, oil, and gold).[34]

34. Dijur, op. cit., pp. 127–37. The volume in which this article is printed was compiled in New York in 1942 by a group of Russian-Jewish immigrants.

Corroborating evidence can be found in the 1897 census to indicate that Russian Jews were not merely on the economic margin, but on the contrary, occupied an important place close to the center of the Russian economy.

Commerce in the Pale was even more heavily Jewish. Indeed, nearly three-quarters of all those employed in commerce were Jews.[35] In some provinces, such as Lithuania and White Russia, the figure was as high as 90 percent. About half the Jews in commerce were dealers in agricultural products such as grain, cattle, hides, furs, and other commodities. Others were merchants or peddlers, selling to the local population.

It would be misleading to give the impression that Jews were prospering in Eastern Europe, for this was hardly the case. Most "merchants" were little more than petty traders, and intense competition kept profits meager at best. For those who worked in factories, wages were pitifully low. Conditions varied from one region to another—for example, Jews in Lithuania were generally less impoverished than Jews in Poland—but on the whole, Eastern European Jews were unquestionably poor, though decidedly better off than the surrounding peasant population.

The Social Class Advantages of Jewish Immigrants

Despite their poverty, however, Jewish immigrants were concentrated in economically advanced sectors of their countries of origin, and therefore had industrial experience and concrete occupational skills that would serve them well in America's expanding industrial economy. In contrast, the vast majority of other immigrants who came during the same period were peasants or, more often, farm laborers. The difference between Jewish and non-Jewish immigrants is clearly shown in data collected by the United States Immigration Commission in 1911 (see Table 4). Among Jewish immigrants arriving between 1899 and 1910, two-thirds or

---

Also see Salo W. Baron, Arcadius Kahar, et al., *Economic History of the Jews* (Jerusalem: Keter Publishing House, 1975); Salo W. Baron, *The Russian Jew under Tsars and Soviets* (New York: Macmillan, 1976), chap. 6; Mendelsohn, op. cit.

35. Rubinow, op. cit., p. 553.

67 percent of the adult labor force were classified as skilled. The figures for English, Germans, and Scandinavians are much lower: 49, 30, and 20 percent, respectively. The figures are still lower for southern Italians (15 percent), Irish (13 percent), and Poles (6 percent). In absolute numbers there were more skilled workers among Jewish immigrants than among Italians and Poles combined, despite the fact that the volume of Jewish immigration was only one-fourth as great.

Jews ranked first in 26 of the 47 trades tabulated by the commission:

> They constituted 80 percent of the hat and cap makers, 75 percent of the furriers, 68 percent of the tailors and bookbinders, 60 percent of the watchmakers and milliners, and 55 percent of the cigarmakers and tinsmiths. They totaled 30 to 50 percent of the immigrants classified as tanners, turners, undergarment makers, jewelers, painters, glaziers, dressmakers, photographers, saddlemakers, locksmiths, butchers, and metal workers in other

Table 4

PERCENTAGE OF SKILLED WORKERS AMONG
IMMIGRANTS ENTERING THE UNITED STATES
BETWEEN 1899 AND 1910

	Percentage of Skilled Workers*
Jews	67%
English	49
Germans	30
Scandinavians	20
Northern Italians	20
Southern Italians	15
Irish	13
Poles	6
All immigrants	20%

* Figures are based on those with occupations, and thus exclude most women and children.

SOURCE: Adapted from the *Reports of the Immigration Commission*, Vol. 1 (1911), p. 100.

than iron and steel. They ranked first among immigrant printers, bakers, carpenters, cigar-packers, blacksmiths, and building trades workmen.[36]

No other immigrant group arrived with such an array of industrial skills.

Furthermore, these skills corresponded with remarkable precision to needs in the American economy. Precisely at the time when Jewish immigrants were arriving en masse, the garment industry was growing at a rate two or three times as great as the average for all industries.[37] By 1914 the American clothing industry employed over half a million workers; the annual payroll came to over 300 million dollars, and the product value to over a billion dollars.[38] The scale of this industry is more easily grasped by referring to statistics on the volume of goods produced. By 1935, the annual product included 175 million dresses, 20 million men's suits, 17 million women's coats, 170 million dress shirts, 50 million overalls, and 71 million work shirts.[39] Well over two-thirds of the industry was concentrated in New York City, the port of arrival for most Russian Jews.

It would be difficult to exaggerate the significance of this single industry for the economic adjustment of Jewish immigrants. Among those arriving between 1880 and 1910, 145,000 were classified as tailors and another 80,000 as seamstresses.[40] Most of them presum-

36. Moses Rischin, *The Promised City: New York Jews, 1870–1914* (Cambridge: Harvard University Press, 1962), p. 59. Similar data are presented by Thomas Kessner in his history of Italian and Jewish immigrant mobility in New York City between 1880 and 1915 (*The Golden Door*, New York: Oxford University Press, 1977). Kessner reports occupational differences between Jewish and Italian immigrants, both in their countries of origin and in New York City, but he explains these differences in terms of cultural factors; specifically, "attitudes toward family and community, attitudes toward economic goals and ambitions, and attitudes toward education" (p. 94). Consistent with others, he sees "middle-class values" as the main determinant of Jewish success (e.g., pp. 99, 111, 173).

37. "Garment Industries," *Encyclopedia of Social Science* (New York: Macmillan, 1931), p. 575.

38. Irving Howe, *World of Our Fathers* (New York: Harcourt Brace Jovanovich, 1976), p. 155.

39. Jacob M. Budish and George Soule, *The New Unionism in the Clothing Industry* (New York: International Publishers, 1935), p. 4.

40. *Reports of the Immigration Commission*, vol. 3, op. cit., pp. 98–178.

ably found employment in the burgeoning garment industry, as did many who had no previous experience in the clothing industry but could work at jobs that required little skill. As early as 1890 the work force was predominantly Jewish, and remained so for nearly half a century.

Despite the notoriety of the sweatshop, wages in the clothing industry compared favorably with other industries. In 1908 the United States Immigration Commission collected data on over 220,000 workers in 21 major industries. The findings showed that the average weekly wage for foreign-born male workers was $11.92, but the comparable figure for workers in the clothing industry was $12.91. Yet this does not tell the whole story, because within the clothing industry Jews were concentrated in the more skilled jobs that paid higher wages. Average weekly earnings for Russian Jewish males was $13.28; for "other" Jews, $14.90.[41] Thus, the wages of Jewish garment workers were, if anything, higher than those of immigrants generally.

Furthermore, the structure of the clothing industry was conducive to individual enterprise, especially during the period when trade unions were nonexistent or weak. The "sweating system," as it was called, was a system of contract labor whereby manufacturers farmed out work to labor contractors who employed a small number of immigrant workers in a shop or at home. The result was a proliferation of such shops—in 1913 there were over 16,000 in New York City alone—providing as many opportunities for entrepreneurship. As a report by the 1901 Industrial Commission observed, the obstacles to entrepreneurship were not great, given the low capital requirements of opening a small shop:

> These small shops are able, on account of low rent and meager wages, to compete successfully, although with foot power, against the large shops and factories with steam or electric power. Usually it is not necessary to have more than $50 to start a shop with foot-power machines. As there is no investment in goods, the contractor runs no risk. Little managing ability is required because the number of employees is small.[42]

41. Ibid., vol. 1, pp. 385, 394.
42. *Reports of the Industrial Commission on Immigration*, vol. 15 (Washington, D.C.: Government Printing Office, 1901), p. 321.

Eastern European Jews introduced an assembly line process that resulted in substantial production economies, and by the First World War they had replaced German Jews as the dominant force in the nation's garment industry.

Similar opportunities for business entrepreneurship existed in other areas of commercial life, allowing Jewish immigrants to capitalize on their experience as peddlers, merchants, and middlemen. Despite some spectacular successes, most of the businesses they established remained small and simply provided an adequate living. Nevertheless, they provided the necessary economic resources for educational and occupational mobility in the next generation, and as is shown in Chapter 5, a disproportionately high number of Jewish scholars and scientists have their origins in this entrepreneurial class.

It is evident that, contrary to what is generally assumed, Jews did possess occupational skills that gave them a decisive advantage over other immigrants who were entering industrial labor markets for the first time. A second, and related, advantage was that Jews had a higher rate of literacy than most other immigrant groups.

Literacy has both ideal and material dimensions. In the case of the Jews, study was a religious imperative and, at least in Eastern Europe where Jews were often excluded from state schools, learning usually occurred within a religious framework. As Zborowski and Herzog write in *Life Is With People:*

> Not every Jew in the shtetl is a scholar or even a learned man, but intellectual achievement is the universally accepted goal. There are few Jews from Eastern Europe who have not attended the kheyder at least for a short time. . . . And the traditional expectation for a boy in the shtetl is that from the kheyder to the grave he will devote some portion of his time to study.[43]

The level of literacy for Jews in Russia was higher than that of the non-Jewish population, though not as high as might be inferred from Zborowski and Herzog's embellished description. According to the 1897 Russian census, the rate of literacy for those over ten years of age was 50 percent for Jews and 28 percent for non-Jews.[44] Excluding women, the rate was 65 percent for Jews

43. Zborowski and Herzog, op. cit., p. 102.
44. Rubinow, op. cit., p. 578.

and 39 percent for non-Jews. Whether this difference reflects the operation of distinctive religious factors, however, is open to question. Presumably, if the Russian census had compared Jews with non-Jews who were engaged in urban occupations the difference would have been less striking.

Indeed, the literacy rates for other immigrant groups closely correspond to the overall level of economic development in their countries of origin. Illiteracy was the exception among immigrants from Western Europe, and for those who came between 1899 and 1910, it never exceeded 5 percent for any nationality. The illiteracy rate was also low among immigrants from northern Italy (12 percent), but among Polish immigrants the figure rose to 36 percent, and among immigrants from southern Italy, illiteracy soared to 54 percent. The rate for Eastern European Jews fell between these extremes—26 percent.[45] Thus, while Jewish values may well have placed special emphasis on learning, and infused it with deeper religious significance, the overall rate of literacy among Jews was not unusual for groups, including northern Italians, that had their origins in the industrial sectors of their countries of origin.

For an immigrant in an alien country, literacy was a valuable asset. First of all, it facilitated the acquisition of a new language, and historical data show that Jews learned to speak English faster than any other immigrant group with the exception of the Swedes and Norwegians.[46] Secondly, to be literate obviously facilitated entry into business and more lucrative occupations that demanded an ability to read and write. Finally, literacy among immigrants translated into an educational head start for their children. A 1911 study on *The Children of Immigrants in the Schools* found that school performance was higher among children of parents who spoke English; presumably the same was true for children of parents who were literate.[47] Thus, the comparatively high rate of literacy among Jewish immigrants alone would have resulted in a higher level of academic achievement among their children.

45. *Reports of the Immigration Commission*, vol. 1, op. cit., p. 99.
46. Ibid., p. 480.
47. "The Children of Immigrants in Schools," *Reports of the Immigration Commission*, vol. 1 (Washington, D.C.: Government Printing Office, 1911), pp. 35–36.

Conclusion

In terms of their European background, Jews were especially well equipped to take advantage of the opportunities they found in America. Had Jews immigrated to an industrial society without industrial skills, as did most other immigrants, their rich cultural heritage would have counted for little. Indeed, a parallel situation exists today in Israel, where Jews immigrating from underdeveloped countries in North Africa typically lack the occupational and educational advantages of the earlier settlers, and despite the fact that all share the same basic religion, the recent immigrants find themselves concentrated at the bottom of Israeli society. Thus, in large measure Jewish success in America was a matter of historical timing. That is to say, there was a fortuitous match between the experience and skills of Jewish immigrants, on the one hand, and the manpower needs and opportunity structures, on the other. It is this remarkable convergence of factors that resulted in an unusual record of success.

This is not to deny that Jews possessed values that served them in their quest for social and economic advancement. But one would not expect an urban proletariat to exhibit the same values as peasants emerging from folk societies and semifeudal conditions. Nor would one expect a group on the threshold of a dramatic economic breakthrough to exhibit the same attitudes and values as groups that were destined to remain indefinitely poor. If Jews set high goals, it is because they had a realistic chance of achieving them. If they worked hard, it is because they could see the fruits of their labor. If they were willing to forgo the pleasures of the moment, it is because they could realistically plan for a better future, for their children if not for themselves. In short, there was much in the everyday experience of Jewish immigrants to activate and sustain their highest aspirations. Without this reinforcement, their values would have been scaled down accordingly, and more successful outsiders would today be speculating about how much further Jews might have gone if only they had aimed higher.[48]

48. Other examples of ethnic success can be traced back to factors in the countries of origin that, in one way or another, placed these groups in a favorable position to achieve rapid economic mobility.

In a critical review of William Petersen's book on Japanese-Americans, Kiyoshi Ideda insists that "the Japanese-Americans are not a self-made people" (*Social Forces,* vol. 51, June 1973, p. 499). Over against Petersen's emphasis on ethnic pride and solidarity as the reason for Japanese success, Ideda points out that the higher rate of mobility among Mainland Japanese, as compared to Hawaiian Japanese, is due to the fact that the former group had parents "who came from less impoverished districts, and who were more advantaged in class standing and literacy levels, and who were less likely to be drawn from peasant-agriculturalist households in Japan" (p. 498). Roger Daniels also writes of immigrant Japanese: "They came with almost all the skills and technological know-how necessary to reach the bottom rungs of the ladder of success" (in John Higham, ed., *Ethnic Leadership in America* [Baltimore: Johns Hopkins University Press, 1978], p. 63).

Much the same can be said of Koreans, who in recent years have made conspicuous inroads into small business in a number of American cities. One study reports that two-thirds of Korean immigrants between 1965 and 1974 were professional, technical, or managerial workers at the time of their entry (Jai P. Rhu, "Koreans in America: A Demographic Analysis," in Hyung-Chan Kim, ed., *The Korean Diaspora* [Santa Barbara: ABC-Clio, Inc., 1977], p. 211). Another study of 52 Korean businesses in four cities found that 70 percent of the owners had a college education (Hyung-Chan Kim, "Ethnic Enterprises among Korean Immigrants in America," ibid., p. 97). This study also found that only one of the firms obtained its capital from a rotating credit system (p. 99), which Ivan Light contends in *Ethnic Enterprise in America* (Berkeley: University of California Press, 1972) is a major factor explaining Asian success in business.

The relative economic success of West Indian immigrants is often cited as "proof" that racism alone cannot explain the economic plight of black Americans. Thomas Sowell, for example, writes of West Indians: "Their example also suggests that the current disabilities of black Americans are due not only to current discrimination but also to past deprivation and disorganization that continue to take their toll" (Sowell, op. cit., p. 102). But elsewhere Sowell reports that once region and education are held constant, there is little difference in the incomes of the two groups. In other words, West Indian migrants tend to have more education than Afro-Americans. When this factor is taken into account, and West Indians are compared to urban blacks with the same amount of education, then the economic difference between the two is no longer marked. Sowell found, for example, that a northern black who graduated from college makes almost as much money as a West Indian with the same amount of education (Thomas Sowell, *American Ethnic Groups* [Washington, D.C.: The Urban Institute, 1978], p. 44).

Cubans have been cited as the latest ethnic success story. For example, an article in *Fortune* magazine (October 1966), entitled "Those Amazing Cuban Emigrés," lauded Cubans for their impressive economic gains, for rarely needing welfare, and for sprucing up run-down neighborhoods in cities where they have settled. Yet prior to the 1980 Cuban influx, there were few farmers or blue-collar workers in the immigrant pool. Indeed, half the émigres had professional, semiprofessional, or business backgrounds. Furthermore, as Denise Cronin has shown, Cubans have received preferential treatment from the Small Business Administration (unpublished dissertation, State University of New York, Stonybrook, 1978).

Once the concrete reasons for the various ethnic successes are understood, it is no longer tempting to invoke supernatural imagery to explain what Andrew Greeley has called "The Ethnic Miracle" (op. cit.).

Chapter 4

The Culture of Poverty Reconsidered

"The wronged are always wrong, and so we blame the Negro. If we are fair, however, we must place the responsibility of a social effect upon those responsible for the cause."

New Republic, June 24, 1916

IF SOCIAL science has created ethnic heroes, there have been ethnic villains too. Indeed, the same logic that underlies the myth of ethnic success has produced an opposite myth about groups that never escaped from poverty. Such groups are said to be encumbered with a set of disabling or dysfunctional cultural values that impede social and economic mobility. As with the myth of ethnic success, the idea that the poor are held back by the "wrong" cultural values has long been part of the conventional wisdom, but has been refined and given intellectual credence by a number of serious writers.

The term "culture of poverty" was coined by the anthropologist Oscar Lewis in a 1959 study of poor families in rural Mexico. He later elaborated upon the concept in a study of Puerto Rican families living in New York, published in 1965 under the title *La Vida*.[1] Lewis's research style involved intensive personal observation, which he presented in graphic detail in his books. Of course, the concept

1. Oscar Lewis, *Five Families* (New York: Basic Books, 1959); Oscar Lewis, *La Vida* (New York: Knopf, 1968).

of a "culture of poverty" was an abstraction from his empirical materials, and at least one critic has suggested that Lewis's theoretical postulates are contradicted by his own data.[2] Others have interpreted and applied the culture-of-poverty idea in ways that Lewis himself repudiated. Though the meaning of the "culture of poverty" has gone through many transmutations, for over a decade this concept has dominated intellectual discussion of the nature and dynamics of poverty, and has also been a major influence in the formulation of public policy.

According to Lewis, the poor, by virtue of their exclusion from the mainstream of the societies in which they live, develop a way of life all their own, one that is qualitatively different from that of the middle-class societies in which they live. Like all cultures, the culture of poverty is a "design for living" that is adapted to the existential circumstances of the poor. The pressure of coping with everyday survival leads to a present-time orientation; the lack of opportunity, to low aspirations; exclusion from the political process, to feelings of powerlessness and fatalism; disparagement of the poor on the part of the society at large, to feelings of inferiority; the inability of men to provide adequately for their families, to mother-centered households; unrelenting poverty, to passivity and a sense of resignation. Thus, for Lewis, the culture of poverty comes into existence as a reaction and adaptation to conditions of poverty.

Here Lewis makes a theoretical leap. Once a culture of poverty is formed, he argues, it assumes a "life of its own" and is passed on from parents to children through ordinary channels of cultural transmission. As Lewis writes: "By the time slum children are age six or seven, they have usually absorbed the basic values and attitudes of their subculture. Thereafter they are psychologically unready to take full advantage of changing conditions or improved opportunities that may develop in their lifetime."[3] The adaptations of one generation thus become the inherited culture of the next, creating a self-perpetuating cycle of poverty.

If poverty acquires a life and dynamic all its own, then it would no longer suffice to change external conditions and to open up

2. Charles Valentine, *Culture and Poverty* (Chicago: University of Chicago Press, 1968), pp. 50–63.

3. Oscar Lewis, "The Culture of Poverty," *Scientific American* 215 (October 1966), p. 5.

channels of opportunity. Lewis wrote that "the elimination of physical poverty *per se* may not be enough to eliminate the culture of poverty which is a whole way of life."[4] By this he meant that the typical liberal remedies, such as welfare and the job training programs, might not go far enough in modifying the context in which the poor lived. Lewis was struck by the success of the civil rights movement in the United States and of the Cuban Revolution in eliminating some of the worst aspects of a culture of poverty despite the persistence of poverty itself. As he wrote:

> By creating basic structural changes in society, by redistributing wealth, by organizing the poor and giving them a sense of belonging, of power and of leadership, revolutions frequently succeed in abolishing some of the basic characteristics of the culture of poverty even when they do not succeed in curing poverty itself.[5]

Conservative theorists, however, seized upon Lewis's view of poverty as self-perpetuating and carried it to drastically different conclusions. It has long been an article of faith among conservatives that "throwing money at poverty will not make it go away." For example, Edward Banfield wrote that poverty is rooted in "deeply ingrained habits," and added:

> In large degree it is "inwardly" caused, and improvements in external circumstances are likely to affect it gradually if at all. Poverty of this type tends to be self-perpetuating. . . . In principle, it is possible to eliminate the poverty (material lack) of such a family, but only at great expense, since the capacity of the radically improvident to waste money is almost unlimited. Raising such a family's income would not necessarily improve its way of life, moreover, and could conceivably even make things worse.[6]

If raising the incomes of the poor is futile or even counterproductive, on the assumption that poverty is rooted in the culture and behavior of the poor, then it follows that the imperative for social

4. Ibid.
5. Ibid., p. 9.
6. Edward Banfield, *The Unheavenly City Revisited* (Boston: Little Brown, 1974), p. 143.

policy is to rehabilitate the poor culturally. Indeed, this was an underlying premise of many of the war-on-poverty programs, including Head Start for children and various job training programs for adults. One such program, described by David Wellman in an article entitled "Putting-on the Poverty Program," subjected ghetto youth to a regimen of classroom instruction and field trips that were designed to improve their motivation and work habits, instruct them in middle-class styles of decorum, and otherwise remold their cultural attitudes and bearing, ostensibly so that they could compete for jobs in the market place. But the program itself offered no job placement or specific job training, and therefore the enrollees cynically played along for whatever temporary benefits they derived. As Wellman concluded:

> Most modern liberals seem to view black people as temporarily hindered by psychological and cultural impediments. Inequities in the employment and opportunity structure of America, they seem to suggest, are minor in comparison with the deficiencies of black people themselves. What black people need, according to liberals, is cultural enrichment and the ability to "sell themselves" to white society. In the end, northern liberals and southern racists agree; the problem is mainly with Negroes.[7]

Along with Wellman, other critics of the culture-of-poverty thesis argue that it places blame on the victim and, in doing so, obscures the social causes of poverty. The aim of social policy becomes one of reforming the poor rather than changing society. That is, instead of instituting the sweeping changes that could redistribute income, the focus of social policy becomes indoctrinating the poor with middle-class values. Obviously, such a melioristic approach is less expensive and more acceptable politically, in that it does not entail any changes in the nation's basic political or economic institutions. But that was hardly what Oscar Lewis had in mind when he suggested that raising the income level of poor families would not solve all the manifold problems associated with poverty.

7. David Wellman, "Putting-on the Poverty Program," in David Gordon, ed. *Problems in Political Economy* (Lexington, Mass.: D. C. Heath, 1977), p. 128.

The Culture of Poverty in Historical Perspective

Although the culture-of-poverty thesis has been presented with all the trappings of modern social science, it has disconcerting affinities to commonplace stereotypes regarding the poor, especially as these have been affixed to particular minority groups. Take, for example, the concept that the poor exhibit a "present-time orientation" or an "inability to defer gratification." How different is this from the traditional stereotype of blacks as "spendthrift"? In 1907, Charles Morris, author of *The Old South and the New,* also thought he detected a "present-time orientation" among blacks, though his language lacked the aura of sociological objectivity:

> . . . looking upon the blacks as a whole we find them displaying various traits of character which belong to the childhood of mankind. Such a trait is their widespread lack of prevision, of preparation for the morrow. To the genuine African there is no to-morrow. The world is a great to-day. He lives for the passing time. His only use for money is to spend and enjoy it. . . . [T]he love of present enjoyment is the ruling power in his soul.[8]

Immigrants, too, were once seen as improvident. Commenting on the Ford Motor Company's plan to pay workers a minimum of five dollars a day, a sociologist from the University of Michigan wrote in 1913:

> The great trouble with the vast majority of our laborers is that they do not know how to spend their wages judiciously. If they receive $5 a day, the likelihood is in the majority of cases that it will be spent when the next pay day comes, and there will be no more left in the fall to tide over a hard winter, or laid away to bridge a sick spell, than there was when the laborer was receiving $2.50 a day.[9]

In this instance the motives behind such a characterization are rather transparent: after all, if workers are so improvident, there is no reason to pay them higher wages. But one has to ask whether

8. Charles Morris, *The Old South and the New* (Philadelphia, 1907), p. 370.
9. Quoted in Alan Nevins, *Ford* (New York: Scribner, 1954), p. 553.

contemporary social scientists are not acting out of similar motives when they write, as one urban specialist did in 1970, that "money alone will not overcome the attitudes and cultural conditions which keep people in poverty."[10]

In other respects too, the culture of poverty appears to be a refined formulation of ordinary stereotypes. The claim that the poor are deficient in their "work ethic" and have low aspirations translates all too easily into the familiar stereotype of the poor as lazy, shiftless, and lacking in ambition.

Finally, just as nineteenth-century theorists treated poverty as a moral defect, their twentieth-century counterparts suggest as much by their preoccupation with the prevalence of "social pathologies" among the poor. Even studies that merely enumerate the incidence of crime, illegitimacy, and family instability among the poor—so long as these studies are predicated on the assumption that poverty is "inwardly caused"—convey the impression of rampant promiscuity and moral turpitude. And like its nineteenth-century antecedents, the culture-of-poverty idea provides a theoretical rationale for limiting the role of the state to sponsoring educational programs that seek to reform the habits and morals of the poor. Then, as now, the onus of responsibility for poverty is placed on the poor themselves.

However, now that immigrants have escaped from the poverty of earlier generations, they tend to look back on their experience in poverty as different from that of lower-class minorities today. Thus, Nathan Glazer distinguishes between "slums of hope" and "slums of despair," by which he implies that immigrant slums were not afflicted with the social disorganization and cultural distortions that are identified with present-day slums.[11] According to this view, despite their material privations, immigrant families stayed together, workers organized for better wages, and a stubborn ethnic pride cemented immigrants together in collective self-defense against the deprecations of the outside world. This solidarity of family and community is assumed to be the chief reason that im-

10. Henry Cohen, "Coping with Poverty," in Lyle C. Fitch and Annmarie Hauck Walsh, eds., *Agenda for a City* (Beverly Hills: Sage Publications, 1970), p. 141.

11. Nathan Glazer, "Slums and Ethnicity," in Thomas D. Sherrard, ed., *Social Welfare and Urban Problems* (New York: Columbia University Press, 1968), p. 84.

migrant ghettos were spared the social pathologies associated with today's ghettos.

But were they so spared? A number of recent studies suggest that social pathologies of various kinds were more widespread in immigrant communities than has previously been acknowledged. Once again, it will be useful to focus on the Jewish experience, since Jews have so often been held out as an example of a group that, despite the poverty of the immigrant generation, did not produce high rates of crime and other such social pathologies.

"Slums of Hope"

Chroniclers of the Jewish experience in America have rarely suggested that crime among Jews was ever more than an idiosyncratic event. Milton Gordon comments that Jewish immigrants had "an aversion to violence already internalized";[12] Nathan Glazer writes of the 1920s and '30s that "it was not dangerous to walk through the New York slums at night when they were inhabited by Jews";[13] Thomas Sowell asserts that "there was much crime on the Lower East Side, but Jews were victims more often than perpetrators."[14] In *World of Our Fathers* Irving Howe concedes that "crime befouled the life of the East Side during the eighties and nineties," but adds that "in the life of the immigrant community as a whole, crime was a marginal phenomenon. . . . [I]t was never at the center of Jewish immigrant life."[15]

However, this was not the prevailing view in the early part of the century.

In 1908 the "crime wave" among immigrant Jews emerged as an explosive political issue after Theodore Bingham, New York City's police commissioner, published an article in which he claimed that

12. Milton M. Gordon, *Assimilation in American Life* (New York: Oxford University Press, 1964), p. 186.

13. Nathan Glazer, "The American Jew and the Attainment of Middle-Class Rank: Some Trends and Explanations," in Marshall Sklare, *The Jews* (New York: Free Press, 1958), p. 144.

14. Thomas Sowell, *Race and Economics* (New York: McKay, 1975), p. 69.

15. Irving Howe, *World of Our Fathers* (New York: Harcourt Brace Jovanovich, 1976), p. 101.

Jews accounted for as much as half the crime in New York. Bingham wrote:

> It is not astonishing that with a million Hebrews, mostly Russian, in the city (one quarter of the population) perhaps half of the criminals should be of that race when we consider that ignorance of the language, more particularly among men not physically fit for hard labor, is conducive to crime. . . . They are burglars, firebugs, pickpockets and highway robbers—when they have the courage; but though all crime is their province, pocket-picking is the one to which they take most naturally. . . . Among the most expert of all the street thieves are Hebrew boys under sixteen who are brought up to lives of crime. . . .[16]

Bingham's article unleashed a storm of protest from an outraged Jewish community, and eventually he was forced out of office. Even before his article appeared, however, Jewish leaders had begun to express concern about the growing incidence of crime. In his presidential address to the National Conference of Jewish Charities in 1906, Judge Julian Mack of Chicago implored his audience to confront the problem squarely:

> We must not, in our pride, hide the facts which are brought out daily in the juvenile and police courts. Delinquency is on the increase among our boys; no longer is the Jewish girl a synonym for virtue.[17]

The same month that Bingham's article was published, Louis Marshall wrote that crime was "a cancer . . . gnawing at our vitals."[18] A few years later one of the city's Yiddish newspapers editorialized: "No matter how bitter it may be, we must recognize the fact that among Jews we can find all kinds of bandits."[19]

The growing concern with Jewish crime spawned the Kehillah

16. Quoted in Arthur A. Goren, *New York Jews and the Quest for Community* (New York: Columbia University Press, 1970), p. 25.

17. Julian W. Mack, "Prevention of Delinquency," in Robert Morris and Michael Frennal, eds., *Trends and Issues in Jewish Social Welfare in the United States, 1890–1912* (Philadelphia: The Jewish Publication Society of America, 1966), p. 110.

18. Quoted in Goren, op. cit., p. 148.

19. Quoted in Goren, op. cit., p. 155.

movement, which is the subject of Arthur Goren's study, *New York Jews and the Quest for Community*. For fourteen years the Kehillah sought to unite Jewish groups in a concerted fight against crime on the Lower East Side. Subsidized by contributions from uptown Jews, it employed its own staff and supplied information to the police concerning illicit activities in the Jewish quarter. At its zenith the Kehillah prevailed on the mayor to appoint its own counsel as a deputy police commissioner for the district encompassing the Lower East Side.

What were the circumstances that impelled a community to mobilize such an elaborate anticrime apparatus? Whatever malice or prejudice led Commissioner Bingham to write his notorious article, there was more than a kernel of truth in his allegations. In the first place, prostitution was rife on the Lower East Side. This was acknowledged in an 1898 issue of the *Jewish Daily Forward* which admonished its readers "to stay away from Allen, Chrystie, and Forsyth Streets, if you go walking with your wife, daughter or fiancée. There is an official flesh trade in the Jewish quarter. In the windows you can see human flesh instead of shoes."[20]

Statistical data also indicate that prostitution was widespread. After the Bingham affair, a Jewish newspaper began to monitor arrests in the night court, with the aim of refuting Bingham's allegation that half the criminals in New York were Jewish. In triumphant headlines the paper reported that though Jews made up more than a third of Manhattan's population, they accounted for "only" 27 or 28 percent of prostitutes in night court.[21]

Another study found that in 1907 Jews made up 16 percent of those convicted of felonies, and a much higher percentage of those arrested for lesser crimes.[22] It is true that these figures proved Bingham's allegations to be exaggerated, since the rate of Jewish crime was considerably lower than the percentage of Jews in the population. But the figures also proved that crime was more than an anomalous event. Aside from petty thefts and minor infractions of the city's restrictions on peddling, which were the two most common offenses, Jews could be found among the most notorious

20. Quoted in Howe, op. cit., p. 98.
21. Goren, op. cit., p. 147.
22. Ibid.

gangsters of the period. As Goren reports:

> Behind such *noms de guerre* as Kid Twist (gang leader), Yuski Nigger ("king of the horse poisoners"), Big Jack Zelig (gang leader), Dopey Benny (leader of labor union strong-arm gangs), Kid Dropper (gang leader), and Gyp the Blood (bouncer and gangster), appeared the East European Jewish names, respectively, of Max Zweiback, Joseph Toblinsky, William Albert, Benjamin Fein, Nathan Kaplan, and Harry Horowitz.[23]

In the popular mind Jews were very much a part of the crime wave that had besieged American cities, and Jewish groups were kept busy defending Jewish honor against the exaggerated and often malicious allegations that periodically appeared in the press.

The debate within the Jewish community over the "criminality problem" produced the usual ideological split. Most of the Yiddish press, as well as moderate Jewish leaders, attributed the rising rate of crime among Jews to the breakdown of the traditional order. The problem, they believed, was that in America parents had lost control over their children, and religion and other traditional values had been shattered. To remedy this situation, they called for a revitalization of traditional values through religious instruction and various social work programs; they also advocated a more concerted effort within the Jewish community to stamp out crime.

The socialist *Forward,* however, took a quite different view of the rising rates of crime among Jews. The problem, the *Forward* insisted, was not with the Jewish community or even an erosion of traditional values, but with capitalism. The *Forward* explicitly rejected the notion of "Jewish crime." It seemed obvious that the destitute condition of immigrant Jews was the root cause of crime, and for this reason the *Forward* opposed the Kehillah and other specifically Jewish efforts to control crime. If crime was a product of conditions endemic to capitalism, then narrow strategies that treated crime as an internal disorder of the Jewish community were misdirected and doomed to failure.[24]

The experience of other immigrant groups certainly is consistent with the *Forward*'s view that crime had nothing to do with ethnicity as such, but was primarily a function of poverty. The history of

23. Ibid., p. 137. Also, Robert A. Rockaway, "The Rise of the Jewish Gangster in America," *Journal of Ethnic Studies* 8:2 (1980), p. 31–44.

24. Goren, op. cit., p. 156.

prostitution in America is a case in point. The "oldest profession" has always been the province of the newest group to reside in urban ghettos. In the middle of the nineteenth century it was the Irish who, despite a strong tradition of chastity, figured most prominently among the streetwalkers of New York and Boston.[25] Later in the century they were replaced by Jews and other immigrants. Only in recent decades has this dubious mantle been passed on to blacks and other newcomers to the city.

Generally speaking, there has been an ethnic succession in all areas of crime, beginning with the Irish, who were the first identifiable minority to inhabit urban slums. In the 1860s *Harper's Magazine* observed that the Irish "have so behaved themselves that nearly 75% of our criminals are Irish, that fully 75% of the crimes of violence committed among us are the work of Irishmen. . . ."[26] Speculation as to the causes of the alarming rate of crime among the Irish centered on ethnic traits, especially the intemperate disposition of the Irish "race."

By the end of the century, the connection between immigration and crime became something of a national obsession. The United States Immigration Commission, which carried out a series of studies on the "immigration problem," devoted a whole volume to "Immigrants and Crime." On the basis of extensive statistics collected in New York, Chicago, and Massachusetts, the commission drew up a composite picture of "races and nationalities . . . exhibiting clearly defined criminal characteristics."[27] Italians figured most prominently with respect to crimes of personal violence, including murder. The Irish stood out among those arrested for drunkenness and vagrancy. The French and Jews were disproportionately represented among those arrested for prostitution. In addition, Jews were second only to native Americans when it came to crimes against property, including burglary, larceny, and receiving stolen goods.

25. Oscar Handlin, *Boston's Immigrants* (New York: Atheneum, 1968), p. 122; Richard Stivers, *A Hair of the Dog* (University Park: Pennsylvania State University Press, 1976), p. 107.

26. Quoted in Andrew Greeley, *That Most Distressful Nation* (Chicago: Quadrangle Books, 1972), p. 225. Corroborating evidence of the high rate of crime among Irish immigrants can be found in Handlin, op. cit., p. 259.

27. "Immigration and Crime," *United States Immigration Commission*, vol. 36 (Washington, D.C.: Government Printing Office, 1911), p. 2.

Greeks, Italians, and Jews all ranked high with respect to infractions against city ordinances regulating peddling and trade. The commission concluded that "immigration has had a marked effect on the nature of the crime committed in the United States."[28] Though the report did not attempt to explain the observed relationship between crime and ethnicity, neither did it consider the possibility that the correlation was simply a by-product of poverty. For the commission, the relationship between nationality and crime was self-evident, and implied its own remedy: crime could be reduced by restricting the immigration of those "races" that were prone to criminality.

Today, of course, it is blacks, Puerto Ricans, and Chicanos who are blamed for high rates of crime, and as before, crime is treated as a cultural aberration rather than a symptom of class inequality. No doubt, the incidence of crime in immigrant ghettos was lower than it is today; nor, perhaps, were homicides and other crimes of violence as prevalent. But neither were immigrants mired in poverty over many generations. On the contrary, having entered an expanding economy, most immigrants were on the threshold of upward mobility. Yet if the Irish, Italians, Jews, and others produced as much crime as they did in a single generation, what could have been expected of these groups had they remained in poverty for five or eight or ten generations, like much of the nation's black population?

That crime in immigrant communities was primarily a response to economic disadvantage, and not a product of deeper cultural abnormalities, is easier to see now that these groups have attained middle-class respectability. To realize this should make it easier to avoid confusion of social class with culture and ethnicity when considering the problems of minorities today.

"Slums of Despair"

If social scientists have idealized immigrant communities as "slums of hope," they have also portrayed the communities of today's racial minorities as "slums of despair," characterized by a tangle of pathology involving high rates of crime, unstable families,

28. Ibid., pp. 16–20.

weak and disorganized communities, and a debilitating culture of poverty that is said to impede social and economic progress. In this respect, contemporary sociological thought is reminiscent of nineteenth-century Social Darwinism. Then, as now, the prevailing attitude toward the ghetto was of moral condemnation, and the onus for the ethnic plight was placed on the ethnic groups themselves. Of course, there is no small irony in the fact that the "New Darwinists" invariably have their roots in the very ethnic groups that were previously maligned by the Social Darwinists.

As noted earlier, nineteenth-century perspectives on poverty have been modified and updated to conform with the tenets of modern social science, and it is no longer fashionable to attribute ethnic differences to the operation of biological factors. Kenneth Clark was one of the first to speak out against the tendency to replace notions of biological inferiority with notions of cultural inferiority. Specifically, he attacked those who sought to explain the educational difficulties of black children as symptomatic of a "cultural deprivation" with roots in their homes and communities. Clark wrote in 1965:

> To what extent are the contemporary social deprivation theories merely substituting notions of environmental immutability and fatalism for earlier notions of biologically determined educational immodifiability? To what extent do these theories obscure more basic reasons for the educational retardation of lower-status children? To what extent do they offer acceptable and desired alibis for the educational default: the fact that these children, by and large, do not learn because they are not being taught effectively and they are not being taught because those who are charged with the responsibility of teaching them do not believe that they can learn, do not expect that they can learn, and do not act toward them in ways which help them to learn.[29]

As genetic explanations for the behavior of the poor have been discarded, the "poverty subculture" has received even greater emphasis. And whenever the poor are identifiable in terms of some ethnic or racial characteristic, the tendency has been to look within these particular cultures for an explanation of the group's relative

29. Kenneth Clark, *Dark Ghetto* (New York: Harper & Row, 1965), p. 131.

failure. The underlying assumption is that if it were not for the undesirable qualities endemic to the group to which they belong, these individuals too would be able to climb the ladder of success.

Like Clark, Glazer and Moynihan in *Beyond the Melting Pot* address themselves to the educational problems of black school-children, but they locate the source of the problem in the defective institutions of the black community. "There is little question," they write without equivocation, "where the major part of the answer must be found: in the home and family and community. . . . It is there that the heritage of two hundred years of slavery and a hundred years of discrimination is concentrated; and it is there that we find the serious obstacles to the ability to make use of a free educational system to advance into higher occupations and to eliminate the massive social problems that afflict colored Americans and the city."[30] For Glazer and Moynihan, American society provides ample opportunity for class mobility, and it is black cultural institutions—"home and family and community"—that are problematic. The implicit comparison is with Jews, Asians, and other groups where cohesive families and strong communities are presumed to account for the higher rates of individual mobility.

Glazer and Moynihan cannot be accused of being oblivious to racism; after all, they explicitly acknowledge "two hundred years of slavery and a hundred years of discrimination." Nevertheless, this view of the role of racism warrants careful examination. According to their model, historic patterns of racism have done irreparable damage to the cultural integrity of family and community among blacks. What might have begun as a problem of a brutally racist society ends up as the problem of a battered minority that has lost its cultural bearings and is too scarred to take full advantage of the opportunities now placed before it. Implicitly, Glazer and Moynihan acknowledge the operation of racism in the distant past, but minimize its present significance. Their prescription for social policy is consistent with this model. If the remedy was once to combat racism, today it is to repair the damage previously inflicted on black families and communities, which in their view constitutes the major obstacle to racial progress today.

The logic of this argument, and its regressive implications for

30. Nathan Glazer and Daniel Patrick Moynihan, *Beyond the Melting Pot* (Cambridge: MIT Press, 1970), pp. 49–50.

social policy, became fully apparent with the 1965 publication of the Moynihan Report, a position paper written by Daniel Patrick Moynihan during his tenure as assistant to President Johnson on domestic affairs. The report contended that the black family was in deep crisis and that this was the single most important problem confronting the black community. In the rather bald language of the report:

> At the heart of the deterioration of the fabric of Negro society is the deterioration of the Negro family. It is the fundamental source of the weakness of the Negro community at the present time.[31]

Moynihan based this assessment on data from a number of official surveys indicating very high rates of illegitimacy and family breakdown among blacks. The data themselves were not new, and though questions were raised concerning their accuracy, the imbroglio that followed the publication of the report principally had to do with the dubious interpretations that Moynihan advanced.

Controversy surrounded Moynihan's insistence that the problems of black families today are a by-product of the ravages of slavery on the black family. This is a seductive argument, since it appears to place the onus of blame on a racist society. But for Moynihan it is not our sins but the sins of our fathers that are at the root of the problem. That is to say, the report tends to minimize the role of present-day conditions as they operate to undermine black families; instead, the emphasis is upon racism as it operated in the distant past. Aside from this misplaced emphasis, more recent historical evidence calls into question the assumption that slavery shattered the black family as a cultural institution.

In his history of *The Black Family in Slavery and Freedom*, Herbert Gutman marshaled an enormous body of evidence to show that despite the abuses inflicted on black families during slavery, the cultural fabric of the family remained intact, and blacks left slavery with very powerful family traditions.[32] Even before Gut-

31. Daniel Patrick Moynihan, *The Negro Family: The Case for National Action,* in Lee Rainwater and William C. Yancy, *The Moynihan Report and the Politics of Controversy* (Cambridge: MIT Press, 1967), p. 51.

32. Herbert Gutman, *The Black Family in Slavery and Freedom* (New York: Pantheon, 1976).

man's book was published, there was evidence that contemporary problems in black families do not have their roots in slavery. Had Moynihan examined available data prior to the 1940s, he would have realized that illegitimacy and family instability are only recent trends that began with the mass movement of blacks to cities since the First World War.[33] In other words, if there is a crisis in the black family, it has its roots not in slavery, but in the conditions that black migrants encountered in northern ghettos.

When immigrants lived in urban slums, they, too, experienced strains in the family system. In the early 1900s, for example, desertions were widespread among Jewish immigrants, and Jewish journals and social agencies expressed alarm over the "desertion evil."[34] Some indication of the magnitude of this problem can be gleaned from the records of the United Hebrew Charities of New York, which reported that in 1903–4 alone it had received over one thousand applications for relief from deserted women. The *Jewish Daily Forward* routinely ran a "Gallery of Missing Husbands" to assist women in locating their errant spouses.[35]

Once again, it would not be correct to imply that family instability was as common among Jews and other immigrants as it is among today's racial minorities, for this was not so.[36] But neither was their experience in poverty the same. Despite the hardships of immigrant life, most immigrants had left still more depressed conditions in their countries of origin, and their American experience of poverty was generally short-lived. In the case of New York's Jewish population, the proportion residing on the Lower East Side declined from 75 percent in 1892 to only 23 percent in 1916.[37] If this was a "slum of hope," then it is clear that there was something to be hopeful about.

The vulnerability of the family to poverty was revealed during the Depression. A study by Edward Bakke, called *Citizens With-*

33. Jessie Bernard, *Marriage and Family among Negroes* (Englewood Cliffs, N.J.: Prentice-Hall, 1966), chap. 1.

34. *Jewish Charity,* vol. 5, February 1905, pp. 143–45; November 1905, p. 50; February 1905, p. 138.

35. Howe, *World of Our Fathers,* op. cit., p. 179.

36. See Gutman, op. cit., pp. 521–30.

37. Moses Rischin, *The Promised City: New York Jews, 1870–1914* (Cambridge: Harvard University Press, 1962), p. 153.

out Work, traced the devastating impact of unemployment on the family system. Bakke wrote:

> The family, dissociated from many of its former community contacts, is now thrown in upon itself where conflict and confusion dominate and established relationship patterns have disintegrated. There is no comfort in the family circle. The breaking up of the family unit may be considered at this time by one or both of the parents since there is a present failure to receive satisfaction customarily expected of the family and very little prospect that the future will offer anything different.[38]

The dissolution of families occurred despite the fact that the "citizens without work" had been unemployed for only a short time, and could hardly blame themselves for a collapse in the national economy. In contrast, racial minorities today not only experience chronic unemployment, but do so at a time of general prosperity, a condition that exacerbates feelings of self-blame, with dire consequences for the family.

The thrust of the Moynihan Report, however, was not to show that poverty undermined families, but on the contrary, to suggest that a weak family system is responsible for the problems that beset black communities. In the unequivocal language of the report:

> . . . at the center of the tangle of pathology is the weakness of the family structure. Once or twice removed, it will be found to be the principal source of most of the aberrant, inadequate, or anti-social behavior that did not establish, but now serves to perpetuate the cycle of poverty and deprivation.[39]

As Moynihan's critics have argued, such a formulation inverts cause and effect. Instead of seeing poverty as the source of family instability, as well as other social problems, Moynihan turned this proposition around and argued that family instability was at the bottom of it all.

Moynihan's analysis had grave implications for social policy. Instead of programs to reverse the chronic unemployment and poverty that were undermining the family system, Moynihan pro-

---

38. Edward Bakke, *Citizens Without Work* (New Haven: Yale University Press, 1940), p. 209.

39. Moynihan Report, op. cit., p. 76.

posed a national program to strengthen the black family. Here, alas, was the end result of the confusion of social class with ethnic factors. Instead of a frontal attack on the institutional inequalities between the haves and have-nots in American society, a prominent sociologist-politician was mapping a policy aimed at repairing the frayed culture of a racial minority. Of course, such a formula was appealing to the political establishment in Washington, since it did not threaten to tamper with major institutions, and indeed absolved the society at large of responsibility for the plight of black Americans, beyond what was required to help them put their own cultural house in order.

The Social Context of Poverty

Much of the issue between Moynihan and his critics concerns the relative importance of factors internal and external to the black community. Moynihan carried the culture-of-poverty thesis to the extreme of viewing the poverty subculture as a self-contained and self-perpetuating system that existed independently of white society. As he wrote:

> Three centuries of injustice have brought about deep-seated structural distortions in the life of the Negro American. *At this point, the present tangle of pathology is capable of perpetuating itself without assistance from the white world.* The cycle can be broken only if these distortions are set right. [Italics added.][40]

Clearly, this formulation is fundamentally at odds with Oscar Lewis's position, for although Lewis acknowledged the operation of self-perpetuating mechanisms, he viewed them within the total context of economic, political, and social inequality. In response to his own critics, Lewis stated his position in unmistakable terms:

> The crucial question from both the scientific and the political point of view is: How much weight is to be given to the internal, self-perpetuating factors in the subculture of poverty as compared to the external societal factors? My own position is

40. Ibid., p. 93.

that in the long run the self-perpetuating factors are relatively minor and unimportant compared to the basic structures of the larger society.[41]

Consistent with this position, Lewis did not take refuge in melioristic reforms that pretended that poverty could be remedied through a cultural rehabilitation of the poor. For him, genuine and lasting change could occur only through a transformation of the structural inequalities in which the culture of poverty was ultimately rooted.

The issue with respect to the culture of poverty, however, goes beyond the question of how much weight is to be given to internal versus external factors. The more compelling question has to do with the relationship between these two sets of factors, and particularly with the ways in which external structures impinge upon and shape the values and life-styles of the poor. The stark figures presented in the Moynihan Report, for example, do not shed light on the process that results in a high rate of illegitimacy and family breakdown. To suggest that a weak family system produces family instability is meaningless, when the only evidence for the claim that the family system is weak is the high rate of family instability. To break out of this pattern of circular reasoning, and to understand the process through which family relationships are undermined, it is necessary to explore the linkages between economic forces, cultural values, and individual states of mind.

This was the approach that Elliot Liebow used in *Tally's Corner,* published in 1967.[42] Liebow, an anthropologist, penetrated the inner world of "streetcorner men" in Washington, D.C., and his analysis focused on a key point of articulation between the individual and society—the job market. *Tally's Corner* is thus a study of the impact of unemployment and underemployment on what are ordinarily regarded as strictly personal spheres of behavior—sexual relationships, marriage, and the family. It is important to note that the streetcorner men whom Liebow observed are not representative of the ghetto population, but of an underclass. The men worked only sporadically at odd jobs, most had fathered several children with

41. Quoted in Eleanor Burke Leacock, *The Culture of Poverty: Critique* (New York: Simon & Schuster, 1971), pp. 35-36.

42. Elliot Liebow, *Tally's Corner* (Boston: Little, Brown, 1967).

different women, and their lives centered around neither jobs nor families but the street corner where they "hung out" with others like themselves. If a culture of poverty exists at all in American society, one would expect to find it in such a place, and thus Liebow's study, while it does not purport to deal with black America generally, does provide a good test of the culture-of-poverty thesis.

At least superficially, the streetcorner men exhibited many of the characteristics of a culture of poverty. They unquestionably had a present-time orientation, in that immediate pleasures were pursued without regard to long-range implications. Their aspirations were low, at least as gauged by the fact that they worked irregularly and did not look for better jobs. Their absence from their families meant households were headed by women. And the feelings of inferiority, helplessness, and fatalism that Lewis saw as endemic to a culture of poverty were in plain evidence. Yet Liebow forcefully rejects the view that these are "traits" that add up to a culture of poverty. He insists that the fundamental values of the streetcorner men are the same as those of middle-class society, and that their behavior, though in apparent contradiction to those values, is only a response to external circumstances that prevent them from living according to conventional values.

Of paramount importance is the fact that these men are unable to find jobs that pay a living wage. As Liebow points out, the way a man makes a living and the kind of living he makes defines a man's worth, both to himself and to his neighbors, friends, lovers, and family. This operates with the same force as in the rest of society, but inversely, since the streetcorner men do not have jobs that are worth very much, either in status or pay. For Liebow, this is the controlling factor in their lives, distorting their values, their family relationships, and their concept of themselves.

Thus, if they do not plan for the future, it is not because they are observing a different cultural norm that emphasizes the pleasure of the moment, but because their futures are bleak and they lack the resources and opportunities for doing much about it. Similarly, their low aspirations are an inevitable response to restricted opportunity, particularly the improbability of finding a decent job. This is not a self-fulfilling prophecy, but a resignation born out of bitter personal experience. All the men in Liebow's study had tested themselves repeatedly on the job market, and had come to realize that the only jobs available were menial, low-paying, dead-end jobs that would not allow them to support their families.

Nor does the fact that families are headed by women indicate a "matriarchal family pattern" rooted in black culture. Rather it is an inevitable by-product of the inability of men to function as bread-winners for their families. Their inability to do so, furthermore, plays havoc with their sense of manhood, and their relationships with their wives and children. As Bakke observed with respect to unemployed families during the Depression:

> Economic resources provide not only food and shelter but also the means of establishing and maintaining the satisfying relationships and status of a social nature within the family and in the community.[43]

It is the loss of this status and function within the family that finally led Liebow's subjects to seek refuge on the street corner.

Thus, Liebow presents a strong case that the streetcorner men have the same concept of work and family as does the middle class. Indeed, it is precisely because they share these conventional values that they experience such a profound sense of personal failure. The attraction of the street corner, with its "shadow system of values," is that it compensates for an impaired sense of manhood. In all these respects Liebow's interpretation of the street corner is in direct opposition to the culture-of-poverty thesis. As Liebow writes:

> . . . the streetcorner man does not appear to be a carrier of an independent cultural tradition. His behavior appears not so much as a way of realizing the distinctive goals and values of his own subculture, or of conforming to its models, but rather as his way of trying to achieve many of the goals and values of the larger society, of failing to do this, and of concealing his failure from others and from himself as best he can.
>
> If, in the course of concealing his failure, or of concealing his fear of even trying, he pretends—through the device of public fictions—that he did not want these things in the first place and claims he has all along been responding to a different set of rules and prizes, we do not do him or ourselves any good by accepting this claim at face value.[44]

43. Bakke, op. cit., p. 176.
44. Liebow, op. cit., p. 222.

Thus, similarities between parents and children are not the product of cultural transmission, but of the fact that "the son goes out and independently experiences the same failures, in the same areas, and for much the same reasons as his father."[45]

For Liebow, then, the poor do not need instruction in the Protestant ethic or other values, but jobs that would allow them to incorporate these values into their everyday lives. It is not their culture that needs to be changed, but an economic system that fails to provide jobs that pay a living wage to millions of the nation's poor.

Conclusion

There is intellectual perversity in the tendency to use the cultural responses of the poor as "explanations" of why they are poor. Generally speaking, groups do not get ahead or lag behind on the basis of their cultural values. Rather, they are born into a given station in life and adopt values that are consonant with their circumstances and their life chances. To the extent that lower-class ethnics seem to live according to a different set of values, this is primarily a cultural manifestation of their being trapped in poverty. In the final analysis, the culture-of-poverty thesis—at least as it has been used by Banfield, Moynihan, and others—is nothing more than an intellectual smoke screen for our society's unwillingness or inability to wipe out unemployment and poverty.

45. Ibid., p. 223.

Chapter 5

———

Education and Ethnic Mobility:
The Myth of Jewish Intellectualism
and Catholic Anti-Intellectualism

*"If our children don't go to school, no harm results. But
if the sheep don't eat, they will die. The school can
wait but not our sheep."*

AN ITALIAN PEASANT, QUOTED IN LEONARD COVELLO,
The Social Background of the Italo-American School Child, 1967.

HORACE MANN, the architect of the common school, once described
education as "the great equalizer." Implicitly Mann recognized that
the schools would function within the context of class inequality,
providing the less privileged members of society with opportunities
for social and economic advancement. In *Democracy and Education*
John Dewey also wrote that "it is the office of the school environment . . . to see to it that each individual gets an opportunity to
escape from the limitations of the social group in which he was
born, and to come into living contact with a broader environment."[1]
To this day, it is an article of faith in American society that educa-

———

1. Quoted in Samuel Bowles and Herbert Gintis, *Schooling in Capitalist
America* (New York: Basic Books, 1976), p. 21.

tion is the key to material success, and the key to eliminating social inequalities as well.

Consistent with this liberal faith in education, two general assumptions run through the social science literature on education and ethnic mobility. The first is that those ethnic groups that have taken advantage of educational opportunities have, for that reason, enjoyed comparative mobility and success. The second assumption is that the values of some groups have been conducive to intellectual achievement, whereas other groups have been saddled with anti-intellectual values or other cultural traits that discouraged their children from pursuing educational opportunities. This "theory" is thus a variant of the more general theory of ethnic success discussed earlier.

As before, issue arises not with the fact that ethnic groups vary in educational attainment, but with the assumption that this reflects the operation of cultural factors, such as the degree to which education is valued. How do we know that some ethnic groups value education more highly? Because they have a superior record of educational attainment. Obviously, it is incorrect to infer values from the outcome, and then to posit these values as causal factors. To prove the cultural thesis, it is necessary to furnish independent evidence that some groups placed special value on education, and that this factor operated in its own right as a determinant of educational achievement.

Yet a number of writers have claimed such evidence by pointing to the cultural systems of certain ethnic groups that are thought to be compatible or incompatible with the requirements of modern education. This argument is commonly made with respect to Asians and Jews, both of whom have in fact achieved higher levels of education than most other groups in American society.

For example, in his book on Japanese-Americans William Petersen begins with the factual observation that "since 1940, the Japanese have had more schooling than any other race in the American population, including whites."[2] He then proceeds to explain the high educational levels of Japanese-Americans as an outgrowth of a particular set of cultural values. On the basis of his examination of the records of Japanese students at Berkeley during the late 1950s

2. William Petersen, *Japanese Americans* (New York: Random House, 1971), p. 113.

and early 1960s, Petersen writes: "Their education had been conducted like a military campaign against a hostile world, with intelligent planning and tenacity. . . . In a word, these young men and women were squares."[3] Irrespective of Petersen's questionable metaphor (would enterprising Jewish or Italian students be described as waging a military campaign, or is this imagery reserved for the Japanese?), his characterization of such students as "squares" is most revealing. According to Petersen, the "cultural traditions" of Japanese produced diligent, persevering, and industrious students who eschewed the pleasures of the moment in their dogged pursuit of long-range goals. Like the "old-fashioned boys" in Horatio Alger's novels, it is the squares who ultimately triumph.

In her praise of Chinese educational achievement, Betty Sung is even more explicit in tracing this to a specific "cultural heritage." According to Sung:

> Chinese respect for learning and for the scholar is a cultural heritage. Even when a college degree led to no more than a waiter's job, the Chinese continued to pursue the best education they could get, so that when opportunities developed, the Chinese were qualified and capable of handling their jobs. Other minorities have not had the benefit of this reverence for learning.[4]

For Sung, the Chinese reverence for learning is not merely characteristic of Chinese-Americans, but is a product of a cultural heritage rooted in centuries of history.

Of course, it is the Jews who are most often acclaimed, in folklore and social science alike, as a "people of the book." The implication here is that Jews owe their intellectual prominence to a reverence for learning that is rooted in their religious culture and that has been passed down through the ages. There is hardly a study of Jews in America that does not cite a "Jewish passion for education" as a major factor, if not *the* major factor, in explaining Jewish mobility. A typical exposition of this idea is found in Marshall Sklare's 1971 book on *America's Jews:*

3. Ibid., pp. 115–16.
4. Betty Lee Sung, *The Story of the Chinese in America* (New York: Macmillan, 1967), pp. 124–25.

Jewish culture embraced a different attitude toward learning from that which characterized the dominant societies of eastern Europe. This Jewish attitude was part of the value-system of the immigrants. It pertains to learning in general, though in the traditional framework it is most apparent with respect to the study of religious subjects.[5]

According to Sklare and numerous others, the high valuation that Jews traditionally placed on religious learning was, in the New World, transferred to secular learning, and with this cultural head start, the children of Jewish immigrants were quick to climb the educational ladder.

A large number of empirical studies have documented Jewish intellectual achievements. It is known that, compared with most other groups, Jews are more likely to go to college, especially highly competitive colleges, to excel once they are there, and to go on to graduate and professional schools. Studies have also shown that Jews are disproportionately represented among the teaching faculties of the nation's colleges and universities and this is especially so in the leading research institutions.[6] Still other studies have shown that Jews have produced more than their share of eminent scholars and scientists, and of course there has been much preoccupation with the fact that Marx, Freud, and Einstein, three of the towering figures of modern history, have been Jewish.[7] As in the case of Jewish economic success, the fact of Jewish intellectual prominence can hardly be disputed. Rather it is the interpretation of this fact—specifically, the notion that Jewish educational achievements result from a reverence for learning embedded in Jewish history and culture—that is problematic.

An alternative to this cultural theory is a social class theory that does not deny the operation of cultural factors, but sees them as conditional on preexisting class factors. Whereas the cultural theory

5. Marshall Sklare, *America's Jews* (New York: Random House, 1971), p. 58.

6. Stephen Steinberg, *The Academic Melting Pot* (New York: McGraw-Hill, 1974), chap. 5.

7. Tina Levitan, *The Laureates: Jewish Winners of the Nobel Prize* (New York: Twayne Publishers, Inc., 1960); Nathaniel Weyl and Stefan Possony, *The Geography of Intellect* (Chicago: Henry Regnery, 1913), pp. 123–28.

holds that certain groups placed unusually high value on education, which resulted in greater mobility, the class theory turns this proposition around, and holds that economic mobility occurred first, and that this opened up channels of educational opportunity and engendered a corresponding set of values and aspirations favorable to education. Obviously, education allowed these groups to consolidate and extend their economic gains, but these were gains that initially occurred in the occupational marketplace without the benefit of extensive education.

This is not to deny the well-documented fact that Japanese, Chinese, and Jews all placed high value on education; nor does the class theory deny that reverence for education may be rooted in the traditional belief systems of these groups. Where the class theory differs from the cultural theory is in its emphasis on the *primacy* of class factors. That is to say, it is held that cultural factors have little independent effect on educational outcomes, but are influential only as they interact with class factors. Thus, to whatever extent a reverence for learning was part of the religious and cultural heritage of Asians and Jews, it was activated and given existential significance by their social class circumstances. Without this congruence between culture and circumstance, it is hardly conceivable that these groups could have sustained their traditional value on education, or that it would have actually resulted in higher levels of educational achievement.

The Myth of Jewish Intellectualism

Can Jewish intellectual traditions, rooted in premodern and prescientific systems of thought, explain the academic achievements of Jews in twentieth-century America? This is the question raised by anthropologist Miriam Slater, who did a "content analysis" of Jewish scholarly traditions. Slater shows that the style and content of traditional Jewish scholarship were fundamentally at odds with the requirements of modern secular education, and if anything would have operated as a deterrent to educational achievement in America. For example, whereas shtetl learning involved a ritualistic preoccupation with Talmudic legalisms, Western education is highly pragmatic, innovative, and oriented toward lucrative employment in the marketplace. In Slater's view it was a striving for material success, and not a passion for learning, that spurred Jews up the educational ladder.[8]

Slater is not the first to suggest that the specific content of traditional Jewish education was incompatible with modern secular education. For example, in his study on the historical evolution of science, Lewis Feuer writes of Talmudic scholarship that "this sterile type of 'learning' and disputation was an obstacle to the development of science among Jews, a hurdle they had to surmount."[9] In *World of Our Fathers* Irving Howe also comments that "scholarship often degenerated into abysmal scholasticism. Intellect could be reduced to a barren exercise in distinctions that had long ago lost their reality."[10] A less dispassionate view of traditional Jewish pedagogy is found in Michael Gold's autobiographical novel *Jews Without Money:*

> Reb Moisha was my teacher. . . . What could such as he teach any one? He was ignorant as a rat. He was a foul smelling, emaciated beggar who had never read anything, or seen anything, who knew absolutely nothing but this sterile memory course in dead Hebrew which he whipped into the heads and backsides of little boys.[11]

In his own fashion, Gold concurs with Slater's view that Jewish scholarship was "discontinuous" with secular education in America.

Yet the issue that Slater raises is a spurious one. What sociologists have argued is not that Jewish intellectual traditions were important in and of themselves, but rather that they fostered a positive orientation toward learning that was easily adapted to secular education. In his novel *The Rise of David Levinsky,* Abraham Cahan explores how Old World values were recast in the New World. Formerly a Talmudic scholar in Russia, David Levinsky yearns to

8. Miriam Slater, "My Son the Doctor: Aspects of Mobility Among American Jews," *American Sociological Review* 34 (June 1969): 359–73.

9. Lewis S. Feuer, *The Scientific Intellectual* (New York: Basic Books, 1963), p. 303.

10. Irving Howe, *World of Our Fathers* (New York: Harcourt Brace Jovanovich, 1976), pp. 8–9.

11. Michael Gold, *Jews Without Money* (New York: Avon Books, 1961; orig. edition 1930), p. 43.

go to City College. Gazing at the "humble spires" of a City College building, he thinks to himself: "My old religion had gradually fallen to pieces, and if its place was taken by something else . . . that something was the red, church-like structure on the southeast corner of Lexington Avenue and Twenty-third Street. *It was the synagogue of my new life.*"[12] This last phrase epitomizes the transfer of a traditional value on learning from religious to secular education, which, according to the conventional wisdom, accounts for the rapid economic mobility that Jews experienced in America.

Yet in Cahan's novel, Levinsky never fulfills his ambition to go to City College; instead he makes a fortune as an entrepreneur in the garment industry. Is this mere fiction or does Cahan's character typify the pattern of Jewish mobility? In other words, was it generally the case that Jews achieved economic mobility *before* their children climbed the educational ladder? Indeed, this is the conclusion of a recent study by Selma Berrol on "Education and Economic Mobility: The Jewish Experience in New York City, 1880–1920."[13]

Berrol's inventory of educational facilities in New York City at the turn of the century shows that the schools could not possibly have functioned as a significant channel of mobility. Still in an early stage of development, the public school system was unable to cope with the enormous influx of foreigners, most of whom were in their childbearing ages. Primary grade schools were so overcrowded that tens of thousands of students were turned away, and as late as 1914 there were only five high schools in Manhattan and the Bronx. If only for this reason, few children of Jewish immigrants received more than a rudimentary education.

Berrol furnishes other data showing that large numbers of Jewish students ended their schooling by the eighth grade. For example, in New York City in 1908 there were 25,534 Jewish students in the first grade, 11,527 in the seventh, 2,549 in their first year of high school, and only 488 in their last year.[14] Evidently, most immigrant

12. Abraham Cahan, *The Rise of David Levinsky* (Colophon Books: New York, 1960), p. 169 (italics added).

13. Selma C. Berrol, "Education and Economic Mobility: The Jewish Experience in New York City, 1880–1920," *American Jewish Historical Quarterly,* March 1976, pp. 257–71.

14. Ibid., p. 261.

Jewish children of this period dropped out of school to enter the job market.

Nor could City College have been a major channel of Jewish mobility during the early decades of the twentieth century. Until the expansion of City College in the 1930s and 1940s, enrollments were not large enough to have a significant impact on Jewish mobility. Furthermore, Jewish representation at the college was predominantly German; Berrol estimates that in 1923 only 11 percent of CCNY students had Russian or Polish names.

In short, prior to the 1930s and 1940s, the public schools, and City College in particular, were not a channel of mobility for more than a privileged few. It was not until the expansion of higher education following the Second World War that City College provided educational opportunities for significant numbers of Jewish youth. However, by this time New York's Jewish population had already emerged from the deep poverty of the immigrant generation, and had experienced extensive economic mobility.

It was the children of these upwardly mobile Jews who enrolled in City College during the 1930s and 1940s. For them, education was clearly a channel of mobility, but it accelerated a process of intergenerational mobility that was already in motion, since their parents typically had incomes, and often occupations as well, that were a notch or two above those of the working class in general. As Berrol concluded:

> . . . most New York City Jews did not make the leap from poverty into the middle class by going to college. Rather, widespread utilization of secondary and higher education *followed* improvements in economic status and was as much a result as a cause of upward mobility.[15]

The conclusion that economic mobility preceded the Jewish thrust in education is also suggested by Herbert Gutman's analysis of 1905 census data.[16] Gutman did a comparison of two immigrant Jewish neighborhoods on New York's East Side: Cherry Street, one of the section's poorest neighborhoods, made up largely of rank-and-file workers; and East Broadway, a somewhat more prosperous neigh-

15. Ibid., p. 271.
16. Gutman's unpublished data are summarized by Irving Howe in *World of Our Fathers*, op. cit., pp. 141–44.

borhood largely inhabited by businessmen and professionals. The contrast between the two neighborhoods in terms of the mobility patterns of the next generation is striking. On Cherry Street almost all of the children in their late teens had left school and gone to work, generally at low-status, blue-collar jobs that barely raised them above the level of their parents. However, the children of the more affluent families on East Broadway were making a breakthrough into higher-status white-collar occupations and the professions.

Though Gutman's data are far from conclusive, they are consistent with other historical data suggesting that economic success was a precondition, rather than a consequence, of extensive schooling. There is no evidence to indicate that the children of Jewish rank-and-file workers received more education than other immigrant children of the same social class. If this assumption is correct, then the greater overall success that Jews experienced stems from the fact that Jews had an occupational head start compared to other immigrants, that this resulted in an early economic ascent, which in turn allowed more of their children to remain in school and avail themselves of educational opportunities.

Precisely at the time that Jews were overcoming the poverty of the immigrant generation, there was a vast increase in educational opportunity, another fortuitous wedding of historical circumstances that facilitated Jewish mobility. As the economy matured, the demand increased for a more educated labor force. This set in motion a long series of educational reforms leading to an expansion and overhaul of the nation's educational institutions. Especially in the northern industrial states where Jews were concentrated, there was a trend toward much heavier public investment in schools and colleges. The curricula were also changing away from their classical traditions toward science, vocational training, and professional education, and thus were more compatible with the talents and aspirations of children born outside the upper class.

One ramification of the educational expansion of the period was that teaching itself emerged as a significant profession. Between 1898 and 1920, the number of teachers in the New York City schools increased from 10,008 to 24,235, the largest numerical increase in any profession.[17] And among Russian Jews who graduated from City College between 1895 and 1935, more entered teaching than either medicine or law.[18] But it was not until a second major expansion of higher education after the Second World War that Jews began to show up in large numbers on the faculties of American colleges and universities.[19] Not surprisingly, they tended to enter new and expanding fields in the social and natural sciences. In all these ways, the stages of economic and educational development within the Jewish population coincided with stages of growth and change in American educational institutions.

What conclusion, then, can be drawn concerning the relationship between Jewish cultural values and Jewish educational achievements? It goes without saying that the educational levels that Jews finally attained would not have been possible without a corresponding set of supportive values that encouraged education, defined college as a suitable channel for social and economic mobility, and idealized intellectual achievement. But were these values distinctively part of a religious and cultural heritage, or were they merely cultural responses of a group that had acquired the economic prerequisites for educational mobility at a time when educational opportunities abounded?

There is a sense in which both these questions can be answered affirmatively. Even if Jews placed no special value on education, their social class position undoubtedly would have led them to pursue educational opportunities anyway. But Jews *did* place a special value on education, and this helped to impart the pursuit of educational opportunities with deeper cultural significance. Given the role of study in Jewish religion, the transfer of these values to secular learning tended to legitimate and sanctify a worldly desire for social and economic improvement. But these values only assumed operational significance in their interaction with a wider set of

17. Sherry Gorelick, *Social Control, Social Mobility and the Eastern European Jews: Public Education in New York City, 1880–1924*, unpublished Ph.D. dissertation, Columbia University, 1975 (scheduled for publication by the Rutgers University Press), p. 167. *The World Almanac, 1923* (New York: The Press Publication Co., 1923), p. 549.

18. Gorelick, ibid., p. 165.

19. Steinberg, op. cit., p. 106.

structural factors, especially the advantageous position of economically mobile Jews and the favorable structure of educational opportunity that they encountered. It was because education carried with it such compelling social and economic rewards that the traditional value on education was activated, redefined, and given new direction.

Had immigrant Jews remained trapped in poverty and deprived of educational opportunities, it is unlikely that Jewish intellectual life would have advanced beyond the archaic scholasticism that immigrant Jews carried over with them from Europe. Conversely, other immigrant groups that started out with less favorable cultural dispositions with respect to education rapidly developed an appetite for education once they achieved a position in the class system comparable to that of Jews a generation earlier.

The Myth of Catholic Anti-Intellectualism

In matters of education, Catholics stand in historical counterpoint to Jews, lagging behind in areas where Jews have excelled. This has sometimes led to invidious comparisons between the two groups. For example, Thomas O'Dea, a leading Catholic scholar, wrote in 1958:

> It is doubtful that even the Irish immigrants, perhaps the poorest of the nineteenth-century arrivals to these shores, were much poorer than the eastern European and Russian Jews who came after 1890, except possibly in the worst years of the Irish potato failure of the 1840s. Yet these eastern Jews . . . have contributed a larger proportion of their children and grandchildren to academic and scholarly life than have Catholic immigrants as a whole.[20]

Having assumed that Catholics and Jews started out in the same place in the class system, O'Dea implicitly dismisses class factors as irrelevant to the question of why Jews have produced a greater number of scholars. As already shown, however, although Jewish immigrants were poor, they had social class advantages in the form

20. Thomas O'Dea, *American Catholic Dilemma* (New York: Sheed & Ward, 1959), p. 87.

of literacy and occupational skills, that resulted in more rapid economic mobility. Thus, O'Dea's unfavorable comparison between Catholics and Jews is based on a false assumption.

Yet O'Dea's failure to consider class factors has been characteristic of nearly half a century of social research, and has resulted in a castigation of Catholicism itself for the underrepresentation of Catholics among the nation's scientists and scholars. For example, in 1931 *Scientific Monthly* published an article on "Scientific Eminence and Church Membership," in which the authors reported that Unitarians were 1,695 times more likely than Catholics to be listed among the nation's eminent scientists. The data seemed to give credence to the popular stereotype of the Catholic Church as a dogmatic and authoritarian institution that restricts free thought and scientific inquiry. The authors thus concluded that "the conspicuous dearth of scientists among Catholics suggests that the tenets of the church are not consonant with scientific endeavor."[21]

Several decades later, in his book on *Anti-Intellectualism in American Life*, Richard Hofstadter also scored Catholics for having "failed to develop an intellectual tradition in America or to produce its own class of intellectuals. . . ."[22] Like earlier writers, Hofstadter automatically assumed that the low level of Catholic representation among scholars is symptomatic of an anti-intellectualism rooted in Catholic religion and culture.

The same inference is made in Kenneth Hardy's 1974 study of the "Social Origins of American Scientists and Scholars," published in *Science* magazine.[23] Hardy ranked American undergraduate colleges in terms of their "scholarly productivity," as measured by the relative number of their graduates who went on to receive Ph.D.s. Like women's colleges and southern colleges, Catholic colleges turn out to be low in scholarly productivity. Hardy's interpretation of these findings is altogether circular. He assumes ipso facto that those institutions low in productivity are marked

21. Harvey C. Lehman and Paul A. Witty, "Scientific Eminence and Church Membership," *Scientific Monthly* 33 (December 1931), pp. 548–49.

22. Richard Hofstadter, *Anti-Intellectualism in American Life* (New York: Random House, 1963), p. 136.

23. Kenneth Hardy, "Social Origins of American Scientists and Scholars," *Science*, vol. 185, August 9, 1974, pp. 497–506. Also, my critique in *Change* magazine, June 1976, pp. 50–51, 64.

by anti-intellectual, antidemocratic, and antihumanitarian values that are antithetical to scholarship. But the only evidence he has that institutions have such retrograde values is that they are low in productivity. On this flimsy basis, he portrays Catholic colleges, as well as women's colleges and southern colleges, as culturally to blame for the fact that relatively few of their students go on to earn Ph.D.s.

A more plausible explanation, however, is that such colleges tend to attract students from less privileged backgrounds who have lower academic qualifications from the start, and who are less likely to aspire to careers that entail graduate education. Indeed, Alexander Astin has shown that it is not the attributes of colleges that determine their productivity of future Ph.D.s, but rather the attributes of the students they recruit.[24] In fact, those Catholic colleges that maintain high entrance standards—for example, Georgetown University, Boston College, Loyola University, and the Catholic University of America—all have above-average records for producing future Ph.D.s. Thus, there is no basis for attributing the generally lower rates of scholarly productivity of Catholic colleges to the intellectual quality of these institutions, much less to a specific set of anti-intellectual values rooted in the Catholic religion.

Why, then, have Catholics produced fewer scholars and scientists than other groups? What was the meshing of culture and circumstance that obstructed educational progress for Catholics? As a first step in addressing this issue, it is necessary to consider the varied ethnic composition of the Catholic population. It makes little sense to treat Catholics as a monolith, especially given the fact that the ethnic groups that made up the nation's Catholic population occupy such different positions in the class system. As Andrew Greeley has shown, Irish and German Catholics rank well above the national average on measures of income, occupation, and education, while Poles, Italians, Slavs, and French are closer to average.[25] These differences themselves suggest that religion may be less important as a factor in explaining social class outcomes than factors associated

24. Alexander Astin, " 'Productivity' of Undergraduate Institutions," *Science* 136 (April 1962); *Predicting Academic Performance in College* (New York: Free Press, 1971), pp. 129-35.

25. Andrew Greeley, *Why Can't They Be Like Us?* (New York: Dutton, 1971), pp. 67-68; "The Ethnic Miracle," *Public Interest,* Fall 1976, pp. 20-36.

with the nationality of particular groups. In order to explore this further, it will be useful to focus on Italians, since they constitute the largest Catholic group in the last great wave of immigration, and because Italians have often been singled out as a group whose values are said to be inimical to education.

Most Italian immigrants came from the underdeveloped provinces of Southern Italy, where they worked as landless peasants. This helps to explain not only why Italians were less mobile than other groups, but also why they would have exhibited different attitudes toward education. Obviously, immigrants from peasant backgrounds were not likely to have the same outlook upon education as other immigrants, including Northern Italians, who came from more industrially advanced sectors of their countries of origin. In his book *The Social Background of the Italo-American School Child,* Leonard Covello had this to say about the sources of the Southern Italian's low valuation of formal education:

> As a peasant, unable to perceive things *in abstracto,* and as a man of the soil, he perceived education in association with material benefits. He saw the need to educate his children only insofar as the school provided means for bettering one's economic condition, or for breaking through the caste system. But since few precedents existed where a peasant's son became anything but a peasant, the *contadino* almost never entertained the possibility of his son's becoming a doctor, a lawyer, or embarking on some other professional career.[26]

Given the fact that Italian peasants were tied to the soil, formal education had little value for individual or collective survival.

A more basic reason for the high rate of illiteracy that prevailed among Italian immigrants was that schools were poor or nonexistent. As John Briggs has shown in a recent study, in areas where education was available, illiteracy was far less prevalent. On the basis of a painstaking analysis of educational statistics in the early 1900s, Briggs reached the following conclusion:

> Literacy, then, was closely associated with the quality and quantity of schooling available in southern Italy. The lower social

26. Leonard Covello, *The Social Background of the Italo-American School Child,* edited with an introduction by Francesco Cordasco (Totowa, N.J.: Rowman and Littlefield, 1972), p. 256.

classes had little control over the provision of public schooling. They took advantage of it where it existed. Illiteracy resulted where it was lacking or was offered only under extremely inconvenient circumstances. Clearly, the prevalence of illiteracy among emigrants is not a good criterion of their attitudes toward education, nor is it an indication of the inappropriateness of their traditional culture for their futures as urbanites. Such evidence is better viewed as a measure of past opportunity than as a prediction of future response to schooling.[27]

To whatever extent Southern Italians exhibited negative attitudes toward education, in the final analysis these attitudes only reflected economic and social realities, including a dearth of educational opportunities.

A number of ethnographic studies of Italians in the United States have also found evidence of unfavorable attitudes toward education, and have implicitly chastised Italians for not being more zealous in pursuit of educational opportunities. But, once again, it is necessary to ask whether Italian attitudes toward education were simply a carryover from Europe, as is commonly assumed, or whether they were responses to conditions of Italian life in this country as well.

This issue arises, for example, in interpreting the results of a 1958 study by Richard Otis Ulin on "The Italo-American Student in the American Public School," which was based on a comparison of students from Italian and Yankee backgrounds in Winchester, Massachusetts. Ulin found that the Italian students generally had poorer academic records, and he ascribed this to cultural orientations inherited from Southern Italy. The most important cultural flaw, according to Ulin, is a tendency toward fatalism and an inability to plan for the future. As Ulin writes:

One can see much of the same Wheel of Fortune attitude that left the South Italian peasant praying for rain but neglecting to dig an irrigation ditch, hoping for a remittance from America or for a windfall in the national lottery. These are sentiments which are echoed today in the currently popular tune, which

27. John W. Briggs, *An Italian Passage* (New Haven: Yale University Press, 1978), p. 64.

interestingly enough, has Italian lyrics, "Che Sera, Sera" ("What Will Be, Will Be").[28]

Aside from Ulin's stereotypical view of the Italian peasant, what evidence is there that his Italian subjects in Winchester exhibit a "wheel of fortune attitude" toward life?

Ulin bases his conclusion on comments by Italian students such as the following: "I know other guys who worked their ———— off in school and they got good grades and now they got lousy jobs. It's just the way the ball bounces." But Ulin offers no evidence to support his claim that such attitudes are rooted in Southern Italian culture. On the contrary, it could be argued that his Italian subjects are expressing attitudes that are typical of the working class and in all likelihood accurately reflect the world as it actually exists for these working-class students in Winchester, Massachusetts. At least this is what is implied by another student, whom Ulin also construes as expressing a fatalistic attitude:

> Listen, they [the teachers] can talk all they want about how everybody in Winchester has an equal chance. Do they think us kids from the Plains have an equal chance? In the pig's eye! The West Side kids get all the breaks. They don't have to work after school. The teachers go out of their way to help them. And if they want to go to college, their old man will give 'em the dough.[29]

What these students appear to be expressing is not a cultural disregard for education, but a recognition of the fact that, unlike their more affluent Yankee peers, their chances of reaching college are slim, and consequently their futures are not likely to depend upon their school performance. Like the men on *Tally's Corner,* they have adjusted their aspirations and their strategies to what they can realistically hope to achieve.

The view that cultural factors explain the low academic achievement of Italians has also been advanced in a study by Fred Strodtbeck that compared Italian and Jewish students on a number of

28. Richard Otis Ulin, "The Italo-American Student in the American Public School," unpublished Ph.D. dissertation, Harvard University, 1958, p. 157.

29. Ibid., p. 156.

value measures that predict educational performance. The largest differential was on the item: "Planning only makes a person unhappy because your plans hardly ever work out anyway." Only 10 percent of Jewish students in his sample, but 38 percent of Italians, answered in the affirmative. Strodtbeck interprets such responses as an indication of the extent to which individuals have developed a sense of self-mastery, which he speculates is more often found in Jewish families because they are more democratic, and for this reason produce more motivated, secure, and achieving children. Not only does this interpretation involve a perilous leap from rather scant data, but there is evidence in Strodtbeck's data that what he measured were not ethnic differences, but class differences. When Strodtbeck compared Italian and Jewish students of the same social class background, there was no longer any difference between them.[30] In other words, the reason that the Jews in his original comparison were more likely to exhibit such traits as a future-time orientation, self-mastery, and democratic family relationships was that these qualities are generally characteristic of the middle class, regardless of the ethnic character of the groups involved.

In short, if Italians and other Catholics have not excelled academically, this cannot be blamed on a value system that discouraged education, since these values themselves only reflect the operation of social class factors and the unfavorable structure of educational opportunity that confronts the lower classes generally. As in the case of Jews, Catholics had to secure an economic foothold before their children could make significant advances up the economic ladder. But given the relative disadvantages associated with the peasant origins of most Catholic immigrants, more time was required to establish this foothold. Since the Second World War, however, Catholics have substantially improved their collective position in the class system. On the basis of national surveys extending from 1943 to 1965, one study concluded that:

At the end of World War II, Protestants in the United States ranked well above Catholics in income, occupation, and education; since then Catholics have gained dramatically and have

30. Fred L. Strodtbeck, "Family Interaction, Values, and Achievement," in Marshall Sklare, *The Jews* (New York: Free Press, 1958), pp. 161–62.

surpassed Protestants in most aspects of status.[31]

If the above historical interpretation is correct then the fact that Catholics are achieving economic parity with the rest of the population should bring an end to patterns of Catholic underrepresentation among the nation's scholars and scientists.

The Changing Religious Composition of American Higher Education

About a decade ago the Carnegie Commission on Higher Education conducted a massive survey of approximately 60,000 faculty in 303 institutions of higher learning across the nation.[32] From this landmark study it is possible to chart historical trends in the religious background of American scholars and scientists and, indirectly, to test the proposition that Catholicism is inherently anathema to intellectual achievement.

Table 5 reports the religious background of faculty in four different age groups, and of graduate students planning a career in college teaching. In evaluating these figures it should be kept in mind that Catholics make up roughly 26 percent of the national population, Protestants 66 percent, and Jews 3 percent.

The data in Table 5 show unmistakably that there has been a gradual uptrend in Catholic representation over the past several decades. Among the oldest cohort of faculty, Catholics are only 15 percent, but this figure increases among younger age groups to 17, 19, and 20 percent. Among graduate students who plan a career in college teaching, the figure again rises to 22 percent. Since Catholics make up 26 percent of the national population, it is clear that they are rapidly approaching the point of being represented among faculty in the same proportion as in the nation as a whole.

In the case of Jews, the data indicate a pattern of overrepresentation. Though only 3 percent of the national population, Jews were already 5 percent of the oldest cohort of faculty, and this proportion gradually rose to 10 percent, where it has leveled off. The largest

31. Norval D. Glenn and Ruth Hyland, "Religious Prejudice and Worldly Success," *American Sociological Review* 32 (February 1967), pp. 84–85.

32. For methodological details regarding these surveys, see Martin Trow and Oliver Fulton, *Teachers and Students* (New York: McGraw-Hill, 1975), pp. 297–371.

Table 5

THE RELIGIOUS BACKGROUND OF COLLEGE FACULTY OF DIFFERENT AGES (ALL INSTITUTIONS)

Religious background	Age of faculty				Graduate students planning a career in college teaching
	55 or more	45–54	35–44	34 or less	
Protestant	76%	69%	63%	63%	58%
Catholic	15	17	19	20	22
Jewish	5	8	10	10	10
Other	2	3	4	4	4
None	2	3	4	3	6
Total	100%	100%	100%	100%	100%

SOURCE: Stephen Steinberg, *The Academic Melting Pot* (New York: McGraw-Hill, 1974), p. 104.

increase in Jewish representation occurred with the 45–54 age group, which would indicate that Jews made their major breakthrough in college teaching during the expansion of higher education after World War II.

The increasing representation of Catholics and Jews among college faculty has resulted in a proportionate decrease of Protestants. Between the oldest cohort and the youngest, Protestants have gone from being overrepresented to being underrepresented relative to their proportion of the national population. Given the Protestant decrease and the Catholic increase, it can now be said that Catholics and Protestants have achieved parity with each other.

The same trends emerge even more clearly when the ranking universities are examined (this includes seventeen "top" institutions such as Columbia, Harvard, Johns Hopkins, Northwestern, etc.). Jewish representation in these institutions is considerably higher than among colleges and universities generally, and Protestant and Catholic representation is somewhat lower. But the *trend* is even more pronounced than before (see Table 6). That is, Catholic representation in these ranking institutions has steadily increased; there has been a corresponding decrease of Protestants; and the Jewish proportion reached a peak with the expansion of higher education after the Second World War and then leveled off. As far as Catholics are concerned, all the evidence leads to the conclusion that they are belatedly taking their place in American higher education.[33]

Further insight into the different mobility patterns of Protestant, Catholic, and Jewish scholars can be gleaned from data on the class origins of faculty in the Carnegie survey. Respondents were asked about the occupation of their fathers; the category labeled "working class" includes both blue-collar workers and those in low-level white-collar occupations such as clerical and sales workers. The data, reported in Table 7, are consistent with the historical data analyzed above.

In the first place, relatively few Jewish scholars, and many more Catholics, have their origin in the working class. The figure for Jews is 25 percent; for Protestants, 32 percent; for Catholics, 45 percent. What is especially notable is that even among older age cohorts, relatively few Jewish faculty come from working-class backgrounds.

An unusually large number of Jewish faculty had fathers who owned small businesses. Indeed, this is the case of slightly over half the Jews in the oldest age category, and a third of those in the youngest age category. As observed earlier, many Jewish immigrants were able to use their prior experience in commerce as an avenue of economic mobility. The data now indicate that it is the children of these businessmen who went on to become scholars and scientists in disproportionate numbers. On the other hand, the Jewish working class has never been a major source of Jewish scholars.

The pattern is quite the opposite for Catholics. In every age cohort four out of every ten Catholic scholars come from working-class backgrounds, and on the basis of what is known about the occupational concentrations of Catholics in the society at large, it is safe

33. Though the Carnegie surveys did not query respondents about their ethnic background, it is safe to assume that the Irish have contributed disproportionately to the Catholic increase, since they have higher levels of income and education in the population at large. See Andrew Greeley, "The Ethnic Miracle," op. cit.

Table 6

THE RELIGIOUS BACKGROUND OF COLLEGE FACULTY OF DIFFERENT AGES (THE 17 TOP-RANKING UNIVERSITIES ONLY)

Religious background	Age of faculty				Graduate students planning a career in college teaching
	55 or more	45–54	35–44	34 or less	
Protestant	72%	64%	57%	55%	52%
Catholic	10	11	13	16	20
Jewish	12	16	19	18	16
Other	2	3	5	4	5
None	4	6	6	7	7
Total	100%	100%	100%	100%	100%

SOURCE: Stephen Steinberg, *The Academic Melting Pot,* op. cit., p. 107.

to assume that Catholic scholars are typically coming not from the bottommost strata, but rather from stable working-class occupations that offer an adequate, if marginal, livelihood. This is a more precarious economic base than existed for Jews, which helps to explain the lower representation of Catholics in the academic profession.

Conclusion

Given the disadvantages with which Catholic immigrants started life in America, it is not surprising that they required another generation or two to produce their numerical share of scholars and scientists. Thomas O'Dea is too quick to dismiss immigration and problems of assimilation as factors bearing on "the absence of intellectual life" among Catholics.[34] The fact that the great majority of Catholic immigrants came from peasant backgrounds was of enormous consequence. Not only did high levels of illiteracy slow the pace of cultural adjustment, but Catholic immigrants also lacked

34. O'Dea, op. cit., p. 93.

Table 7

SOCIAL CLASS ORIGINS OF COLLEGE FACULTY BY RELIGION AND AGE

Religious background Father's occupation	Age				Total
	55 and more	45–54	35–44	34 or less	
Protestants					
Professional	26%	22%	22%	25%	23%
Managerial*	13	16	17	20	17
Owner, small business	17	16	15	13	15
Farm	19	14	12	9	13
Working class**	25	32	34	33	32
Total	100%	100%	100%	100%	100%
Catholics					
Professional	10%	14%	13%	16%	14%
Managerial*	19	18	19	22	20
Owner, small business	22	16	17	13	16
Farm	9	6	5	4	5
Working class**	40	46	46	45	45
Total	100%	100%	100%	100%	100%
Jews					
Professional	13%	14%	17%	26%	19%
Managerial*	14	11	13	17	14
Owner, small business	52	45	44	33	41
Farm	2	1	0	1	1
Working class**	19	29	26	23	25
Total	100%	100%	100%	100%	100%

*Includes corporate officials and owners of large businesses.

**Includes skilled and unskilled workers and low-level white-collar workers such as clerical and sales workers. Armed Forces personnel are also included, though they constitute a negligible 1 percent of the sample.

SOURCE: Stephen Steinberg, *The Academic Melting Pot*, op. cit., p. 92.

the kinds of occupational skills that facilitated economic mobility for other groups. These conditions also presented formidable obstacles to intellectual achievement, especially in light of the class character of American higher education, and the many factors producing a far lower rate of college attendance among lower-class children. However, as Catholics have gradually improved their position in the class system, their children are going to college with greater frequency, and as in every group, a certain number of them pursue academic careers and become scholars of distinction. The scenario is no different for Catholics than for other groups. It has only taken longer to play itself out.

Chapter 6

Why Irish Became Domestics
and Italians and Jews Did Not

"I hate the very words 'service' and 'servant.' We came to this country to better ourselves, and it's not bettering to have anybody ordering you around."

THE DAUGHTER OF AN IRISH DOMESTIC, QUOTED IN
HELEN CAMPBELL, *Prisoners of Poverty,* 1889.

THE FAMILIAR plaint that "it's hard to find good help these days" dates back to the earliest days of this country, when American-born women refused to work as domestics. According to one writer in 1904, "the servant class was never native American; even in Colonial days domestics came as indentured servants who ultimately moved up to higher-status jobs once their service was over."[1] In the South, of course, domestic work was a "negro job," but even in the North, as one writer commented in 1860, "domestic service certainly is held to be so degrading . . . that no natives will do it."[2] Those native women who did enter the labor market could usually find

1. Frances A. Kellor, "Immigration and Household Labor," *Charities* XII (1904). Reprinted in Lydio F. Tomasi, ed., *The Italian in America* (New York: Center for Migration Studies, 1972), p. 39.
2. Thomas Kettel, *Southern Wealth and Northern Profits* (New York: G. W. & J. A. Wood, 1860), p. 102.

more attractive employment as teachers, bookkeepers, saleswomen, clerks, secretaries, and nurses.

While native-born Americans were loath to work as domestics, immigrants sometimes viewed domestic work more favorably. As a Norwegian wrote to a newspaper back home in 1868:

> America is an excellent country for capable and moral servant girls, because usually young American women show a decided unwillingness to submit to the kind of restraint connected with the position of a servant. . . . People are constantly looking for Norwegian and Swedish servant girls; and as they are treated very well, especially in Yankee families, there is no one whom I can so safely advise to emigrate as diligent, moral, and well-mannered young girls.[3]

As can be inferred from this passage, "the service" was not regarded with the same opprobrium in Europe as in America. This can be traced to a number of demographic and economic factors.

As industrialization advanced in England, France, and other European countries, the hiring of servants became an integral part of the life-style of the new middle classes. At the same time, conditions of poverty and overpopulation in the countryside induced marginal peasants to apprentice their excess children to work as domestics in adjacent cities.[4] As one British historian notes, domestic service became "the major setting for female urban labour force participation during the transitional stages of industrialization."[5] It was often viewed as a respectable path for single young women, one that would indoctrinate them into the values and manners of the middle class, provide them with domestic skills, and in both these respects, prepare them for marriage. Thus, the prevailing cultural attitude sanctioned what was at bottom a matter of economic necessity. For poor country girls, domestic service functioned as a channel of social and economic mobility, and especially before there was a demand for female labor in the nascent textile industries, it provided rural women with an important stimulus for migrating to

3. Theodore C. Blegen, ed., *Land of Their Choice* (St. Paul: University of Minnesota Press, 1955), pp. 435–36.

4. Theresa M. McBride, *The Domestic Revolution* (New York: Holmes & Meier, 1976), p. 38.

5. Quoted in McBride, op. cit., p. 14.

cities. It provided others with their only opportunity to emigrate to the United States.

From the vantage point of their employers, immigrants made ideal servants. In the first place, they could be paid little, since they had few alternative sources of employment. Perhaps for the same reason, or perhaps because they came from societies where rank was taken for granted, foreigners also tended to make more pliable and less disgruntled servants. As one observer wrote in 1904: "Although the immigrant so frequently lacks training, she is strong, asks few privileges, is content with lower wages and long hours, and has no consciousness of a social stigma attaching to her work."[6] The pariah status of immigrants also meant that their employers ran little risk that compromising details of their lives might be revealed to anyone in their own milieu.

While it is easy to see why immigrant women were in demand as servants, it might seem curious that immigrants in pursuit of the American Dream would accept such low-status employment. Actually, at the end of the nineteenth century there was only one other major avenue of employment open to immigrant women. That was in the needle trades, an industry that includes dressmakers, milliners, seamstresses, and tailoresses, and could be stretched to include workers in textile mills. Both domestic labor and the needle trades were extensions of traditional female roles, in that they involved work that was similar to household tasks. Domestics, of course, were employed to do the household work of other women. In the case of the needle trades, women were engaged in clothing production that once had been carried out in the home, but by the end of the nineteenth century had been mechanized and transferred to small shops and factories. Among immigrant women in the labor force in 1900, a solid majority worked in these two occupations.[7]

However, women of different ethnic backgrounds differed greatly in their propensity to work as domestics or as workers in the needle trades. Though some Irish women were employed in mills scattered across small industrial towns in the Northeast, the vast majority worked as domestics. The proportion varied, depending

6. Kellor, op. cit., p. 39.

7. *Report of the United States Immigration Commission*, vol. 1 (Washington, D.C.: Government Printing Office, 1911), pp. 830–38.

on time and place, but its high point occurred during the famine migration of the 1850s. Of the 29,470 domestics that show up in the 1855 census of New York City, 23,386 were Irish.[8] Though Irish were about one-quarter of New York's population, they were over three-quarters of the domestic labor force. Germans were the other major immigrant group during this period, but the German proportion in the domestic labor force was exactly the same as in the city's population—15 percent. Not only were most domestics Irish, but it was also the case that virtually all Irish women who worked did so as domestics.

Of course, the peak of Irish immigration preceded by several decades the burgeoning of the garment industry. However, even after the waves of Jewish and Italian immigration at the end of the century, it was still the Irish who dominated the ranks of domestic workers. According to figures collected by the United States Immigration Commission in 1900, 71 percent of immigrant Irish women in the labor force were classified as "domestic and personal" workers; 54 percent were specifically classifid as "servants and waitresses." In contrast, only 9 percent of Italian female workers and 14 percent of Jewish female workers were classified as "servants and waitresses." And whereas 38 percent of Italian women and 41 percent of Jewish women were in the needle trades, the figure for Irish was only 8 percent.[9]

How is this ethnic division to be explained? Why were Italian and Jewish women generally able to avoid working at one of the most menial and low-status jobs in the labor force, and why should so many Irish flock to it? As with occupations connoting success, social scientists have stressed the operation of cultural factors in explaining why some groups were more likely than others to become domestics.

For example, in *Blood of My Blood,* Richard Gambino implies that Italian women never deigned to work as domestics. As he writes:

No matter how poor, the Italian-American woman to this day does not work as a domestic. For to work in the house of an-

8. Robert Ernst, *Immigrant Life in New York City, 1825–1863* (Port Washington, N.Y.: Ira J. Friedman, 1949), p. 219.

9. *Report of the United States Immigration Commission,* op. cit., pp. 834–36.

other family (sometimes an absolute economic necessity in the old land) is seen as a usurpation of family loyalty by her family *and by her*. And if one loses one's place in *la via vecchia*, there is no self-respect. In American history, there is no Italian counterpart of Irish, German, black, Spanish-speaking, English, Scandinavian, and French maids.[10]

How is it that Italians were able to escape a fate that befell all these other groups? Gambino implies that a stubborn ethnic pride, buttressed by a strong family system, protected Italian women from the indignities of domestic labor. Would he then suggest that other groups were lacking in these traits? And if domestic labor was "an absolute economic necessity" in Italy, as Gambino says, why was this not so in America?

In her recent history of Italians in Buffalo, New York, Virginia Yans-McLaughlin also suggests that family pride, reinforced by a strong patriarchal tradition, protected Italian women from having to work as domestics:

> Truly enterprising women seeking year-round wages could become domestics; but the Italian women were more likely to take in boarders because the men rarely permitted their wives to work as maids, cleaning women, or factory hands. The Italian ideal was to keep women at home.[11]

For Yans-McLaughlin, the "decision" not to work as domestics constituted an "occupational choice," one that was governed by "cultural tradition." As she put it: "Culture, then, acted as an interface between family and economy, dictating which options were acceptable and which were not."[12]

Acting on the same assumptions, other writers have suggested that the Irish lacked the cultural repugnance that supposedly deterred Italians and Jews from working as domestics. As one historian comments: "The Irish community viewed domestic service

10. Richard Gambino, *Blood of My Blood* (Garden City, N.Y.: Anchor, 1975), p. 14.

11. Virginia Yans-McLaughlin, *Family and Community* (Ithaca: Cornell University Press, 1977), p. 53.

12. Ibid.

favorably and no ethnic taboos or language barriers prevented Irish women from working in other people's homes."[13]

Are these writers correct in positing ethnic and cultural factors as the explanation of why some ethnic women became domestics and others did not? On reflection, it makes little sense to take the Irish "tolerance" of domestic work at face value. This is hardly a calling that any group would define as an ideal worth striving for, and, for better or worse, the idea that woman's place is in the home is no less characteristic of Irish than of Italians and Jews. As will be seen, it was not a different cultural norm but a different set of historical circumstances that explains why Irish became domestics and Italians and Jews did not.

Though both domestics and needle-trade workers were engaged in traditionally female occupations, there was one fundamental difference between them: needle-trade workers returned to their homes when the workday was finished, whereas domestics typically lived in with a family, usually occupying a single small room in the rear of the residence specifically designed for this purpose. Although some domestics worked in households where there were other servants and a clear-cut division of labor, most households employed a single domestic. Her daily regimen consisted of preparing and serving three meals; doing household cleaning according to a prescribed weekly schedule, and being "on call" for whatever demands might be made outside of her routine duties. The average day began at six in the morning and lasted until late into the evening. Most domestics worked seven days a week, though a generous employer might give servants Sunday and perhaps one evening off.[14]

By comparison, needle-trade workers clearly labored under more adverse physical conditions. Indeed, Marx and Engels singled out textile factories as typifying the most inhumane and brutalizing aspects of capitalism. Sweatshops and factories were notoriously dirty, crowded, and often dangerous, and the work itself had a relentless tedium. For meager wages, workers were reduced to repeating a single minute task under the watchful eye of a boss or foreman, and the average workweek lasted between fifty and sixty

13. Barbara Klaczynska, "Why Women Work: A Comparison of Various Groups—Philadelphia, 1910–1930," *Labor History* 17 (Winter 1976), p. 81.

14. Daniel Katzman, *Seven Days a Week* (New York: Oxford University Press, 1978), pp. 110–12.

hours. In her 1919 study of *Italian Women in Industry,* Louise Odencrantz reported that a typical workday began at eight and went until six; Saturday was sometimes, though not always, a short day.[15]

Yet factory workers had decided advantages over domestics. The fact that they returned to their own homes necessarily limited the authority of their bosses to the workplace, and even there, once unions were organized, workers could place restraints on their employers and strike for better wages. Degraded as they were by the conditions that prevailed in textile factories, they still belonged to a class of free labor, and as the early garment-trade unions demonstrated, could realistically hope to achieve a measure of dignity.

Domestic work, in contrast, had the earmarks of feudalism. Lacking a separation between work and home, the domestic was, in effect, bonded to her employer, and scarcely an aspect of her life escaped scrutiny and regulation. The domestic had virtually no time, and except for the limited privacy of her maid's room, no space that she could claim as her own. Isolated from other workers, she was powerless to change the conditions of her employment. To be sure, she was nominally free to quit, but lacking a home of her own, she could hardly risk the perils of being unemployed.

Furthermore, the nature of her work involved an exploitation of the whole person. Motivated solely by profit, the factory owner took little interest in the personal lives of his workers so long as they executed their assigned tasks. Though the textile worker might be reduced to a commodity, paradoxically, her inner self was left intact. But the employers of a domestic need to be sure that the person with whom they share the intimacies of their lives, and to whom they entrust their children, are decent, kind, affable, well mannered, and so on. In this sense, it is not just labor that is purchased, but the laborer as well.[16]

15. Louise C. Odencrantz, *Italian Women in Industry* (New York: Russell Sage Foundation, 1919), p. 317.

16. Lewis Coser has suggested that the servant is engulfed by a "greedy institution" that demands total allegiance. As he writes: "The master's family operates as a 'greedy organization' in relation to the servant. It does not rest content with claiming a segment of the time, commitment, and energy of the servant, as is the case with other occupational arrangements in the modern world, but demands—though it does not always receive—full-time allegiance. Moreover, while in other occupational roles the incumbent's duties are largely

Domestic servants implicitly understood the feudalistic aspects of their employment, as was revealed by a survey of over 5,000 domestics conducted in 1889 by an enterprising professor from Vassar College, Lucy Maynard Salmon.[17] Though only 1,000 responded to Salmon's survey, they provide valuable insight into the private sentiments of domestic laborers during this period.

A common complaint among Salmon's respondents was that they felt lonely. This may seem curious since domestics lived in such close quarters to others and often developed personal ties with the families they served. However, one of Salmon's respondents eloquently describes the loneliness of the household domestic:

> Ladies wonder how their girls can complain of loneliness in a house full of people, but oh! it is the worst kind of loneliness— their share is but the work of the house, they do not share in the pleasures and delights of a home. One must remember that there is a difference between a *house,* a place of shelter, and a *home,* a place where all your affections are centered. Real love exists between my employer and myself, yet at times I grow almost desperate from the sense of being cut off from those pleasures to which I had always been accustomed.[18]

Another complaint among Salmon's respondents was that they had little time of their own; several said bluntly that they felt like prisoners. This feeling was articulated by an Irish woman in another 1889 survey who explained why she chose to work in a paper box factory instead of "the service":

> It's freedom that we want when the day's work is done. I know some nice girls . . . that make more money and dress better and everything for being in service. They're waitresses, and have Thursday afternoon out and part of every other Sunday. But they're never sure of one minute that's their own when they're in the house. Our day is ten hours long, but when it's done it's done, and we can do what we like with the evenings.

---

independent of personal relationships with this or that client or employer, particularistic elements loom very large in the master-servant relationship." *Greedy Institutions* (New York: Free Press, 1974), p. 69.

17. Lucy Maynard Salmon, *Domestic Service* (New York: Macmillan, 1901).

18. Ibid., p. 151.

That's what I've heard from every nice girl that ever tried service. You're never sure that your soul's your own except when you are out of the house, and I couldn't stand that a day. Women care just as much for freedom as men do. Of course they don't get so much, but I know I'd fight for mine.[19]

When Salmon asked her respondents why more women do not choose housework as regular employment, the most common answer alluded to a loss of pride. Above all else, they bristled at being called "servants," a term that has a spasmodic history.

During Colonial times "servant" referred to indentured servants, but fell into disuse after the Revolution, apparently reflecting the democratic spirit of that period. Instead the term "help" was used, though "servant" was still applied to blacks in the South. With the influx of Irish and other foreigners in the second half of the nineteenth century, however, "servant" again came into vogue. Salmon herself acknowledged that it was "a mark of social degradation" that discouraged women from entering this occupation. There were efforts to substitute the term "maid" or "working housekeeper," but according to Salmon, this "excited little more than ridicule."[20]

A less offensive nomenclature, however, could hardly disguise the stigma of servitude that was inescapably associated with domestic work. It is endemic to a master-servant relationship that even friendly gestures on the part of employers inevitably assume a patronizing cast, and unwittingly frustrate the servant's need to maintain a modicum of social distance. For example, Salmon's respondents complained that their employers took the liberty of addressing them by their Christian names. "It may seem a trifling matter," Salmon commented, "yet the fact remains that domestic employees are the only class of workers, except day laborers, who are thus addressed."[21] Domestics also objected to the cap and apron as still another badge of social inferiority.

What kinds of women, then, were willing to submit to the indignities of a cap and apron, and what kinds opted instead for the drudgery of the sweatshop? And why should Irish go one way, and Italians and Jews another?

19. Helen Campbell, *Prisoners of Poverty* (Boston: Roberts Brothers, 1889), p. 224.

20. Salmon, op. cit., p. 156.

21. Ibid.

The answer, in a nutshell, has to do with the fact that comparatively large numbers of Irish female immigrants were unmarried and unattached to families. Italian and Jewish women rarely immigrated unless they were accompanied or preceded by husbands or fathers, but it was common for Irish women to migrate on their own. For an unattached woman in an alien country—impoverished, uprooted, and often isolated from friends and family—domestic work had practical appeal. At least, it provided them with a roof over their head and a degree of personal security until they were able to forge a more desirable set of circumstances.

The reasons why Irish women were far more likely than either Italians or Jews to be single has to do with conditions in their respective countries of origin. In the case of Italians, an economic crisis in agriculture induced men to emigrate in pursuit of industrial labor and higher wages, and there was an overwhelming preponderance of males in the immigration pool. Between 1899 and 1910, nearly two million Italian men, but fewer than half a million Italian women entered the United States.[22] In some cases the men planned to send for their families once they had accumulated some savings; more often, they planned to return to Italy. An excerpt from a 1903 study on the Italian colonies in New York City describes this immigration pattern:

> The Italian population in this country is predominantly male. The reason for this is plainly seen. In nine cases out of ten, the father of a family decides to emigrate to America; he would like to take with him his wife and children, but since the least cost of a steerage ticket is something over $30, it becomes an impossibility for the entire family to come at once. The result is the wife and children are left behind and the father comes. On the other hand, few women indeed come here of their own accord—they are brought or sent for by husband or prospective husband.[23]

Thus, few Italian women immigrated as independent breadwinners. Invariably, a husband or family member preceded them, sometimes by many years, and by the time the women arrived, they

22. *Report of the United States Immigration Commission,* op. cit., p. 97.
23. Antonio Mangano, "The Italian Colonies of New York City," in *Italians in the City* (New York: Arno Press, 1975), p. 13.

were already part of families that had established at least a tenuous economic foothold. Married women generally stayed out of the job market altogether, though some took in lodgers or homework. Those women who did enter the job market generally found employment in the manufacturing sectors, especially in the expanding needle trades. In other words, neither economic necessity nor circumstances forced Italian women into domestic labor.

In Italy the situation was different. According to a study of women's employment in Milan in 1881, 23,000 women, or 20 percent of all female workers, were employed as domestics.[24] If few Italian woman worked as domestics in America, this can hardly be attributed to a distinctively Italian attitude toward women and the home.

Immigrant Jewish women, like their Italian counterparts, rarely immigrated alone, though for very different reasons. Eastern European Jews were refugees from religious persecution and political violence, and unlike Italians, those who left harbored no thoughts of returning. As a consequence, Jews typically immigrated as families. Whereas there were nearly four Italian men for every woman among those who immigrated between 1899 and 1910, Jews had a much more even sexual balance—608,000 men and 467,000 women.[25] That Jews tended to immigrate as families is also indicated by the fact that a quarter of all Jewish immigrants during this period were children under fourteen years of age. Thus, most Jewish women came to America with husbands or fathers. Few were independent breadwinners, and when they did work, they usually found employment in the burgeoning garment industry. Often they worked in small shops with other family members.

The demographic character of Irish immigration was different from that of either Italian or Jews in that it included large numbers of single women. Unfortunately, no data exist on the marital status of immigrants, and consequently there is no exact measure of how many were unmarried. However, a rough estimate can be gleaned from examining the sex ratios of the various immigrant pools. In contrast to the situation among Italians and Jews, there were ac-

24. Louise A. Tilly, "Urban Growth, Industrialization, and Women's Employment in Milan, Italy, 1881–1911," *Journal of Urban History* 3 (August 1977), pp. 476–78.

25. *Report of the United States Immigration Commission,* op. cit., p. 97.

tually more women than men among Irish immigrants around the turn of the century. Specifically, among Irish arriving between 1899 and 1910, there were 109 women for every 100 men. Among Jews, there were 77 women for every 100 men; among Italians, only 27 women for every 100 men.[26] Not only were Irish women far less likely to be married when they immigrated, but the sex ratio did not favor their finding Irish husbands after they arrived.

A similar situation existed earlier in the century as well. For example, according to the 1860 census, New York's Irish-born population consisted of 87,000 males, but 117,000 females. Not surprisingly, the marriage rates of Irish in American cities were generally lower than those for other groups throughout the nineteenth century. Hence, from a demographic standpoint, Irish women were an ideal source of live-in domestics. That they also spoke English made them all the more desirable.

Further impetus was given to the immigration of Irish domestics by agencies that sprang up on both sides of the Atlantic. Beginning in the 1850s, a number of British emigration societies were organized to encourage and assist the emigration of surplus population, especially single women of childbearing age who were unlikely to emigrate on their own. They bore imposing names like the London Female Emigration Society, the British Ladies Emigration Society, the Girls' Friendly Society, and the Travelers' Aid Society for Girls and Women. With philanthropic pretense, these societies recruited indigent women, paid for their steerage, escorted them to the port of embarkation, and dispatched them to the New World where they were commonly placed in private households as domestic servants.[27] Not all the recipients of this dubious largess were Irish, and many were sent to Canada and other British colonies. Nevertheless, the very existence of these societies testifies to the popular currency given to the idea of sending poor young girls across the Atlantic to work as domestic servants.

There were also employment agencies in the United States that recruited and transported young foreign girls to work as domestics in New York. According to one account, in 1904 there were as many

26. Ibid.

27. Stanley C. Johnson, *A History of Emigration from the United Kingdom to North America, 1763–1812* (London: Frank Case, 1966), orig. 1913, chap. XI, p. 264.

as 300 "intelligence offices" in New York City alone.[28] To some extent, then, "Bridget" was the creation of employment agencies that engaged in this human commerce and collected fees for supplying households with Irish domestics.

There is still other evidence that many Irish women emigrated with the express purpose of finding work as domestics. Among immigrants arriving between 1899 and 1910, 40 percent of the Irish were classified as servants; in contrast, the figure for both Italians and Jews was only 6 percent.[29] Only 14 percent of Irish immigrants were classified as having "no occupation," a category that consisted mostly of children and women who considered themselves homemakers. The comparable figure for Southern Italians was 23 percent; for Jews it was 45 percent. From this it is reasonable to assume that most Irish women who immigrated around the turn of the century planned to enter the labor force, presumably in the servant occupation that they named when asked their occupation at the port of entry.

The reasons why so many young women left Ireland just to become servants in America must be traced to a series of economic crises in the nineteenth century, and the social and cultural changes that ensued. The infamous potato famine of the late 1840s was only one such crisis. Almost as important was a process of land consolidation that, between 1849 and 1851 alone, involved the dispossession of some million people from the land and the physical destruction of their homes.[30] To make matters worse, English colonial policy had reduced Ireland to a producer of wool and food, and the island had no industrial base that might have absorbed its surplus rural population. Irish emigration reached its peak during the potato famine, but it was already gaining momentum before the famine and it continued at substantial levels long after. Incredibly, Ireland's population in 1900 was almost half of what it had been in 1850.[31]

Ireland's prolonged economic depression played havoc with the family system. Traditionally, marriage was bound up with the

28. Kellor, op. cit., p. 39.

29. *Report of the United States Immigration Commission,* op. cit., p. 173.

30. Oscar Handlin, *Boston's Immigrants* (New York: Atheneum, 1968), p. 46.

31. Walter F. Willcox, ed., *International Migrations,* vol. II (New York: National Bureau of Economic Research, 1931), p. 274.

inheritance of land, and as land became more scarce, there was a tendency to postpone marriage. For nearly a century after the famine, as one recent study has shown, "the average age at marriage increased, the marriage rate decreased, and the percentage who remained permanently celibate increased."[32] In 1891, for example, two-thirds of men and half the women between the ages of 25 and 34 were single. Even among those between 35 and 44, a third of the men and a quarter of the women were single. One out of six of each sex never married.

The impact of these trends was especially harsh on women, since they were forced onto a labor market that was hardly favorable to them. Against this background it is easy to understand why young women, even more often than men, decided to emigrate. And given their vulnerability as single women in an alien country, as well as the limited alternatives that existed, it is also easy to understand why "the service" provided at least a temporary solution to their dilemma. It made emigration possible, provided them with food and lodging, and carried them over until such time as they could find either husbands or more desirable employment.

If historical circumstances and economic necessity forced immigrant Irish women to accept work as domestics, this was not a trend that continued into the second generation. Table 8 below reports the occupations in 1900 of first- and second-generation Irish, Italian, and Jewish women. The most striking observation is that whereas 71 percent of immigrant Irish women were classified as working in "domestic and personal service," only 25 percent of their children were so classified. Thus, by the second generation, Irish were not much more likely than other groups to work as domestics.

What the female children of Irish immigrants did was to follow in the footsteps of Italian and Jewish immigrants. As can also be seen in Table 8, by 1900 they were entering the needle trades and other branches of manufacturing, precisely at the point when second-generation Italian and Jewish women were abandoning these occupations in favor of work as saleswomen, bookkeepers, clerks, and the like. In a sense, Irish women started out on a lower occupational threshold than either Italians or Jews, and remained

32. Richard Stivers, *A Hair of the Dog* (University Park: Pennsylvania State University Press, 1976), p. 56.

Table 8

OCCUPATIONS OF FIRST- AND SECOND-GENERATION IRISH, ITALIAN, AND JEWISH FEMALE BREADWINNERS, 1900

Ethnic group	Irish		Italian		Jews	
Generation	First	Second	First	Second	First	Second
Occupation*						
Domestic & personal service (includes waitresses)	71%	25%	21%	15%	18%	21%
Needle trades & textiles	16	29	48	33	44	26
Other manufacturing	6	17	20	28	23	17
Saleswomen, bookkeepers, clerks, etc.	5	19	10	20	14	31
Professional	2	10	1	4	1	5
	100%	100%	100%	100%	100%	100%
Number of cases	(245,792)	(388,108)	(20,307)	(5,751)	(35,030)	(5,781)

* The small number of cases whose occupations could not be classified are excluded from the percentages.

SOURCE: Adapted from the *Reports of the United States Immigration Commission*, Vol. I (Washington, D. C.: Government Printing Office, 1911), pp. 834–36.

one generational step behind. But as far as domestic service is concerned, by the second generation few women in any of these groups were so employed.

Conclusion

Culture and family morality have little or nothing to do with explaining why Irish became domestics and Italians and Jews did not. It was not that Irish husbands were less protective of their wives, but rather that immigrant Irish women were less likely to have husbands in the first place. It was not that as a group Irish had less aversion to working in other people's homes, but that their choices were far more limited. For these courageous women who migrated alone to the New World, domestic work was merely a temporary expedient to allow them to forge new lives. That the Irish had no cultural tolerance for domestic work is pointed up by the fact that they fled "the service" just as quickly as they could establish families of their own or gain access to more desirable employment. If other groups were spared the indignities of domestic labor, it is not that they had better cultural defenses or a superior moral code, but because their circumstances did not compel them to place economic survival ahead of their pride.

PART THREE

———◆———

THE CLASS CHARACTER OF
RACIAL AND ETHNIC CONFLICT

Introduction

———◆———

The "Iron Law of Ethnicity" Revised

B OT H T H E conventional wisdom and a considerable body of social theory adhere to what might be called "the iron law of ethnicity." According to this "law," where there is ethnic difference there will be ethnic conflict. The internal dynamics of group existence, if not human nature itself, are presumed to make ethnic conflict inevitable. According to one widely held view, since a sense of "we" presupposes a sense of "they," it follows that ethnocentrism, prejudice, and conflict are natural by-products of group identity and belonging.[1] Admittedly, there is a great deal of superficial evidence to give credence to such a theory. In a wide range of nations—those in the East as well as the West, traditional as well as modern, socialist as well as capitalist—ethnic pluralism has been associated with dissension and instability, and not infrequently, such societies have been torn apart at their ethnic seams. Undeniably, the ideal of a plural society, where ethnic groups live in cooperation, harmony, and mutual respect, has proved a most elusive one.

1. Gordon W. Allport, *The Nature of Prejudice* (New York: Anchor, 1958), chaps. 2 and 3.

Nonetheless, it is doubtful that the connection between ethnic difference and conflict is as automatic or as inevitable as is commonly supposed. What often appears to be an eruption of "traditional hatreds" on closer examination turns out to involve political and economic issues that are real and immediate. Perhaps the never-ending conflict in Northern Ireland provides the best illustration of this point. That there are "traditional hatreds" between Protestants and Catholics is obvious. The question, however, is whether these animosities would have endured, and would today be carried to such violent extremes, if not for the structural inequalities between the Protestant majority and the Catholic minority in terms of class, status, and power. In other instances—South Africa, for example—it is the minority that has enjoyed material advantages over a resentful and sometimes rebellious majority. Whether conflict occurs between a privileged minority and a disadvantaged majority, or vice versa, almost invariably institutionalized inequalities are at or near the center of the conflict. Indeed, whenever ethnic divisions occur along class lines, there is the likelihood, or at least the potential, that ordinary class conflict will manifest itself as ethnic conflict, in reality as well as appearance.

If there is an iron law of ethnicity, it is that when ethnic groups are found in a hierarchy of power, wealth, and status, then conflict is inescapable. However, where there is social, economic, and political parity among the constituent groups, ethnic conflict, when it occurs, tends to be at a low level and rarely spills over into violence.

Conditions in Switzerland help exemplify both sides of this "law." Amongst the German, French, and Italian minorities, there is a reasonable distribution of power and wealth, and though ethnic tensions exist, they have been successfully contained within institutionalized channels of conflict resolution. Yet, as portrayed in the Italian-made film *Bread and Chocolate,* migrant workers from Italy and other countries who have been imported to do the undesirable labor that native Swiss workers refuse to do not only exist as an underclass, but also experience intense prejudice and discrimination.

The lesson to be drawn from the Swiss case is that the fact of class difference is far more important than the fact of ethnic difference, and that ethnic conflict is often only a surface manifestation of a deeper conflict of an essentially social class character.

To emphasize the class character of ethnic conflict, however, is not to deny the operational significance of ethnic factors. Clearly, racial and ethnic stigma, even when rooted in patterns of class exploitation, assume a life of their own and have a capacity to inflict great harm, a notion Lorraine Hansberry expresses in her play *Les Blancs*. Against the backdrop of an anticolonial war in a mythical African colony, Tshembe, an African revolutionary educated in Europe, and Charlie, a liberal white journalist from the United States, debate the limits of race and class as explanations for colonial domination:

TSHEMBE: Race—racism—is a device. No more. No less. It explains nothing at all.

CHARLIE: Now what the hell is that supposed to mean?

TSHEMBE (*Closing his eyes, wearily*): I said racism is a device that, of itself, explains nothing. It is simply a means. An invention to justify the rule of some men over others.

CHARLIE: But I agree with you entirely! Race hasn't a thing to do with it actually.

TSHEMBE: Ah—but it *has!*

CHARLIE: (*Throwing up his hands*): Oh, come on, Matoseh. Stop playing games!

TSHEMBE: I am not playing games. (*He sighs and now, drawn out of himself at last, proceeds with the maximum precision and clarity he can muster*) I am simply saying that a device is a device, but that it also has consequences: once invented it takes on a life, a reality of its own. So in one century, men invoke the device of religion to cloak their conquests. In another, race. Now, in both cases you and I may recognize the fraudulence of the device, but the fact remains that a man who has a sword run through him because he refuses to become a Moslem or a Christian—or who is shot in Zatembe or Mississippi because he is black —is suffering the utter *reality* of the device. And it is pointless to pretend that it doesn't *exist*—merely because it is a *lie!*[2]

2. Lorraine Hansberry, *Les Blancs* (New York: Random House, 1973), pp. 121–22.

The chapters that follow confront both the reality and the "lie" of racial and ethnic conflict in three historical contexts. Chapter 7 deals with the historic conflict between blacks and European immigrants who constituted alternative labor pools for Northern industry. It seeks to explain why and how, in the aftermath of the Civil War, blacks were excluded from the industrial labor market in the North that provided opportunity to millions of immigrants, and instead forced into a new kind of servitude that was almost as oppressive as slavery itself. This was a critical turning point in American race history, since it condemned the vast majority of blacks to generations of poverty, while allowing immigrants to pursue the American Dream.

Chapter 8 extends this analysis of the historic conflict between blacks and immigrants into the twentieth century. The steady migration of blacks to Northern cities placed the two groups in direct competition, and has resulted in new and ever more dangerous patterns of racial and ethnic conflict. The chapter assesses the changing nature of racial conflict in the twentieth century, culminating in the ethnic and racial polarization that began anew in the 1970s and that seems destined to continue into the 1980s.

If immigrants and blacks were historic rivals for jobs in the nation's burgeoning industries, Jews were among the first to rise above their proletarian origins and to attempt to enter polite society. Chapter 9 examines what happened when the unpolished sons of Jewish immigrants "invaded" Harvard and other elite colleges in the 1920s. The conflict that ensued typifies the ongoing conflict between the WASP elite and the descendants of immigrants as they come into direct competition for power, wealth, and status.

Finally Chapter 10 explores some of the "dilemmas and contradictions" of ethnic pluralism in America. Its main tenet is that as long as pluralism is based on systematic inequalities, there is an inherent tension between democratic norms and the requirements of a pluralistic society—a tension that often forces an unhappy choice between pluralism and democracy.

Chapter 7

———◆———

The Reconstruction of Black Servitude
after the Civil War

"They could call it some other name—it is fertile in names; it has been called 'the peculiar institution,' the 'impediment,' etc., and it will again turn up under some new and hateful guise to curse and destroy this nation."

FREDERICK DOUGLASS, *The New York Times,*
May 11, 1865

THE END of the Civil War was a critical juncture in American race history. Slavery had been abolished at a time when the North was on the verge of an economic breakthrough that would transform the United States into the world's most industrialized nation within a single generation. The labor shortages associated with this rapid growth presented the nation with a unique opportunity to integrate black workers into the industrial mainstream. As the British economist Brinley Thomas has written: "After the Civil War the best thing that could have happened to the black workers of the United States would have been a fair opportunity to contribute to satisfying the great demand for labour in the rapidly growing cities of the

North and West."[1] However, blacks were almost totally excluded from these burgeoning industries, and instead the nation looked to European immigrants to fill its manpower needs. In the half century between the end of the Civil War and the beginning of the First World War, over 24 million immigrants entered the United States; at the end of this period 89 percent of the nation's 10 million blacks remained in the South.

The reasons for this categorical exclusion of blacks from northern industry are far from clear, as Gunnar Myrdal noted in *An American Dilemma:* "There was enough industrial activity . . . in many of the smaller centers of the North to permit a significant immigration of Negroes. That Negroes have not migrated to these places is . . . a mystery. . . ."[2] It is often implied that, as a rural people, blacks were tied to the soil and reluctant to migrate to northern cities. Any such interpretation, however, is belied by a considerable body of evidence showing that emancipated slaves explored every conceivable channel of escape from southern oppression.

Both as individuals and as groups, blacks experimented with migration to underpopulated and developing areas of the South and West (especially Florida and Texas), to Kansas and other home-steading areas of the Midwest, to the urban North, to Canada, to Haiti and other Caribbean islands, and even to Africa. If none of these "colonization schemes" developed into significant movements, it is because none offered a realistic solution to the plight of the black masses. It was for this reason, and not out of any lack of knowledge or motivation, that more blacks did not flee the South after the Civil War.

Whenever promising alternatives to the South were found, information spread like wildfire through the Black Belt. In the case of the "exoduster movement" to Kansas in the late 1870s, itinerant black leaders met with prospective migrants in churches throughout the South, and blacks working on steamboats and railroads

1. Brinley Thomas, *Migration and Economic Growth* (London: Cambridge University Press, 1973), p. 330.

2. Gunnar Myrdal, *An American Dilemma* (New York: McGraw-Hill, 1974), pp. 189–90. Commenting on the paucity of research on black migration prior to the First World War, one demographer attributed this to a failure to study nonmigration. Peter Uhlenberg, "Noneconomic Determinants of Nonmigration: Sociological Considerations for Migration Theory," *Rural Sociology,* 38 (Fall 1973), p. 296.

circulated leaflets and passed on word of cheap land and black settlement in Kansas. No amount of propaganda, appeasement, or intimidation on the part of white Southerners succeeded in stemming the exodus.[3]

It is tempting to dismiss the preference given immigrants over blacks in northern industry simply as a case of racism, as Robert Allen does in his book *Black Awakening in Capitalist America:*

> It would have made sense at the close of the Civil War to plan for the assimilation of black people as a group into the American mainstream. Racism made this impossible. . . . Hence racism, the stepchild of slavery, prevented black people from following in the footsteps of other ethnic groups.[4]

To be sure, there was a color line in northern industry that barred blacks from employment in any but the most menial positions. However, racism per se cannot explain the existence of this color line. In the South where racism was carried to its most malevolent extremes, there was a general preference for black laborers over foreigners, despite public rhetoric to the contrary. Indeed, from the end of the Civil War until the Great Depression, the South frequently resorted to violence to obstruct the movement of blacks to labor markets in the North. On the other hand, whenever black labor was needed in northern industry—for example, when immigration was cut off by the First World War—employers were all too willing to put aside their racist attitudes and to integrate blacks into the labor force.

Thus, what needs to be explained is why black labor was indispensable in the South and, until the First World War, superfluous in the North. Simple "racism" cannot explain why black laborers were excluded from northern industry in the first decade of the twentieth century and employed by the hundreds of thousands in the second decade.

The key to solving the "mystery" of why blacks were excluded from the early stages of industrialization has to do with the critical role that cotton played, not just in the South but in the national economy as a whole. The South was unable, despite considerable

3. Nell Painter, *The Exodusters* (New York: Knopf, 1977), chap. 15.

4. Robert L. Allen, *Black Awakening in Capitalist America* (Garden City, N.Y.: Doubleday, 1970), p. 51.

effort, to attract immigrants to the cotton fields, and came to realize that it was utterly dependent on black labor. On the other hand, as long as the North had access to cheap foreign labor, there was no reason to raid the labor supply of the South, especially when its own economic well-being depended on an abundant supply of cheap cotton.

In short, major economic interests were served by the deployment of blacks to southern agriculture and immigrants to northern industry. Yet there was no conspiratorial design to regulate the racial composition of the labor force on a regional basis. What needs to be explained, therefore, is how emancipated slaves were forced to remain in a region of the country and a sector of the economy that was so inimical to their collective interests.

The "Negro Question" After the Civil War: The North

The end of the Civil War and the abolition of slavery raised a great question that was debated by journalists and politicians in both the North and the South. The question, in Lincoln's own words, was: "What shall we do with the Negroes after they are free?"[5] The nation's quandary over the future of four million emancipated slaves stemmed from the fact that the status of blacks in America had always been defined in terms of slavery. Had their emancipation made them expendable? In 1867 one vitriolic Southerner actually proposed the mass expulsion of blacks:

> No permanent lodgment, no enduring part nor lot, must the black and baneful negroes be permitted to acquire in our country. Already have they outlived their usefulness—if, indeed, they were ever useful at all. . . .[6]

Expulsion was not altogether a new concept. Since 1816 the American Colonization Society had been active, with the help of a con-

5. Quoted in Charles W. Wesley, "Lincoln's Plan to Colonize the Emancipated Negroes," *Journal of Negro History,* January 1919, p. 20. Also see *DeBow's Review* IV (AWS), 1867, p. 363; Congressional Globe, 38th Congress, 1st Session (February 17, 1864), p. 43; *New York Tribune,* May 25, 1865, p. 4.

6. Hinton Helper, *Nojoque* (New York: G. W. Carleton, 1867), p. 251.

gressional subsidy, in the "repatriation" of freed blacks to Africa. Lincoln himself became a champion of colonization, and in 1862 he prevailed upon Congress to pass legislation subsidizing the voluntary emigration of ex-slaves to various destinations in the Caribbean. The naked truth is that white America valued blacks only as property. Notwithstanding the sectional conflict, few Northerners —indeed, few abolitionists—could conceive of living with blacks as equals.

Even before the war was over, the North was practically obsessed with a fear that emancipation would unleash an "invasion" of southern blacks to the northern states. These fears were especially pronounced among ordinary laborers, many of them immigrants, who found themselves in competition for jobs with the small black population living in northern cities. This was particularly true of Irish immigrants, who rapidly became as racist as any segment of northern society simply because they competed with blacks for jobs at or near the bottom of the occupational ladder. The antagonisms that built up prior to the Civil War finally exploded into the bloody Draft Riots, when Irish mobs ravaged New York City for four days, randomly lynching blacks, razing a black orphanage, and driving blacks out of the city.[7]

By 1862 blacks who had escaped from the South or been liberated by the Union Army were already drifting into northern cities, and in Cincinnati there was a riot following the employment of blacks on the wharves. In August the *Boston Pilot,* an Irish-Catholic newspaper, reported that "we have already upon us bloody contention between white and black labor. . . . The North is becoming black with refugee Negroes from the South. These *wretches* crowd our cities, and by overstocking the market of labor, do incalculable injury to white hands."[8]

7. Albion P. Mann, "Labor Competition and the New York Draft Riots of 1863," *Journal of Negro History* 36 (October 1951). For a graphic description of the "black pogrom," see Adrian Cook, *The Armies of the Streets* (Lexington: University Press of Kentucky, 1974), chap. 4. In her *History of Chicago* (New York: Knopf, 1937), Bessie Louise Pierce writes that in 1864 a mob of Irish assaulted a dozen blacks working in a lumber dock. The *Annual Cyclopedia* for 1862 (p. 754) reports disturbances in Chicago, Brooklyn, Cincinnati, Toledo, and New Albany, Indiana, all provoked by the hiring of blacks.

8. Article reprinted in *The Liberator,* August 22, 1862, p. 1.

Even before the Civil War, northern politicians frequently exploited fears of labor competition to rally popular opposition to the extension of slavery to the territories. William Seward, the governor of New York who was later to become Lincoln's influential secretary of state, explicitly defined immigration and slavery as two competing sources of labor, and in 1856 he delivered a speech entitled "Immigrant White Free Labor or Imported Black African Slave Labor" to an audience in Oswego, New York, made up largely of immigrants. After extolling the contributions immigrants had made to the prosperity of Oswego and the entire nation, Seward issued the following admonition:

> Only grant now that this great end of the slaveholders can be attained, and you will need no argument to prove that African slaves will be found in the ports, not merely of New York, New Orleans, and Philadelphia, and in the fields of Kansas and Nebraska, but even in the ports of Oswego, Rochester, and Buffalo, and in the fields of Western New York, forcing the free white labor, equally of native Americans, and of Englishmen, Irishmen, and Germans, no matter whether they be Protestants or Roman Catholics, into Canada, Russian America, Australia, and wherever else throughout the whole earth, free white industry can find refuge.[9]

As reflected in Seward's speech, much of the North's opposition to the extension of slavery had all along been predicated on racist assumptions. Prevailing sentiment favored not the abolition of slavery, but rather its containment to the South where blacks posed no economic threat. As an English observer of the American working class wrote in 1865: "At present the working-men in the Northern States, though they have neither sympathy nor fellow feeling for the coloured race, make no objection to their emancipation providing they remain south of Dixie's line."[10]

Given their working-class constituency, Democratic politicians

9. Speech of William Seward, "Immigrant White Free Labor or Imported Black African Slave Labor," at Oswego, New York, November 3, 1856, p. 4. Schomburg Center for Research and Black Culture, New York City Public Library.

10. James D. Burns, *Three Years Among the Working Classes in the United States During the War* (London, 1865), p. xii.

actively played on fears of labor competition, and according to one historian, "opposition to negro immigration [to the North] and citizenship was one of the cardinal principles of the Democratic party."[11] For example, in 1862 the Democratic Party of Pennsylvania denounced Republicans as:

> ... the party of fanaticism, or crime, whichever it may be called, that seeks to turn the slaves of the Southern states loose to overrun the North and enter into competition with the white laboring masses, thus degrading and insulting their manhood by placing them on an equality with Negroes in their occupations is insulting to our race, and merits our most emphatic and unqualified condemnation.

On the same day, the Democratic State Convention of Ohio passed a similar resolution:

> Because ... emancipation would throw upon the border free states, and especially upon Ohio, an immense number of negroes ... to compete with ... the white laborers of the State ... we would deem it most unjust to our gallant soldiers to see them compelled to free the negroes of the South and thereby fill Ohio with a degraded population, to compete with these same upon their return to peaceable avocation of life.[12]

Republican leaders and abolitionists countered that, once freed, blacks would have little reason to leave their "natural home" in the South. However, the principal tactic for allaying fears of a black invasion of the North was to link emancipation with colonization. As a writer in the abolitionist newspaper *The Liberator* observed in 1863:

> Everywhere ... denunciations of slavery and advocacy of the emancipation policy are coupled with the proposition that the two races cannot occupy the same territory in peace, and that we must choose between slavery with all its countless brood of evils, and the deportation of the black race.[13]

11. Norman Dwight Harris, *The History of Negro Servitude in Illinois, 1719–1864* (Chicago: Lakeside Press, 1904), p. 241.

12. Quoted in Williston Lofton, "Northern Labor and the Negro During the Civil War," *Journal of Negro History* 34 (July 1949), pp. 254–55.

13. *The Liberator,* November 27, 1863, p. 2.

In his annual address to Congress in 1862, Lincoln proposed his plan to colonize ex-slaves to islands in the Caribbean, and explicitly justified it as a way of reducing labor competition between the races. As he said: "Reduce the supply of black labor by colonizing the black laborer out of the country and precisely by so much you increase the demand for and wages of white labor."[14]

It was not for lack of popular support that colonization was never implemented on a major scale. Black labor was simply too valuable to be discarded so recklessly, as was recognized by Representative Thomas Eliot of Massachusetts:

> You ought not to do it, because besides its intrinsic and fatal injustice, you will deprive the country of what it most needs, which is labor. Those freedmen on the spot are better than mineral wealth. Each is a mine out of which riches can be drawn. . . .[15]

The real function of the colonization proposals was to make the war and abolition more palatable to public opinion in the North, and to win the support of groups such as the Tammany Club in New York, which in 1862 went on record as "opposed to emancipating negro slaves, unless on some plan of colonization, in order that they may not come in contact with the white man's labor."[16]

Several other schemes were proposed which would "mine the riches" of black labor without posing a threat to white workers in the North. The most far-reaching proposal, advanced by a small group of Radical Republicans, would have broken up the large plantations and redistributed confiscated land to ex-slaves. That more than considerations of justice went into this proposal is reflected by an 1863 editorial in the *New York Daily Tribune* that favored a land distribution program because it would allay fears

14. Quoted in Wesley, op. cit., pp. 14–15.

15. Quoted in Wesley, op. cit., pp. 11–12. Much the same point of view was expressed in *The Liberator:* "'Expatriate him,' say the haters of the Negro. Expatriate him for what? He has cleared the swamps of the South, and has put the soil under cultivation; he has built up the towns and cities and villages, he has enriched the North and Europe, and for this you would drive him out of the country?" May 16, 1863.

16. Quoted in James McPherson, "Abolitionist and Negro Opposition to Colonization During the Civil War," *Phylon,* 4th quarter, 1965, p. 391.

among workers that "they are to be swamped by a vast importation of blacks."[17]

Another plan, proposed by Senator James Lane of Kansas in 1864, would have set aside large tracts of land in Texas for Negro colonization.[18] Still another proposal, advanced by Carl Schurz and John Palmer Usher, the secretary of the interior, would have employed blacks in railroad construction and other public works projects.[19] The common feature in all these plans is that blacks would have been safely removed from the industrial labor markets. Even Charles Sumner, who in 1863 weighed the possibility of using freedmen to build the transcontinental railroad, later reversed himself on the ground that "their services can be more effectively bestowed at home, as laborers and soldiers."[20]

Thus, even these benevolent schemes for dealing with the "Negro question" never contemplated an integration of black workers into the nation's industrial labor force. On the contrary, policy in the North was expressly designed to preclude this possibility, and even before emancipation, Pennsylvania, Ohio, and Illinois passed laws restricting black migration into their states.[21] Surveying this situation in 1863, Montgomery Blair, the postmaster general, was moved to ask: "When the Northern free States have framed laws prohibiting the colored freedman from obtaining a foothold on their soil, upon what terms can it be supposed the master race, in the slave states, would consent to associate with negroes made free by the hand of war?"[22]

17. February 12, 1863, p. 4.

18. *Congressional Globe,* 38th Congress, 1st Session, pp. 672–75.

19. "Schurz Report," *Senate Executive Documents,* 39th Congress, 1st Session, No. 2, pp. 2–105; "Report of the Secretary of the Interior," *House Executive Documents,* vol. 3, no. 1, 38th Congress, 1st Session, 1863–64, p. 414.

20. Charles Sumner, *Complete Works,* vol. IX (New York: Negro Universities Press, 1969), p. 319.

21. Edward Raymond Turner, *The Negro in Pennsylvania* (Washington: American Historical Association, 1911), pp. 153–67; Frank U. Quillin, *The Color in Ohio: A History of Race Prejudice in a Typical Northern State* (Ann Arbor: Univ. of Michigan, 1913), published thesis, p. 45; Pierce, op. cit., p. 12; Harris, op. cit., pp. 234–43.

22. *The Liberator,* June 26, 1863, p. 1.

The "Negro Question" in the South

If the North was apprehensive about black encroachment on "white" labor markets, the problem was quite different in the South, where blacks constituted the chief source of agricultural labor. Here the "Negro question" assumed the form: "Will the Negro work now that he is free?"[23] To some extent southern thought was trapped in its own myths, in that slavery had always been justified as having rescued blacks from a slothful existence in the bush, and it was argued that blacks would never work unless forced to do so. As the author of an 1866 letter in the *Southern Cultivator,* a planters' journal, put it: "With some two hundred years experience, it has been found that the only way to make the negro work is to keep the fear of corporeal punishment continually before him; rewards for diligence uniformly ruin him."[24] Now that Negroes had been freed from the salubrious constraints that slavery placed on their nature, the author speculated, they would inevitably die off.

Like the northern schemes to colonize blacks out of the country, however, such rhetoric should not be taken at face value. It reflected the South's difficulty in reconciling itself ideologically to dealing with blacks in a state of freedom, but behind the rhetorical excesses were more rational concerns. Would ex-slaves be willing to return to their previous station as farm laborers? What wages would they exact, and given the dearth of capital after the war—complicated by the fact that cotton has a two-hundred-day growing season—how were they to be paid? Finally, now that the economic advantages of slavery had been eliminated, why employ blacks at all? Why not tap the vast pool of immigrant labor that had proved so valuable to the North?

When *DeBow's Review,* the South's leading economic journal, resumed publication after the war, labor problems were in the forefront of the journal's concerns. The first edition contained no fewer than three articles—one written by DeBow himself—proclaiming the advantages that white immigration would have for the South, as well as a fourth article assessing the sundry plans for

23. *DeBow's Review,* vol. I, no. 1, AWS (January 1866), p. 7; vol. IV (1867), p. 363.

24. *Southern Cultivator* 24 (January 1866), p. 5.

colonizing blacks out of the country. For the next half century, the South would try, often through official agencies established by state governments, to promote European immigration, but with almost no success. Immigrants who were destined for farming generally moved to the developing areas west of the Mississippi where land was cheap and where no established social hierarchy denied them status and opportunity. Those who did not have the requisite experience and capital to become independent farmers typically opted for jobs in northern industry. Given these alternatives, there was no reason why immigrants should voluntarily enter the South's feudalistic system of agriculture as ordinary laborers.[25]

Nor given the South's access to cheap black labor was there any incentive for developing a reward system that might have attracted immigrants to the region. Indeed, the South rapidly became disenchanted with those few immigrants who settled there, for reasons that were foreshadowed in DeBow's 1866 article. DeBow quoted a southern planter as saying: "Germans do not aim to become merely day laborers, but landowners."[26] The same observation was made by a traveller to the South in 1866 who reported that "Germans of a better class . . . wouldn't contract with you, unless they saw a chance to become, after a time, the owners of the soil they cultivated."[27] Another traveler in 1867 described the European immigrant as "simply an unbloated aristocrat without the slightest intention of working for anybody except himself," an accusation

25. This was well recognized by contemporary observers: "The immigrant laborer does not strive long to rival him [the black worker] because no such laborer is content to live on the same humble plane of existence; in this, the latter resembles the native white laborer, only that he is far more irritable and complaining"—Philip A. Bruce, *The Plantation Negro as a Freedman* (New York: Knickerbocker Press, 1889), p. 188. "The farm laborer of the North would be foolish indeed to go to the South to compete with the negro in the cultivation of cotton or any other staple at the prices which labor receives in that region. Not only can he earn the equivalent thereof in half the time upon a Northern farm, but with his labor there he receives also bed and board of a character that would seem ruinously extravagant to the Southern landlord."—Albion Winegar Tourgée, *An Appeal to Caesar* (New York: Fords, Howard, & Hulbert, 1884), p. 161.

26. *DeBow's Review,* vol. 1, no. 1, AWS (January 1866), p. 11.

27. Whitelaw Reid, *A Southern Town, May 1, 1865 to May 1, 1866* (New York: Moore, Wilstack, and Baldwin, 1866), p. 564.

that would later be made of Italians in particular.[28] The crux of the matter was that unlike blacks, immigrants could not be forced into a quasi-serfdom. If their conditions as agricultural laborers became intolerable, there were always alternatives. As a result the South's experiment with immigration ended in dismal failure.[29]

A proposal to import Chinese to do the work previously done by slaves aroused particular enthusiasm. "We can drive the niggers out and import coolies that will work better at less expense, and relieve us from the cursed nigger impudence," exclaimed one planter in 1866.[30] A year later *DeBow's Review* proposed importing half a million Chinese laborers, whom the journal extolled as "docile and obedient" workers.[31] Just as the North used the reservoir of black labor to subdue white workers, the South now turned to Chinese for much the same purpose. With the coming of the Chinese, a Kentucky editor wrote gleefully, "the tune . . . will not be 'forty acres and a mule,' but . . . 'work nigger or starve.' "[32]

However, the experiment with Chinese labor also yielded meager results. Few Chinese went South, opting instead for more lucrative and less degrading employment on the railroads or in the mines of the West. And those who did migrate to the cotton or cane fields of the South rapidly made their way into more rewarding niches in the regional economy—often as storekeepers, and in the case of Louisiana's Chinese, as independent fishermen and truck farmers.[33] If Chinese laborers proved to be less "docile and obedient" than their

28. Henry Latham, *Black and White* (New York University Press, 1869; orig. 1867), p. 141. For similar statements concerning the Italians, see Robert L. Brandfon, "The End of Immigration to the Cotton Fields," *Mississippi Valley Historical Review* 50 (March 1964), p. 606.

29. Ibid., pp. 591–611; Bert James Loewenberg, "Efforts of the South to Encourage Immigration," *The South Atlantic Quarterly* 33 (October 1934), pp. 363–85.

30. Quoted in Oscar Zeichner, "The Transition from Slave to Free Labor in the Southern States," *Agricultural History* XIII (1939), p. 26.

31. *DeBow's Review*, vol. IV, AWS (1867), p. 364.

32. Quoted in Gunther Barth, *Bitter Strength: A History of the Chinese in the United States, 1850–1870* (Cambridge: Harvard University Press, 1964), pp. 188–89. A similar refrain is found in a message to the freedmen printed in *DeBow's Review* in 1867 (vol. IV, p. 421).

33. James W. Loewen, *Mississippi Chinese* (Cambridge: Harvard University Press, 1971).

employers hoped, it was because there were channels of escape open to them.

In the end the South had to reconcile itself to the fact that it was as dependent as ever on black labor. On a note of resignation, *DeBow's Review* wrote in 1867: "Our sole reliance hereafter, as heretofore, for farm hands must be on the negroes."[34] The one difficulty, however, was that blacks had never worked in the cotton fields by choice. Now that they were ostensibly free, how could they be forced to take employment that no other segment of the labor force would accept on more than a temporary basis? This was the dilemma facing the postbellum South. Vanquished in war, the South could not achieve this fateful objective of getting blacks to work for their former masters without the active support and collaboration of the North.

The Politics of Cotton

With characteristic acumen, Alexis de Tocqueville wrote in *Democracy in America:* "It is not for the good of Negroes but for that of the whites that measures are taken to abolish slavery in the United States."[35] This applies with equal force to the granting of full citizenship to ex-slaves, which was motivated less by altruism than by a self-serving desire on the part of the victorious North to curtail the political power of the southern oligarchy and, in effect, to drive a thirteenth nail in the Confederate coffin. For example, the Fifteenth Amendment enfranchising black men was viewed by the reigning Republicans as a device for securing a permanent Republican foothold in the South.[36] In short, nothing in the race history of the North—not even its advocacy of black civil rights—augured well for the future of blacks once the sectional conflict was settled. Rather, there were powerful economic and political pressures in the North to restore the southern economy, and cotton production in particular,

34. Zeichner, op. cit., p. 494.
35. Alexis de Tocqueville, *Democracy in America,* vol. 1 (New York: Vintage, 1954), p. 360.
36. William Gillette, *The Right to Vote* (Baltimore: Johns Hopkins Press, 1965), chaps. 2–3.

to prewar levels, even if this meant compromising the freedom that had been reluctantly granted to ex-slaves.

As already indicated, cotton was the most expansive force in the American economy during the early nineteenth century. It provided the raw material for the nascent textile industry, which functioned as a base for industrial development; it alone accounted for over half of American exports, which served as a critical source of foreign capital; and it unleashed a chain of economic forces that led to sustained growth. By 1860, however, the North had emerged as a fullfledged industrial and commercial center with its own self-sustaining economic base, and as Douglass North points out, "the dependence of both the Northeast and the West on the South waned."[37] Nevertheless, cotton still accounted for 58 percent of the dollar value of all American exports, and the domestic textile industry's demand for raw cotton was never greater.[38]

Southern apologists for slavery had long contended that the North profited from slavery as much as the South, and complained that southern profits were siphoned off to build up the northern economy —a claim that was not without justification. In the first place, much of the capital for the plantation economy came from northern banks and financial institutions. Secondly, northern traders and ports reaped most of the benefit from the profitable commerce in raw cotton, and cotton manufacturing was concentrated almost exclusively in northern cities. Finally, most of the profits made by southern planters were eventually spent purchasing farm machinery, supplies, and consumer goods produced in the North. Despite its best efforts, the South lacked the capital resources and the home market to develop its own industrial base and to diversify economically, and was reduced to being little more than a supplier of cotton and a few other raw materials to the North.[39] This prompted one southern senator to comment that "the South is nothing else now

37. Douglass North, *The Economic Growth of the United States, 1790–1860* (New York: W. W. Norton, 1966), p. 70.

38. Ibid., p. 233.

39. See Eugene Genovese, "The Significance of the Slave Plantation for Southern Economic Development," *Journal of Southern History* 28 (1962), p. 424.

but the very best colony to the North any people ever possessed."[40]

This helps to explain why, in the aftermath of the Civil War, there was such an urgent need to normalize economic relations between North and South. Northern businessmen were in the forefront of those calling for political conciliation and a rebuilding of the shattered southern economy. The drift of business sentiment can be gleaned from the pages of the *Commercial and Financial Chronicle,* a new publication that, according to one historian, functioned as "a business propaganda offensive for Jacksonianism."[41] The first issue appeared in July 1865, and began on this sanguine note: "The end of the war, through which the country has just passed, inaugurates an era of peace and prosperity which only needs wise legislation to find encouragement." The *Chronicle* did not leave it to the imagination of its readers to decipher what was meant by "wise legislation":

> It is to our advantage as much as theirs that their lands shall be tilled, their channels of trade reopened, their villages, towns and cities redeemed from the ravages of war, their railroads, canals and highways repaired and put in working order, and their minds relieved from vague apprehensions of impending chastisement for past misconduct. They have sinned much, they have suffered much. . . . Help them to retrieve their fallen fortunes, and in doing so we make them more efficient helpmates in achieving the general prosperity.[42]

Further, the task of rehabilitating the crippled southern economy took precedence over social reform and social justice:

> The question, therefore, which, as practical men, the administrators of our public affairs have to settle, at this moment, as it seems to us, is not the ideally desirable in the way of reconstructing Southern society, but the really practicable in the way

40. Senator Robert Rhett of South Carolina, quoted in John W. Stormont, *The Economics of Secession and Coercion* (Victoria, Tex.: Victoria Advocate Publishing Co., 1957), p. 11. Also, Robert Albion, *The Rise of the New York Port 1815–1860* (New York: Scribner, 1939).

41. George Ruble Woolfolk, *The Cotton Regency* (New York: Bookman Associates, 1958).

42. *Commercial and Financial Quarterly,* July 1, 1865, pp. 1, 5.

of remitting the Southern communities at the earliest possible day to their normal relations of production and consumption with the rest of the republic.[43]

An immediate restoration of southern state governments, the *Chronicle* believed, would redound to the benefit of all concerned. But what about the Negro? The *Chronicle's* answer was vague in expression but clear in its import: "Social questions must be left, in great degree, to adjust themselves."[44]

Implicit in the *Chronicle's* endorsement of "benign neglect" was a repudiation of the idea that the federal government should intervene on behalf of ex-slaves, either to guarantee their rights or to redistribute land seized from slave owners. No doubt, the *Chronicle's* editors recognized that a land redistribution might establish an ideologically dangerous precedent, as was pointed out, on a note of sarcasm, in an 1867 issue of *DeBow's Review:* "We are inclined to think that if the agrarian ball should be set in full motion in ten states of the Union," then laborers in the North "would be very apt to consider their claim upon the wealth of the North quite as good as that of the negro upon the wealth of the South."[45] When it came to protecting wealth and property, there was no dispute between northern businessmen and southern planters, and it was this harmony of interest between the ruling elites of the two regions that ultimately defeated the hopes of freedmen for their own land.

Northern businessmen had all along assumed that a system of free labor would be not only more effective, but more profitable as well. From the vantage point of northern industrialists, slavery was a wasteful and inefficient labor system that needlessly tied up large amounts of capital in "fictitious property," and instead of providing incentives for hard work, did the exact opposite. Industrialists boasted that for modest wages, their employees reported to work promptly, labored long hours, and did not have to be supervised after the workday ended, or supported during their unproductive years. They were convinced that a system of free labor would eliminate the inefficiencies inherent in slavery and, not incidentally, make

43. Ibid., April 26, 1866, p. 260.
44. Ibid., September 23, 1865, p. 388.
45. *DeBow's Review,* vol. IV (1867), p. 587.

cotton production more competitive by breaking the monopolistic control of large southern planters.

This was the logic that allowed Edward Atkinson, a leading business critic of slavery, to say of himself, "I am a cotton manufacturer, at the same time an anti-slavery man."[46] In 1861 Atkinson published a pamphlet under the revealing title: *Cheap Cotton by Free Labor*. Atkinson argued that the experience of the West Indies proved that slaves would work after emancipation, just as the experience of Texas proved that, contrary to the claims of slave owners, whites could work in the cotton fields. Not only could cotton be grown by free labor, according to Atkinson, but it would actually be cheaper. Finally, Atkinson issued a statement that might well be called "the cotton manifesto":

> Have not the cotton spinners of the world the right to say to the slaveholder: "You have proved by the experience of the last few years that with your slave labor you cannot give us cotton enough."[47]

The Civil War presented Atkinson with an opportunity to prove that cotton could be produced by emancipated slaves. In 1863 he organized the Free Labor Cotton Company which followed on the heels of the Union Army as it conquered the lower Mississippi Valley. Under a program administered by the federal government's Commission on Plantations, Atkinson leased confiscated land and employed ex-slaves at prescribed wages. Due to the unstable economic conditions as well as Confederate raids, the scheme was not very successful. Northern investors had better luck on the Sea Islands off the Georgia coast, which were insulated from the hostilities on the mainland and produced a large and profitable harvest on land worked by ex-slaves.[48]

No sooner were the Confederate armies defeated on the battlefield than northern businessmen rushed in to take advantage of the

46. Harold Francis Williamson, *Edward Atkinson* (New York: Arno Press, 1972), p. 4.

47. Edward Atkinson, *Cheap Cotton by Free Labor* (Boston: A. Williams and Co., 1861), p. 25.

48. See Willie Lee Rose, *Rehearsal for Reconstruction: The Port Royal Experiment* (Indianapolis: University of Indiana Press, 1965).

opportunities afforded by the collapse of the plantation system. The war had left southern planters on the verge of bankruptcy, and more dependent than ever on credit from outside sources. The situation was ripe for northern capital, especially since land values had plummeted at a time when cotton was selling at a premium due to wartime shortages. Some investors bought huge parcels of land at depressed prices, others provided credit to southern middlemen who in turn extended credit to planters and tenant farmers.[49] Though it is not precisely known to what extent cotton production in the postbellum South was owned and financed by northern interests, it was enough to prompt one southern politician to remark in 1868 that "it is the Northern capitalist as well as the Southern planter that the poor freedman has to contend against now."[50]

In other ways, too, the freedmen had to cope with the northern capitalist as well as the southern planter. The South, after all, had been prostrated by the war, and at least during the Reconstruction period, it was the North that wielded the political power that would determine the ultimate fate of the freedmen. This was the historical moment when the North's legacy of racism and its own stake in the exploitation of black labor would deal a devastating blow to the hopes of the ex-slaves for economic and social redemption.

The two possible outcomes that would have been most advantageous to blacks—a massive redistribution of land in the South, or integration into the industrial labor force in the North—were never given more than fleeting consideration. Excluded from the industrial labor markets, blacks were pushed back onto the South; denied an opportunity to become independent farmers, they were forced to work as farm laborers, or as sharecroppers or tenant farmers under a system that in some respects was almost as bad as slavery itself. The South's historic role in oppressing blacks after slavery is well understood. What is not generally recognized is the role that the North played in creating the larger framework in which southern racism operated.

Aside from fateful acts of omission in failing to institute con-

49. Fred Shannon, *The Farmer's Last Frontier, 1860–1897* (New York: Farrar & Rinehart, 1945), p. 100.

50. Quoted in James Allen, *Reconstruction* (New York: International Publishers, 1937), p. 71.

structive policies that might have redistributed land to ex-slaves or integrated blacks into the industrial labor force, the North was an active agent in the development of the sharecropping system that functioned as an economic surrogate for slavery. And the chief instrument for the North's reorganization of southern agriculture into a sharecropping system was the agency that was established ostensibly to promote the welfare of emancipated slaves—the Freedmen's Bureau.

Whose Freedmen's Bureau?

The initial step toward the development of the Freedmen's Bureau came from a committee representing several freedmen's aid societies, voluntary groups dedicated to the "elevation" of ex-slaves, who petitioned President Lincoln in 1863 to establish an official bureau that would put the machinery of government behind their lofty mission. The petitioners included prominent clergy and abolitionist leaders—such as Henry Ward Beecher, the brilliant antislavery preacher, and Levi Coffin, a Quaker leader in the Underground Railroad. But along with these selfless individuals whose repudiation of slavery rested on high moral principle appears the name of Edward Atkinson, the Boston cotton manufacturer who that same year had organized the Free Labor Cotton Company.[51] Here was the first sign that more than altruism went into the creation of the Freedmen's Bureau.

From its inception the bureau was designed to facilitate the transition from slavery to freedom in a manner that would not disrupt the Southern economy or jeopardize the North's supply of cheap and abundant cotton. To be more precise, the abolitionist voice which had been so reviled prior to the Civil War was now used to provide an ideological facade for an agency whose covert function was to ease the emancipated Negro into a new form of subjugation.

That the Freedmen's Bureau would serve narrow business interests was forewarned by some of its opponents in Congress. A New York congressman denounced it as a "money-making scheme" which was "for the use of the black race by northern masters," while a

51. George R. Bentley, *A History of the Freedmen's Bureau* (New York: Octagon Press, 1970), p. 31.

Kentucky congressman criticized it for putting "the control of three or four million men seated in southern and western states in the hands of the commercial and manufacturing parts of the country. . . ."[52] Indeed, beneath the philanthropic pretensions of the bureau and the sanctimony of its most ardent supporters were raw economic interests that had a stake in prodding ex-slaves back to the cotton fields. As a congressional proponent of the Bureau argued: "The welfare of the people of the North demands it. They need the commodities yielded by this territory. Their industry is paralyzed by want of cotton which will be produced on these fields and by the labor of these people."[53]

In theory, distribution of land to ex-slaves could have restored cotton production, and the promise of "forty acres and a mule" in fact attained a prominent place in the political discourse of the postbellum period. Indeed, the legislation establishing the Freedmen's Bureau specifically provided that "abandoned or confiscated land"—that is, land of Confederate soldiers and supporters that had been seized by the government—should be distributed to freedmen in 40-acre tracts. However, the government possessed only 800,000 acres of such land, which, at best, could have provided 20,000 homesteads for the four million ex-slaves. Besides, this provision of the bill never received more than token implementation. No sooner did Otis Howard, the embattled commissioner of the Freedmen's Bureau, initiate a land distribution to freedmen than President Johnson forced him to rescind the order. By 1866 half the land in government possession had been returned to the original owners, and in a number of cases, blacks were forced—sometimes at the point of a bayonet—to relinquish land that they had been previously granted.

Instead of effecting a land redistribution program, the Freedmen's Bureau became the chief instrument for organizing a system of contract labor that reduced the black population of the South to a state of virtual peonage. The bureau's strategy was to draw up model contracts, and to prevail upon planters and laborers alike to sign them. On the surface, the contract provided benefits to both parties. Freedmen were guaranteed specific wages, or in lieu of wages, a share of the crop raised. In addition, their employers were

52. Ibid., pp. 38–39.
53. Ibid., p. 39.

enjoined to provide shelter, food, and medical care for their employees. In return, employers received a binding obligation from their laborers to work for the duration of the contract. The bureau arrogated to itself the right to supervise the contracts and to adjudicate any disputes.

Here was the North's answer to the Negro question—a system of contract labor that had all the earmarks of a voluntary agreement that conferred benefits on both parties, that would restore agricultural production and revitalize commerce in the South's precious commodity.

The one stumbling block was that ex-slaves were less than eager to sign the contracts. Above all else, they were repelled by the idea of returning to work for their former masters. Furthermore, by signing the contracts, they were essentially surrendering their freedom to quit their jobs or to strike for higher wages, and would be bonded to their employers and subject to a regimentation, including the possibility of harsh punishment, that was not very different from slavery itself. Thus it is hardly surprising that freedmen balked at signing contracts, and jealously guarded their newly acquired freedom to choose the conditions of their own employment.[54]

Nevertheless, the Freedmen's Bureau zealously promoted its system of contract labor. Its first task was to disabuse ex-slaves of their expectations of "forty acres and a mule," which was accomplished "by constant exertions on the part of officers of the bureau."[55] In addition, agents exhorted ex-slaves to prove by their labor that they were deserving of the freedoms that had been bestowed upon them. For example, the very first communication issued to freedmen by the Freedmen's Bureau of South Carolina began with these unctuous words of advice:

Freedmen, let not a day pass ere you find some work for your hands to do, and do it with all your might. Plough and plant,

54. Joel Williamson, *After Slavery* (Chapel Hill: University of North Carolina Press, 1965), p. 69; Martin Abbott, *The Freedmen's Bureau in South Carolina, 1865–1872* (Chapel Hill: University of North Carolina Press, 1967), pp. 70–72; Zeichner, op. cit., pp. 25–26.

55. "Report of the Commissioner of the Bureau of Refugees, Freedmen, and Abandoned Lands," House Executive Documents, vol. 3, 39th Congress, 2nd Session, 1866–67, p. 3; Charles William Ramsdell, *Reconstruction in Texas* (New York, 1910), pp. 48, 73.

dig and hoe, cut and gather in the harvest. Let it be seen that where in slavery there was raised a blade of corn or a pound of cotton, in freedom there will be two.[56]

This evangelical tone, characteristic of the bureau's dealings with ex-slaves, was typically invoked for the purpose of sanctifying labor contracts and compliance with authority. "This thing you must learn above all else," sermonized an assistant commissioner of the bureau, "a contract must be sacredly observed."[57]

Where moral suasion failed, the bureau resorted to more coercive methods. Even before the bureau was established, the government had begun systematically to cut back on the rations provided to ex-slaves crowded into refugee camps, and this policy was continued by the Freedmen's Bureau. The bureau's stated policy was to issue rations "so as to include none that are not absolutely necessitous and destitute."[58] According to official records, in August 1865 there were about 148,000 freedmen receiving relief. But by September, when the bureau had become fully operational, the number had been reduced to 75,000. A year later the figure was 30,000; a year later, 12,000.[59] Though the bureau routinely doled out money to transport refugees back to their former homes, it refused to pay transportation expenses for refugees who wished to go to other parts of the country, including the areas of the West and South that had recently been opened for homesteading.[60]

In effect, then, relief provided to ex-slaves was used as a lever to force them to resume their previous roles as farm laborers in southern agriculture. In June 1865, *The New York Times* took obvious satisfaction in reporting that "the throngs of colored people that were visible in our midst some time ago have scattered and

56. Quoted in Laura Josephine Webster, "The Operation of the Freedmen's Bureau in South Carolina," *Smith College Studies in History* (January 1966), p. 107.

57. Quoted in William McFeeley, *Yankee Grandfather* (New Haven: Yale University Press, 1968), p. 180.

58. "Report of the Commissioner of the Bureau of Refugees, Freedmen, and Abandoned Lands," 1868, 40th Congress, 3rd Session, p. 9.

59. Ibid.

60. The 1866 Report of the Freedman's Bureau indicated that "no transportation has yet been given in the work of transferring freedmen to the public lands. . . ." "Report of the Commissioner of the Bureau of Refugees, Freedmen, and Abandoned Lands," 1866, op. cit., p. 7.

settled down on the plantations. The short supply of rice in the government's storehouses doubtless had much to do with their departure."[61] Blacks who had sought refuge in government camps had been pushed to the brink of starvation by the very people to whom they had turned for protection. In a sense, it was the Freedmen's Bureau that carried out the southern planters' dictate, "Work, nigger, or starve."

An equally oppressive device, specifically designed to force blacks to sign labor contracts, was the use of vagrancy laws and the threat of vagrancy arrest. According to Daniel Novak, in his recent history of black forced labor after slavery, this practice was pioneered by the Freedmen's Bureau in Mississippi, which threatened black laborers with arrest if they did not sign labor contracts.[62] Between 1865 and 1867 most southern states passed Black Codes which included vagrancy laws that not only provided for the arrest of "idle" blacks, but also provided that "vagrants" could be hired out at public auction for as long as a year. Novak presents this synopsis of Mississippi's vagrancy laws:

> Mississippi's opening effort, ironically titled "An Act to Confer Civil Rights on Freedmen," barred the freedman from renting land outside city limits, thus ensuring that blacks could not begin farming on their own. Further, by the following January, and annually thereafter, each freedman had to hold written proof of lawful employment (i.e., a labor contract). The absence of such evidence was prima facie proof of vagrancy. Should a freedman breach his contract "without good cause," he was subject to arrest by the police or other civil officer. The arresting officer was entitled to a reward of five dollars (plus ten cents per mile traveled), to be paid out of the laborer's wages. As a further insurance against flight, the old Fugitive Slave Laws were reborn: any person attempting to "entice" a laborer from his master, employ him, or otherwise aid or harbor him was subject to criminal as well as civil penalties.[63]

61. Quoted in Williamson, op. cit., p. 67.

62. Daniel A. Novak, *The Wheel of Servitude* (Lexington: University Press of Kentucky, 1978), p. 11.

63. Ibid., pp. 2–3. Also see W. Kloosterboer, *Involuntary Labour Since the Abolition of Slavery* (Leiden: E. J. Brill, 1960), chap. 5.

In Florida the definition of a "vagrant" was broadened to include laborers found guilty of "a willful disobedience of orders," "impudence," "disrespect to his employer," or "idleness." Still other laws empowered courts to remove children from parents declared unwilling or unable to provide for them, and bind them out to employers, preferably their former owners, under an apprenticeship system.[64]

In some states the Freedmen's Bureau nullified the Black Codes, but in other states it either acquiesced or actively encouraged their enforcement. Novak concluded that "the Black Codes regulating labor were little more than local validations of the regulations initiated and enforced by the federal authorities."[65]

Finally, if these indirect methods failed to produce the desired results, the bureau could intervene militarily. In South Carolina, for example, agents visited each plantation, presented laborers with contracts drawn up by planters, mediated any differences, and evicted any laborers unwilling to sign.[66] By the summer of 1866, agents had approved about 8,000 contracts involving 130,000 black farm laborers.[67] Indeed, after the initial period of providing relief to refugees, implementation and enforcement of the contract system received the agency's highest priority. By its own account, as stated in the bureau's annual report for 1868, "every bureau officer became an employment agent for the purpose of securing homes and employment for all who were without work."[68]

Despite the various forms of coercion that were applied to ex-slaves, the bureau's agents could pretend, perhaps even to themselves, that they were engaged in a noble experiment to prove the viability of a free labor system, and hence the obsolescence of slavery. As William McFeeley, Otis Howard's biographer, has noted, "the Freedmen's Bureau always tried to veil its enforcement of the contract system with talk of mutually beneficial arrangements freely entered. . . ."[69] In actual practice, however, blacks were hardly act-

64. Novak, op. cit., pp. 3–6.
65. Novak, op. cit., p. 9.
66. Williamson, op. cit., p. 69.
67. Abbott, op. cit., p. 91.
68. "Report of the Commissioner of the Bureau of Refugees, Freedmen, and Abandoned Lands," 1868, op. cit., p. 8.
69. McFeeley, op. cit., p. 180.

ing out of free choice, and the system was far from equitable. As long as they were prevented from withholding their labor, black workers were not in a position to negotiate their wages or the conditions of their employment. Furthermore, planters' organizations generally conspired to impose a ceiling on wages, and laws were passed prohibiting planters from "enticing" laborers already under contract. Consequently, black laborers never received a fair wage for their labor, nor benefited from the high price of cotton or the great demand for their labor in the aftermath of the Civil War. Finally, blacks had little protection from outright fraud, and the Freedmen's Bureau was far from evenhanded in enforcing the contracts. In 1866 a northern teacher wrote of the Bureau:

> They are more proslavery than the rebels themselves, and only care to make the blacks work—being quite unconcerned about making the employers pay. Doing justice seems to mean . . . seeing that the blacks don't break contract and compelling them to submit cheerfully if the whites do.[70]

Sharecropping arrangements were also subject to abuse. Problems arose over the distribution of shares, and it was not uncommon for planters to renege altogether after the cotton was harvested. Of even greater consequence was the routine exploitation inherent in the sharecropping system itself. Lacking any resources of their own, ex-slaves were dependent upon their employer, or upon local merchants extending credit on their employer's account, for food, clothing, seed, and other provisions to carry them through the growing season. More often than not, the costs of goods advanced, typically at usurious rates of interest, exceeded the value of the laborer's share at the end of the season. Thus sharecroppers had little or nothing to show for a year's labor, and as they borrowed again for the next season, they were kept permanently in debt. Except for the fact that sharecropping usually freed blacks from working in closely supervised field gangs, it amounted to a form of economic bondage that made a chimera of their emancipation.

Given the role that the Freedmen's Bureau played in the evolution of these new forms of servitude, it is not surprising that southern planters overcame their initial antipathy toward the bureau and

70. Ibid., p. 157; see also Zeichner, op. cit., pp. 495–96.

came to see it as an ally in resolving the "Negro question." The annual reports of the Freedmen's Bureau are peppered with statements of appreciation on the part of planters for the bureau's work. For example, the 1866 report indicated that "many of the planters in the wealthy districts, where a large number of freedmen are employed, acknowledge the aid rendered to the planting interests by the bureau."[71] This was reiterated in the 1868 report: "Many planters have expressed their approbation of the conduct of the freedmen, and given officers of the bureau credit for aiding in settling labor upon just principles."[72] Indeed, southern planters had good reason to exonerate the Freedmen's Bureau from the charge that it was an instrument of Yankee domination of the South. Not only were their landholdings secure, but through the contract system, the bureau had helped to resolve their most serious problem—a stable supply of cheap labor. One planter in 1866 calculated that labor was as cheap as it was during slavery:

> Before the war able-bodied negroes were commanding from fifteen hundred to three thousand dollars in the New Orleans market. Counting only ten percent interest on the investment, we find it nearly as cheap to hire the negroes as it was in the old days to own them and get their labor for nothing.[73]

Not only was labor cheap, but cotton production was increasing. In its 1868 annual report, the Freedmen's Bureau could trumpet the success of the newly installed labor system:

> . . . the great mass of freedmen are now self-supporting. And in spite of the misfortunes that have fallen upon the south during the last two planting seasons—the floods, the caterpillar, and the army worm—the voluntary labor of the freedmen has produced nearly all the food which has supported the whole people, besides nearly two millions of bales of cotton in 1866, and above two millions of bales in 1867, which have paid a tax of more than forty millions of dollars into the United States

71. "Report of the Commissioner of the Bureau of Refugees, Freedmen, and Abandoned Lands," 1867, 40th Congress, 2nd Session, op. cit., p. 41.

72. "Report of the Commissioner of the Bureau of Refugees, Freedmen, and Abandoned Lands, 1868, p. 8.

73. Reid, op. cit., p. 278.

treasury, and furnished exports amounting in value to more than 300 millions of dollars.[74]

In effect, the Freedmen's Bureau had vindicated northern businessmen who had argued that a free labor system would work in the South and that cotton would be as plentiful as ever. Never mind that in proving its point the bureau had mutilated the concept of free labor. Never mind that the nation had again made a sham of its equalitarian principles, and reneged on its promises to the emancipated slaves. Never mind that in the aftermath of the Civil War blacks had been reduced to a state of virtual peonage. These compromising details were easily brushed aside as the North bathed in self-congratulation for having freed the slaves.

Conclusion

Thus, the most notable and enduring achievement of Reconstruction was the reconstruction of black servitude. Though the Civil War had ended slavery, the underlying economic functions that slavery had served were unchanged, and a surrogate system of compulsory paid labor developed in its place.

While the Freedmen's Bureau was a powerful instrument in the development of this surrogate system of exploitation, it is doubtful that the coercive tactics used to get ex-slaves back onto the cotton fields would have succeeded had other avenues of escape been open. Four million emancipated slaves were, in effect, trapped in the South, and unlike Alex Haley's family at the end of *Roots,* they had no teams of horses to carry them to less oppressive homes, and no capital to buy land or develop homesteads. As it was, a large number of ex-slaves made their way to Texas and other developing areas of the South and West where their labor was in demand, but as in the Old South, they worked primarily as agricultural laborers. Though the federal government possessed over one billion acres of public lands which it generously doled out to European settlers, railroads, and other special interests, almost none was made available for black settlement.[75] Though northern industry absorbed tens

74. "Report of the Commissioner of the Bureau of Refugees, Freedmen, and Abandoned Lands," 1868, op. cit., p. 9.

75. Kloosterboer, op. cit., p. 59.

of millions of immigrants in the decades following the Civil War, a color line barred the employment of black labor until the supply of white labor had been exhausted. In short, ex-slaves were encircled by discriminatory barriers in other parts of the country, and, pushed to the brink of starvation, were forced to struggle for survival as wage laborers, sharecroppers, and tenant farmers in southern agriculture.

Once again, blacks paid the price and carried the burden of the nation's need for cheap and abundant cotton.

Chapter 8

Racial and Ethnic Conflict
in the Twentieth Century

*"If beliefs, per se, could subjugate a people, the beliefs
which Negroes hold about whites should be as effective
as those which whites hold about Negroes."*

OLIVER COX, *Caste, Class, and Race,* 1948

''THE AVERAGE Pole or Italian arriving at Ellis Island does not realize that he is the deadly foe of the native Negro." Thus began an editorial in the *New Republic* in 1916 under the caption "The Superfluous Negro." Blacks had become superfluous, the editorial explained, because "by filling all the jobs in the North the immigrant forces the Negro back on the South, where wages are lower and industrial development more backward. It is a silent conflict on a gigantic scale."[1]

Though the "average Pole or Italian" may have been oblivious to the detrimental effects of immigration on black Americans, the same cannot be said of the "average black." Beginning in the mid-nineteenth century, when blacks and Irish were locked in competition for jobs in New York and Boston, the feeling became rooted in the black community that immigrants were usurping opportuni-

---

1. *New Republic,* June 24, 1916, p. 187.

ties that might otherwise have gone to them. At times blacks expressed this resentment by embracing nativist rhetoric, as when the *Colored American Magazine* warned in 1907 that "already the day is upon us when the scum of Europe is with us, her paupers, her convicts, her socialists, her anarchists."[2] At other times black opposition to immigration was given more dignified expression, as when the Tennessee Republic League passed the following resolution in 1916 calling for immigration restriction:

> We favor restricted immigration since the labor market of the United States, for which foreigners are imported in large numbers, or allowed in large numbers to pass Ellis Island would be well supplied if American laborers, without regard to color, were allowed freely to work in their own country.[3]

Actually, the League's resolution was itself superfluous, because a year earlier the First World War had brought immigration to a virtual standstill.

The labor shortages that resulted from the cutoff of immigration provided blacks with their first real opportunity to be hired in northern industry. Not only did employers lower the racial barriers that had previously excluded blacks from all but the most menial jobs, but they dispatched labor agents to the South to recruit prospective black workers. Responding to this favorable turn of events, southern blacks by the hundreds of thousands migrated to northern cities where they were readily integrated into the industrial labor force. This is the clearest evidence that blacks all along had been willing to respond to favorable economic opportunities in the North, that they were "qualified" for the jobs that previously had gone to immigrants, and that the racism of employers and workers alike posed no insurmountable obstacle to the hiring of blacks once their labor was needed.

Now blacks and immigrants would come into direct competition to an unprecedented extent, and what the *New Republic* had recognized as a "silent conflict on a gigantic scale" would become still larger and ever more strident.

2. *Colored American Magazine,* August 1907, p. 90.
3. *Immigration Journal,* October 1916, p. 104.

The Proletarization of Black Labor

Emblazoned across the front page of a 1916 issue of the *Chicago Defender*, the nation's leading black newspaper, was a headline: SOMEBODY LIED. And in smaller type: "When the South Howls About the Race Moving North Does It Forget the Time When It Wanted to Ship 1,000,000 to Africa?" With undisguised pleasure, the *Defender* took note of the economic panic that gripped the South as the northern exodus gained momentum. Ever since slavery, southern rhetoric had belittled blacks as poor and unproductive workers, and complained that they were a curse to the South and a bane to progress. Now that blacks were leaving, urgent appeals were issued imploring blacks not to abandon their "natural home" in the South, and warning of the perils awaiting them in the North, not the least of which was the danger of freezing to death in a climate for which they were constitutionally unfitted. Laws were passed restricting the activities of labor agents representing northern industries, and blacks were sometimes subjected to intimidation and violence at railroad stations.

Undaunted, the *Defender* exhorted more blacks to leave: "It is estimated that there are places for 1,500,000 working men in the cities of the North. Go to it, my Southern Brothers, the North needs you." The paper assured its readers that its "statistics department" could not find a single case of blacks freezing to death, and besides, "better a thousand times, even if it were true, to run the chances of being nipped by the fingers of Jack Frost than to shake off this mortal coil at the end of the lynchers' rope. . . ."[4]

The First World War thus marked the beginning of a black exodus from the South that would continue for over half a century. The end result has been an almost complete transformation of the nation's black population—from agriculture to industry, from countryside to city, from South to North. Between 1910 and 1970 the percentage of blacks living in rural areas decreased from 73 to 19 percent, and the percentage living in the North increased from 11 to 48 percent. In less than a century, blacks would become even more urban than whites.[5]

4. *Chicago Defender,* October 1, 1916, p. 1.
5. "The Social and Economic Status of the Black Population in the United States, A Historical View, 1790–1978," *Current Population Reports,* Series P-23, No. 80 (Washington, D.C.: Government Printing Office, 1979), p. 14.

The proletarization of American blacks—that is, their escape from semifeudal conditions in the South and their entry into the industrial work force—was the result of a series of "push" and "pull" factors that conveniently correspond, more or less, to decennial periods:

1910s. As already mentioned, the initial impetus for black migration came from the cutoff of European immigration during the First World War. In 1914, immigration was at near-record levels; there were 1.2 million immigrant arrivals, a figure that would never again be duplicated. In a single year, immigration plummeted to 327,000; by 1918 it was only 111,000, or one-tenth the volume prior to the war. This cutoff occurred in the midst of a spectacular economic boom, augmented in part by the wartime mobilization. The number of wage earners employed in manufacturing increased from 7 million in 1914 to 9 million in 1919.[6] It was this urgent demand for labor that led to a lowering of the color line in industry, and this in turn triggered the first large-scale movement of blacks to the North. According to census estimates, between 1910 and 1920 there was a net migration of 454,000 southern blacks to the North, which exceeded the figure for the previous forty years combined.[7]

1920s. Similar conditions prevailed in the 1920s. Legislated restrictions on immigration and a high level of economic growth kept up the demand for black labor, and with the color line already broken, blacks made further advances into northern industry. Given these favorable conditions, the exodus from the South gained momentum, and net migration for the decade increased to 749,000.

1930s. The Depression eliminated the pull factors that had been drawing blacks to the industrial cities in the North. Indeed, blacks lost a third of the jobs that they had held in industry prior to the onset of the Depression. However, there were new push factors associated with the Depression that sustained black migration, though at reduced levels. Between 1929 and 1939, cotton land in production was cut almost in half, from 43 million acres to 23 million, and tens of thousands of black farmers and sharecroppers were

6. Harold Baron, "The Demand for Black Labor," *Radical America,* Vol. 5 (March–April 1971), reprinted by New England Free Press, p. 20.

7. "The Social and Economic Status of the Black Population in the United States, A Historical View, 1790–1978," op. cit., p. 14. Unless otherwise noted, figures on black migration come from this volume.

driven off the land.[8] New Deal farm policies also contributed to this trend by subsidizing reductions in acreage and by giving landowners an incentive to eliminate their tenant farmers. Thus, despite the employment crisis in northern industry, the exodus continued; net migration for the decade totaled 347,000.

1940s. The wartime economic boom generated an enormous demand for black labor, as it had during the First World War. In only two years, between 1940 and 1942, nonfarm employment increased from 32 to 40 million workers, and according to Harold Baron, this resulted in "the most dramatic improvement in economic status of black people that has ever taken place in the urban industrial economy."[9] A million and a half black workers were part of the war-production work force alone, and the income of black workers increased twice as fast as that of whites. Between 1940 and 1950 net migration from the South reached an all-time high of 1,600,000.

The Postwar Decades. Throughout the twentieth century, the introduction of labor-saving technology steadily reduced manpower needs in farming, but it was not until the postwar period that the full impact of the mechanization of agriculture was felt. With respect to cotton production, the use of tractors and herbicides first reduced cotton hands from year-round to seasonal workers whose labor was necessary mainly during the harvest. Then, in the 1950s, the harvest itself became mechanized, with the introduction of automatic cotton pickers.[10] New waves of black migrants moved to cities throughout the nation, in the West as well as the North. During the 1950s the net migration of blacks from the South totaled 1.5 million; the figure for the 1960s was almost as great. It was not until the early 1970s that the black exodus finally tapered off, in fact producing a slight return migration and thus reversing a trend that began with the first runaway slaves.

In 1860 a prescient writer, Thomas Eubank, published a pamphlet called "Inorganic Forces Ordained to Supersede Slavery." Eubank predicted that the day would come when machines would do the work of black field hands:

8. Baron, op. cit., pp. 25–27.
9. Ibid., p. 29.
10. Richard Day, "The Economics of Technological Change and the Demise of the Sharecropper," *American Economic Review,* June 1967, pp. 427–449.

. . . slaves will disappear from our plantations, for a piece of fuel costing less than the daily food of a negro will do more work in a day than several negroes. And as all people will ultimately have them, inducements to enslave negroes will finally pass away.[11]

Indeed, it was not until the mechanization of agriculture that blacks were finally released from the South and the oppressive system that bound them to the soil.

Of course, whites, too, have been profoundly affected by the mechanization of agriculture, and since the Second World War some 26 million whites, in addition to four million blacks, have been driven off the land. Today only about 4 percent of the nation's work force, and 3 percent of black laborers, make their living off the land, and even these figures are expected to be sharply reduced in the near future. This sweeping reorganization of agriculture, involving the elimination of the small farmer and the black peasantry in particular, has drastically altered the basis of race relations as black workers emerged from a semifeudal existence and entered the industrial work force. To be sure, racial exploitation and oppression would continue, but in an altogether different context.

In effect, a caste system evolved in industry that designated certain jobs as "negro jobs," and relegated black workers to the lowest-paying, menial, and not infrequently, back-breaking or dangerous jobs. Rarely did blacks rise to skilled job levels or to supervisory positions. Thus, as immigrant workers or their children climbed one or two occupational rungs, they were in effect replaced by black laborers who increasingly formed the base on which the occupational pyramid rested.

This transition from a feudal to an industrial caste system can be documented with a few summary statistics. In 1890, at the outset of the last great wave of immigration, 85 percent of black men and 96 percent of black women were employed in just two occupational categories: agriculture and domestic or personal service. Forty years later—at the onset of the Depression—90 percent of black women were still confined to these two areas, but in the case of black men, the figure had dropped to 54 percent.[12] However, virtually all of the

11. Thomas Eubank, "Inorganic Forces Ordained to Supersede Slavery," 1860 pamphlet, New York Historical Society, p. 31.

12. "Social and Economic Status of the Black Population," op. cit., p. 72.

remaining 46 percent were unskilled workers. A mere 5 percent were classified as white-collar workers, and this consisted largely of a small class of clergy, teachers, and businessmen serving the ghetto population. In short, racial segregation within and across occupational lines was nearly complete.

The Rise of a New Black Bourgeoisie

It was on a note of irony that Franklin Frazier chose *The Black Bourgeoisie* for the title of his 1957 study of the black middle class. Frazier's point was that the black middle class, notwithstanding a good deal of self-delusion, was far from an economic elite. Lacking any basis in the national economy, it consisted of a handful of professionals and owners of small businesses. Even those businesses that approached corporate size—a few banks, insurance companies, and newspapers—were based in the ghetto economy. Ironically, the "black bourgeoisie" owed its existence to patterns of racial segregation, and thus did not contradict the assumptions of a caste system.[13]

By the 1960s the caste character of the black labor force had undergone profound change. The labor shortages associated with the Second World War marked the beginning of a process of occupational diversification that continued during the postwar period. Today, for the first time, large numbers of blacks are found in every job sector—skilled as well as unskilled, white collar as well as blue collar. This is not to say that the nation is on the threshold of racial equality, for it is not. However, blacks are no longer confined to precapitalist sectors of the national economy—that is, to farm labor, domestic service, and other menial occupations reminiscent of slavery.

Again, a few statistics will help document this point. Whereas in 1940 62 percent of black men worked as farmers or unskilled laborers, by 1977 the figure had declined to 19 percent. The difference for women is even more striking, if only because their starting point was lower. In 1940 73 percent of black women in the labor force worked as domestics or as farm laborers, but by 1977 this

13. Franklin Frazier, *Black Bourgeoisie* (New York: Free Press, 1957).

figure was 11 percent.[14] It is premature to proclaim the end of racism, as some have done, since there remain large and even widening gaps between blacks and whites. But neither should this obscure the fact that the postwar period has witnessed a major breakdown, after two centuries, of America's caste system.

The clearest indication of the waning of caste is the emergence of a sizable black middle class, though the size of this middle class necessarily depends on how it is defined. In an article published in *Commentary* in 1973, Ben Wattenberg and Richard Scammon contended that a majority of blacks had attained middle-class status.[15] However, they stretched the definition of middle class to include all white-collar workers, including such groups as secretaries, retail workers, and security personnel whose wages leave them at or below the poverty line. This error was avoided in a more recent article, aptly entitled "The Illusion of Black Progress," where the author, Robert Hill, compiled data showing the number of blacks working in "high paying occupations," a category consisting mainly of professionals, businessmen, and craft workers. Contrary to Wattenberg and Scammon's optimistic conclusions, Hill found that in 1977 only a third of black men (32 percent) worked in these high-paying occupations, as compared to 52 percent of whites.[16]

Nevertheless, even 32 percent represented a big improvement over 1940, when only 7 percent of blacks worked in high-paying occupations, and cannot be dismissed as mere tokenism. Of equal importance is the fact that, for the first time in American history, the black middle class is based not in the ghetto economy but in mainstream occupational structures. Thus, despite the continuing gap between blacks and whites, there has been a collapse of the caste

14. "Social and Economic Status of the Black Population in the United States, 1790–1978," op. cit., pp. 74, 218.

15. Ben J. Wattenberg and Richard M. Scammon, "Black Progress and Liberal Rhetoric," *Commentary*, April 1973, p. 35.

16. Robert Hill, "The Illusion of Black Progress," *Social Policy*, November/December 1978, pp. 14–25. Also Everett Ladd, "The Kerner Commission: Ten Years Later," *Public Opinion Quarterly*, May/June 1978; and Reynolds Farley, "Trends in Racial Inequalities: Have the Gains of the 60s Disappeared in the 70s?" *American Sociological Review*, April 1977, pp. 189–208; Barbara Becnel, "Black Workers, Progress Derailed," in Jerome Skolnick and Elliot Currie, eds., *Crisis in American Institutions* (Boston: Little, Brown, 1979), pp. 149–68.

system that once relegated blacks almost without exception to the economic periphery.

The emergence of this new black bourgeoisie is not only important in itself, but will inevitably force changes in the prevailing images that whites have of blacks. In *The American Dilemma* Gunnar Myrdal observed that racism has a tendency to feed upon itself, as whites react to the conditions of lower-class life with still greater racism.[17] However, this "cycle of racism" operates in reverse as well. As more blacks achieve middle-class respectability, it becomes increasingly difficult for whites to maintain blanket assumptions of racial inferiority. Indeed, recent studies report a sharp decline in the extent to which Americans cling to traditional stereotypes of blacks.[18] Despite the unique potency of racist ideologies, there is every reason to expect that reductions in economic inequalities between whites and blacks will be accompanied by a waning of prejudice, as occurred with Irish, Jews, Japanese, and others who have risen in the class system.

The problem, however, is that the extent of racism in a society cannot be measured solely by the number of people who give unprejudiced answers to pollsters, or even by the extent to which norms of tolerance govern the nation's legal institutions. The sheer existence of a vast black underclass is prima facie evidence of institutionalized racism, and the continuing plight of this underclass casts a long shadow over the progress of the black middle class.

The Other Black America

According to figures published by the Bureau of Labor Statistics, roughly half of all black families in the United States can be said to be poor, twice the number for whites. These figures are based on the bureau's "lower budget," which in 1976 was set at just over $10,000 for an urban family of four. At best, this is a lean budget that allows for few amenities. Yet 54 percent of all black families

17. Gunnar Myrdal, *An American Dilemma* (New York: McGraw-Hill, 1974), pp. 75-78.
18. For example, Andrew M. Greeley and Paul B. Sheatsley, "Attitudes Toward Racial Integration," *Scientific American*, December 1971, pp. 13-19.

had incomes below this level, as compared to 27 percent of white families.[19]

The gloomiest statistics, insofar as the racial prognosis is concerned, pertain to black teenage unemployment. As the economy slipped into a recession in July 1980, the rate of unemployment for black teenagers reached 40 percent, more than twice the percentage for white teenagers.[20] This difference can no longer be attributed to educational deficiencies among blacks, since the educational gap between the two groups has narrowed considerably. Besides, contrary to popular belief, most of the new jobs being generated by the economy do not require extensive education or skills that cannot be acquired on the job.

The soaring rate of unemployment among black youth is largely a function of a massive overcrowding of the labor markets in cities where blacks are concentrated. New York City, for example, has lost 650,000 jobs since 1969, most of these in the manufacturing sector. The critical state of the job market, and the fact that black youth want to work, are demonstrated each summer when thousands of these teenagers line up for the relatively small number of federally subsidized summer jobs—which are low-paying, dead-end jobs that typically involve menial work.[21] This is hardly consistent with Midge Decter's claim that "there are all sorts of jobs that from one month or year to the next cannot find any takers."[22] Decter wrote this in the aftermath of the blackout and looting in New York City in August 1977, and she went on to dismiss the "liberal" argument that the poor cannot find jobs as "a laughable proposition." Yet in the same month that Decter's article went to press, 8,000 black youth turned out to apply for 2,000 jobs created

19. Hill, op. cit., p. 24. The Social Security Administration defines poverty at a level considerably below that used by the Bureau of Labor Statistics. In 1976 the poverty threshold was $5,815 for a nonfarm family of four. By this minimal definition 31 percent of blacks were poor, as compared to 9 percent of whites. ("Characteristics of the Population Below the Poverty Line," *Current Population Reports,* series P-60, No. 115, July 1978, p. 1.)

20. *Wall Street Journal,* August 21, 1980, p. 1.

21. For example, in 1978, 100,000 applications were received for 55,000 jobs under New York City's summer youth-employment program. *New York Times,* June 17, 1978, p. 2.

22. Midge Decter, "Looting and Liberal Racism," *Commentary,* September 1977, p. 52.

by the federal government to clean up the debris from the looting.[23]

Thus, at the same time that some blacks have made dramatic inroads into middle-class occupations, many others have been frozen out of the job market altogether. As Frances Piven and Richard Cloward have commented: "In effect, the black poor progressed from slave labor to cheap labor to (for many) no labor at all."[24]

Among blacks who are employed, many—probably a majority—work at jobs in the "secondary market" that are generally not unionized, involve unstable or irregular employment, pay low wages, offer few benefits, and provide no entrée to more desirable job categories. Not only are these workers falling further behind whites, but they have hardly progressed relative to their own parents and grandparents. Obviously, their lives and opportunities have not been enhanced by the good fortunes of the black middle class. If anything, the society at large has cynically used the example of blacks who have "made it" to minimize the significance of racism, and to blame the black underclass for its own plight. On the other hand, by threatening the stability of American society, this volatile underclass has functioned as a forceful reminder of the enduring significance of race.

The Changing Nature of Racial Conflict

In a society organized on racist principles—that is, white domination and black subordination—"racial harmony" depends on the routine maintenance of this hierarchical relationship. Since blacks have been less than content in this subordinate position, an elaborate system of controls has always been necessary to assure black compliance. When these controls have been most effective, racial

23. *New York Times*, August 10, 1977. Decter implies that these youths, having been coddled too long by liberals, will not settle for ordinary jobs, presumably as immigrants did, but insist on "good" jobs that will catapult them into the middle class. But the much-coveted cleanup jobs paid just $30 a day for a maximum of 33 days, and 6,000 applicants were turned away. The job crisis in New York City was dramatically pointed up in March, 1978 when 337,000 applicants took postman and clerk tests for 3,150 openings in the U.S. Postal Service (*New York Post*, March 1, 1978, p. 1).

24. Frances Fox Piven and Richard A. Cloward, *Poor People's Movements* (New York: Vintage Books, 1979), p. 184.

harmony has prevailed. Conversely, some of the most racially turbulent periods in American history have been those during which blacks have been most effective in challenging the racial status quo.

Historically, the term "race riots" has been applied indiscriminately to any violent episode between blacks and whites, regardless of who the rioters are, who gets hurt, and whose rights are at stake. The term "pogrom," for example, is devoid of such ambiguities. Now, it is one thing to repudiate violence by whites and blacks alike, but another to fail to distinguish between violence that affirms, and violence that negates, racism. Indeed, this distinction is crucial to an understanding of the changing character of racial conflict over the past century.

Prior to the Second World War, race riots were invariably instigated by whites determined to maintain and enforce patterns of racial segregation. "Nearly every overt racial clash in the North in the early twentieth century," writes historian Allan Spear, "involved conflict between blacks and working-class whites."[25] Fears of labor competition, often manipulated by employers who hired blacks as strikebreakers, were typically at the root of the conflict— the most notable examples are the riots in East St. Louis in 1917, in Chicago in 1919, and in Detroit in 1943. "In all three cities," Elliott Rudwick has observed, "unskilled whites manifested tension after they considered their jobs threatened by Negroes. . . . Economic conflict was inevitable because the industrial corporations had employed Negroes not only to supplement white labor but also to crush strikes and destroy unions."[26]

Since the Second World War, it is primarily blacks who have been the "disturbers of the racial peace." Of course, black protest itself is hardly a new development. As Herbert Aptheker has shown, even during slavery, revolts occurred often enough to compel slave society to institute an elaborate system of safeguards.[27]

25. Allan Spear, "The Origins of the Urban Ghetto, 1870–1915," in Nathan Huggins et al., eds., *Key Issues in the Afro-American Experience* (New York: Harcourt Brace Jovanovich, 1971), p. 163. See also William Tuttle, Jr., "Labor Conflict and Racial Violence," *Labor History* 10 (Summer 1969), pp. 408–32.

26. Elliott Rudwick, *Race Riot at East St. Louis* (Carbondale: Southern Illinois University Press, 1964), p. 218.

27. Herbert Aptheker, *Negro Slave Revolts in the United States* (New York: International Publishers, 1939).

Indeed, there is no period in Afro-American history that is devoid of significant protest, though it was not until the emergence of the civil rights movement in the late 1950s and early '60s that black protest reached political maturity. Here for the first time was a full-fledged protest movement, with the leadership, organization, resources, and popular base to mobilize and sustain a direct assault on racist structures.

Why the civil rights movement began in the 1950s, and not sooner, cannot be answered simply. Certainly, a "great man theory" of history does not shed much light. The black community has always had leaders with the charisma and vision of Martin Luther King, Jr., as well as courageous individuals like Mrs. Rosa Parks, whose refusal to move to the rear of a bus in Montgomery, Alabama, in 1955 helped to spark the black revolt (the Congress of Racial Equality, for example, used sit-in tactics during the 1940s). In explaining why the civil rights movement did not take root until the 1950s, great weight must be given to the fact that with the modernization of southern agriculture, the caste system became increasingly obsolete. As blacks were freed from feudal constraints, it became feasible, as Piven and Cloward have suggested, "to construct the occupational and institutional foundation from which to mount resistance to white oppression."[28]

Other factors also worked to make the 1950s an opportune time for racial change. For one thing, Jim Crow practices were becoming increasingly problematic to the nation's conduct of international affairs during the Cold War, especially when African and Asian diplomats in this country were subjected to racial indignities.[29] For another thing, as the black vote in the North grew in size and importance, the northern wing of the Democratic Party gradually broke ranks with the southern segregationists. In addition, the 1954 Supreme Court decision in *Brown* v. *Board of Education of Topeka, Kansas* placed a mantle of legitimacy on racial protest and signaled a new era in race relations. Numerous other factors would have to be cited to explain the genesis and success of the civil rights movement, and the specific direction that it assumed, but the factor of overriding significance was that by the 1950s economic change

28. Piven and Cloward, op. cit., 205.

29. C. Vann Woodward, *The Strange Career of Jim Crow* (New York: Oxford University Press, 1966); Piven and Cloward, op. cit., chap. 4.

had obviated the Jim Crow practices established during the post-Reconstruction era. Harold Baron has put it well:

> While the civil-rights movement and the heroic efforts associated with it were necessary to break the official legality of segregation, it should be recognized that in a sense this particular form of racism was already obsolete, as its base in an exploitative system of production had drastically changed.[30]

The civil rights movement can claim at least two monumental achievements, both defined against the crimes of the past: it brought an end to the reign of terror in the South, and it elevated blacks to full citizenship under the law. In both respects the civil rights movement set the stage for a process of orderly change, especially as the black vote became increasingly important in local, state, and national elections. Yet at the same time the movement helped to unleash forces of change that would operate outside conventional political channels. The increased militancy of the movement for equal rights did much to heighten consciousness and galvanize protest among blacks who lived in urban ghettos across the nation, but even in its successes, it did little to alleviate their plight. Furthermore, the organizations that had effectively spearheaded the movement for equal rights were not equipped, ideologically or tactically, to deal with the massive problems of the ghetto. It is in this context that a series of "race riots" exploded in cities across the nation between 1965 and 1968.

At the time most Americans, including most national leaders, viewed the riots as sheer anarchism, an extension of deep-seated antisocial tendencies in the black community. Even liberal supporters of civil rights were appalled by the violent turn of events, which they feared would wipe out the gains acquired through nonviolence. Since the destruction of property was limited almost entirely to black neighborhoods, the riots seemed all the more irrational, and the widespread looting, projected daily on network television, reinforced the popular belief that the riots were nothing more than the collective acts of aberrant individuals. Edward Banfield, the Harvard-based interlocutor of the conventional wisdom, entitled his essay "Rioting for Fun and Profit," and wrote:

30. Baron, op. cit., p. 33.

It would appear, then, that what requires explanation is not so much rebellion by Negroes (whether against the whites, the slum, their "own masochism," the police, or something else) as it is outbreaks of the "carnival spirit" and of stealing by slum dwellers, mostly boys and young men and mostly Negroes.[31]

A radically different set of conclusions was reached by the National Advisory Commission on Civic Disorders, popularly known as the Kerner Commission.[32] The studies conducted by the commission invalidated the "riffraff theory," which assumed that the riots were the doing of a small number of aberrant black youths. The commission found that while the number of active participants was small, they constituted a significant proportion of the young male population; furthermore, participants were no more likely than nonparticipants to be school dropouts, to have arrest records, or to be unemployed. Finally, public opinion polls conducted in the aftermath of the riots found that while few blacks expressed outright support for the riots, many felt they would bring beneficial results, and most were resigned to their inevitability so long as conditions remained unchanged. To attempt to grasp the meaning of the riots only by focusing on the characteristics of the actual participants, therefore, is to miss the point that the riots grew out of smoldering resentments that run throughout the ghetto population.

Nor was the violence as unrestrained or indiscriminate as was widely believed. As Robert Fogelson, one of the consultants to the Kerner Commission, writes in *Violence as Protest:* ". . . [T]hough the rioters destroyed millions of dollars of property, and devastated whole sections of the ghettos, they burned mainly stores that charged excessive prices or sold inferior goods (or did both) and left homes, schools, and churches unharmed."[33]

---

31. Banfield, *The Unheavenly City Revisited* (Boston: Little, Brown, 1974), p. 225.

32. *Report of the National Advisory Commission on Civil Disorders* (New York: Bantam Books, 1968). For a summary of the commission's findings, see Robert M. Fogelson, *Violence as Protest* (New York: Doubleday, 1971), chap. 1.

33. Ibid., p. 17.

If there was sometimes a "carnival spirit," as Banfield claims, it expressed a sense of exhilaration among people who are normally powerless and vicitimized at having fought back. This mood is captured in Tom Hayden's firsthand account of the Newark riot:

> People voted with their feet to expropriate property to which they felt entitled. They were tearing up the stores with the trick contracts and installment plans, the second-hand television sets going for top-quality prices, the phony scales, the inferior meat and vegetables. A common claim was: this is owed me. But few needed to argue. People who under ordinary conditions respected law because they were forced to do so now felt free to act upon the law as they thought it should be. When an unpopular store was opened up, with that mighty crash of glass or ripping sound of metal, great shouts of joy would sound. "Hey, they got Alice's!" "They gave that place what he deserved." "They did? G-o-o-d!"[34]

The essentially political character of the riots is demonstrated even more clearly by examining their effects rather than by dwelling on their causes. At the height of the violence, when lives were tragically lost and whole sections of cities destroyed, and when the protests were effectively snuffed out by brute force, they certainly appeared to be senseless and even counterproductive. But the final judgment must be reserved until the indirect and long-term consequences can be assessed. In retrospect, there were at least three major outcomes of riots that can be said to have advanced the struggle for racial equality.

First, in the wake of the riots, the federal government launched major new initiatives to deal with "the urban crisis," and the plight of blacks in particular. This has been carefully documented in James Button's book *Black Violence,* which examines the policy reactions of three federal agencies active in urban affairs—the Office of Economic Opportunity, Housing and Urban Development, and the Department of Justice. Button found that all three agencies pumped massive amounts of money into cities that had been torn by riots,

34. Tom Hayden, *Rebellion in Newark* (New York: Random House, 1967), p. 30.

and introduced a plethora of new programs designed to remedy conditions that were believed to have spawned the riots.[35]

Though these programs were unveiled with much fanfare and political bombast, they were deficient in several respects. First of all, the level of funding, while substantial, was far from adequate given the enormity of the problem. For example, from 1965 to 1972, federal grants for the "war on poverty" totaled only 15 billion dollars, compared to more than 120 billion that was spent in Vietnam. In addition, most programs were not designed to attack the root causes of poverty; at best, they could alleviate some of the hardships associated with poverty by providing services and cash assistance to the poor. The underlying purpose of these programs was to keep the cities "cool," and as Button shows, once the level of violence subsided and the ideological winds changed, most of the programs were dismantled or the level of funding drastically reduced. As one writer suggested, they amounted to a form of "ghetto pacification."[36] Nevertheless, billions were spent on the "war on poverty" as a direct result of the riots, and even if only palliatives, expanded welfare and improved services did provide partial and temporary relief for millions of the nation's poor.

A second positive result of the riots is that they advanced the cause of equal rights. Though most black leaders condemned the riots and feared a white backlash that might wipe out the gains achieved through peaceful protest, the opposite happened. For example, in the 1950s Martin Luther King was widely viewed as an extremist who was pushing the nation to a race war, but against the background of burning cities he emerged as the epitome of "moderate" and "responsible" leadership, and the goals of the civil rights movement were granted a new legitimacy. In this way the ghetto uprisings made it easier for established black leaders to win concessions from white power structures.

Thus a third benefit emanating from the riots is that the nation's corporate elite, fearful of the mounting level of violence in the nation's cities, launched ambitious programs for recruiting and

35. James W. Button, *Black Violence* (Princeton: Princton University Press, 1978), p. 3.

36. Robert L. Allen, *Black Awakening in Capitalist America* (Garden City: Doubleday, 1970), p. 239.

training black workers. The result was the first significant integration of the nation's white-collar work force, including lower and middle management. Writing from a leftist perspective, Robert Allen has dismissed this as an attempt to "generate a black capitalist buffer class firmly wedded (in both financial and ideological terms) to the white power structure."[37] It is yet to be seen whether the black middle class will develop class interests in opposition to the black masses, or whether it will provide leadership and assistance, but one thing is clear: the new black bourgeoisie owes its existence to the ghetto revolts of the 1960s.

As Button observed, the tendency among social scientists to be philosophically opposed to violence and to believe in the possibility of peaceful change has deterred them from even asking whether violence in specific situations might function as an instrument of change. To be sure, the ghetto uprisings exacted great costs in human life and they risked a dangerous backlash, but this should not obscure the fact that they constituted a form of protest and advanced the cause of racial equality. As Robert Weaver has commented: "The ills of our society must be dramatized. In this sense the riots aroused conscience, or guilt, or fear that resulted in *action*. We need something to 'galvanize' society and government."[38] Even more to the point, perhaps, is the fact that our society and government seem incapable of action until their stability is threatened, and in this sense it is not violence that galvanizes political action but rather political inertia that galvanizes violence.

What Ethnic Backlash?

The migration of blacks to northern cities and the rising level of racial protest have exacerbated the historic rivalry between immigrants and blacks. Wherever blacks went, it seemed that one or another ethnic group occupied the stratum just above them, and therefore black efforts for self-advancement tended to arouse ethnic loyalties and provoke an ethnic response. In this way a conflict that was fundamentally one between the haves and the have-nots—or more accurately, between the have-nots and those who have a little

37. Ibid., p. 220.
38. Quoted in Button, op. cit., p. 159.

—assumed the external marks of an ethnic conflict, giving the appearance that culture rather than class was at the root of the conflict.

Specifically, the migration of some four million blacks to cities in the North and West since the Second World War has placed blacks and working-class ethnics on a collision course, as they competed for jobs, neighborhoods, schools, and government services. Just as native-born Americans a half-century earlier reacted against the "immigrant invasion" on the basis of ancestry and nationality, these ethnic groups see themselves threatened by a "black invasion," and use their ethnicity to justify the exclusion of blacks. William Wilson provides this description of the situation in Chicago:

> . . . white working-class ethnics are stressing that their ethnic institutions and unique ways of life are being threatened by black encroachment on their neighborhoods, the increase of black crime, and the growth of black militancy. The emphasis is not simply that blacks pose a threat to whites but that they also pose a threat to, say, the Polish in Gage Park, the Irish in Brighton Park, the Italians in Cicero, or the Serbians, Romanians, and Croatians in Hegewisch. These communities are a few of the many ethnic communities in the Chicago area threatened by the possibilities of a black invasion, and their response has been to stress not only the interests of whites in general but the interests of their specific ethnic groups as well.[39]

The claim that blacks threaten the ethnic character of neighborhoods should perhaps be regarded with skepticism. The Poles and Slavs in Chicago, like the Irish in South Boston and the Jews in Forest Hills, rarely experience their ethnicity so acutely as when threatened with racial integration. Typically, these neighborhoods already have a broad ethnic mix, even though one or another ethnic group may predominate, and what is being resisted is not the introduction of ethnic outsiders, but specifically the introduction of blacks.

Yet even the blatant racism on the part of white ethnics should not be taken at face value. It is far from clear that white resistance to integration stems from race prejudice per se. Often it is the same

39. William Julius Wilson, *The Declining Significance of Race* (Chicago: University of Chicago Press, 1978), p. 117.

people who work amicably beside blacks on the job, and who are appropriately deferential to blacks whom they encounter in positions of status and authority, who become rabid in their opposition to integration. Their fears are not rooted in prejudice—that is, in superstition and irrationality—so much as in the realities of a class society. What is feared is not racial contamination, but reduced property values; not racial mixing, but deteriorating neighborhoods and schools. At bottom, the so-called ethnic backlash is a conflict between the racial have-nots and the ethnics who have a little and are afraid of losing even that.

Other factors have heightened tensions between Jews and blacks, threatening the traditional alliance between these two groups as well. Of course, Jews living in affluent suburbs are generally insulated from encroachments by the black lower class. However, in New York and other cities in the Northeast, blacks inherited the neighborhoods abandoned by upwardly mobile Jews, though property generally remained in the hands of the original owners. As a result, a disproportionate number of slum landlords and merchants were Jews. Though studies indicate that blacks tend to perceive Jews as a persecuted minority and as an ally to black causes, the Jewish role in the ghetto economy inevitably produced resentments.[40] As James Baldwin wrote in *The New York Times Magazine* in 1969, "the Jew is singled out by Negroes not because he acts differently from other white men, but because he doesn't. . . . He is playing the role assigned him by Christians long ago: he is doing their dirty work."[41] Despite fears that Jews would be singled out for attack during the ghetto uprisings, this generally did not happen. Even in their rage the rioters had the political savvy not to equate "the enemy" with "the Jew."

In other ways, too, Jews often have found themselves in the role of middleman between blacks and an exploitative society. Their own marginality in business meant that Jews were often the employers of blacks on jobs that paid substandard wages, and the concentration of Jews in the civil service bureaucracy—as teachers,

40. For two empirical studies of black-Jewish tensions, see Gary Marx, *Protest and Prejudice* (New York: Harper & Row, 1967), chaps. 6 and 7; and Gertrude Jaeger Selznick and Stephen Steinberg, *The Tenacity of Prejudice* (New York: Harper & Row, 1968), pp. 111–31.

41. James Baldwin, "Negroes are Anti-Semitic Because They Are Anti-White," *New York Times Magazine,* April 9, 1967, p. 137.

welfare workers, and government officials—also stirred reaction as blacks revolted against the "colonization" of their communities. Even the Jewish role in civil rights organizations came to be resented as blacks demanded control over their own liberation movement.

Finally, as the civil rights movement grew more militant, and as the black agenda began to threaten Jewish interests, the alliance between Jews and blacks became increasingly strained. A series of clashes in New York City over the issue of school decentralization widened the breach between the two groups, and on a national scale, many Jews were outspoken opponents of affirmative action, which they saw as a threat to their position of higher education and in the professions. Thus, even as blacks climbed out of poverty, the competitive struggle with groups just above them on the ladder of privilege would continue.

Conclusion

The historic rivalry between blacks and immigrants had now gone full circle. If blacks had been allowed, at the turn of the century, to compete for the industrial jobs that provided opportunity to millions of immigrants, they would today occupy a position in the class system similar to that of Irish, Italians, Poles, and other immigrants who were entering the industrial labor market for the first time. Their exclusion, however, set the stage for generations of conflict as blacks and white ethnics became unequal competitors for social and economic advantage.

In 1971 the *Amsterdam News*, New York's leading black newspaper, printed a cartoon that serves as a poignant rebuttal to the claim of immigrant groups that "we made it, why haven't you?" It portrayed a black figure prostrated on the ground as a chain of other figures representing various immigrant groups climbed the tree of success.[42] Nor does this imagery apply only to the distant past. Since 1970 the United States has absorbed more than four million immigrants and refugees, and perhaps twice that number of illegal aliens.[43] And like earlier immigrants, the newcomers have crowded the labor markets, competing with blacks for already scarce opportunities.

42. *Amsterdam News,* October 23, 1971.
43. *New York Times,* December 28, 1980, p. A1.

Chapter 9

———◆———

The "Jewish Problem" in American Higher Education

*"His world was dead. Not a Polish Jew fresh from
Warsaw or Cracow—not a furtive Yacoob or Ysaac
still reeking of the Ghetto, snarling a weird Yiddish
to the officers of the customs—but had a keener instinct,
an intenser energy, and a freer hand than he—American
of Americans, with Heaven knew how many Puritans
and Patriots behind him. . . ."*

The Education of Henry Adams, 1918

THE UNITED STATES opened its doors to Europe's impoverished
masses because labor was needed for the nation's burgeoning industries. It was never envisioned, except perhaps by rabid nativists,
that the children of immigrants might soon demand entry into
such a bastion of privilege as Harvard University. Yet the rapidly
expanding economy that formed the basis for mass immigration
also provided opportunities for class mobility, and given their initial
advantages as skilled workers and traders, Jews were among the
first to attempt to enter WASP society. Indeed, by the 1920s enough
Jews were enrolled at Harvard to create a "Jewish problem," as

Samuel Eliot Morison notes in his history *Three Centuries of Harvard*:

> The first German Jews who came [to Harvard] were easily absorbed into the social pattern; but at the turn of the century the bright Russian Jewish lads from the Boston public schools began to arrive. There was enough of them in 1906 to form the Menorah Society, and in another fifteen years Harvard had her "Jewish problem."[1]

From the perspective of Abbott Lawrence Lowell, president of Harvard from 1906 to 1933, the problem was that the increasing numbers of Jewish students at Harvard threatened to alter the traditional character of the college. To the Jews of the period, it was that the university for the first time was preparing to impose religious quotas.

By 1922 Columbia and New York University had already begun to restrict Jewish enrollment. But they had done so covertly, relying on character tests and regional quotas to conceal their intentions. Harvard was, however, the first openly to advocate and defend a quota system. In June 1922, the university issued an official announcement that began by citing the recent increase in student enrollment and the consequent shortage of classrooms and dormitories. It was then stated, rather ominously, that "[t]his problem is really a group of problems, all difficult, and most of them needing for their settlement more facts than we now have." And finally: "It is natural that with a widespread discussion of this sort going on there should be talk about the proportion of Jews at the college. At present the whole problem of limitation of enrollment is in the stage of general discussion and it may remain in that stage for a considerable time."[2]

This event at Harvard was not an isolated event, but culminated a forty-year period of evolving confrontation between American Jews and the system of higher education. In a sense, Harvard's "Jewish problem" was only a reflection of the "Jewish problem" in early-twentieth-century American society.

1. Samuel Eliot Morison, *Three Centuries of Harvard* (Cambridge: Harvard University Press, 1936), p. 147.
2. *New York Times*, June 2, 1922, p. 1.

The Emergence of a "Jewish Problem"

Prior to the influx of Eastern European Jews beginning in 1881, the nation's Jewish population was a small, inconspicuous, and highly assimilated group. Most were either descendants of early settlers or recent German immigrants. In all they numbered roughly a quarter of a million in a population of 63 million, or less than one percent. As Nathan Glazer comments, ". . . before 1880 or 1890 there were too few American Jews for them to constitute a question."[3]

Aside from their small numbers, German Jews were mostly middle class and blended in culturally with the American mainstream. The prevailing mood in the Jewish community was to abandon outmoded beliefs and customs, and to seek ways to reconcile traditional Judaism with the demands of modern society. This was the period during which the Reform movement flourished and reached its most radical expression, as reflected in its adoption of a set of principles which rejected all Mosaic laws "not adapted to the views and habits of modern civilization."[4]

A small Jewish population, its integration into the class system, the absence of sharp cultural differences between Jews and non-Jews, the mood of accommodation in the Jewish community—these factors contributed to a low level of religious conflict during most of the nineteenth century. However, beneath the surface of religious harmony was a layer of anti-Semitic beliefs and stereotypes that was a legacy of the past. As John Higham writes: ". . . the Jews in early nineteenth century America got along very well with their non-Jewish neighbors although American conceptions of Jews in the abstract at no time lacked the unfavorable elements embedded in European tradition."[5]

The presence of anti-Semitic conceptions, however inert, did not augur well for the immigrants from Eastern Europe. Even before

3. Nathan Glazer, "Social Characteristics of American Jews, 1654–1954" *American Jewish Yearbook,* vol. 56 (1955), p. 9.
4. Nathan Glazer, *American Judaism* (Chicago: University of Chicago Press, 1962), p. 151.
5. John Higham, "Social Discrimination Against Jews in America, 1830–1930," *Publication of the American Jewish Historical Society,* vol. 47, no. 1 (September 1957), p. 3.

their arrival, upwardly mobile Jews of German origin confronted social barriers erected by a nervous Protestant upper class. The economic expansion after mid-century created a new class of wealthy capitalists, some Jews among them, who challenged the position of the "Old Guard." It was largely in response to this development that, as Oscar and Mary Handlin put it, "after 1880 the longings for exclusive, quasi-aristocratic status increasingly found satisfaction in associations with an hereditary basis."[6] Yankee ancestry became a condition for respectability, and the old class sought refuge in exclusive societies and resorts. According to Higham, "during the 1880s anti-Semitic discriminations spread like wildfire through the vacation grounds of New York State and the Jersey shore."[7] Discrimination also became the practice in prestigious clubs, including some university alumni clubs, and in certain private schools in the East.

By 1924, the year that immigration quotas were imposed, the nation's Jewish population had increased to nearly four million. Moreover, Jews were heavily concentrated in the urban centers of the Northeast, where they did in fact constitute a significant portion of the population. The Jewish population of New York, the port of arrival for most immigrants, grew from 80,000 in 1880 to 1,225,000 in 1910.[8]

Even more important than the increase in numbers was the social character of the newer immigrants. Impoverished, refugees from persecution, natives of an alien and sometimes backward culture, adherents of pre-modern religious beliefs and customs, the East European Jews were a new and highly visible element in American life. The spectacle of over one million Jews clustered in New York City aroused a predictably xenophobic reaction. America now had a "Jewish problem," and American nativism a new target.

The essence of the "Jewish problem" was how to control the influx of Jews into areas of social life that were preserves for upper-class Protestants. By 1920 a pattern of anti-Jewish discrimination

6. Oscar Handlin and Mary F. Handlin, "The Acquisition of Political and Social Rights by the Jews in the United States," in *American Jewish Yearbook*, vol. 56 (1955), p. 72.

7. Higham, op. cit., p. 12.

8. Nathan Glazer and Daniel Patrick Moynihan, *Beyond the Melting Pot* (Cambridge: MIT Press, 1970), pp. 138–9.

had become still more prevalent, especially in the Northeast, where the Jewish settlements were located. Discrimination became commonplace in neighborhoods, clubs, resorts, and private boarding schools, and was making headway wherever else Jews turned out in large numbers.

The social barriers that Jews encountered reinforced a tendency to withdraw into their own communities and to establish their own institutions. This mood was reflected in the Reform movement, which no longer held the reconciliation of Judaism to the demands of modern society as a primary objective. Traditions were reinstituted that only a few years before had been dismissed as unenlightened, and the spirit of Reform was replaced by the self-protective concerns embodied in the Jewish defense agencies founded during this period.[9]

Thus at a time when immigrant Jewish children were entering college, a climate of intolerance toward Jews was intensifying. Manifested in patterns of social discrimination and fueled by an outpouring of anti-Semitic propaganda, anti-Semitism now figured prominently in American life. Jews, whether German or Russian, middle class or lower class, were lumped together with other aliens who were threatening Anglo-Saxon supremacy. The eastern colleges—elitist, repositories of Puritan values and upper-class standards—could not remain impervious to these trends, especially when their enrollments contained increasing numbers of Jewish students.

The Jewish Penchant for Education

"The Jew undergoes privation, spills blood, to educate his child," boasts an editorial in a 1902 *Jewish Daily Forward*. "In [this] is reflected one of the finest qualities of the Jewish people. It shows our capacity to make sacrifices for our children . . . as well as our love for education, for intellectual efforts."[10]

9. Stephen Steinberg, "Reform Judaism: The Origin and Evolution of a 'Church Movement,'" *Journal for the Scientific Study of Religion* 5 (Fall 1965), pp. 117–29. The American Jewish Committee was founded in 1906; the Anti-Defamation League in 1913.

10. Quoted in Ronald Sanders, *Downtown Jews* (New York: Harper & Row, 1969), pp. 259–60.

While the Jewish passion for education is often romanticized, the fact is that Jewish immigrants did place high value on education and sent more of their children to college than did other immigrant groups. As the *Forward*'s editorial observed: "You don't find many German, Irish or Italian children in City College. About 90 percent of the boys there are Jews, and most of them children of Jewish workers." What the *Forward* neglected to mention was that, as Jewish enrollment at City College increased, the children of Anglo-Saxon, Dutch, German, and Huguenot descent went elsewhere for their education.[11]

As more and more Jews enrolled in City College, it acquired a reputation for being a "Jewish school." Indeed, by 1920 both City College and Hunter College had become between 80 and 90 percent Jewish. A number of other eastern colleges showed rapid increases in their Jewish enrollment.[12] Before Columbia instituted restrictive quotas after World War I, it had a Jewish enrollment of 40 percent. The figure for New York University was probably higher; the figure for Harvard was 20 percent. Without its pejorative implications, the notion of a "Jewish invasion" would not be inappropriate for describing the trends in these institutions prior to World War I.

The high rate of college attendance among Jews occurred at a time when American society did not place much value on higher education. The vast majority of Americans were employed in occupations that required few skills, especially of the kind that come with formal education. For most people anything beyond a rudimentary knowledge of the three R's had little practical value, and the tendency in the schools was to emphasize "life adjustment" rather than intellectual development. The individual who graduated from high school was the exception, not the rule. Those who did complete high school came mostly from the more affluent strata of society. They alone could afford to postpone employment and could see in a high school or college education some ultimate economic benefit.

Although most immigrant Jewish children in the early 1900s did not receive a high school education, the proportion who did

---

11. S. Willis Rudy, *The College of the City of New York: A History, 1847–1947* (New York: City College Press, 1949), pp. 292–93.

12. Heywood Broun and George Britt, *Christians Only* (New York: Vanguard Press, 1931), pp. 104–63.

so exceeded the average for most other groups. A 1922 study of one eastern high school found that, in comparison with most other immigrant groups as well as native-born Americans, Russian-Jewish students were more likely to reach high school, more likely to finish high school if they entered, and more likely to enroll in college preparatory rather than community or scientific courses. However, the operation of class factors is suggested by the fact that the record of Jewish children was surpassed by the children of German and Scandinavian parents.[13]

Nor did it demand any special talent to gain admission to college, even a prestigious college. Fifty years ago the gates to most of the nation's colleges were open to anyone with minimal academic credentials. In 1922 admission to Harvard was guaranteed to anyone with appropriate high-school training who passed an entrance examination. Thus, Jews did not face intense competition from non-Jews, at least not on today's scale. With determination, average intellect, and modest financial resources, a student could make his way through the academic system.

The fact that the Jewish entry into institutions of higher learning began with the children of immigrants rather than with later generations was of utmost significance, since they inevitably carried the mark of their immigrant background. The editorial in the *Jewish Daily Forward* could take pride in Jewish students marching off to City College with clothes that were "mostly poor and old." But they were greeted with indignation and hostility by their upper-class schoolmates, especially in the Ivy League schools. A writer in a 1923 edition of *The Nation* put it bluntly: the upwardly mobile Jew "sends his children to college a generation or two sooner than other stocks, and as a result there are in fact more dirty Jews and tactless Jews in college than dirty and tactless Italians, Armenians, or Slovaks."[14]

13. George Sylvester Counts, "The Selective Character of American Secondary Education," *Supplementary Educational Monographs*, no. 19 (Chicago: University of Chicago Press, 1922), p. 108.

14. Lewis S. Gannett, "Is America Anti-Semitic?" *The Nation*, March 14, 1923, p. 331.

The Transformation of Higher Education

No matter how strong the Jewish penchant for education, it would have been of little consequence if educational opportunities were not plentiful. It was fortuitous that the tide of Jewish immigration from Eastern Europe coincided with a period of unprecedented expansion in American higher education. Between 1890 and 1925 college enrollments grew nearly five times as fast as the population.

Just as important as the physical expansion of the university were the related innovations in educational content. For several decades a revolt had been gaining momentum against the classical curriculum which consisted principally of Latin, Greek, rhetoric, mathematics, and natural philosophy. By the 1880s the attitude that all knowledge must begin with the classics was giving way to demands for practical education. As one historian of education writes:

> Vocational and technical education had become a legitimate function of American higher education, and everywhere the idea of going to college was being liberated from the class-bound, classical-bound traditions which for so long had defined the American college experience.[15]

Behind this changing conception of higher education was the advancing industrial and scientific revolution that created a need for an educated managerial class as well as for trained professionals and technicians. Thus Latin and Greek were no longer required for admission to most colleges, and the "elective principle" was instituted to free students from traditionally required subjects. The curriculum was overhauled to prepare students for careers in business, engineering, scientific farming, and the arts, and a variety of new professions such as accounting and pharmacy that were making their appearance in American colleges for the first time. By thus abandoning its lofty pretensions, the American college became compatible with the abilities and aspirations of those born outside the upper class.

15. Frederick Rudolph, *The American College and University* (New York: Random House, 1962), p. 263.

The Genteel Tradition

One writer in 1910 observed that in American colleges there were "two classes, the one, favored according to undergraduate thinking, holding its position by financial ability to have a good time with leisure for carrying off athletic and other showy prizes; the other class, in sheer desperation taking the faculty, textbooks and debating more seriously. Each class runs in the same rut all its life."[16] Second-generation Jews obviously did not have the economic resources or the social standing to participate in the collegiate "leisure class." For them a college education was less a mark of status than a vehicle of escape from the lower class, and this inevitably gave Jewish students a unique sense of purpose.

The outstanding academic record of Jewish students was commonly acknowledged during the early 1900s. According to one observer: "At every university and college that I have visited, I have heard ungrudging praise of the exceptional ability of the Jewish, especially of the Russian Jewish, students."[17] Yet praise was not always ungrudging. Another writer comments that "history is full of examples where one race has displaced another by underliving and overworking."[18] Indeed, Jewish academic success aroused considerable resentment on the part of non-Jews, especially given the "taboo on scholarship," as one Yale professor called it, that characterized student culture during this period.

Early in the century, the prevailing mood in the American college, especially in the prestigious eastern colleges, was anything but one of seriousness and devotion to learning. According to one historian:

> The undergraduate temperament was marked by a strong resistance to abstract thinking and to the work of the classroom in general, by traits of practicality, romanticism, and high-spiritedness, and by passive acceptance of moral, political, and religious values taken from the non-academic society at large.[19]

16. Lawrence R. Veysey, *The Emergence of the American University* (Chicago: University of Chicago Press, 1965), pp. 270–71.

17. Alexander Francis, *Americans* (London: Andrew Melrose, 1909), p. 187.

18. William M. Cook, *American Institutions and Their Preservation* (Norwood, Mass.: Norwood Press, 1927), p. 125.

19. Veysey, op. cit., p. 272.

Another historian of the period writes:

> Now what mattered for so many young men was not the course of study but the environment of friendships, social development, fraternity houses, good sportsmanship, athletic teams. The world of business was a world of dealing with people. What better preparation could there be than the collegiate life outside the classroom—the club room, the playing field, where the qualities that showed what stuff a fellow really was made of were bound to be encouraged.[20]

It would be difficult to exaggerate the extent to which honor societies, Greek-letter fraternities, eating clubs, and sports dominated undergraduate life. "The cultivation of gentility," as Thorstein Veblen called it, was pursued to the exclusion of virtually all other values. The prevailing attitude toward scholarship was at best one of indifference, as symbolized by the concept and reality of the "gentleman's C."

The class origins of students in the elite colleges was of central importance. Recruited largely from upper-class families, their route to college typically traversed the private preparatory school. In 1909, for example, 78 percent of Princeton students and 65 percent of Yale students came from prep schools.[21] Significantly, the figure for Harvard was lower—47 percent. In these colleges, upper-class students established a clubbish atmosphere and patterns of expensive and frivolous habits. Veblen bluntly called them "gentlemen's colleges" where "scholarship is . . . made subordinate to genteel dissipation, to a grounding in those methods of conspicuous consumption that should engage the thought and energies of a well-to-do man of the world."[22]

It was no doubt reflective of class formations elsewhere in society that higher education assumed the features of a caste system. At the top of the hierarchy stood Harvard, Yale, and Princeton, with Columbia struggling to retain its elite position. Within each institution was a wealthy class that dominated social life and set patterns imitated at less prestigious schools. The leading institutions

20. Rudolph, op. cit., p. 289.
21. Ibid.
22. Thorstein Veblen, *The Higher Learning in America* (New York: Sagamore Press, 1967), pp. 87–88.

were measured as much in terms of these status characteristics as by academic excellence.

Jews constituted a threat to this genteel tradition. They did so, first of all, because they were generally lower class and violated what Veblen called "the canons of genteel intercourse." Even when this was not the case, Jews were unwanted simply because they were Jews, and it was feared that their presence might sully the reputation of the college and its students. Finally, the seriousness and diligence with which Jews pursued their studies not only represented unwelcome competition, but implicitly called into question the propriety of a "gentleman's college."

Some of the flavor of this conflict is conveyed in an autobiographical essay entitled "The Coming of the Jews." The author, Francis Russell, came from an old-guard Protestant family and attended the Boston Latin School, an elite public high school that sent its best students to Harvard. By 1920 it had become heavily Jewish and with a mixture of admiration and scorn, Russell compares his complacent middle-class assumptions to the drive and competitiveness of his Jewish classmates:

> My own background was middle-class, Protestant, noncompetitive, like that of most Roxbury Latin boys. I had always taken for granted that I should go to Harvard because my father in his time had gone there; and I never doubted the possibility of this any more than I stopped to consider whether I really wanted to or not. That Harvard could be the goal of anyone's ambitions never occurred to me.

In contrast, Jews

> worked far into each night, their lessons next morning were letter perfect, they took obvious pride in their academic success and talked about it. At the end of each year there were room prizes given for excellency in each subject, and they were openly after them. There was none of the Roxbury solidarity of pupils versus the master. If anyone reciting made a mistake that the master overlooked, twenty hands shot into the air to bring it to his attention.

Such a competitive situation does not generate good feeling, especially when the group with superior status takes second place. As

Russell says: "It was a fierce and gruelling competition. . . . Some of us in the Gentile rump were fair students, most of us lazy and mediocre ones, and by our position at the foot of the class we despised the industry of those little Jews." It was just as inevitable that Jews would begrudge the status and privilege of their competitors: "They hated us in return with the accumulated resentment of the past, and because they knew that the way for us was easier."[23]

The picture that emerges from Russell's essay is of a self-satisfied ruling class living off past achievements and suddenly challenged by talented newcomers, resented all the more because they were Jewish. For the first time the conflict between the status interests and the educational functions of the elite colleges became apparent. As one writer in a 1922 journal put it:

Each student in an American college is there, or is supposed to be there, for some other purpose than acquiring knowledge. He is to be the transmitter to others of ideals of mind, spirit, and conduct. *Scholarship is perhaps the most strongly emphasized of these ideals but it is not the only one, or even the one most generally prized.* [Italics added.][24]

No one suggested that Jewish students threatened academic standards. Rather it was argued that the college stood for *other* things, and that social standards were as important and valid as intellectual ones.

Raising the Barriers

A college song during the 1910s had these lyrics:

> Oh, Harvard's run by millionaires,
> And Yale is run by booze,
> Cornell is run by farmers' sons,
> Columbia's run by Jews.
> So give a cheer for Baxter Street,
> Another one for Pell,
> And when the little sheenies die,
> Their souls will go to hell.

23. Francis Russell, "The Coming of the Jews," *Antioch Review* 15 (March 1955), pp. 32–34.

24. "Exclusion from College," *The Outlook*, July 5, 1922, p. 406.

A climate of intolerance prevailed in many eastern colleges long before discriminatory quotas were contemplated by college officials. From the turn of the century, anti-Semitism was a common feature of campus social life. Although exceptions were sometimes made, Jews were generally excluded from the honor societies and eating clubs at Yale and Princeton.[25] In 1902 a dormitory at Harvard came to be know as "Little Jerusalem" because of its large number of Jewish residents.[26] In 1913 a fraternity suspended its charter at CCNY because "the Hebraic element is greatly in excess."[27] Such anti-Semitic incidents checker the history of American colleges after 1900. A 1930 survey under Jewish sponsorship found that "manifestations of anti-Jewish feeling took the following forms: slurring remarks, social aloofness, exclusion from honorary fraternities . . . discrimination in campus politics . . . offensive jokes in student publications and student dramatics, general unfriendliness."[28] In reaction, Jews formed their own fraternities and social groups, though ironically, this only reinforced the prevalent notion that Jewish students were clannish and unassimilable.

However unpleasant, social discrimination was not a serious disability. For one thing, Jews tended to avoid such campuses as Yale and Princeton, which had reputations for bigotry, and to seek out others—City College, New York University, and Columbia—that offered a less hostile atmosphere. Under President Eliot's administration, Harvard earned a reputation as the most liberal and democratic of the "Big Three," and therefore Jews did not feel that the avenue to a prestigious college was altogether closed. While campus anti-Semitism probably left Jews with a feeling of social inferiority, it was a small price to pay for education and economic advancement. The author of a 1916 article in *Harper's Weekly* went so far as to see social discrimination as an asset: ". . . indeed, their exclusion from societies stimulates their education on the intellectual side; and a final judgment on the whole matter would depend in

25. Norman Hapgood, "Jews and College Life," *Harper's Weekly,* vol. 62, 1916, p. 54.

26. Ernest Earnest, *Academic Procession* (Indianapolis: Bobbs-Merrill, 1953), p. 216.

27. Rudy, op. cit., p. 294.

28. Broun and Britt, op. cit., p. 91.

part on the relative importance we give to 'college work' and 'college life.' "[29]

Of potentially greater significance than the social discrimination on campus was the prejudice that existed among faculty and administrators. In 1890 the editor of the *American Hebrew* mailed a questionnaire to a number of prominent Christians, including several college presidents and professors. Those who replied were unanimous in condemning prejudice as indefensible and irrational, but a question concerning "standards of conduct" elicited some critical comments about Jews. The president of the University of Vermont wrote:

Wherever . . . Jews have . . . fallen in with the social customs of the community, they have . . . been received and treated like other Americans. Whereas in certain summer resorts within my observation—they have kept themselves together, and apart from others, and massed themselves on the piazza, and in the drawing rooms, and at the tables, they have been objected to, not because they were Jews, but for the same reason and in the same way that obtrusive and objectionable parties of Christians are often objected to in such places.

The president of the University of Virginia offered this unsolicited advice for Jews:

Let your people become known for culture as well as for business sagacity, for refinements of speech and manners, for those gracious qualities that have been in all ages the outcome of intimacy with literature and art, and they will not lack sympathy and regard from all members of society who care for the best that is in man.

A Harvard professor was less tactful:

Many Jews have personal and social qualities and habits that are unpleasant. . . . These come in large measure from the social isolation to which they have been subjected for centuries, by the prejudice and ignorance of Christian communities. Most Jews are socially untrained, and their bodily habits are not good.

29. Norman Hapgood, "Schools, Colleges and Jews," *Harper's Weekly,* January 22, 1916, p. 78.

The president of Tufts University concurred:

> The social characteristics of the Jews are peculiar. The subtle thing which we call manners, among them differs from the manners of Americans generally.[30]

These men would have been indignant if their remarks had been construed as prejudiced, for they repudiated prejudice as un-Christian and irrational. They were convinced that their opinion of Jews was based not on myth or religious bigotry, but on social reality. As a dean of Columbia wrote in 1904: "What most people regard as a racial problem is really a social problem."[31]

Indeed, to a certain extent it was a social problem involving a clash of class and culture. Yet even Jews from respectable backgrounds with the right manners were victims of social discrimination. Whether or not Jews fit into polite society was not the real issue. Their mere presence was disturbing because, as one of the first immigrant groups to encroach on Brahmin terrain, Jews represented the decline of the old order and of inherited social distinction.[32]

During the 1910s there was increasing pressure in certain eastern colleges to control the Jewish influx. The Jewish "takeover" of City College, whose student body was by then over 80 percent Jewish, served as a warning. In addition, a resurgence of nativism during the First World War tended to heighten anti-Jewish feeling. For largely independent reasons, the mood within the colleges was also undergoing change. Reaction was setting in against the reforms of the past twenty years—the expansion of enrollment, the changing curriculum, and the related trend toward increased class and ethnic heterogeneity in the student population. Soon after his inauguration as president of Harvard in 1909, Abbott Lawrence Lowell complained that Harvard men were not as intellectually or socially rounded as they ought to be, or by implication, as they once were.

---

30. Philip Cowen, *Prejudice Against the Jew* (New York: Philip Cowen, 1928), pp. 97–106.

31. Frederich Paul Keppel, *Columbia* (New York: Oxford University Press, 1914), p. 180.

32. Barbara Miller Soloman, *Ancestors and Immigrants* (Chicago: University of Chicago Press, 1956), chaps. 1–2.

By the 1920s a number of eastern colleges adopted policies designed to reduce their Jewish enrollment. Some established alumni committees to screen candidates, which transferred the onus of discrimination to agreeable alumni. Others placed an absolute limit on total enrollment and then employed waiting lists that permitted a more biased selection of students. Still others, under the pretext of seeking a regional balance, gave preference to students outside the East, thereby reducing the number of Jews admitted.

The most commonly used subterfuge was the introduction of character tests and psychological exams.[33] Before the 1920s only criteria of scholastic performance were used in the admissions process; now admissions boards began to scrutinize the "outside" interests of students. In addition, school principals were asked to rank students on such characteristics as "fair play," "public spirit," "interest in fellows," and "leadership." These traits were exactly opposite those stereotypically ascribed to Jews. According to the prevailing image, Jews did not use "fair play" but were notoriously unethical. "Public spirit" and "interest in fellows" were Christian virtues; Jews were outsiders who cared only for themselves. "Leadership" was seen as a prerogative of non-Jews; Jews exhibiting this quality would be regarded as "pushy." School principals, who were invariably Protestant and middle class, could be expected to draw upon these stereotypes in evaluating their Jewish students.

It is not possible to determine exactly how prevalent quotas were during the 1920s, though enrollment figures would suggest that by 1930 most private colleges with a large and growing Jewish enrollment had instituted some kind of restrictive admissions procedure. The most dramatic reversal occurred at Columbia, where the Jewish enrollment declined from 40 to 22 percent in a two-year period.[34] New York University was also reported to have sharply reduced the number of Jewish students. In 1922 a dean explained NYU's policy of selective admission in this way:

> We do not exclude students of any race or national origin because they are foreign, but whenever the student body is found to contain elements from any source in such proportions

33. "May Jews Go to College?", *The Nation*, vol. 114 (1922), p. 708.

34. *New York Times*, January 23, 1923, p. 22; Broun and Britt, op. cit., p. 74.

as to threaten our capacity for assimilating them, we seek by selection to restore the balance.[35]

By 1920 Harvard's Jewish enrollment reached 20 percent; no restrictions were yet in effect. Syracuse was roughly 15 percent Jewish in 1923 though the chancellor had to fight off an attempt to "rid the hill of Jews." In 1930 Rutgers admitted only 33 Jewish students in order to "equalize the proportion" in the college. Rumor had it that Princeton used a quota based on the percentage of Jews in the United States; whether true or not, the proportion of Jewish students was minuscule. At Dartmouth in 1930 it was just 7 percent.[36]

It is evident that a tide of bigotry swept college campuses during the 1920s, just as it did the nation as a whole. Yet the extent and significance of quotas should not be exaggerated. For one thing, quotas were confined to private schools in the East. And, as objectionable as quotas were, they did not exclude Jews altogether, but rather placed an upper limit on Jewish enrollment. If excluded from the elite eastern colleges, Jewish students could, and did, go elsewhere. Though Jews had the bitter experience of being treated as outcasts, and some had to settle for a less prestigious education, in the final analysis the quotas of the 1920s did not constitute a major obstacle to Jewish aspirations.

The Harvard Affair

So long as quotas were administered surreptitiously, they were difficult to combat. Few people, least of all Jews, were deceived by the subterfuges that colleges employed, but these methods were effective in preventing public exposure and political agitation. This situation was suddenly changed with a terse announcement issued by Harvard University in June 1922. The full text reads as follows:

> The great increase which has recently taken place in the number of students at Harvard College, as at the other colleges, has brought up forcibly the problem of the limitation of enrollment.
>
> We have not at present sufficient classrooms or dormitories, especially freshman dormitories, to take care of any further

35. Broun and Britt, op. cit., p. 108.
36. Ibid.

large increase. This problem is really a group of problems, all difficult, and most of them needing for their settlement more facts that we now have. Before a general policy can be formulated on this great question it must engage the attention of the Governing Board and the Faculties and it is likely to be discussed by alumni and undergraduates.

It is natural that with a widespread discussion of this sort going on there should be talk about the proportion of Jews at the college. At present the whole problem of limitation of enrollment is in the stage of general discussion and it may remain in that stage for a considerable time.[37]

Why did Harvard risk public exposure instead of adopting the subterfuges employed elsewhere? One clue is to be found in the personality of President Lowell, perhaps in his New England candor, more likely in his naiveté and underlying prejudice. Lowell believed that he was acting courageously, a conviction that was reflected in his commencement address of 1922: "To shut the eyes to an actual problem of this kind and ignore its existence, or to refuse to grapple with it courageously, would be unworthy of a university."[38] The "problem" was that Jewish enrollment at Harvard had increased from 6 percent in 1908 to 20 percent in 1922. Lowell, however, was determined to avoid the "indirect methods" employed elsewhere.[39] The storm of protest that ensued must have given him occasion to question the practicality of such moral rectitude.

Elected officials were among the first to react. On the day after the papers reported the news from Harvard, a state legislator from Massachusetts proposed a bill for a legislative inquiry. On the next day President Lowell traveled to the State House where he conferred privately with the speaker of the Massachusetts House of Representatives. The speaker obliged Lowell with a public statement that dismissed the press report as "idle rumor," adding that "Harvard would remain, as in the past, a great university for all the people. . . ."[40] Nevertheless, the protest in the state legislature continued unabated. One pending bill proposed to eliminate all reference to Harvard University from the state constitution, in order to dis-

37. *New York Times,* June 2, 1922, p. 1.
38. *New York Times,* June 23, 1922, p. 1.
39. *New York Times,* June 17, 1922, p. 3.
40. *New York Times,* June 4, 1922, p. 18.

associate the Commonwealth of Massachusetts from Harvard's discriminatory policies. Another proposal called for a review of the tax exemptions that Harvard enjoyed on its property. The Boston City Council passed its own resolution condemning the Harvard administration. Finally, the governor appointed a committee to investigate charges of discrimination at Harvard. *The New York Times* reported that Harvard officials were "surprised" since they had assumed that "any plan for a State investigation would die a natural death."[41]

This was an impressive response from the public sector, unusual for the 1920s. Still, the resolute president of Harvard stood his ground. An exchange of letters with a dissenting Jewish alumnus was printed in *The New York Times*. Lowell's letter began with the disclaimer that "there is perhaps no body of men in the United States . . . with so little anti-Semitic feeling as the instructing staff of Harvard University." The letter continued: "There is, most unfortunately, a rapidly growing anti-Semitic feeling in this country . . . fraught with very great evils for the Jews, and very great perils for the community." Finally the logic becomes clear: quotas are designed not to harm Jews, but to reduce anti-Semitism. They were in the best interests of Jews themselves:

> The anti-Semitic feeling among the students is increasing, and it grows in proportion to the increase in the number of Jews. If their number should become 40 percent of the student body, the race feeling would become intense. When on the other hand, the number of Jews was small, the race antagonism was small also. . . . If every college in the country would take a limited proportion of Jews, I suspect we should go a long way toward eliminating race feeling among the students, and as these students passed out into the world, eliminating it in the community.[42]

For President Lowell, restricting Jewish enrollment at Harvard was a way of restricting the growth of anti-Semitism. But his Jewish correspondent was unconvinced by this logic: "If it be true . . . that the anti-Semitic feeling among the students is increasing,

41. *New York Times*, June 7, 1922, p. 1.
42. *New York Times*, June 17, 1922, p. 1.

should it not be the function of an institution of learning to discourage rather than encourage such a spirit?"

The criticism that was marshaled against President Lowell and Harvard owed itself in part to the political influence that Jews enjoyed both within and outside the university. The Jewish concentration in and around Boston was given particular significance by gerrymandering practices that drew political boundaries so as to maximize ethnic homogeneity. As a consequence there were a number of "Jewish districts" that elected Jewish candidates to the state legislature. This was at least one factor responsible for the strong action that state and city officials took against Harvard's proposed quotas.

In addition, Jews were strategically located within the power structure of the university. Besides the Jewish alumni who expressed their opposition to quotas, Harvard's governing body, the Board of Overseers, had one Jewish member, Judge Julian W. Mack of Chicago, who was a leader in the American Jewish Congress. According to *The New York Times,* he was "much exercised over the matter."[43] In a letter to Mack on March 29, 1922, President Lowell explained himself with characteristic bluntness: "It is the duty of Harvard to receive just as many boys who have come, or whose parents have come, to this country without our background as we can effectively educate; including in education the imparting, not only of book knowledge, but of the ideas and traditions of our people. Experience seems to place that proportion at about 15%."[44]

Another political resource was the presence of Jews on the Harvard faculty. When President Lowell appointed a committee of thirteen to review the college's admissions policies, it included three Jews. All had German names, and judging from the committee's final report, it is doubtful that they did much to defend Jewish interests. Nevertheless, the mere presence of Jews on the faculty made it all the more difficult to justify the sudden imposition of quotas.

Student opinion at Harvard was divided on the issue of quotas.

43. *New York Times,* June 6, 1922, p. 1.

44. President A. Lawrence Lowell to Judge Julian Mack, March 29, 1922; by permission of Harvard University. I am grateful to Penny Hollander Feldman for bringing Lowell's letters to my attention (see *Recruiting an Elite: Admission to Harvard College,* unpublished dissertation, Harvard University, 1975).

A professor of social ethics asked his class to discuss whether religious restrictions were ethically justified. In a class of eighty-three students, forty-one defended religious quotas. Thirty-four, including seven with Jewish names, held that such a policy was not justifiable; the remaining eight were undecided.[45]

Some students who defended quotas expressed resentment of Jewish academic success: "They memorize their books! Thus they keep the average of scholarship so high that others with a high degree of common sense, but less parrot-knowledge, are prevented from attaining a representative grade." A second criticism was that Jews were clannish and did not fit into student life: "They do not mix. They destroy the unity of the college." "They are governed by selfishness." "Jews are an unassimilable race, as dangerous to a college as indigestible food to a man." Other responses were not explicitly anti-Jewish. A few expressed the view that Harvard's founding fathers "wanted certain traditions maintained and it is a duty to maintain them. . . ." A more common argument was that "Harvard must maintain a cosmopolitan balance."

As these comments suggest, the arguments in defense of quotas were basically of two kinds. One emphasized objectionable traits of Jews; the other, more insidious argument did not accuse Jews of objectionable behavior, but assumed the *absence* of qualities necessary for the preservation of the institution's special character. The latter view was expressed by some of the leading journalists of the day. One writer commented that Jewish immigrants "had little training in the amenities and delicacies of civilized existence," and if the proportion of Jews at Harvard increased to 40 percent as President Lowell warned, "this means that its character would be completely changed."[46] Another journalist asserted that:

> It is one of the severest and most distressing tasks of college authorities today to exercise that discrimination which will keep college ideals and atmosphere pure and sound and yet not quench this eager spirit. . . . Racial and religious oppression and prejudice have no place in America, and least of all in academic environments. But the effort to maintain stand-

45. William T. Ham, "Harvard Student Opinion on the Jewish Question," *The Nation*, Sept. 6, 1922, pp. 224–27.

46. "The Jews and the Colleges," *World's Work*, vol. 44 (1922), p. 353.

ards against untrained minds and spirits is not oppression or prejudice.[47]

Even *The Nation,* in commenting on the genteel tradition at Harvard, Yale, and Princeton, conceded that "the infiltration of a mass of pushing young men with a foreign accent accustomed to overcome discrimination by self-assertiveness would obviously change the character of any of these institutions and lessen its social prestige."[48] However, *The Nation's* editorial did not defend quotas. It was resigned to the inevitability that "some of the beauty of the aristocratic tradition" would be lost, and argued that America should not imitate the methods of "the most backward in Europe." As might be expected, Jewish opinion challenged the legitimacy of judging applicants in terms of character. As one Jewish writer put it: "We think that a university which keeps a man out because it doesn't like his character is almost as benighted as the one which would sift him out because he is a Jew."[49]

"*Almost* as benighted." It was difficult to deny the difference between rejecting applicants on sheer religious grounds and rejecting them because they lacked a preferred set of social characteristics. Advocates of quotas did not question the right of Jews to a college education. Rather, the issue was the right of certain eastern colleges to preserve their unique character, which was Protestant and upper class. The problem was not simply that Jews were displacing upper-class Protestants. More important was the effect that this had on the reputation of the college. City College was stigmatized as "the Jewish University of America," and the University of Pennsylvania was said to have "the democracy of the street car."[50] As these colleges suffered in prestige, they ceased to attract students from prestigious families.

One might assume that the president of Harvard was motivated by a sincere desire to preserve Harvard's historic identity rather than by anti-Semitism. After all, was he not the president of an institution with a reputation for liberalism and tolerance? Was this not the A. Lawrence Lowell who in 1902 warned his predecessor

47. "Exclusion from College," *The Outlook,* July 5, 1922, p. 407.
48. "May Jews Go to College?", op. cit., p. 708.
49. "Harvard 'Talk' about Jews," *Literary Digest* 73 (June 24, 1922), p. 28.
50. Veysey, op. cit., p. 288.

of the "great danger of a snobbish separation of the students on lines of wealth" and who, in his own administration, had constructed compulsory freshman dormitories and commons?[51] And had he not, in the same commencement address in which he defended his proposal for selective admissions, also expressed the view that "Americanization does not mean merely molding them [foreigners] to an already settled type, but the blending together of many distinct elements . . . [each] with qualities which can enrich our common heritage."[52]

However, considerable doubt is cast on Lowell's motives by an incident that occurred on Christmas Day, 1922. Traveling on the New York–New Haven railroad, President Lowell was engaged in conversation by a man—Victor Albert Kramer—who, unbeknownst to Lowell, was both a Jew and a graduate of Harvard. Several weeks later, at a synagogue forum on discrimination against Negroes, Kramer described his encounter with President Lowell. Thanks to the presence of a *New York Times* reporter, the event was reported in the press.

According to Kramer, Lowell predicted a deterioration of conditions for Jews as long as they remained apart and resisted intermarriage. Jews had outworn their religion, he believed, and must give up their peculiar practices if they expected to be treated as equals. The man who, in his commencement address six months earlier, extolled the contributions each immigrant group could make to the evolving American character now in private conversation asserted that a Jew could not be both a Jew and an American. Finally, he expressed satisfaction in the fact that New York University had reduced Jewish enrollment and took credit for Harvard's plan to do likewise.[53]

Lowell never denied the encounter on the train, though a statement issued by his office claimed that the newspaper report grossly misrepresented his views. The statement continued sanctimoniously: "His earnest desire is to see anti-Semitic prejudice and Semitic

51. Earnest, op. cit., p. 216.
52. *New York Times,* June 23, 1922, p. 1.
53. *New York Times,* January 16, 1923, p. 23. In personal communication, Mr. Kramer has confirmed the accuracy of the original *Times* report of his conversation with President Lowell. Kramer also published his account of the incident in the *American Hebrew,* Jan. 26, 1923.

segregation abolished in this country, and he believes that Jews and Gentiles should work together to this end. . . ."[54] Inasmuch as anti-Semitic prejudice and "Semitic segregation" go hand in hand, in Lowell's view, a ceiling on the number of Jews at Harvard was in the interest of both groups.

While President Lowell disapproved of "Semitic segregation," or any segregation of students along lines of privilege, it was he who instituted a color ban in the compulsory freshman dormitories. For the handful of Harvard's black students, it was compulsory to find living quarters elsewhere.

Like the proposed religious quotas, the color ban became a cause célèbre. Black civil rights groups agitated against it and 149 Harvard alumni signed a protest petition. But to no avail. As Lowell wrote in a letter to the father of one of Harvard's black freshmen:

> . . . I am sorry to have to tell you that in the Freshman Halls, where residence is compulsory, we have felt from the beginning the necessity of not including colored men. To the other dormitories and dining rooms they are admitted freely, but in the Freshman Halls I am sure you will understand why . . . we have not thought it possible to compel men of different races to reside together.[55]

In private correspondence Lowell compared Harvard's "Jewish problem" to that of a resort hotel:

> The summer hotel that is ruined by admitting Jews meets its fate, not because the Jews it admits are of bad character, but because they drive away the Gentiles, and then, after the Gentiles have left, they leave also. This happened to a friend of mine with a school in New York, who thought, on principle, that he ought to admit Jews, but discovered in a few years that he had no school at all. A similar thing has happened in the case of Columbia College. . . .[56]

Lowell was convinced that the proportion of Jews at Harvard was reaching "a dangerous point," and that the college's future was at stake.

54. *New York Times,* January 16, 1923, p. 23.
55. *New York Times,* January 12, 1923, p. 5.
56. President A. Lawrence Lowell to Professor William E. Hocking, May 19, 1922; by permission of Harvard University.

The exposure of Lowell's underlying bigotry does not by itself invalidate the arguments put forward in defense of quotas or discredit those who sought to preserve Harvard's aristocratic traditions. However, it does reveal how tenuous the distinction is between base prejudice on the one hand, and protection of cultural values on the other. The crux of the matter is that racial and religious prejudice was an intrinsic part of upper-class society. On the surface, upper-class Protestants may have been protecting their status prerogatives and their cultural symbols; but prejudice was a factor in the very definition of status, just as it was a factor in the choice of cultural symbols. Harvard was elite not simply because it was upper-class and genteel, but also because it was predominantly white and Protestant.

In the final analysis, the class origins and ethnic peculiarities of Jews were not the main issue. Given the climate of intolerance that prevailed in the 1920s, the class character of higher education, and the fact that upwardly mobile Jews were penetrating one of the citadels of the Protestant establishment, Jews would have aroused antagonism no matter what their level of assimilation. As Horace Kallen wrote in 1923: " . . . it is not the failure of Jews to be assimilated into undergraduate society which troubles them [President Lowell and his defenders]. They do not want Jews to be assimilated into undergraduate society. What troubles them is the completeness with which the Jews want to be and have been assimilated."[57]

Regional Quotas

Only five days elapsed between Harvard's announcement intimating that quotas might be instituted, and a decision by the college's Board of Overseers to refer the issue to a special faculty committee. When the board dramatically met in emergency session and announced that no changes in the college's entrance requirements would be made until after the committee had reported, the opponents of quotas probably assumed that the administration was in retreat. Actually, the committee functioned as a decoy for the administration. It removed the issue of quotas from the public

57. Horace M. Kallen, "The Roots of Anti-Semitism," *The Nation*, February 28, 1923, p. 242.

arena and insulated Harvard's officialdom from public scrutiny and political pressure. Almost a year passed before the committee issued its report. Its conclusions were probably foreshadowed by the very instructions given to the committee: "To consider . . . principles and methods for more effective sifting of candidates for admission to the university."[58]

The six-page report issued by the committee was unequivocal in repudiating quotas as inconsistent with Harvard's tradition of "equal opportunity for all regardless of race and religion." Indeed, the authors of the report seemed to go out of their way to avoid any proposal that might be construed even by suspicious minds as prejudiced: "Even so rational a method as a personal conference or an intelligence test, if now adopted here as a means of selection, would inevitably be regarded as a covert device to eliminate those deemed racially or socially undesirable. . . ."

However, the committee's mandate was not simply to study religious quotas, but to review *all* of Harvard's admissions procedures. This the committee did with apparent good conscience. It announced its opposition to the policy of giving preference to the sons of graduates and recommended several minor changes in the college's entrance requirements that were intended to upgrade the student body. The reforms, the report asserted, "would solve one part of our problem."

The report continued: "The other part of the problem, namely the building up of a new group of men from the West and South and, in general, from good high schools in towns and small cities, is more difficult." The difficulty was that the students from these regions did not receive a high school education that, in quality or substance, prepared them for Harvard College. As a consequence they were unable to pass Harvard's entrance examination. The committee's solution was to waive the entrance examination for students in the highest seventh of their graduating class if they had completed an approved course of study and had the recommendation of their school. The committee reasoned that such students had demonstrated their fitness within the context of their

58. Report of the Committee Appointed "To Consider and Report to the Governing Boards Principles and Methods for More Effective Sifting of Candidates for Admission to the University" (Cambridge: Harvard University, April 1923).

own schools, and that "the best product is likely to succeed in college better than the poorer portion of the group admitted under our present examinations." On this dubious assumption the committee felt confident that Harvard's standards would not be lowered by accepting students who could not pass the usual entrance examination.

The men who drafted this proposal must have been aware that, if implemented, it would drastically alter the religious composition of Harvard's undergraduates. Jews were overwhelmingly concentrated in the urban centers on the eastern seaboard, and "to raise the proportion of country boys and students from the interior" would obviously reduce Jewish representation. Columbia had already instituted this practice, and when later accused of discrimination, a spokesman for the college acknowledged that there had in fact been a decline in the Jewish enrollment, but attributed this to a "natural change in the geographical distribution for the student body."[59]

Apparently Harvard desisted from taking any drastic action to reduce Jewish enrollment, probably because of the unfavorable publicity that followed its original announcement that such action was under consideration. In a confidential letter to Henry James in 1925, Lowell complained that the Jewish percentage at the college had actually increased, from 21.7 percent in 1922 to 27.1 percent in 1925. The measures adopted to reduce the number, he confided, had proved ineffective, and therefore he proposed a new remedy—to empower the Admissions Committee to screen applicants on the basis of their character and their likely contribution to Harvard and the community at large. To quote Lowell:

> To prevent a dangerous increase in the proportion of Jews, I know at present only one way which is at the same time straightforward and effective, and that is a selection by a personal estimate of character on the part of the Admission authorities, based on the probable value to the candidate, to the College and to the community of his admission.[60]

59. *New York Times,* January 23, 1923, p. 22.
60. President A. Lawrence Lowell to Henry James, November 3, 1925; by permission of Harvard University.

It is not known if or when Harvard implemented Lowell's proposal, though it has become common practice among private colleges to evaluate students by nonacademic criteria, including their personal characteristics and their geographical background. Such practices can be, and often are, defended on legitimate grounds. They are said to improve the quality of the student body, to diversify and enrich student culture, and to help the college establish a national reputation. Whatever merit these arguments may have, the concept of "regional balance" and the practice of evaluating students on the basis of character originated as subterfuges for discrimination and undoubtedly continue to produce the "right" ethnic mix in the student body.

As recently as 1971, a group of Jewish faculty at Harvard met with the dean of admissions to discuss rumors that the college had decided to reduce the number of Jewish students. Though the dean denied that any particular region had been singled out for reductions, he did say that "the doughnuts around the big cities" were not as successful with the Admissions Committee as they used to be. The "doughnuts," he explained, included such areas as Westchester County and Long Island, New York, suburban New Jersey, and Shaker Heights, Ohio. Upon hearing this, one of the Jewish faculty members retorted: "Those aren't doughnuts, they're bagels."[61]

The Jewish Problem with Affirmative Action

In combating patterns of discrimination, Jews have unquestionably been a force in the democratization of American higher education. Their success signified the triumph of principles of academic merit over class privilege and ethnic bias. Though indirect forms of discrimination persist, Jews today are numerically overrepresented in the nation's leading institutions, both as faculty and students.[62] At Harvard, for example, David Riesman estimated in 1973 that Jews comprise about one-quarter of the student body and a third

61. Dorothy Rabinowitz, "Are Jewish Students Different?", *Change,* Summer 1971, pp. 48–49.

62. Stephen Steinberg, *The Academic Melting Pot* (New York: McGraw-Hill, 1971), chap. 5.

of the faculty.[63] Of course, no private college accepts students solely on the basis of academic performance, and most still use a variety of nonacademic criteria that, whether intentionally or not, function as a disguise for privilege. Nevertheless, the overriding trend since the Second World War has been to make access to the elite schools a matter of open competition that allows for "the survival of the fittest," as gauged by academic performance and scores on standardized tests.[64]

The meritocracy benefited Jews because they had the economic and educational prerequisites to compete effectively for scarce places at all levels of higher education. However, other minorities who had to cope with the disabilities of economic disadvantage gained little from the elimination of overt discrimination. The cumulative disadvantages of the past, including inferior schooling, left them unprepared to compete on the same basis with members of more privileged groups. Consequently, the routine application of "objective" criteria resulted in a pattern of exclusion, or institutionalized racism, that vitiated the democratic claims of the merit system.

It was against this background that colleges and universities, under pressure from the federal government, launched affirmative action programs to increase the representation of racial minorities in their enrollments. Sometimes a fixed number of places were designated for minorities; more often, a "goal" was established that would be met only if there were enough qualified minority candi-

63. "Education at Harvard," *Change*, September 1973, p. 27.

64. It should be noted that the "objectivity" of these tests has been called into question, most recently by a Ralph Nader report on the Educational Testing Service, which designs the Scholastic Aptitude Test. According to *The New York Times*, Nader concluded that "the tests were conceived by the upper class for the upper class, and have served as a formidable barrier to millions of students, unjustly diminishing their higher education and career opportunities." Other critics deny E.T.S.'s claim that the tests predict success. According to one investigator who studied E.T.S.'s internal documents: "E.T.S.'s own research has noted that judging candidates by the standard of previous *accomplishment*—things they have *done* in their school, community and in artistic and scientific endeavors—would virtually *eliminate* the elements of class and ethnic discrimination which prevail in the ranking by E.T.S. scores. The evidence suggests that the choice of the standard of merit may depend on which class one is interested in serving." (*New York Times*, January 15, 1980, p. 1.)

dates. In either case minority students who would have been rejected under the traditional system were admitted.

The implementation of affirmative action programs triggered a flurry of lawsuits charging "reverse racism." Though opposition came from many sources, including an array of white ethnic groups, Jewish organizations were in the forefront of the campaign against the "new quotas," as they were construed. For example, when the case of Alan Bakke, the white student who was refused admission to medical school at the University of California at Davis, reached the Supreme Court, the Anti-Defamation League, the American Jewish Committee, and the American Jewish Congress all filed *amicus curiae* briefs in support of Bakke. For Jews, affirmative action smacked of the *numerus clausus*—the restrictive quotas that excluded Jews from universities in Eastern Europe—not to mention the unofficial quotas they have had to contend with in this country as well. As a small minority, numerically overrepresented in institutions of higher learning, Jews were particularly threatened by any suggestion that groups should be represented in rough proportion to their numbers in the general population. For them, there was no room for equivocation or inconsistency on the principle that racial or ethnic considerations should be irrelevant to educational opportunity. As a lawyer for the Anti-Defamation League wrote in *The New York Times:* "the stakes are far too high for a society trying to rid itself of racial discrimination to accept on faith the claim that the only way to achieve equality in the professions is by practicing still more racial discrimination."[65]

But does affirmative action constitute a regression to discriminatory quotas? And does extending preferential treatment to racial minorities amount to a form of "reverse racism"?

On the first question, the "quotas" established under affirmative action can hardly be compared to the discriminatory quotas that Jews encountered in the past. When President Lowell threatened to institute a quota system at Harvard, it was for the express purpose of excluding Jews, a clear violation of democratic norms. The "quotas" or "goals" instituted under affirmative action have the opposite purpose—to advance educational equality by extending educational opportunities to groups that have historically been excluded.

65. Larry M. Lavinsky, "The Dangers of Racial Quotas," *New York Times,* June 15, 1977, p. A21.

Whereas Lowell sought to give preferential treatment to an already privileged group—the WASP upper class—affirmative action programs are aimed at groups so underprivileged that they would otherwise be denied educational opportunity. Whatever other objections might be raised, it is clear that affirmative action is consonant with democratic ideals and, as the Supreme Court has now ruled, with the Constitution as well.

Obviously, granting preferential treatment to racial minorities means that some whites will lose positions they would otherwise have had. But is it accurate to construe this as "reverse racism"? When members of racial minorities were excluded, it was because they were stigmatized as inferior or undesirable, and their exclusion was part of a systematic pattern of exploitation and domination. No such claims can be made with respect to the small number of whites adversely affected by affirmative action. They can hardly be said to have been excluded because of their race when roughly 90 percent of students in professional schools, for example, are white. Their exclusion does not imply a racial stigma, and as members of a powerful and privileged majority, they cannot rightfully claim to be victims of a systematic pattern of discrimination. In short, there is no such thing as "reverse racism." All that can be said is that, as individuals, they paid the price of a societal commitment to achieving racial parity in the professions, and while some whites are injured in the process, it is due not to racism, but to an effort to combat racism.[66]

Jews, of course, have special reason to feel threatened by affirmative action. Not only do they have a particularly large stake in higher education and the professions, but they realize that other avenues of opportunity, especially in the corporate world, are still limited by anti-Semitism. There is also a fear that Jews are likely to pay disproportionately for the places allotted to racial minorities, given the preferential treatment that already goes to children of illustrious families and children of wealthy alumni, not to mention students from areas outside of Jewish population centers. The question, then, is whether Jews as a community will erect barriers behind them to protect their hard-won gains, or whether they will continue their historic battle against privilege.

66. See Robert L. Allen, "The Bakke Case and Affirmative Action," *Black Scholar* (September 1977), pp. 9–16.

Chapter 10

Dilemmas and Contradictions
of Ethnic Pluralism in America

"One of the decisive social tasks of affirmative culture is based on this contradiction between the insufferable mutability of a bad existence and the need for happiness in order to make such existence bearable. Within this existence the resolution can be only illusory."

HERBERT MARCUSE, *"The Affirmative Character of Culture,"* 1965.

THE IDEAL of cultural pluralism is a society that allows for a maximum of ethnic diversity, a conception that was first advanced in 1915 by Horace Kallen in his celebrated article on "Democracy Versus the Melting Pot." For Kallen the melting pot could be achieved only through a tyrannical repression of individual freedoms, and therefore was fundamentally incompatible with democratic precepts. His vision of America was of a "democracy of nationalities," where ethnic groups would share an overriding loyalty to the nation and participate in its political and economic life, but still be free to cultivate their ethnic differences. Drawing an analogy to a symphony orchestra, he argued that union would be achieved not through uniformity, but through a harmony among the parts. Kallen's basic credo, and that of cultural pluralists ever since, is that "democracy involves not the elimination of differences but the perfection and conservation of differences."[1]

Ideologically, Kallen's doctrine of cultural pluralism represented an alternative to the Americanization movement which sought the deracination of immigrant culture. More than a plea for tolerance, his concept of democracy affirmed the value of ethnic difference and granted it political legitimacy. Especially at a time when the United States was preparing to enter the First World War, and the loyalties of hyphenated Americans were suspect, his idea of America as a "nation of nations" helped to validate and protect the millions of immigrants whose rights were in jeopardy. In this way the doctrine of cultural pluralism marked an important turning point in American social thought. Instead of being reviled for their differences and attacked as "unassimilable," immigrants came to be celebrated in American folklore for their contributions to the making of America. If a benign myth was substituted for a benighted one, this at least signified an improved climate of tolerance for the nation's minorities.

Pluralist principles, however, have been on the ascendancy precisely at a time when ethnic differences have been on the wane, and though the United States may now proclaim itself a "nation of nations," never before has it been closer to welding a national identity and culture out of the melange of ethnic groups that populated its soil. Instead of celebrating the triumph of pluralism therefore, it might be more appropriate to ask why Kallen's dream of a "democracy of nationalities" has been unattainable.

The trouble with American pluralism derives from the fact that it was built upon systematic inequalities that constituted an un-

1. Horace Kallen, "Democracy Versus the Melting Pot," in *Culture and Democracy in the United States* (New York: Boni and Liveright, 1924), p. 61. For two historical treatments of cultural pluralism in American social thought, see John Higham, *Send These to Me* (New York: Atheneum, 1975), chap. 10, and James Henry Powell, "The Concept of Cultural Pluralism in American Social Thought, 1915–1965," unpublished dissertation, University Microfilms, 1971. For a more recent statement of the doctrine of cultural pluralism, see Nathan Glazer, *Affirmative Discrimination* (New York: Basic Books, 1975), chap. 1, and *Pluralism Beyond the Frontier,* pamphlet published by the American Jewish Committee, New York City.

tenable basis for long-term ethnic preservation. This was the pitfall
—the fatal flaw—that robbed ethnic pluralism of its cultural innocence.

The literature of the ethnic pluralists devotes remarkably little
space to the problem of inequality, though their vision of a pluralist
society implicitly assumes a basic equality among constituent groups.
Otherwise pluralism might degenerate into a domination of some
ethnic groups by others, as is typical of plural societies throughout the
world. Obviously this is not what Kallen meant when he extolled the
compatibility of pluralism and democracy.

For example, the ethnic pluralists rarely have confronted the
issue of how blacks would fit into the pluralist schema. The players
in Kallen's "orchestration of mankind" were all white and European, and as John Higham has suggested, "the pluralist thesis from
the outset was encapsulated in white ethnocentrism."[2] Indeed, black
intellectuals and leaders have had good reason to balk at the pluralist
doctrine. As a group, blacks have always experienced the bitter side
of pluralism, and ideological justifications for maintaining ethnic
boundaries carried insidious overtones of racial segregation. Although some black nationalists have embraced pluralist ideas to
justify black separatism, they have usually done so out of a sense
of resignation to the impossibility of achieving genuine integration.[3]
Sooner or later the nationalist vision is punctured by the sobering
realization that, as Robert Allen has written, "black control of black
communities will not mean freedom from oppression so long as the
black communities themselves are subservient to an outside society
which is exploitative."[4]

On the other hand, the idea of cultural pluralism has intrinsic
appeal to groups who stand to benefit from maintaining and rein-
forcing ethnic boundaries. As Higham has noted:

2. Higham, op. cit., p. 208.

3. As August Meier has observed: "Generally in periods of discouragement
Negroes have adopted doctrines of self-help, racial solidarity, and economic
development as better techniques for racial advancement than politics, agitation, and the demand for immediate integration." *Negro Thought in America,
1880–1915* (Ann Arbor: University of Michigan Press, 1968), p. 24.

4. Robert L. Allen, *Black Awakening in Capitalist America* (Garden City,
N.Y.: Doubleday, 1970), p. 33.

We may anticipate, then, that cultural pluralism would appeal to people who were already strongly enough positioned to insure that permanent minority status might be advantageous. It was congenial to minority spokesmen confident enough to visualize themselves at the center rather than the periphery of American experience. Accordingly, cultural pluralism proved most attractive to people who were already largely assimilated. It was itself one of the products of the American melting pot.[5]

Inasmuch as the most outspoken advocates of pluralism tend to come from groups already largely assimilated, their impassioned defense of cultural diversity should perhaps be regarded with skepticism. Indeed, throughout American history ethnic groups have espoused the pluralist doctrine in order to protect their class interests, but have been all too willing to trample over ethnic boundaries—their own as well as others—in the pursuit of economic and social advantage.

In short, a pluralism based on systematic inequalities is inherently unstable because ethnic groups at or near the bottom of the social ladder have little reason to endorse the ethnic status quo. On the contrary, groups aspiring to class mobility are typically forced to adopt strategies that are designed to advance their class interests, but at the same time whittle away at the pluralist structure. Two such strategies may be observed, one within the disadvantaged group, the other in its relationship with more advantaged groups.

In the first place, when ethnicity is associated with class disadvantage—with poverty, hardship, a low standard of living, and so on—then powerful inducements exist for the members of such groups to assimilate into the mainstream culture, since this will improve their chances for a better life. Especially when a racial or ethnic stigma is attached to a group in order to justify its exploitation, then to escape this stigma and the economic consequences that flow from it individuals are forced to shed the marks of ethnic difference. Indeed, most disadvantaged minorities have been willing to compromise their ethnicity for the sake of economic security, social acceptance, and a sense of participating fully in society instead of living precariously on the periphery. These were powerful incentives, not mere blandishments, especially when considered against the

5. Higham, op. cit., p. 211.

background of the extreme hardships and deprivations that marked the early experience of these groups in American society.

It is fashionable and convenient to blame "the WASP" for the destruction of ethnic subcultures, but more subtle and complex forces were at work. Ethnic groups were not just passive victims of cultural repression, but played an active role in their own demise —not out of any collective self-hatred, but because circumstances forced them to make choices that undermined the basis for cultural survival. To be sure, these choices were difficult ones, and they were accompanied by a painful sense of cultural loss. This is what Mario Puzo meant in *The Fortunate Pilgrim* when he wrote: "They spoke with guilty loyalty of customs they themselves had trampled into dust."[6]

Not only have ethnic groups sacrificed much of their own ethnicity in a quest for economic mobility, but they have also been instrumental in subverting the ethnicity of groups above them in the class hierarchy. Because Jews escaped poverty more rapidly than others, they were often in the vanguard of an attack on WASP exclusivity in residential areas, in schools and colleges, and in resorts and social clubs. Needless to say, WASPs stubbornly resisted the intrusions of outsiders and sought to preserve the ethnic character of their neighborhoods and institutions. However, antidiscriminatory legislation, combined with a long series of court decisions, has narrowly restricted the basis for lawful discrimination.

It has always been and continues to be permissible to engage in discrimination in the "private domain," as distinguished from businesses or places of public accommodation. But the effect of court decisions over the years has been to broaden the concept of "public" to include areas once considered "private." For example, there is nothing in American legal canons to prevent private clubs from discriminating in their membership policies on the basis of race, religion, creed, color, national origin, or sex. However, recent court decisions have declared discrimination unlawful if clubs hold liquor licenses or enjoy tax exemptions, on the grounds that the state would thereby be implicated in discriminatory acts, which does violate the equal-protection guarantees of the Constitution. The

6. Mario Puzo, *The Fortunate Pilgrim* (New York: Lance Books, 1954), p. 11.

effect of these rulings has been to prohibit discrimination in most social clubs where minorities are likely to be affected.[7]

Similarly, by invalidating housing covenants that once functioned as a subterfuge for discrimination, the courts have made it almost impossible lawfully to maintain restricted neighborhoods and communities. By their nature, such decisions protect the rights of minorities and enhance American democracy. At the same time, however, they narrowly circumscribe the areas in which ethnic exclusivity is possible, and therefore make it difficult for ethnic groups to maintain institutions that are essential to their collective survival.

As these situations demonstrate, there is a fundamental tension between pluralism and democracy. That is to say, our society in principle sanctions the right of ethnic groups to maintain their separate cultures and communities, but it also guarantees individual freedoms and specifically proscribes various forms of discrimination. The problem is that these two sets of rights are often in conflict. This is because ethnic groups in a position of social and economic advantage, when exercising their prerogatives of associating with their own ethnic kind, deprive outsiders of rights and opportunities protected by democratic norms.

Thus, for example, Jewish defense agencies have persuasively argued that the exclusion of Jews from prestigious WASP clubs involves more than simple ethnic preference, since it carries with it adverse economic consequences for Jewish professionals and businessmen. By the same reasoning, a desire to maintain the "ethnic purity" of a neighborhood—to use President Carter's unadulterated terminology—necessarily deprives ethnic outsiders of their right to live where they choose. When the courts have confronted this conflict between pluralism and democracy, the clear tendency, at least in recent times, has been to give precedence to democratic principles.

Just as ethnic groups have class reasons for tearing down ethnic barriers ahead of them, they also have class reasons for raising ethnic barriers behind them. Thus, it is not uncommon for ethnic groups to invoke democratic principles to combat the ethnic exclusivity of more privileged groups, but to turn around and cite pluralistic principles in defense of their own discriminatory practices. A clear-

7. Robert H. O'Brien, "May Private Clubs Lawfully Discriminate?", *Los Angeles Bar Journal* 51 (July 1975), p. 16. Discrimination is also unlawful if clubs lease facilities on a private basis or discriminate in their guest policies.

cut example of this occurred in San Francisco in 1971 when the Chinese community opposed school desegation on the ground that the reassignment of students would destroy the cultural and educational life of the city's Chinese community. When the case came before the Supreme Court, however, Justice William O. Douglas refused their appeal, citing an 1875 Supreme Court decision that prohibited the State of California from denying a license to operate a hand laundry to someone just because he was Chinese.[8] In effect, Douglas was saying that the Chinese could not have it both ways, and that the same laws that protected them from discrimination also prohibited them from discriminating against others.

In other instances, too, as once underprivileged groups attain middle-class status, they find their institutions—neighborhoods, clubs, and other facilities—coveted by less privileged groups, and like the Chinese in San Francisco, their primary allegiance shifts from democratic to pluralist principles. In an attempt to reconcile these two principles, Nathan Glazer and Daniel Patrick Moynihan have gone so far as to propose a distinction between "positive discrimination" and "negative discrimination." The latter refers to discrimination based on naked prejudice, whereas the former is "for the purpose of defending something positive rather than simply excluding someone because of his race."[9] Glazer and Moynihan forget that when Jews and Irish were excluded, upper-class Protestants also expressed a desire to preserve the ethnic character of their neighborhoods and clubs. On closer examination, "negative discrimination" is when "we" are the ones to be excluded; "positive discrimination" is when we are excluding someone else.

In his other writings Glazer has acknowledged that "the same law permitted a Jew to challenge exclusion from a Fifth Avenue cooperative apartment and a Negro to challenge exclusion from a much more modest apartment building."[10] He well understands that "the accidents of history have put the Jew just ahead of the

8. *New York Times*, August 18, 1971, p. 12. In that same year, Jews in the Forest Hills section of New York City also opposed construction of a low-rent housing project on the grounds that it would destroy the religious life and culture of the community. *New York Times*, December 2, 1971, p. 59.

9. Nathan Glazer and Daniel Patrick Moynihan, *Beyond the Melting Pot* (Cambrdge: MIT Press, 1970), p. xxxviii.

10. Nathan Glazer, "Negroes and Jews: The New Challenge to Pluralism," *Commentary* (December 1964), p. 30.

Negro, and just above him."[11] Yet he construes the demands of upwardly mobile blacks as "a new challenge to pluralism," and justifies Jewish resistance to racial integration as stemming from a desire—legitimate in terms of pluralistic principles—to protect their ethnic communities. To quote Glazer:

> . . . the ultimate basis of the resistance to their demands, I am convinced—certainly among Jews, but not Jews alone—is that they [blacks] pose a serious threat to the ability of other groups to maintain *their* communities.[12]

Glazer now wishes to think that when Jews were "battering against the walls of privilege" their goals were limited, and did not constitute a challenge to pluralism. Of course, this is not how WASPs viewed matters as their neighborhoods and clubs were penetrated and, not infrequently, "taken over" by Jews.

Typically it is the exclusivity of privileged groups that comes under challenge, but the institutions of less privileged groups are not immune from challenge either. For example, in 1978 a federal judge ruled that Alabama State University, the oldest and largest black college in Alabama, discriminated against whites in its admissions policies, a ruling that imperils the future of black colleges. A lawyer for the NAACP concurred with the court's decision, saying that "black institutions must face the fact that they cannot have it both ways. They have to adhere to the same laws and principles that apply to white state institutions."[13] A case could be made that "discrimination" on the part of a small and weak minority should not be equated with the same behavior on the part of a powerful and privileged majority. However, the trend in the courts has been to insist on the goose-gander rule, with the result that pluralist patterns are disrupted among advantaged and disadvantaged groups alike.

Thus, democracy and pluralism are not as compatible as the ethnic pluralists would like to think, primarily because pluralist structures tend to reinforce existing class inequalities. In the final analysis, Kallen's model of a "democracy of nationalities" is workable only in a society where there is a basic parity among constituent

11. Ibid.

12. Ibid., p. 32.

13. *New York Times*, May 3, 1978. Also, "Students Organize to Save Public Black Colleges," *Chronicle of Higher Education*, May 11, 1970, pp. 3–4.

ethnic groups. Only then would ethnic boundaries be secure from encroachment, and only then would pluralism be innocent of class bias and consistent with democratic principles.

But would a pluralism based on equality—if such a thing can be imagined in the American context—be any more stable or enduring? After all, pluralism in America evolved out of systematic inequalities, and to some extent these inequalities have been its very lifeblood. Typically it is those groups who have remained on the economic margin who have been insulated from assimilating forces, and thus relatively successful at preserving their ethnic distinctiveness. Groups that have experienced widespread mobility, in contrast, are producing such high rates of intermarriage that their futures are very much in doubt. Without these class inequalities, therefore, one can imagine only an accelerated rate of ethnic defection as the forces of assimilation are freed from the restraints of class.

Thus, in a sense, the hopes of the ethnic pluralists depend not just on a preservation of ethnic traditions, but also on a preservation of the class cleavages that have reinforced ethnic boundaries. Of course, ethnic groups cannot be blamed for the inequities that are built into American society, but as Irving Howe cautions, "the ethnic community too often shuts its eyes or buries its head while clinging anxiously to received customs—as if there were no more important things in the world than customs!"[14] Howe is not one to be irreverent of culture, but he is clear about his priorities:

> The central problems of our society have to do, not with ethnic groupings, but with economic policy, social rule, class relations. They have to do with vast inequities of wealth, with the shameful neglect of a growing class of subproletarians, with the readiness of policy-makers to tolerate high levels of unemployment. They have to do with "the crisis of the cities," a polite phrase masking a terrible reality—the willingness of this country to dump millions of black (and white) poor into the decaying shells of once thriving cities. Toward problems of this kind and magnitude, what answers can ethnicity offer? Very weak ones, I fear.[15]

14. Irving Howe, "The Limits of Ethnicity," *New Republic,* June 25, 1977, p. 19.
15. Ibid.

Moreover, ethnic groups become part of the problem when they function as false havens from the crises that beset the larger community, and foster a parochial disregard for events outside the ethnic province.

The ethnic community also functions, certainly more positively, as a refuge against the alienation that pervades modern society. The chronic malaise of our time is epitomized by the question, Who am I? It is also implied by the question, Assimilate into what? That these questions are raised in so many quarters is indicative of the fact that our society has not created alternatives for the rich cultures and closely knit communities that we identify with our immigrant grandparents. No doubt, this helps to explain why people cling to remnants of the ethnic past, why they crave ritual and a sense of belonging.

But can ethnicity, especially in its attenuated forms, provide the nexus for social life that it did in another era for people quite unlike ourselves? Can it be more than a palliative for spiritual yearnings that are not fulfilled elsewhere? The ultimate ethnic myth, perhaps, is the belief that the cultural symbols of the past can provide more than a comfortable illusion to shield us from present-day discontents.

Epilogue

Ethnic Heroes and Racial
Villains in American Social Science

MYTHS DIE hard, as the saying goes. To be sure, myths about race and ethnicity are deep-seated and often appear immune to change, but this is not because of some inherent potency or appeal. Myths are socially constructed. They arise in specific times and places, in response to identifiable circumstances and needs, and they are passed on through processes that can be readily observed. Whether a myth prospers or withers is always problematic; most, in fact, are relinquished or forgotten. To explain why some myths persist, we have to explore the relationship that these myths have to larger social institutions that promote and sustain them, and that in turn are served by them.

This book has dealt with myths that purport to explain why racial and ethnic groups occupy higher or lower places in the class system—why, in the popular idiom, "we have made it and they have not." The popular explanation, translated into respectable academic language by mainstream social scientists, is that "we" had the cultural virtues and moral fiber that "they" are lacking. If this theory were predicated on fact alone, it would be fairly easy to dispense with—for example, by showing that Jews, the archetype of ethnic success, arrived with occupational experiences and skills that gave them a headstart relative to other immigrants from eastern and southern Europe, that these latter groups were favorably positioned relative to blacks, who were excluded from industrial employment altogether during the critical early phases of industrialization, and that racial minorities—blacks in particular—have been encumbered by discriminatory barriers across generations that constitute the chief reason for their current economic plight. However compelling these facts might be, even when fully documented and analyzed, they are overpowered by other assumptions and beliefs that are almost universally shared in American society and that pervade American social science as well.

My point is that racial and ethnic myths about "making it" are embedded in a larger "success myth," one that is deeply rooted in American history and culture, and not easily countervailed. As Richard Weiss writes at the outset of his book on *The American Myth of Success:*

> . . . the idea that ours is an open society, where birth, family, and class do not significantly circumscribe individual possibilities, has a strong hold on the popular imagination. The belief that all men, in accordance with certain rules, but exclusively by their own efforts, can make of their lives what they will has been widely popularized for well over a century. The cluster of ideas surrounding this conviction makes up the American myth of success.[1]

As Weiss goes on to say, the word "myth" does not imply something entirely false. The success myth was forged when the United States was a nation of yeomen and artisans, and it was sustained through two centuries of virtually uninterrupted territorial expansion and economic growth. There is much in our national experience to sustain notions of America as an open society where the individual can surmount impediments of "birth, family, and class." The problem arises when this simple schema glosses over major contradictions. To wit, colonial America was not just a nation of yeomen

1. Richard Weiss, *The American Myth of Success* (New York: Basic Books, 1969), p. 3

and artisans—one-fifth of its inhabitants were slaves, and the wealth that flowed from slavery had a great deal to do with the expanding opportunities for those early Americans who exemplified Puritan virtues of industry, frugality, and prudence. A problem also arises when success is equated with virtue, and failure with sin and personal inadequacy. Not only does this individualize success or failure, thus obscuring the whole issue of social justice, but it also treats virtue and its opposite as a matter of personal endowment, rather than as traits that need to be explained in terms of their historical and social sources.

It has never been easy to accommodate the success myth to the embarrassing realities of racial inequality. If the United States is an open society where the individual is not irreparably handicapped by "birth, family, and class," then how is racial hierarchy to be explained? When Gunnar Myrdal suggested in the 1950s that racism constituted an unhappy contradiction between American ideals and practices, this was heralded as a major advance. Indeed, the thrust of previous research had been to find in the cephalic index or in intelligence tests clear evidence of a biological inferiority that predestined blacks to subordinate status. The discrediting of scientific racism is unquestionably one of the great triumphs of liberal social science. However, subsequent theorists developed a social-scientific variant of scientific racism that essentially substituted culture for genes. Now it was held that groups that occupy the lowest strata of society are saddled by cultural systems that prevent them from climbing the social ladder. As before, failure is explained not in terms of societal structures, but in terms of traits endemic to the groups themselves.

For the exponents of social-scientific racism, furthermore, culture is almost as immutable as the genes themselves. Thus, for example, Thomas Sowell writes:

> Specific skills are a prerequisite in many kinds of work. But history shows new skills being rather readily acquired in a few years, as compared to the generations—or centuries—required for attitude changes. Groups today plagued by absenteeism, tardiness, and a need for constant supervision at work or in school are typically descendants of people with the same habits a century or more ago. *The cultural inheritance can be more*

important than biological inheritance, although the latter stirs more controversy.[2]

As Sowell contends in this passage and his more extended disquisitions, a defective culture is the chief reason that blacks have not followed in the footsteps of immigrants in their pursuit of the American Dream. Jews, on the other hand, are the perfect counterexample—"the classic American success story—from rags to riches against all opposition."[3] Their formula for success amounts to having a certain cultural magic, called "human capital." To quote Sowell again:

> Whether in an ethnic context or among peoples and nations in general, much depends on the whole constellation of values, attitudes, skills, and contacts that many call a culture and that economists call 'human capital.' . . . The importance of human capital in an ethnic context is shown in many ways. Groups that arrived in America financially destitute have rapidly risen to affluence, when their cultures stressed the values and behavior required in an industrial and commercial economy. Even when color and racial prejudices confronted them—as in the case of the Chinese and Japanese—this proved to be an impediment but was ultimately unable to stop them.[4]

In the hands of Thomas Sowell, "human capital" is little more than an obfuscation for writing a morality tale whereby groups—notably Jews and Asians—who have "the right stuff" overcome every impediment of race and class to reach the economic pinnacle. Other groups—especially blacks—suffer from historically conditioned cultural defects that condemn them to lag behind in the economic competition. Of course, Sowell's morality tale is not an original creation. His ethnic heroes and racial villains are merely an updated version of traditional folklore that pitted rugged cowboys against treacherous Indians (which also had racist overtones).

Nor is this racist folklore, masked as social science, politically innocent. Its covert ideological function is to legitimize existing

2. Thomas Sowell, *Ethnic America* (New York: Basic Books, 1981), p. 284. Italics added.

3. Ibid., p. 98

4. Ibid., p. 282. For another view, see my "Human Capital: A Critique," *The Review of Black Political Economy* 14:1 (Summer 1985), pp. 67–74.

racial inequalities. By placing cultural blame on the victims, the nation's vaunted ideals are reconciled with patently undemocratic divisions and inequities. By projecting collective Horatio Algers, in the unlikely forms of Jews and Asians, it is demonstrated that "success" is attainable to everyone, without regard to "birth, family, and class." Like all myths, the ethnic myth has an implicit morale: "we" are not responsible, morally or politically, for "their" misfortune.

New Heroes: Asians and West Indians

Social science's enchantment with the success myth, replete with its cast of heroes and villains, has been renewed in recent years with the arrival of millions of immigrants, the majority of whom are Asians, West Indians, and Hispanics. That these new immigrants have generally settled in cities with large concentrations of poverty-stricken blacks has only highlighted the contrast between upwardly mobile immigrants and inner-city blacks. Invidious comparisons have been common in the popular press, and social scientists have churned out more spurious scholarship extolling cultural virtue and reciting the stock tale of triumph over adversity. That these new heroes—Asians and West Indians—belong to racial minorities has thickened the plot, since it demonstrates, according to these scholars, that "race" is not an insurmountable obstacle and cannot explain why so many blacks are still mired in poverty.

Before taking up the myth of success as it involves Asians and West Indians, let us put the new immigration in historical context.

In 1965 Congress passed the Hart-Celler Act, which abolished restrictive quotas based on national origin. These quotas had been enacted forty years earlier in order to curb the flow of immigration from eastern and southern Europe. The original legislation, passed in 1921, assigned each nation a quota based on the percentage of the foreign-born of that nation in the U.S. population, according to the 1910 Census. Three years later the law was amended to use the 1890 Census instead, thereby restricting even further the volume of immigration from eastern and southern Europe. The Immigration Act of 1924 also reaffirmed the near total exclusion of Asians that began with the Chinese Exclusion Act of 1882.

In abolishing national origins quotas, the Hart-Celler Act opened up the borders to all nations on an equal basis, allowing for an annual quota of 20,000 persons per nation, regardless of size. It also established a system of "preferences" that gave priority to individuals who were relatives of American citizens or who had occupational skills that were deemed by the Department of Labor to be in short supply. Other provisions, expanded over the years, allowed for the entry of refugees.

The net result of this new law, not fully anticipated at the time of its enactment, was to drastically alter both the volume and the racial mix of the new immigration. A few statistics will convey the dimensions of this change.[5] Between 1951 and 1965, prior to the Hart-Celler Act, immigration totaled about 4 million people. In the fourteen years after the new law went into effect, immigration increased to 5.8 million. The percentage of immigrants from Europe and Canada declined from 62 to 27 percent. Asians, West Indians, and Hispanics now accounted for nearly two-thirds of all immigrants. Before 1965 immigration from Asia was about 21,000 a year; after 1965 it rose to 150,000 a year.

Most accounts attribute the abolition of national orgins quotas to President Kennedy's "idealism," or to the "liberalism" associated with the early 1960s. Immigration reform, however, was the result of more than a vague political mood or trend. It must be seen within the context of the civil rights movement, which discredited official racism and made national origins quotas a national embarrassment. This is at least one reason that the proposal to abolish these discriminatory quotas was morally compelling and politically acceptable. Of course, it is ironic that blacks, through their protest movement, helped to lower immigration barriers against nationalities that previously were racially ineligible, when these same groups are then used to suggest that black economic problems cannot be blamed on "race."

Thomas Sowell is prominent among those who have advanced this point of view. In the passage quoted earlier, Sowell notes that Chinese and Japanese confronted "color and racial prejudices," but

---

5. These figures come from Emanuel Tobier, "Foreign Immigration," in Charles Brecher and Raymond D. Horton, eds., *Setting Municipal Priorities, 1983* (New York: New York University Press, 1982), p. 163.

asserts that this "was ultimately unable to stop them." It is the West Indians, however, who provide Sowell with the clincher to his argument that it is culture, not race, that explains why blacks languish in poverty:

> While not racially distinct from American Negroes, West Indians have had a different cultural background. . . . These differences provide some clues as to how much of the situation of American Negroes in general can be attributed to color prejudice by whites and how much to cultural patterns among blacks.[6]

Several pages later Sowell is less equivocal:

> The contrast between the West Indians and American Negroes was not so much in their occupational backgrounds as in their behavioral patterns. West Indians were much more frugal, hard-working, and entrepreneurial. Their children worked harder and outperformed native black children in school.[7]

The passages above are examples of a unique logical fallacy, which might be called a "Sowellgism." It goes as follows:

Premise 1: Blacks, Asians, and West Indians are all races.
Premise 2: Asians and West Indians have succeeded.
Conclusion: Race cannot explain why blacks have not succeeded.

The trouble with this reasoning is that it uses an overgeneralized abstraction, "race," to gloss over crucial differences among the racial groups being compared to one another. Only in the most general sense can it be claimed that Asians, West Indians, and African Americans are all "races" that have been victims of racial stereotyping and discrimination. Although true, this proposition obscures the unique oppression that blacks have endured throughout American history, beginning with two centuries of slavery and another century of official segregation, reinforced by the lynch mob and systematically unequal treatment in all major institutions. West Indians, of course, were also slaves, but living in island homelands

---

6. Thomas Sowell, op. cit., p. 216.

7. Ibid., p. 219. For a similar popular account, see "America's Super Minority," *Fortune* 114 (November 24, 1986), p. 148.

that were predominantly black, they have been insulated from the legalized and all-encompassing segregation that is unique to the African American experience.

Nor can this be dismissed as "history" that has no bearing on the present generation. If mobility is placed in correct sociological perspective, and regarded not as an individual event but as a process that occurs incrementally across generations, it becomes clear that America's legacy of racism has had a significant impact on the life chances even of today's black youth. To say this is not to engage in "comparative suffering." It is merely to acknowledge the unique oppression that blacks have experienced on American soil. Otherwise it is scarcely possible to explain why blacks have been a perennial underclass in American society, and why they continue to lag behind other "racial" minorities.

The Myth of Asian Success

In 1986 the five top recipients of the prestigious Westinghouse Science Talent Search were of Asian descent. This prompted a spate of articles in magazines and newspapers seeking to explain how a tiny minority, representing less than 2 percent of the national population, could achieve such bewildering success. The question, as framed by Malcolm Browne in an op-ed piece in the *New York Times,* is: "Do Asians have genetic advantages, or does their apparent edge in scientific skills stem from their special cultural tradition?"[8] Thus are we offered a choice between genes and culture as explanations for the academic excellence among Asians. Browne rejects genetic determinism, but has no such qualms with respect to cultural determinism. Paraphrasing an unnamed Westinghouse spokesman, he writes: "Tightly-knit families and high respect for all forms of learning are traditional characteristics of Asian societies . . . as they are for Jewish societies; in the past a very high proportion of top Westinghouse winners were Jewish." Of course, as Browne himself remarks, "the odd thing is that until the twentieth century, real science scarcely existed in Asia." Undaunted by this apparent

8. Malcolm W. Browne, "A Look at Success of Young Asians," *New York Times* (March 25, 1986), p. A31.

contradiction, he argues that Asian children are endowed with "an underlying devotion to scholarship—the kind of devotion imprinted on Asian children by a pantheon of ancestors"—that has made them receptive to Western scientific thought. Thus is a theory bent to accommodate inconvenient facts.

Two years later the *New York Times* ran another piece under the heading, "Why Do Asian Pupils Win Those Prizes?"[9] The author, Stephen Graubard, a professor of history at Brown University and editor of *Daedalus,* opines that Asians, who were eleven of the fourteen Westinghouse finalists from Cardozo High School in Queens, New York, have the advantage of stable families and Asian mothers who rear their children for success. With an air of resignation, he then turns the question onto blacks and Puerto Ricans: "What is to be done for those hundreds of thousands of other New York children, many of illegitimate birth, who live with one parent, often in public housing, knowing little outside their dilapidated and decaying neighborhoods?" Since Graubard does not believe that the schools can do much to compensate for the defective culture of children from poverty backgrounds, these children are presumably condemned to languish in the cultural wasteland.

The same single-minded preoccupation with culture is found in yet another article in *The New York Times Magazine* on "Why Asians Succeed Here." The author, Robert Oxnam, president of the prestigious Asia Society, writes as follows:

> The story of these new immigrants goes far beyond the high school valedictorians and Westinghouse Science scholars we read about in our newspapers. It is the story of a broader cultural interaction, a pairing of old Asian values with American individualism, Asian work ethics with American entrepreneurship. And, where those cultural elements have collided, it has also been a story of sharp disappointments and frustration.[10]

Once again, culture is the fulcrum of success. Like the other writers quoted above, Oxnam identifies "the strong family ties and pow-

9. Stephen G. Graubard, "Why Do Asian Pupils Win Those Prizes?" *New York Times* (January 29, 1988), p. A35.

10. Robert B. Oxnam, "Why Asians Succeed Here," *New York Times Magazine* (November 30, 1986), p. 70.

erful work ethics of Asian cultures" as "key factors in Asian-American achievement."

This theory of Asian success is a new spin on earlier theories about Jews, to whom Asians are explicitly compared. As with the theory of Jewish success, there are a number of conceptual and empirical problems that throw the theory into question:

1. The theory of "Asian" success lumps together some twenty-five nationalities that are very disparate in history and culture. It is only in the United States that they are assumed to share a common "Asian" heritage. Little or no evidence is put forward to substantiate claims that they share common values with respect to family and work, that these values are significantly different from those found among non-Asian groups, or that these values are the key factors in explaining which Asians get ahead or why more Asians do so than others. Here is a classic case of circular reasoning. Values are not measured independently, but inferred from success, and then posited as the cause of success.

2. Theories of Asian success gloss over the fact that large segments of the Asian populations in the United States are far from prosperous. Alongside dramatic and visible success, touted in the popular media, are deep pockets of poverty, exploitation, and despair. Moreover, if successful Asians are presumed to owe their success to distinctively Asian values with respect to family and work, then are we to assume that less affluent Asians are deficient in these values? Are they therefore less "Asian"?

3. As in the case of Jewish success, the prevailing theory of Asian success overlooks the operation of premigration class factors that go a long way toward explaining the destinies of these immigrants after their arrival. The issue here has to do with selective migration—that is, with who decides to emigrate and who is permitted entry. As Ezra Vogel, a scholar of China and Japan, has noted, Asian immigrants "are a very biased sample, the cream of their own societies."[11] They are drawn disproportionately from the intellectual and professional elites that, for one reason or another, have restricted opportunity in their home countries. Many of them have been admitted under the occupational preferences built into

11. Quoted in Fox Butterfield, "Why Asians Are Going to the Head of the Class," Education Supplement, *New York Times* (August 3, 1986), section 12, p. 20.

Table 9

PERCENTAGE OF PROFESSIONALS AMONG ASIAN IMMIGRANTS WITH OCCUPATIONS

	1961–65	1966–68	1969–71	1971–74	1975–77
China	31%	35%	47%	37%	31%
India	68	67	89	84	73
Japan	44	50	45	37	28
Korea	71	75	70	51	38
Philippines	48	60	70	63	47
All Asians	40	52	62	54	44
All Immigrants	20	25	29	27	25

SOURCE: Adapted from Morrison G. Wong and Charles Hirschman, "The New Asian Immigrants," in *Culture, Ethnicity, and Identity,* ed. William McCready (New York: Academic Press: 1983), pp. 395–97.

the new immigration law. In short, they are "successful" even before their arrival in America.

Data collected by the Immigration and Naturalization Service demonstrate the class character of Asian immigration. Table 9 reports the percentage of immigrant workers classified as professionals.[12] In the case of Indians, over three-quarters of immigrants with occupations are professionals; this reached a high point in 1969–71 when nine out of every ten Indians with occupations were professionals. Among Filipinos, Koreans, and Japanese the figures range between half and three-quarters; among Chinese, the figures are somewhat lower, but still much higher than for non-Asians. The influx of professionals of all nationalities reached a peak between 1969 and 1971, and declined thereafter. Nevertheless, the evidence is clear that a major segment of Asian immigration represents an educational and occupational elite.

12. These percentages are based on the number of immigrants who report having a job, thereby excluding nonworking women, as well as the old and young.

Other data indicate that between 1965 and 1981 some 70,000 medical professionals—physicians, nurses, and pharmacists—came from the Philippines, South Korea, and India.[13] Another major source of immigrants has been students who enter the United States with student visas and then do not return to their home country. Of the 70,000 Chinese students from Taiwan between 1950 and 1983, it is estimated that 90 percent remained in the United States. The same is true of tens of thousands of students from Hong Kong, Korea, and other Asian countries. What these figures indicate is not a dramatic success story, but merely the transfer of intellectual and professional elites from less developed nations.

These immigrants start out with the educational and occupational resources that are generally associated with educational achievement in the next generation. To put the cultural theory to a fair empirical test, one would have to compare the children of Asian professionals to the children of other professionals. Only in this way could we assess the significance of distinctive ethnic factors. It is hardly valid to compare the children of upper-middle-class Asian professionals to the children of unemployed black workers, as is done when "Asians" are compared to "blacks."[14]

Not all Asian immigrants, however, come from advantaged backgrounds. Indeed, in recent years the flow of immigrants has included large numbers of uneducated and unskilled workers. These are the "downtown Chinese," as Peter Kwong calls them in his recent book, *The New Chinatown*.[15] These immigrants have difficulty finding employment in the racially segmented labor market outside of Chinatown, and are forced to accept jobs, commonly in sweatshops

13. Illsoo Kim, "Ethnic Class Division among Asian Immigrants: Its Implications for Social Welfare Policies," unpublished paper presented at the Conference on Asian American Studies, Cornell University, October 24, 1986, p. 3.

14. If there is a distinctively ethnic factor in patterns of Asian mobility, it is that, like Jews of earlier generations, Asians realize that their channels of opportunity are restricted by prejudice. Closed off from the corporate fast lane, they are drawn to the professions. The sciences are particularly attractive to individuals who lack fluency in English. Data reporting SAT scores indicate that Asian American students score far above average on the math test, but far below average on the verbal test. *New York Times*, Section 12: "Education Life" (August 3, 1986), p. 3.

15. Peter Kwong, *The New Chinatown* (New York: Hill & Wang, 1987), pp. 5–6.

and restaurants, that match their nineteenth-century counterparts in their debasing exploitation. It has yet to be demonstrated that the children of these super-exploited workers are part of an Asian success story. Indeed, the outbreak of gang violence among China-town youth has exploded another myth that had great currency in the 1950s; namely, that because of their close-knit families, delinquency is virtually nonexistent among the Chinese.[16]

In demystifying and explaining Asian success, we come again to a simple truth: that what is inherited is not genes, and not culture, but class advantage and disadvantage. If not for the extraordinary selectivity of the Asian immigrant population, there would be no commentaries in the popular press and the social science literature extolling Confucian values and "the pantheon of ancestors" who supposedly inspire the current generation of Asian youth. After all, no such claims are made about the Asian youth who inhabit the slums of Manila, Hong Kong, and Bombay, or, for that matter, San Francisco and New York.

The Myth of West Indian Success

The mythical aspects of West Indian success, and the invidious comparisons between West Indians and blacks, predate the current wave of immigration. In *Beyond the Melting Pot,* published in 1963, Glazer and Moynihan wrote that "the ethos of the West Indians, in contrast to that of the Southern Negro, emphasized saving, hard work, investment and education."[17] Although Glazer and Moynihan offer no evidence to support their claims, their observations are consistent with those made by other observers over several decades.[18] The key issue, though, is not whether West Indians in New York had the exemplary cultural traits that were ascribed to them. The issue is whether these cultural traits *explain* West Indian

16. For example, see Henry Beckett, "How Parents Help Chinese Kids Stay Out of Trouble," series in the *New York Post* (July 11–13, 1955), and Betty Lee Sung, *The Story of the Chinese in America* (New York: Collier, 1971), p. 156.

17. Nathan Glazer and Daniel Patrick Moynihan, *Beyond the Melting Pot* (Cambridge: MIT Press, 1963), p. 35.

18. For example, Ira Reid, *The Negro Immigrant* (New York: Arno Press, 1969), originally published in 1939; James Weldon Johnson, *Black Manhattan* (New York: Knopf, 1930).

success, or whether, on the contrary, West Indians were more middle-class to begin with, and this explains their different attitudes with respect to "saving, hard work, investment and education."

As with Asians, the factor of selective migration must be considered. To begin with, we need to distinguish between two waves of West Indian immigration: the first, during the 1920s; the second, after the 1965 Hart-Celler Act. The first wave of immigrants were a highly selective group. According to immigration records, almost all of the adults—89 percent—were literate, a figure far higher than that for West Indians who did not emigrate, or for the southern blacks to whom they are compared.[19] Over 40 percent of the West Indian immigrants were classified as skilled, and some of these were highly educated professionals. Thus, once again, in drawing overall comparisons between West Indians and African Americans, we are comparing groups that differ in their social class as well as their ethnicity. It has never been shown that West Indians are different in terms of "saving, hard work, investment, and education" when compared with their social class equals who are not West Indian.[20]

19. Nancy Foner, "West Indians in New York City and London: A Comparative Analysis," in Constance R. Sutton and Elsa M. Chaney, eds., *Caribbean Life in New York City* (New York: Center for Migration Studies, 1987), p. 123.

20. In their study of Jamaican and black American migrant farm workers, Nancy Foner and Richard Napoli observed differences between the two groups that, at first glance, appear to support the cultural thesis. The black American farm workers were frequently apathetic on the job, and squandered part of their wages on liquor and gambling. In contrast, the Jamaican workers "worked very hard, were extremely productive, and saved most of their earnings" (p. 492).

To their credit, Foner and Napoli probe beneath surface behavior, and show that the two groups have different origins and are recruited through different procedures. For black Americans, migrant labor was a last resort and a dead end, whereas for Jamaicans the wages meant a higher living standard when they returned home, and the possibility of purchasing land or establishing a small business. Thus, the same work attracted a different calibre of worker, and the same pay provided different incentives.

Second, as offshore workers, Jamaicans were recruited under a program that not only included a physical exam, but also considered their previous work record. They also had to meet a work quota to remain in the camp and to ensure that they would be hired again. In these ways the Jamaican recruiting system "seemed to weed out the kinds of workers who frequently travelled North in the black-American migrant stream" (p. 501). Nancy Foner and Richard Napoli, "Jamaican and Black-American Migrant Farm Workers: A Comparative Analysis," *Social Problems* 25 (June 1978), pp. 491–503.

In other words, before generalizing about "West Indian cultural values," we need to be clear about which West Indians we have in mind. This is sharply illustrated by Nancy Foner's study of West Indians in New York City and London.[21] Since both groups have the same cultural heritage, this factor cannot explain why West Indians in New York have been more successful than those in Britain. Foner shows that the two immigrant pools are different in occupational background. Those who flocked to Britain during the 1950s were responding to labor shortages and an open-door immigration policy for Commonwealth nations. Although many were skilled workers, only about 10 percent were classified as white-collar. In contrast, among West Indian legal emigrants to the United States between 1962 and 1971, 15 percent were professional workers and another 12 percent worked in other white-collar occupations. For this reason alone, it is not surprising that West Indians in New York have been conspicuously more successful than those in London.[22]

The selective character of West Indian immigration to the United States, as already suggested, "stacks the deck" in terms of any comparisons to African Americans. Especially at a time when there was virtually no indigenous black middle class, the influx of a small West Indian elite of professionals, businessmen, and prominent individuals did in fact stand out, and seemed to support notions of West Indian cultural superiority. Two things have changed since the migration of the 1920s, however. In the first place, there is a sizable African American middle class. Second, West Indian migration has become more occupationally diverse than was previously

21. Nancy Foner, "West Indians in New York City and London: A Comparative Analysis," in Sutton and Chaney, eds., *Caribbean Life in New York City,* op. cit. Also, see Roy Simon Bryce-Laporte, "New York City and the New Caribbean Immigration: A Contextual Statement," *International Migration Review* 13:2 (1979) pp. 214–34.

22. Ibid., p. 123. In addition to differences in the occupational background of the two West Indian cohorts, Foner cites two other factors that help to explain why West Indians have fared better in the United States: (1) the migration spans a much longer period, and is already into the second generation, and (2) they benefited from having a preexisting black community that provided patronage for West Indian professionals and entrepreneurs, and that allowed West Indians to be cast into a privileged intermediary position between black and white America (comparable in some ways to the position of the coloreds in South Africa).

the case. Therefore, we have to reconsider our assumptions regarding the social status of West Indians in relation to African Americans.

In a paper entitled "West Indian Success: Myth or Fact?" Reynolds Farley undertakes an extensive analysis of 1980 Census data.[23] He concludes that there is more myth than fact in suppositions about West Indian success.

Farley divided his sample into five groups: native whites, native blacks, black immigrants pre-1970, black immigrants post-1970, and blacks of West Indian ancestry (born in the United States but of West Indian parents or grandparents). On all relevant social and economic indicators, the four black cohorts differ little among themselves, and where differences exist, they are small in comparison to the differences between blacks and whites. For example, the figures below indicate the percentages of families that are female-headed:

Whites 11%
Native blacks 37%
Black immigrants pre-1970 . . . . 33%
Black immigrants post-1970 . . . . 25%
West Indian ancestry 38%

Except for recent immigrants, female-headed households are as prevalent among West Indians as among native blacks. Thus, the data do not support the widespread notion that West Indians have "strong families" in comparison to African Americans.

Nor do the data support the notion that West Indians are endowed with an entrepreneurial spirit that leads to business success. The following figures, adjusted for age, report the rate of self-employment among men:

White . . . . 87 per thousand
Native blacks 30
Black immigrants pre-1970 41
Black immigrants post-1970 22
West Indian ancestry 45

23. Reynolds Farley, "West Indian Success: Myth or Fact," unpublished manuscript (Ann Arbor, Mich.: Population Studies Center, University of Michigan, 1987). Statistical data are taken from pp. 8, 11, and 13. Also see Reynolds Farley and Walter R. Allen, *The Color Line and the Quality of Life in America* (New York: Russel Sage, 1987), chapter 12.

The rate of self-employment among recent West Indian immigrants is strikingly low (in contrast to what is found among recent Korean immigrants, for example). It is true that earlier West Indian immigrants and their descendants have a higher rate of self-employment than do native blacks, but the levels are still much lower than that for whites. In short, self-employment is not so pronounced among West Indians as to support crude popular notions concerning "Jew-maicans," or, for that matter, more refined claims of "ethnic enterprise" and "entrepreneurial spirit" supposedly endemic to West Indian culture.

Similar patterns are found with respect to education, occupation, and income. West Indians are generally higher on these measures of social class than native blacks, but the differences are not great and there is always the suspicion that they are an artifact of selective migration. For example, the figures below report the average earnings in 1979 of employed males between the ages of 25 and 64:

Native whites.............................. 15,170
Native blacks............................. 9,380
Black immigrants pre-1970................. 11,170
Black immigrants post-1970............... 7,460
West Indian ancestry...................... 10,720

Again, West Indians are much closer to native blacks in their earnings than they are to whites, and recent West Indian immigrants have the lowest incomes of all five groups. On the basis of his analysis of these 1980 Census data, Farley reached the following conclusion:

> We have shown that black immigrants and West Indians in 1980 were quite similar to native blacks on the most important indicators of social and economic status. There is no basis now—and apparently there was none in the past—for arguing that the success of West Indians in the United States "proves" that culture, rather than racial discrimination, determines the current status of blacks.[24]

The critical role that premigration factors play in a group's "adjustment" is even more vividly illustrated by the two waves of Cuban immigration. The first wave, occurring in the aftermath of

24. Ibid., p. 15.

the Cuban Revolution, consisted largely of Cuba's economic elites—professionals, businessmen, shopkeepers, and others disenchanted with Cuban socialism. The second wave, "the Mariel invasion," consisted of ordinary Cubans, including a small number of criminals and mental patients whom the Cuban government cynically placed aboard the boats. The first wave was welcomed, especially in southern Florida's depressed economy, and inspired exuberant articles, like the one in *Fortune* magazine on "Those Amazing Cuban Emigrants."[25] The second wave received a far less hospitable reception, and were besmirched by sensational press reports suggesting that the Mariel Cubans were mostly criminals, lunatics, and degenerates.[26] The Cuban cultural magic seemed to have vanished.

In the final analysis, the attempt to use Asians and West Indians to prove that "race" cannot explain the plight of black America is fallacious at best, and sinister at worst. It is based on an untenable juxtaposition of groups that look alike in terms of a simplistic racial classification (they are all "racial" minorities), but who are very different in terms of their social class origins, in terms of the structures of opportunity they encounter after their arrival, and even in terms of the depth of racism that limits access to these opportunities. This is not to deny that Asians and West Indian immigrants confront a difficult situation, one that calls forth all their cultural and personal resources. Nor is it to deny that both groups encounter racist barriers in their quest for a better life. It does not do them or ourselves any good, however, to use these struggling minorities to make specious comparisons to African Americans, and to minimize the significance of racism.

Old Villains, New Terminology: The Underclass

If the American success myth has been revived with a new cast of ethnic heroes, it has the same downtrodden racial villains. They

25. Tom Alexander, "Those Amazing Cuban Emigres," *Fortune* 74 (October 1966), pp. 144–49.

26. Actually, less than 5 percent of the Mariel migrants were hardened criminals, mental patients, or other undesirables. See Robert L. Bach, Jennifer B. Bach, and Timothy Triplett, "The Flotilla 'Entrants': Latest and Most Controversial," *Cuban Studies* 11 (1981), pp. 29–48.

have been refurbished, however, with a new name: "the under-class." This term, which originated in academic studies, made its way into the popular press with a 1982 book by Ken Auletta, entitled *The Underclass*. This was followed by articles in such popular magazines as *U.S. News and World Report, The Atlantic, Fortune, Newsweek, The Reader's Digest,* and *Time.*[27] By 1988 the term entered the political discourse of the presidential election, as candidates were queried about their policies for dealing with the underclass. Though camouflaged behind a smokescreen of innuendo and code words, the issue permeated the campaign as the two major candidates vied with each other to demonstrate their commitment to "values." The values most often cited concerned family, work, and education, precisely those values central to the success myth and presumed to be lacking among the underclass.[28]

In its original conception, the term "underclass" referred to segments of the poverty population who languished on the bottom even during periods of economic growth and declining unemployment. They were a "perennial underclass," consisting largely though not exclusively of racial minorities. Later the definition was extended to refer not only to objective conditions of chronic poverty and joblessness, but to "socially dysfunctional behavior" as well. In summing up the prevailing view of the underclass, Ricketts and Sawhill write: "Thus, most observers agree that the underclass is characterized by *behaviors which are at variance with those of mainstream America* (such as joblessness, welfare dependency,

27. Ken Auletta, *The Underclass* (New York: Random House, 1982); "A Permanent Black Underclass?" *U.S. News and World Report* 100 (March 3, 1986), and "The Black Underclass," 100 (April 19, 1986); Nicholas Lemann, "The Origins of the Underclass," *The Atlantic* (June, July 1986); "America's Underclass: What to Do?" *Fortune* 115 (May 11, 1987); "Why We Can't Wait Any Longer," *Newsweek* (March 7, 1988); Pete Hammil, "American's Black Underclass: Can It Be Saved?" *Reader's Digest* 132 (June 1988); "The Underclass: Breaking the Cycle," *Time* 132 (October 10, 1988).

28. The underclass issue surfaced in less muffled tones in the Republican commercial about Willie Horton, a black man who raped and murdered a woman while on a furlough from a Massachusetts prison. The unmistakable purpose of this commercial was to reap political hay from widespread fears concerning the prevalence of drugs, crime, and violence associated in the public mind with the underclass. Whatever its impact on the 1988 election, this episode demonstrated the ominous potential for a reactionary backlash when lower-class blacks are portrayed in demonic terms.

unwed parenting, criminal or uncivil behavior, and dropping out of high school)."[29] To measure the underclass, Ricketts and Sawhill begin by defining an "underclass area" as a Census tract with a high proportion of (1) high school dropouts; (2) young males outside the labor force; (3) welfare recipients; and (4) female-headed households. An underclass individual is "someone in an underclass area who engages in various socially costly behaviors." On the basis of these criteria, Rickets and Sawhill estimate that 2.5 million people live in underclass areas. Most of the underclass tracts are in urban areas, and 59 percent of their residents are black and 10 percent Hispanic. Not all these people engage in underclass behaviors, but they all live in "neighborhoods where such behaviors were common."

Although such an appeal has all the trappings of objective social science, it is, I would submit, riddled with value assumptions. Furthermore, it obfuscates the historical and structural sources of the underclass, and fudges over the significance of racism in the production and maintenance of this underclass. Let me elaborate:

1. The term "underclass" implicitly accepts the established order as the starting point of analysis. We begin with the empirical observation that certain people languish outside—or "below"—the class system, and we want to know why. The class system itself is accepted as a given—an empirical if not normative fact of life. Thus, attention is directed not at the structures of inequality that produce an underclass, but at the attributes of the individuals who occupy this stratum. Once again, methodological individualism plays havoc with the sociological imagination, reducing societal phenomena to an individual level of analysis. Hence, the individual becomes the focal point of change as well. The presumption is that we can eliminate the underclass by rehabilitating its victims.

The problem with taking traits of the underclass out of historical and institutional context is that the underclass is then reduced to the level of atomized individuals. Indeed, it is all too easy to isolate the aberrant and antisocial behavior of the underclass, to rail against it, and to propose programs to redeem these deficient individuals. But so long as we focus exclusively on individuals who belong to

29. Erol R. Ricketts and Isabel V. Sawhill, "Defining and Measuring the Underclass," *Journal of Policy Analysis and Management* 7 (1988), p. 317; italics added.

the underclass without regard to the structural conditions that produce such individuals in the first place, we end up with superficial truths, facile value judgments, and ineffectual policy.

2. By reducing the underclass to the level of atomized individuals, the term in effect denies the racial character of the underclass. Thus, the defining criteria involve measures of prolonged joblessness, economic privation, and the like. These measures are then used as the basis for extrapolating the racial composition of the underclass, as when Rickets and Sawhill estimate that blacks constitute 59 percent of the 2.5 million people who live in underclass areas. The problem with this approach, however, is that it implicitly denies the historical and group character of the underclass, and in doing so obscures the role of racism in producing and perpetuating this underclass. The "real underclass," one might say, is an exclusive affiliation, not determined by demographics alone. It is the birthright of those who belong to racially stigmatized groups with a history of oppression and labor market segregation. In point of fact, there are different underclasses—different in their origins, their social constitution, their circumstances, and their implications for the society at large. To lump these disparate groups together on the basis of common demographic traits is to obscure the historically specific factors that produce these various underclasses, and in particular, the role that racism has played in producing the black underclass.[30]

3. The most serious flaw in the concept of the underclass is the conflation of race, class, and culture. The result is a conceptual muddle that blurs the distinctive roles of race, class, and culture in producing the underclass, the explanatory weight that is to be assigned to each, and the dynamic relationships among them. Instead, we are left with a nebulous category that, to be sure, fits a social reality. There *are* people, not all of them minorities, who may be said to live "outside the class system" and to engage in "behaviors at variance with those of mainstream society." We do not need

---

30. The more stringent the defining criteria of the underclass, the higher the proportion who are black. Thus, blacks constitute a third of those living below the poverty line. However, they are two-thirds of those who are "persistently poor," defined as being poor in at least eight of the previous ten years. Terry K. Adams, Greg J. Duncan, and Willard L. Rogers, "The Persistence of Urban Poverty," in Fred R. Harris and Roger Wilkins, eds., *Quiet Riots* (New York: Pantheon, 1988), p. 84.

sociology to tell us that, and I fear that the term "underclass" only gives scientific sanction to ordinary perceptions and prejudices regarding race and class. Where sociology can be useful is in shedding light on the social production of this underclass. To do so, we need to disentangle race, class, and culture, instead of blurring these crucial analytical distinctions and focusing only on surface manifestations.

The conflation of race, class, and culture has left the theoretical door open for different theorists to single out whichever factor pleases them for claims of causality. For some, "culture" is the key factor in explaining the underclass. For others, it is "class," and the unfavorable structure of opportunity that keeps people trapped in poverty. Both these positions minimize the significance of "race"—that is, specifically racist structures in the production and reproduction of the underclass. In the analysis that follows, I limit the discussion of "race" to African Americans, in order to bring into focus the historically specific factors that explain the black underclass.

The Underclass as Culture

The concept of the underclass has provided a new rubric for the old, and in my view, discredited, culture-of-poverty thesis.[31] As indicated earlier, for many investigators aberrant culture and antisocial behavior are assumed in the very definition of the underclass, thus obscuring cause and effect. The issue is not whether members of the underclass engage in "socially dysfunctional behavior." Rather, the issue is whether this behavior *explains* why they are in the underclass or whether these individuals first find themselves in the underclass (typically as a matter of birth), and only afterward develop "socially dysfunctional behavior." Also at issue is whether this behavior, while clearly "dysfunctional" for the society at large, is nonetheless functional for the actors themselves, given their restricted life chances. As Douglas Glasgow writes in *The Black Underclass:*

31. See chapter 4 above.

Behaviors of young inner-city Blacks are . . . consciously propagated via special socialization rituals that help the young Blacks prepare for inequality at an early age. With maturity, these models of behavior are employed to neutralize the personally destructive effects of institutionalized racism. Thus, they form the basis of a "survival culture" that is significantly different from the so-called culture of poverty. Notwithstanding its reactive origin, survival culture is not a passive adaptation to encapsulation but a very active—at times devious, innovative, and extremely resistive—response to rejection and destruction. It is useful and necessary to young Blacks in their present situation. . . .[32]

In contrast to Glasgow's attempt to delineate the existential sources and functions of cultural patterns associated with the underclass, note how cause and effect are obscured in the following passage, excerpted from a recent article in *Fortune* magazine:

They are poor; but numbering around five million, they are a relatively small minority of the 33 million Americans with incomes below the official poverty line. Disproportionately black and Hispanic, they are still a minority within these minorities. What primarily defines them is not so much their poverty or race as their behavior—their chronic lawlessness, drug use, out-of-wedlock births, nonwork, welfare dependency, and school failure. *"Underclass" describes a state of mind and a way of life. It is at least as much cultural as an economic condition.*[33]

In this treatment of the underclass as "a state of mind and a way of life," we have a clear retrogression to the culture-of-poverty school of the 1960s, which was itself a retrogression to the cultural deprivation school of the 1950s. It seems that no sooner is the head of this theoretical dragon severed than it regenerates another. Part of the reason for its invincibility is that the cultural thesis has superficial validity and squares with everyday observation, not to

32. Douglas G. Glasgow, *The Black Underclass* (New York: Vintage Books, 1981), p. 25.

33. Myron Magnet, "America's Underclass: What to Do?" *Fortune* 115 (May 11, 1987), p. 130; italics added.

speak of the findings of a plethora of demographic and ethnographic studies. Why social scientists think they have discovered something when they find that an indigent and marginal population lives according to "different rules" from the middle classes is itself perplexing. The descriptive reality is there to be observed and measured. The critical question, which has been thoughtfully addressed by Elliot Liebow and several others, is not whether these cultural patterns exist, but whether they constitute an independent cultural traditional with "a life of their own," or whether they merely represent the cultural manifestations of extreme poverty and marginality, protracted across generations.

This issue, furthermore, does not turn on whether individual members of the underclass can hold down a good job when it is offered them. Some can and some cannot, according to studies that have put this to an empirical test. The problem with this approach is that it falls into the reductionist trap of treating poverty and its cultural correlates as attributes of atomized individuals. As I commented earlier, this trivializes the whole problem and leads to simplistic policy. The behavioral patterns we associate with a culture of poverty are contingent upon the adversities and deprivations that afflict whole populations. They are a *collective* response to *shared* circumstances and exigencies. Thus, it is no test of anything to pluck a handful of individuals out of this environment and to deposit them on an assembly line in some factory. Even if they adapt successfully, which is not a reasonable expectation, they will be replaced on the street corner by someone else. In short, it is myopic and futile to attempt cultural change without attacking the constellation of social and structural conditions in which this culture is embedded.

The Class Interpretation of the Underclass

If some observers of the underclass give theoretical primacy to culture, others give theoretical primacy to class. William Wilson is in the forefront of those who see the underclass as the byproduct of economic dislocations that have transformed the urban economy, wiping out literally millions of jobs in manufacturing and related fields.[34] These dislocations, which are themselves the product of larger transformations in the global economy, have had an especially severe impact on blacks since they are concentrated in cities and job sectors most affected by deindustrialization. Thus many blacks remain trapped in poverty, perhaps more so than any other group in American history.

Furthermore, Wilson sees this endemic unemployment and underemployment as the root cause of the "tangle of pathologies" associated with the underclass—unstable marriages, out-of-wedlock children, welfare, crime, drugs, and so on. Wilson's agenda for change is consistent with his analysis. Because the causes are not race-specific—that is, based on patterns of deliberate racial exclusion—neither can the resolution be race-specific. Thus, Wilson proposes "a universal program of reform" that would attack unemployment and underemployment.[35] Essentially, Wilson's agenda involves a renewal and expansion of the forgotten war on poverty. Thus, Wilson calls for (a) macroeconomic policy to promote growth and generate jobs, and (b) improved welfare and social services, including job training, for those who need it.

Over against the culture-of-poverty theorists, Wilson is mindful of the link between culture and social structure. He traces underclass culture primarily to the job crisis that afflicts ghetto workers, particularly males, destroying the basis for stable families and engendering various coping strategies that affront middle-class society. In terms of the discipline, Wilson's emphasis on economic structures and labor markets has enlarged the scope of analysis well beyond the antiquated race relations model, which presupposed that racial inequality was solely a function of race prejudice. Wilson seems to be saying that even if Myrdal had his way, and all whites were exorcised of their distorted and malicious racial beliefs, the underclass would be about as badly off as they are today. Without doubt, the underclass is more than a product of race and specific patterns of racial exclusion.

34. Wilson's ideas were first advanced in *The Declining Significance of Race* (Chicago: University of Chicago Press, 1980). Generally speaking, my comments address his latest formulation in *The Truly Disadvantaged* (Chicago: University of Chicago Press, 1987).

35. Ibid., chapter 7.

A problem arises, however, when class analysis is carried to a point that obscures the role that racist structures play not only in the production of the underclass, but in its perpetuation as well.

The Racist Sources of the Underclass

The first thing that needs to be said is that the very existence of a ghetto underclass is evidence of institutionalized racism. That is to say, if the cumulative disadvantages that ensue from past racism leave many blacks without the education and skills to compete for the better jobs, we are left with patterns of racial exclusion and inequality even if employers are not personally motivated by racial prejudice. That less than half of black men of working age are part of the labor force speaks for itself. This is a measure of the extent to which American labor markets are perpetuating patterns of racial inequality.[36]

But black workers *are* being discriminated against directly, to a far greater extent than Wilson allows. The fact of a large black middle class, relatively immune from racial stereotypes and acts of overt discrimination, is not really germane. Indeed, white society has come to recognize the new face of black America, and has responded by elaborating and refining racism to take class into account. Instead of blanket stereotypes that once applied to all blacks, whites have learned to discriminate between those respectable blacks who are reasonably tolerated, and those other blacks

36. My point is that the distinction between "race" and "class" should not obscure the racist dimensions of behavior that may be motivated by class but that is racist in its consequences. This issue surfaced in a recent controversy in Yonkers, New York, where whites were fiercely resisting court orders to construct low-cost housing that would introduce poor blacks into their middle-class neighborhoods. The *New York Times* quotes Governor Mario Cuomo as saying that white opposition was based on class, not race, and that these same people would accept Lena Horne or Harry Belafonte as neighbors. Perhaps so. But even if we grant that white resistance is motivated primarily by class, it still has the effect of perpetuating racial distinctions and racial inequalities. Social scientists may debate race and class, but history will judge the United States, not by what happens to Lena Horne and Harry Belafonte, but by its treatment of the anonymous individuals who inhabit America's ghettos.

who bear the stigma of the ghetto and are still objects of racial stereotyping, fear, and scorn. This elaboration of a once monistic system of beliefs may well be part of a long-term attenuation of racist ideology, with parallels to other ethnic groups (as when lace-curtain Irish were distinguished from shanty Irish, uptown Jews from downtown Jews, and so on). Nevertheless, the fact that middle-class blacks may encounter minimal racism does not mean that ghetto blacks are so fortunate.

Indeed, Wilson does not adequately explain why blacks—who were never heavily represented in the manufacturing sector in the first place—have not found more jobs in the rapidly expanding service sector. Along with others, he assumes that there is a "mismatch" between the educational and skill levels of black workers and the demands of a postindustrial labor market. As Wilson writes: "Basic structural changes in our modern industrial economy have compounded the problems of poor blacks because education and training have become more important for entry into the more desirable and higher-paying jobs and because increased reliance on labor-saving devices has contributed to a surplus of untrained black workers."[37] Of course, Wilson is right with respect to the *most* desirable and *highest*-paying jobs in the service sector. However, the vast majority of the new jobs in the service sector do not require a great deal of education and skills. This is true not only of the lowest paying jobs, but also of coveted jobs in major service industries, such as hospital and health care, hotels, restaurants, transportation, and sales. These are precisely the job areas where recent immigrants have made significant inroads, undoubtedly at the expense of blacks.

The problem with the mismatch hypothesis is that it seriously underestimates the color line in the world of work. There is, as Norman Fainstein has argued in a recent paper, a pattern of "employment ghettoization" whereby blacks are excluded from whole job sectors, especially those decently paid jobs that require minimal

37. Ibid., p. 126. For a full explication of the "mismatch hypothesis," see John D. Kasarda, "Urban Change and Minority Opportunities," in P. E. Peterson, ed., *The New Urban Reality* (Washington, D.C.: The Brookings Institute, 1985), pp. 33–67.

education and skills. On the basis of a detailed analysis of labor market data, Fainstein came to the following conclusion:

> ... the economic situation of blacks is rooted more in the character of the employment opportunities in growing industries than in the disappearance of "entry-level" jobs in declining industries. Unlike the immigrants of yesterday, the problem for blacks is not so much inadequate educations as the channeling of the educated into relatively poor jobs and the exclusion of many of the uneducated from work altogether.[38]

Thus, Fainstein shows that blacks who have attended college have a rate of unemployment as high as that for whites who have dropped out of high school. At the other end of the spectrum, less educated blacks have great difficulty in finding jobs that generally do not require much education. The restaurant industry is a case in point. Blacks are generally excluded from entry-level jobs with career ladders, such as waiters and cooks in full-service restaurants, and relegated to menial, low-paying, and dead-end jobs.[39]

In a 1985 study of closed labor markets in New York City, Walter Stafford also provides detailed documentation of labor market segregation. He found that 68 percent of all blacks work in only 20 of the city's 212 industries covered in the study—mainly hospitals, banks, insurance companies, telephone communications, and department stores. On the other hand, blacks have virtually no representation in 130 out of 193 industries in the city's private sector. Those blacks who are employed in core industries are generally found in clerical positions. Blacks are rarely found in supervisory positions anywhere in the service economy.[40]

Other data indicate the extraordinary dependence of blacks on public-sector employment. A total of 149,080 blacks in New York City—a full third of all black workers—were employed by the government in 1980. This number has increased by some 21,000

---

38. Norman Fainstein, "The Underclass/Mismatch Hypothesis as an Explanation for Black Economic Deprivation," *Politics and Society* 15:4 (1986–87), p. 439.

39. Thomas Bailey, "A Case Study of Immigrants in the Restaurant Industry," *Industrial Relations* 24 (Spring 1984), pp. 205–21.

40. Walter W. Stafford, "Closed Labor Markets: Underrepresentation of Blacks, Hispanics and Women in New York City's Core Industries and Jobs," publication of the Community Service Society of New York, 1985.

employees since 1970, despite overall shrinkage in the size of the government work force. On a national level, over 470,000 blacks are employed by the federal government, and another 835,000 are employed by state and local governments. Without this public-sector employment, which in large measure reflects affirmative action policy, much of the black middle class simply would not exist.[41]

Clearly, this pattern of employment ghettoization cannot be blamed solely on a mismatch between workers and jobs. It is equally the result of patterns of discrimination that leave whites with a virtual monopoloy on whole job sectors, especially in the expanding service economy. To the extent that blacks—tenth-generation Americans—do suffer from a deficit of education and skills, this must be seen in historical context. To tell these descendants of slaves and quasi-slaves that they would be hired in industry if such jobs existed, or in white-collar jobs if only they were qualified, amounts to a preposterous negation of history.

This is why I take issue with Wilson's categorical distinction between past and present racism, leading to the conclusion that the current problems of blacks have more to do with class than with race. These class disabilities are real enough, but they are the by-product of past racism, they are reinforced by present racism, and they constitute the basis for perpetuating racial divisions and racial inequalities. Wilson acknowledges all of this in principle, but still reaches the conclusion that race—that is, race per se—is of declining significance.

Nor is this a semantic quibble over how we define and measure racism. The full implications of Wilson's subsuming of race under class become apparent in the final chapters of *The Truly Disadvantaged*. Here Wilson criticizes the race-specific policies of the past, such as antidiscrimination legislation and affirmative action, for benefiting the black middle class, but offering little relief to the underclass. Consistent with his view that the underclass is connected with "the structure and functioning of the American economy," he

41. Roger Waldinger, "Changing Ladders and Musical Chairs: Ethnicity and Opportunity in Post-Industrial New York," *Politics and Society* 15:4 (1986–87), pp. 373, 380; *Annual Report on the Employment of Minorities, Women, and Individuals with Handicaps in the Federal Government, Fiscal Year 1985*, Equal Employment Opportunity Commission, 1985; *Minorities and Women in State and Local Government*, 1985, Equal Employment Opportunity Commission, 1985.

advocates programs that would attack unemployment and under-employment. His "hidden agenda," as he calls it, is to help the ghetto underclass "by emphasizing programs in which the more advantaged groups of all races can positively relate."[42] Thus, he presents his case for "a universal program" that would involve "long-term planning to promote both economic growth and sustained full employment, not only in higher-income areas but in areas where the poor are concentrated as well."[43]

Here we see in bold relief the policy ramifications of Wilson's thesis regarding the declining significance of race. In my view, his agenda for economic restructuring amounts to a variant of trickle-down economics. Instead of targeting programs and benefits directly to blacks, it entails macro-reforms that, in all probability, will help blacks last and least. To provide jobs for blacks, we are told, we have to provide jobs for everyone. Is the message to these oldest of Americans that they have to wait for a social democratic revolution before they can claim their rightful place in the nation's labor force?

I hasten to add that Wilson explicitly endorses affirmative action and other race-specific policies. However, he is convinced that they are limited in what they can accomplish, and that it is impossible to muster political support for programs targeted for blacks. I fail, however, to see why it is more realistic to place our bets on full employment and the other far-reaching policies that Wilson proposes. Indeed, I would argue that the lesson of the sixties was that programs that were initiated in response to the black protest movement and intended for blacks were derailed and ultimately defeated precisely because they were subsumed under a general war on poverty. Here was another missed opportunity in American race history, where there was a grass-roots movement and political momentum for a societal attack on institutionalized racism. Instead, the 9 million poor black Americans (these are 1966 figures) were lumped together with the 19 million poor white Americans. The nation, as it turns out, did not have the political will to underwrite and implement the structural changes that would have been necessary to wipe out poverty. Where a war on institutionalized racism might have succeeded, a war on poverty failed.

42. Op. cit., p. 120.
43. Ibid., p. 121.

By virtue of their unique oppression, blacks have historical and moral claim to have their grievances redressed before those of other groups. Blacks should not have to queue up with the other displaced workers in the nation's rust belt. For their underclass status is not merely the result of plant shutdowns. It is the end product of three centuries of racial oppression.

The Case for Race-Specific Public Policy

Just as Wilson's analysis led him to "a universal program" for change, the foregoing analysis suggests the need for a race-specific public policy. Several elements of such a policy are outlined below:

1. We need a national commitment to eliminate ghettos. It is remarkable how we, as a nation, have become inured to the odious moral connotations of this term. We talk about "ghettos" with the same neutrality that we talk about "suburbs." Ghettos are nothing less than the shameful residue of slavery. It took one century after this nation declared its own freedom from colonial domination to abolish slavery. It took another century, and a protracted and bloody civil rights struggle, to end official segregation. It is time for a third stage that will eliminate racial ghettos, and destroy the less visible and tangible barriers that manifest themselves in a host of inequities ranging from lower incomes to higher mortality.

2. The elimination of ghettos would entail large-scale programs of urban reconstruction, like those proposed by Wilson and others. These programs, however, should have the specific purpose of eliminating ghettos, lest they become a pork barrel for a myriad of "urban" and "minority" constituencies. Furthermore, in my view, these economic policies must not ignore the racial and cultural dimensions of the underclass. For economic policy to work, it is imperative that local groups and individuals be empowered so that the process of reconstruction can occur from within, rather than being imposed from outside. Only community-based groups can bridge the chasm that separates the underclass from mainstream society, and marshal the cultural and spiritual resources to effect meaningful change. This is the correct application of the culture-of-poverty thesis. When Oscar Lewis wrote that "the elimination of physical poverty *per se* may not be enough to eliminate the culture

of poverty,"[44] he pointed to the need to combat apathy and despair "by organizing the poor and giving them a sense of belonging, of power and of leadership."[45] In his book *The Black Underclass,* Douglas Glasgow also showed how street-corner men and former convicts and addicts were mobilized, in the wake of the Watts Riot and the infusion of federal funds, to work as constructive agents for change.[46] My point is that not only the ends, but the means as well, must be race-specific.

3. We should not be diverted by the adamant opposition to affirmative action, and the split in the liberal coalition over this issue. Affirmative action has been hotly contested because it is the most radical development in race policy since Reconstruction. It is radical because it legitimated the principle of compensation for past wrongs, and provided a fool-proof mechanism for achieving racial parity—one which has achieved significant results in major employment sectors.

To take one key example, in 1973 the American Telephone and Telegraph Company, one of the largest employers in corporate America, entered into a six-year agreement with the Equal Employment Opportunities Commission to correct prior discriminatory employment practices. By 1982 the percentage of minority craft workers had increased from 8.4 percent to 14.0 percent. The proportion of minorities in management increased at an even higher rate—from 4.6 percent to 13.1 percent.

Raw numbers point up the impact of affirmative action even more vividly. The number of black employees at IBM increased from 750 in 1962, to 7,251 in 1968, to 16,546 in 1980. Under threat of litigation, governmental agencies have pursued affirmative action programs even more aggressively. To take one example, by 1982 the number of black police officers nationally increased by 20,000. These diverse examples testify to the profound impact that affirmative action has had on black representation in both the private and public sectors.[47]

44. Oscar Lewis, *La Vida* (New York: Vintage, 1968), p. lii.
45. Ibid.
46. Glasgow, op. cit., chapter 8.
47. These figures come from chapter 4 of "A Report of the Citizen's Commission on Civil Rights," published by the Citizen's Commission on Civil Rights, 620 Michigan Ave. N.E., Washington, D.C. 20064. I am grateful to Gertrude Ezorsky for bringing this valuable report to my attention.

Having laid the groundwork and survived the harrowing legal battles, we should not turn away from affirmative action as a strategy for rectifying past wrongs.[48] On the contrary, affirmative action should be extended into all areas of our economy and society. Wilson is right to worry that its benefits will not filter down to the underclass, but this is not an insurmountable problem. Our statisticians have demonstrated their skill at classifying who belongs to the underclass. The challenge is to make this designation a ticket to a good job, instead of what Richard McGahey has called "poverty's voguish stigma."[49]

4. We need manpower policies that will assess immigration policy with respect to its impact on native workers, and minority workers in particular. Again, this raises issues that trouble the liberal conscience, and demands hard moral choices. However, as Otis Graham, Jr., wrote in *Dissent* in 1980, immigration restriction should be considered, "not simply in the interest of national economic efficiency, but as the only way to extend economic opportunity to our own disadvantaged."[50]

48. Of course, as we are finding out, "surviving the harrowing legal battles" is not irreversible. The Supreme Court recently rendered a decision that jeopardizes affirmative action programs in 36 states and 200 local governments. The test case was a Richmond, Virginia, law that channeled 30 percent of public works funds to minority-owned construction companies. When the law was passed less than 1 percent of the city's construction contracts had been awarded to minority-owned businesses in the previous five years. At the time half the city's population was black. The majority on the court insisted on a stringent standard of proof that such underrepresentation was the result of deliberate discrimination. Their claim, of course, is that they are upholding the principle of a color-blind society. In his dissenting opinion, on the other hand, Justice Blackmun wrote: "I never thought I would live to see the day when the city of Richmond, Virginia, the cradle of the Old Confederacy," having voluntarily tried to "lessen the stark impact of persistent discrimination," would then see its effort struck down by "this Court, the supposed bastion of equality." *New York Times* (January 24, 1989), p. 1.

49. Richard McGahey, "Poverty's Voguish Stigma," *New York Times* (March 12, 1982), p. A29.

50. Otis L. Graham, Jr., "Illegal Immigration and the Left," *Dissent* 27:3 (Summer 1980), p. 344. In New York City, for example, there were about 650,000 immigrant workers in 1979, comprising one-fifth of the total work force. The areas of largest immigrant concentration were as follows: manufacturing, 178,000; restaurants, 42,000; hospitals, 35,000; construction, 31,000. There were also large concentrations in various service industries, such as hotels, laundries, beauty shops, and shoe repair and tailor shops. Marcia Freedman, "The Labor Market for Immigrants in New York City," *New York Affairs* 17:4 (1983), p. 99.

In the past quarter century, when some 3 million industrial jobs disappeared, the nation absorbed over 11 million legal immigrants, not to speak of millions of undocumented workers. Thus, at the same time that we have been exporting jobs we have been importing workers—in even greater numbers. It may be true, as some have argued, that many of these immigrants are not in direct competition with the underclass.[51] Others are, however, and while this simple truth seems to elude the experts, it is acutely realized by average blacks who are in direct competition with immigrants. This was evident during the recent "riots" in southern Florida, where protesters voiced their resentment about the influx of Hispanic refugees.[52] Whatever salubrious effects immigration has for the economy as a whole, it can hardly be denied that the absorption of well over 11 million immigrants in the last quarter century has compounded the job crisis for the nation's 13 million black workers. Once again, the nation is pursuing a shortsighted policy of importing foreign labor instead of upgrading the skills of our marginal domestic workers.

I hasten to add that this is not an argument for blanket restriction. There are other compelling moral and political considerations that must be taken into account when shaping immigration policy. For one thing, different nationalities have different historical and moral claims. This is particularly true of nations previously conquered or colonized by the United States, including Mexico. Second, although immigration policy generally has been governed by self-interest, the United States *has* functioned as an asylum for the dispossessed, and we cannot in good conscience slam the door on desperate political and economic refugees. These legitimate concerns, however, must be balanced against the interests of unemployed and marginal native workers who pay the price of current immigration practices.

Nursing is a case in point. To meet a critical shortage of nurses, the United States has been importing tens of thousands of foreign nurses, largely from the Philippines and the West Indies. At the same time, we have been closing down nursing schools throughout

51. For example, see Michael Piore, "Another View on Migrant Workers," *Dissent* 27:3 (Summer 1980), pp. 347–51, and Roger Waldinger, op. cit.

52. "Dreams and Despair Collide as Miami Searches for Itself," *New York Times* (January 23, 1989), p. 1; "A Brightly Colored Tinderbox," *Time* (January 30, 1989), pp. 28–29.

the United States instead of expanding subsidies and creating channels of opportunity for blacks and other marginal groups. No doubt it is cheaper and more expedient to import nurses trained at some other nation's expense. However, such a shortsighted policy would be inconceivable if our nation's unresolved racial problems were high on the national agenda.

Whether or not a race-specific policy like the one proposed here is politically realistic, it is incumbent upon us as social scientists to put forward an analysis and agenda that are faithful to history and responsive to the racial crisis that still afflicts this society, with terrible repercussions for whites and blacks alike.[53] Besides, as we have learned from the past, what is "politically unrealistic" is subject to rapid change. Hopefully, it will not take another spiral of violence to convince this nation that it is time to eliminate that large residue of slavery that is to be found in unemployment halls, welfare centers, prisons, shelters, drug and alcohol rehabilitation centers, psychiatric wards, and street corners throughout the nation's ghettos.

Is Historical Reconciliation Possible?

In 1981, the same year this book was first published, Thomas Sowell published his book *Ethnic America*. His opening sentence read: "The peopling of America is one of the great dramas in all of human history."[54] *The Ethnic Myth* began on an admittedly more jarring note: "Ethnic pluralism in America has its origins in conquest, slavery, and exploitation of foreign labor." These different points of departure lead to analyses that, as one reviewer commented, are "180 degrees opposed" to one another. Whereas Sowell, as I have claimed, presents us with a comforting morality tale that extols America as a land of opportunity that rewards enterprise and cultural virtue, *The Ethnic Myth* presents a far less

53. For an astute analysis of the decline of race-specific public policy in the 1970s and 1980s, see Gary Orfield, "Race and the Liberal Agenda: The Loss of the Integrationist Dream," in Margaret Weir, Ann Shola Orloff, and Theda Skocpol, eds. *The Politics of Social Policy in the United States* (Princeton: Princeton University Press, 1988), pp. 313–56.

54. Thomas Sowell, op. cit., p. 3.

sanguine view, and has been unrelenting, I hope, in exposing the seamy side of American society insofar as racial and ethnic minorities are concerned.

This has not been an exercise in negative debunking, however. There is a paradoxical flip side to my critique and Sowell's celebration of American society. In absolving societal institutions of responsibility for the terrible inequalities that divide and imperil us, Sowell ends up heaping blame on the weakest and most vulnerable members of our society. There is nothing upright or upbeat about this. At best, Sowell's blaming of the victim invites callousness and indifference, and serves as an apologia for benign neglect. At worst, it could provide an intellectual facade for ruthless repression, should the underclass become too menacing or troublesome. On the other hand, those of us who harp on the failings of American society, create the basis, intellectually at least, for taking remedial action and healing national wounds. In *The Fire Next Time* James Baldwin put it with characteristic eloquence:

> In order to survive as a human, moving, moral weight in the world, America and all the Western nations will be forced to reexamine themselves and release themselves from many things that are now taken to be sacred, and to discard nearly all the assumptions that have been used to justify their lives and their anguish and their crimes so long.[55]

Baldwin's exhortation to reexamine our assumptions must begin with the unpleasant fact that, like many nation states, the United States was constituted through violence and oppression. As an outpost for European colonialism, it was implicated in the conquest, decimation, and expropriation of the indigenous people who inhabited the continent—both Indians and Mexicans in the Southwest. Then, to assure necessary labor for the early agricultural economy, the fledging nation imported hundreds of thousands of Africans under a slave system that was to last for two centuries. These were national crimes of enormous proportions, and they set the nation on a path of racial division and conflict for generations to come. As tempting as it might be to shut our eyes to these ignominious chapters in our national history, their repercussions

55. James Baldwin, *The Fire Next Time* (New York: The Dial Press, 1963).

are still painfully evident on the reservations and in the barrios and ghettos, and wherever else this nation's racial pariahs find refuge.

The problem exists on a symbolic as well as a material plane. In recent years we have been treated to a series of spectacles ostensibly celebrating our national history: first the bicentennial of the Declaration of Independence; then the festivities associated with the Statue of Liberty; more recently, the bicentennial of the Constitution. These events have important symbolic functions. They are meant to unify, to heighten national consciousness, to promote national pride and patriotic feeling, and to reaffirm commitment to the nation's highest ideals. In each instance, however, beneath the din of fireworks and official hoopla, were the anguished voices of those groups still on the periphery of American society. These are the historical victims of American nationhood—those for whom "the first new nation" of sociological lore meant not opportunity, but oppression.

The inescapable truth is that our national symbols are tainted, still, by the crimes associated with the founding and development of the nation. Until we come to terms with these national crimes, and make adequate reparation for them, then collective self-congratulation and sentimentality, like that evoked during national holidays and celebrations, are morally fraught, and serve only to gloss over the injustices visited upon our national victims.

This point was made poignantly in a television documentary on Native Americans. An elderly Indian woman, who chose to live by herself on a remote reservation, commented that, for her, Columbus Day is a day of mourning. It is not that we should "give America back to the Indians," to use the vulgar popular expression. Rather, it is that until we as a nation honor legitimate Indian land and water claims, stop plundering the mineral wealth on Indian reservations, eliminate the deplorable conditions of life that prevail among the Indian population, and give appropriate homage to the history and culture of the indigenous peoples of this continent— only then can we celebrate Columbus Day with a clear national conscience.

Much the same moral reasoning applies to Mexicans. After annexing half of Mexico's territory, this nation spent the next 150 years patrolling "our" borders and deporting "illegal migrants" from what one Chicano writer has dubbed "occupied Mexico." If justice had its way, Mexicans would be granted special rights of immigration to their former territories.

For black Americans there was bitter irony in the national celebrations of recent years. The Constitution, after all, explicitly sanctioned slavery and for a century after slavery provided the legal framework for official segregation. There is an even deeper irony, however. The fact that Africans were singled out for a unique oppression obviated the need for super-exploitation of other groups, like whites who previously had been imported as indentured servants. Thus, it is not just that blacks were excluded from the national covenant, as suggested by the apt title of Benjamin Ringer's book *We the People and Others*.[56] The more vexing truth is that "our" freedoms were enhanced by "their" oppression. American democracy would have been profoundly different—perhaps not even possible—without the "peculiar institution." Thus, slavery cannot be dismissed as an unfortunate flaw in an otherwise perfect cloth. It would be closer to the truth to say that slavery provided the fabric out of which the cloth was made.

This was literally the case with respect to the textile industry that was central to the burgeoning industrial growth during the late nineteenth and early twentieth centuries. We need to be reminded that those immigrant workers who labored in the mills and sweatshops in the North worked with raw material produced, under far more exploitative and oppressive conditions, by black labor in the South. What, then, can the Statue of Liberty mean to black Americans, except the preemption of their rights and opportunities by successive waves of foreigners, favored because they were white.

A bitter realization that the American Dream did not include them runs deep in the black community. Recently the op-ed page of the *New York Times* included a piece by a black police sergeant, Don Jackson, who sought to expose police brutality by driving through an affluent section of Long Beach, California. He was soon stopped by police, and had his head shoved through a window during his arrest. Yet what most aggrieves Jackson is not the abuse he suffered personally, but what it signifies about the historical abuse of his people:

56. Benjamin Ringer, *We the People and Others* (New York: Travistock Publications, 1983).

In the past decade, I have watched from a fence post as the hopes and dreams of my people dwindled and declined in the back of America's priorities. The worst of our troubles, however, does not come in the form of socio-economic disadvantage. The plight of the black American is made greatest by the removal of hope. The hope that we have lost is that the dream America offers to a world of immigrants is not available to its most faithful citizens.

Some may dare to ask, How is it that I call the black American more faithful than others? Well, it's like the woman married to an abusive husband. He keeps making promises that things will get better but the beating continues. She may stay with him but she knows he will never change his ways without accepting that he has a problem.

America certainly has a problem. Black Americans have picked cotton, scrubbed the floors, cooked the meals and laid the bricks in hopes that hard work would one day mean liberation and acceptance. We felt that somehow what is our birthright could be purchased by proving ourselves worthy. Yet, America demands more proof that we are worthy.[57]

Blacks have "paid their dues" to America, to put it in the blunt vernacular. It is not just that blacks, as individuals, have made countless "contributions" to American life. It is commonplace to cite those illustrious men and women who have distinguished themselves in some scientific or cultural endeavor. But how does one begin to calculate the *collective* contributions of a people who for two centuries labored as slaves and for another century as second-class citizens, yet sacrificed their sons in national wars and enriched the nation with their unique cultural and spiritual resources? In a word, blacks deserve reparation—not in the form of cash payments to individuals, but in national policies committed to the elimination of racial inequality.

Tragically, this nation has neither the moral commitment nor the political will to confront its legacy of racism, and to make amends to its national victims. This is regrettable, not only because historical wrongs are not rectified and victimized groups are denied justice,

57. Don Jackson, "Police Embody Racism to My People," *New York Times* (January 23, 1989), p. A25

but because all members of this society must fear what Franz Fanon has called "the rage of the oppressed."

The alternative is clear. As a nation we must give up our ethnic heroes and racial villains, and wage a frontal assault against the dangerous divisions of race and class that rend our society. At stake is not just racial and economic justice, but the very soul of the nation.

Index

Abbott, Martin, 193 *n.*, 196 *n.*
Abolitionists, 177, 179, 185, 191
Accommodation, 52, 56, 72; as stage in "race relations cycle," 47, 48
Acculturation process, 47–48, 66. *See also* Cultural assimilation
Adams, Henry, 222
Adler, Roy D., 91 *n.*
Affirmative action, 221, 250–252, 291, 292, 294–295
Affirmative Character of Culture, The (Marcuse), 253
Africa: European colonization of, 6; Negro repatriation attempts, 174, 176–177
Agriculture, 6, 24–31; cotton culture, 27–28, 175–176, 182–183, 185, 189, 198–199, 204, 205; labor needs, 24–27, 28, 31, 35, 41, 42, 176, 182–185, 188–199; labor needs reduced, 204–206; mechanization of, 205–206
Alabama State University, 260
Alba, Richard, 68 and *n.*
Albion, Robert, 187 *n.*
Alexander, Tom, 280 *n.*
Alger, Horatio, 79, 83–84, 85, 87, 130, 267
Allen, James, 190 *n.*
Allen, Robert L., 175 and *n.*, 217 *n.*, 218, 252 *n.*, 255 and *n.*
Allen, Walter R., 278 *n.*
Allport, Gordon W., 169 *n.*
Amalgamation, 47 and *n.*, 48, 72
America: "discovery" of, 13; colonization of, 6–13, 14
American Colonization Society, 176
American Dilemma, An (Myrdal), 174
American Educator (journal), 91
American Federation of Teachers, 91
American Hebrew (journal), 235
American in the Making, An (Ravage), 51
American Indians, 3, 5, 6, 13–21, 40, 43, 299; in colonial period, 13, 14–15; dispossession and vanquishment of, 13–18; 20, 37; in early federal period, 15–17; enslavement attempts, 24;

Mexicans equated with, 21–22 and *n.*, 23–24; population statistics, 6, 18, *table* 19; red ghettos, 21; reservation system, 17, 18, 20–21; in 20th century, 20–21
American Jewish Committee, 71, 226 *n.*, 251
American Jewish Congress, 241, 251
American Judaism (Glazer), 90
Americanization, 48, 53, 244, 254
America's Jews (Sklare), 130
Amsterdam News (newspaper), 221
Anderson, Charles, 8 *n.*
Anglo-Saxons: as founders of U.S., 8, 11, 13; "supremacy," 4, 225–226; taste dominance in cuisine, 64–65. *See also* British-Americans; WASP elite
Anti-Defamation League, 226 *n.*, 251
Anti-intellectualism, 129, 138–145, 148, 150
Anti-Intellectualism in American Life (Hofstadter), 139
Anti-Semitism, 61, 224–226, 240; college campus, 232–235, 242; college faculties and administrations, 235–246, 248–249; corporate, 90–91, 252
Aptheker, Herbert, 212 and *n.*
Arizona, acquisition of, 22
Aronson, Gregor, 95 *n.*
Asia, European colonization of, 6
Asians, 3, 40, 43, 119; compared with blacks, 268–269; educational achievements, 85, 129, 132; ethnic successes, 84–86, 104 *n.*–105 *n.*; myth of success, 270–275; selective migration, 272–274; stereotype traits, 78; Westinghouse science contest, 270–271, 274. *See also specific nationalities*
Assimilation, 261; cultural pluralism as reaction to, 256; stage in "race relations cycle," 47 and *n. See also* Assimilation process
Assimilation in American Life (Gordon), 65–66

Assimilation process, 9, 45–48, 49, 52, 71–74; advanced by decline in prejudice, 55–56; amalgamation as final step in, 47 and *n.*, 48, 72; and atrophy of ethnic cultures, 60–63, 73; ethnic subsociety as transition stage, 67–68, 72; fourth generation as watershed in, 44–45; homogenizing factors, 51–59, 73; intermarriage as factor in, 68–71, 72, 261; loss of native tongue, 9, 45–46, 72; Park's stages, 47 and *n.*; role of public schools in, 54–55; second-generation marginality, 52; terminology, 47 *n.*

Astin, Alexander, 140 and *n.*
Atkinson, Edward, 189 and *n.*, 191
Auden, W. H., 50 *n.*
Auletta, Ken, 281 and *n.*

Backlash, white, 219–221
Bailey, Thomas, 290 *n.*
Bakke, Alan, 251
Bakke, Edward, 121–122 and *n.*, 126 and *n.*
Baldwin, James, 220 and *n.*, 298 and *n.*
Banfield, Edward, 108 and *n.*, 127, 214–215 and *n.*, 216
Baron, Harold, 204 *n.*, 205 and *n.*, 214 and *n.*
Baron, Salo W., 97 *n.*
Barth, Gunther, 184 *n.*
Becnel, Barbara, 208 *n.*
Beecher, Henry Ward, 191
"Benign neglect," 188
Bentley, George R., 191 *n.*
Bergman, Elihu, 69 *n.*
Berkhofer, Robert F., Jr., 20 *n.*
Bernard, Jessie, 121 *n.*
Berrol, Selma C., 134 and *n.*, 135
Beyond the Melting Pot (Glazer and Moynihan), 49, 59, 119, 275 and *n.*
Bilingual education, 55
Bingham, Theodore, 112–113, 114
Biological determinism, 78–79
Biological superiority and inferiority, notions of, 77–79, 118
Black Awakening in Capitalist America (Allen), 175
Black Bourgeoisie, The (Frazier), 207
Black capitalism, 88
Black Codes, 195–196
Black Family in Slavery and Freedom, The (Gutman), 120
Black Violence (Button), 216
Blacks, 5, 42–43, 255; affirmative action, 291–292, 294–295; civil rights movement, 108, 213–214, 217, 221; colonization and deportation schemes, 174, 176–177, 179–180, 182–183; condition in Northern ghettos, 121, 177 and *n.*, 210–211, 214, 220; crime, 117, 219; "culture of poverty," 80, 106–111, 118, 123–124, 127; in domestic service, 151, 155, 206, 207–208; economic disabilities compared with West Indian ethnic success, 104 *n.*; educational handicaps of, 118–

119, 250; employment, 206–208, 210–211, 218; farm labor, statistics, 206, 207–208; government employment, 290–291; Harvard freshman dormitory color ban, 245; income, 205, 209–210; Jews as "model" for, 88; job competition with ethnic whites, 40–41, 177–181, 201–202, 206, 212, 219; job discrimination in North, 172, 173–176, 181, 190, 199–200, 201, 206–207, 221; middle class, 207, 208–209, 211, 218; migration attempts, postbellum, 174–175, 176–177, 202; migration restrictions, 181; militancy, 214, 219; mobility, 207–209, 218; nationalism and separatism, 3, 255; and national symbols, 300–302; opposed to immigration, 201–202; population figures, 174, 176; poverty as source of family instability, 107, 111, 117, 119, 120–122; poverty statistics, 209–210 and *n.*; proletarization and urbanization of, 203–207; prostitution, 116; quasi-servitude after Civil War, 42, 119, 172, 173–176, 185–200; race "riots" of, 212, 214–218, 220; relations with Jews, 219, 220–221, 259–260; sharecropping and contract labor, 190–191, 192–200; slavery, 25–27, 28, 29–31, 37, 119, 120–121, 182, 188–189; slave statistics, 26 and *n.*, 27 *n.*, 28, 176; socio-economic immobility, 106–107, 117–119; Southern postbellum conditions, 182, 185, 190–200; South-to-North shift, population figures, 203–205; stereotypes for, 110, 182, 209; teenage unemployment, 210–211; underclass, 280–297; unskilled labor, 206, 207; vote of, 213, 214; compared with West Indians, 268–269, 275–280; women, employment, 155, 206, 207–208. *See also* Freedmen; Racial minorities; Slavery
Blair, Montgomery, 181
Blancs, Les (Hansberry), 171
Blauner, Robert, 40–42 and *n.*
Blegen, Theodore C., 152 *n.*
Blood of My Blood (Gambino), 154
Boston: black-Irish conflict, 177, 201, 219; and "Jewish problem" at Harvard, 240, 241; prostitution, 116
Boston College, 140
Boston Pilot (newspaper), 177
Bowles, Samuel, 128 *n.*
Bracero program, 23
Brandfon, Robert L., 184 *n.*
Briggs, John, 141–142 and *n.*
British-Americans: colonial majority, 7–9; in domestic service, 155, 162; 19th to 20th century immigrants, 35, 40, 41, 162; population estimate for 1790, 7. *See also* Anglo-Saxons; English-Americans; Scots and Scotch-Irish Americans; WASP elite
British Ladies Emigration Society, 162
Britt, George, 227 *n.*, 234 *n.*, 237 *n.*, 238 *n.*

Broadcasting industry, 91
Broun, Heywood, 227 *n.*, 234 *n.*, 237 *n.*, 238 *n.*
Browne, Malcolm W., 270–271 and *n.*
Brown v. *Board of Education*, 213
Bruce, Philip A., 183 *n.*
Bruchey, Stuart, 28 *n.*
Bryce-Laporte, Roy Simon, 277 *n.*
Budish, Jacob M., 99 *n.*
Buffalo, N.Y., 155
Buffalo Bill, 14
Bulgarians, 35
Bureau of Indian Affairs, 18, 20, 21
Bureau of Labor Statistics, 89, 94, 209, 210 *n.*
Burkey, Richard M., 41
Burns, James D., 178 *n.*
Business, corporate, 90–91, 252
Business, small: Asians in, 85, 104 *n.;* blacks in, 207, 208; Jews in, 85, 89, 90, 147
Button, James W., 216–217 and *n.*, 218 and *n.*

Cahan, Abraham, 52, 133–134 and *n.*
California: acquisition of, 22; gold rush, 23
Calvinism, 93
Campbell, Helen, 151, 159 *n.*
Campbell, Mildred, 7 *n.*, 10 *n.*
Canada: minority schools, 54; Negro migration to, 174
Canadian immigrants to U.S., 40, 41
Capitalism, 38, 40, 78, 156; black, 88; called root cause of crime, 115; Northern, in South, effect on blacks, 186–190
Capitalism and Slavery (Williams), 25
Caribbean, Negro colonization schemes, 174, 177, 180
Carnegie Commission on Higher Education, 145, 147 and *n.*
Carter, Jimmy, 258
Carter, Samuel, 16 *n.*, 17 *n.*
Caste, Class, and Race (Cox), 201
Caste system, 206–207; waning of, 208–209, 213
Catholic Church, 139
Catholic colleges, 139–140
Catholic University of America, 140
Catholics, 8 and *n.*; class status compared with Protestants, 144–145; college faculty percentage, 145, *table* 146, 147, *table* 148; college faculty social background, 147–148, *table* 149; educational status parity with Protestants, 146; ethnic intermarriages among, 68–69; mobility patterns, 147–148, *table* 149; myth of anti-intellectualism, 138–145, 148; myth debunked, 145–150; parochial schools, 54; population percentage, 145; in religious intermarriages, 69, 70–71
Caudill, William, 85 and *n.*
Cheap Cotton by Free Labor (Atkinson), 189
Cherkin, Alvin, 69 *n.*, 89 *n.*
Cherokee Indians, 16–17

Cherokee Nation v. *State of Georgia*, 17
Chicago: anti-black pogroms, 177 *n.*, 212; crime studies, 116; ethnic white backlash, 219; 1910 immigrant population, 47; red ghetto, 21
Chicago Defender (newspaper), 203
Chicanos, 3, 24, 117. *See also* Mexican-Americans
Children of Immigrants in the Schools, The (1911 study), 102
Chinese-Americans, 85–86; educational levels of, 130, 132; few attracted to Reconstruction South, 184–185; recent immigrants, 273, 274–275; suit against school desegregation, 259
Church, as institution, 57. *See also* Religion
Cincinnati, anti-black riot of 1862, 177 and *n.*
Citizens Without Work (Bakke), 121–122
Citizenship, 12–13; Negro, 179, 185, 214
City College of New York, 135, 137, 227, 228, 234, 236, 243
Civil rights movement, 108, 213–214, 217, 221
Civil War, 28, 176, 177, 189
Clark, Kenneth, 118 and *n.*, 119
Class position: basic indicators of, 89; black rise, 207–209, 218; cultural factors alleged, 79, 80–81, 83, 86–88, 92–93, 99 *n.*, 103; differences in, as cause of ethnic conflict, 170–171, 220, 221, 230–236, 246, 257–261; and educational level, 131–132, 135–136, 137–139, 141–145, 147–148, *table* 149, 150; and elite college enrollment, 230–246; low entry position of immigrants, 43, 52–53; low, and pressures to abandon ethnicity, 256–257, 258; New Darwinist view, 79, 80–81; societal factors, 93–103, 104 *n.*–105 *n.;* Yankee ancestry and, 225
Clinton, De Witt, 9
Cloward, Richard A., 211 and *n.*, 213 and *n.*
Clubs, discrimination by, 257–258, 259, 260
Coffin, Levi, 191
Cohen, Henry, 111 *n.*
Colleges, 136, 139–140; admissions policies, 228, 237–238, 248–250, 260; anti-Semitism at, 232–246, 248–249; Catholic, 139–140; curricula, 229, 237; enrollment, 228; enrollment increase, 229, 236, 238; enrollment quotas, 223, 227, 237–248; racial quotas, 250–252; regional quotas, 247–248; religious background of faculty, 145, *table* 146, 147, *table* 148, 249–250; social-class origins of faculty, 147–148, *table* 149. *See also* Higher education
Colonial period, 6–11, 13–15; American Indian relations, 13, 14–15; ethnic mix, 7–9; immigration, 9–11; indentured servants, 9, 25, 151, 159; labor shortages, 6, 10–11.
Colorado, acquisition of, 23

Colored American Magazine, 202

Columbia University, 231, 233, 236, 245, 248; Jewish enrollment at, 223, 227, 234, 237, 248

Columbus, Christopher, 13

Commentary magazine, 61 and *n.,* 208 and *n.*

Commercial and Financial Chronicle, 187–188

Commons, John R., 39 *n.*

Community, local, as institution, 57, 80, 99 *n.;* instability of, and poverty, 80, 111, 118, 119

Congress of Racial Equality (CORE), 213

Conquest, 37; as factor in ethnic pluralism, 5, 40; of Indian lands, 13–21, 24; justification for, 16, 21–22; of Mexican lands, 21–24

Conservative Judaism (Sklare), 60

Constitutional Convention, 12

Contact, stage in "race relations cycle," 47

Convict immigrants, 11 and *n.*

Cook, Adrian, 177 *n.*

Cook, William N., 230 *n.*

Cornelius, Wayne, A., 23 *n.*

Cornell University, 233

Corporate anti-Semitism, 90–91, 252

Coser, Lewis, 157 *n.*

Cotton: basic factor in national economy, 27–29 and *n.,* 30 *n.,* 31, 175, 185–186, 192; postbellum labor, 175–176, 182–185, 189–200; production, 26–27, 28 and *n.,* 32, 182, 189, 109–199, 204; production mechanized, 205; trade, 27–29 and *n.,* 30 *n.,* 186, 190, 199

Cotton gin, 28

Counts, George Sylvester, 228 *n.*

Covello, Leonard, 128, 141 and *n.*

Cowen, Philip, 236 *n.*

Cox, Oliver, 201

Crime, 111, 112–117, 219; allegation of genetic factors in, 78, 79; ethnic succession in, 115–116; as function of poverty, 115–117; immigrant minorities compared with racial minorities, 117; among Irish, 116, 117; among Italians, 116–117; among Jewish immigrants, 112–115, 116–117; Willie Horton case, 281 *n.*

Croatians, 35, 219

Cronin, Denise, 105 *n.*

Cuban Revolution, 108

Cubans, 104 *n.*–105 *n.,* 279–280; in Miami, 221

Cultural assimilation, 44–46, 52–53, 65, 72. *See also* Acculturation process

Cultural Darwinism. *See* New Darwinism

Cultural deprivation theories, 118

Cultural pluralism, 43, 49–51, 59–60, 65, 66, 253–254; atrophy of, 59–63; contradictions of, 254–262; crisis of, 44–46, 56–59, 63; vs. structural pluralism, 66–67. *See also* Ethnic pluralism

Cultural relativism, doctrine of, 60

Cultural superiority and inferiority, notions of, 79–80, 84–85, 118

Cultural values: alleged fulcrum of ethnic success. 80, 83–88, 92–93, 99 *n.,* 103, 129–132, 265–267, 275, 284–286; dysfunctional, in "culture of poverty," 106–109, 117–119; and educational level, 129–132, 137–138, 139, 142–144; taboo on domestic service alleged, 154–156; taboo proposition invalidated, 160–161, 166

Culture of poverty, 80, 106–127, 265, 284–286, 293–294; behavioral and attitudinal symptoms, 107, 110, 111, 125–126; self-perpetuating (internal) factors, 107–108, 122–124; societal (external) factors, 107, 123–125. *See also* Poverty

Cuomo, Mario, 288 *n.*

Currie, Elliot, 23 *n.,* 208 *n.*

Curtin, Philip, 26 *n.*

Czechs, 35

Daniels, Roger, 104 *n.*

Danish-Americans, 41

Dartmouth College, 238

Darwin, Charles, 77–78

Daughters of the American Revolution, 6

Dawes Act (1887), 20

Dawidowicz, Lucy, 63 *n.*

Day, Richard, 205 *n.*

DeBow's Review, 182–183 and *n.,* 184 and *n.,* 185, 188 and *n.*

Decline of the WASP, The (Schrag), 49

Decter, Midge, 210 and *n.,* 211 *n.*

Democracy, vs. pluralism, 172, 253–255, 258–261

Democracy and Education (Dewey), 128

Democracy in America (Tocqueville), 185

"Democracy of nationalities," 253–254, 260

"Democracy Versus the Melting Pot" (Kallen), 253–254

Democratic Party, 178–179, 213; Tammany, 180

Depression, 206; black migration to North during, 204–205; unemployment, 121–122, 126, 205

Deprivation theories, 118

Determinism, hereditary, 78–79

Detroit, race riots by whites, 212

DeVos, George, 85 and *n.*

Dewey, John, 128

Dijur, I. M., 95 *n.,* 96 *n.*

Dillingham Commission, 36

Discrimination, 257–259; against Jews, 225–226, 234–246, 248–249, 257; neighborhood, 219–220, 258, 259 and *n.;* "positive vs. negative," 259; by private clubs, 257–258, 259. *See also* Racial discrimination

Domestic service, 151–166; agencies, 162–163; blacks in, 151, 155, 206, 207; emigration societies, 162; ethnic distribution, 81, 153–156, 159–164, *table* 165; feudalistic nature of, 157–159; Italians in Italy, 155, 161; social inferiority stigma, 151–152, 159; working conditions, 156, 157–158

Douglas, William O., 259
Douglass, Frederick, 173
Drachsler, Julius, 68 and *n.*
Draft Riots, 177
Dutch-Americans, 7, 8, 9; population estimate for 1790, 7

Earnest, Ernest, 234 *n.,* 244 *n.*
East (region), economic development of, 29, 32. *See also* Northeast
Eastern European Jews, 35, 39 and *n.,* 40, 44, 82, 91–103, 115, 138, 161, 224–226, 229; and education, 92–93, 101–102, 135, 137, 228, 230; at Harvard, 223; motives for emigration, 34–35, 161; literacy rates, 101–102; skilled worker percentage of immigrants, 97, *table* 98; urban background of, 93–97, 103. *See also* Jews; Russian Jews
Eating in America (Root), 64
Economic motivation for emigration, 33, 34, 160, 163–164
Economy: antebellum, role of cotton in, 27–29 and *n.,* 30 *n.,* 31, 175, 186; industrial growth, 38–39, 172, 173–174; postbellum, role of cotton in, 175, 185–186, 192; regional specialization, 31–32 and *n.*
Education, 227–229; curriculum changes, 55, 136, 229, 237; emphasis on, and ethnic success, 81, 84, 85, 88, 89, 93, 99 *n.,* 101–102, 128–150; level of achievement, cultural vs. class theory of, 129–132, 135–136, 137–139, 141–145, 147–150; poverty as obstacle to, 118–119, 135–136, 138; problems of racial minorities, 118–119, 250; vs. Talmudic scholarship, 132–134; vocational, 136, 229. *See also* Colleges; Higher education; Schools
Educational system: reforms, 136, 229; role in assimilation, 54–55
Educational Testing Service (E.T.S.), 250 *n.*
Einstein, Albert, 131
Eliot, Charles William, 234
Eliot, Thomas, 180
Emancipation, 173, 176–177; a sham, 178, 181, 185, 190–191, 199
Emigration societies, Britain, 162
Employment: black, 207–208, 210–211, 218; caste system in, 206–207, 208–209; skilled immigrant groups, 97, *table* 98, 103, 104 *n.,* 139; unskilled labor, 35, 38, 141, 177, 206, 207. *See also* Labor
Encyclopaedia Britannica (1911), 30
Engels, Friedrich, 156
English-Americans: convict immigrants, 11; early attitudes toward other groups, 9–10, 11–13; early cultural preeminence, 9, 13; early population majority, 7–9; language adopted as lingua franca, 9; money owned by immigrants, 93; 19th to 20th century immigrants, 35, 40, 41; population estimate for 1790, 7; skilled worker percentage of immigrants, *table* 98

Ernst, Robert, 154 *n.*
Ethnic communities, 72–73, 253–262; cultural atrophy, 59–63, 66, 73; identity crisis, 44–46, 56–59, 63, 73; rebuilding efforts, 46, 47, 48–51, 59–60, 73–74; social fabric, 46, 54; 65–66; structural limits on, 53–55; subsocieties, 65–68, 72, 73; surviving symbolic and psychological functions, 58, 63, 262
Ethnic conflict, class character of, 170–171, 220, 221, 230–236, 246, 257–261
Ethnic foods, 63–65
"Ethnic heritage" curricula, 55
Ethnic intermarriage, 47 and *n.,* 68–71, 72, 73
Ethnic organizations, 46, 65
Ethnic pluralism, 3–4, 64, 169, 253–254; vs. democratic principles, 172, 254–261; future questioned, 43, 55–63, 67, 71–74, 260–262; negative basis of, 4, 5–6, 43, 254–255, 261; obstacles to, 51–55, 73, 169, 256; social dimension, 65–66, 72; structural, 66–68; symbolic remnants, 58, 63. *See also* Cultural pluralism
Ethnic pluralists, 47, 48–51, 59–60, 253–254, 255, 260, 261
Ethnic revival, 3, 4, 50–51, 73–74. *See also* "New ethnicity"
Ethnic success, 82–105, 106; cultural values as alleged fulcrum of, 80, 83–88, 92–93, 99 *n.,* 103, 129–132; education and, 81, 84, 85, 88, 89, 93, 99 *n.,* 101–102, 128–150; Horatio Alger theory of, 83–85, 130; Jews as example of, 87–103, 135; a "morality tale," 86–87; non-Jewish examples, 84–85, 103 *n.*–105 *n.;* societal factors in, 93–103, 131–132, 135–136, 137–138. *See also* Mobility of immigrants
Ethnicity: abandonment of, for class mobility, 256–257, 258, 259–260; clinging to, for class protection, 258–260; mobility in conflict with, 53, 73, 261; "new," 47, 48–51, 60, 73–74; surviving functions, 58, 63, 262
Ethnocentrism, 169; white, 9, 255
Eubank, Thomas, 205–206 and *n.*
Europe: agrarian crisis, 33–34; effects of industrialization in, 33, 34, 152; population surplus, 33, 34
European immigrants, 3, 44–45, 82; assimilation of, 44–48, 49, 51–59, 67–68, 72–74; colonial majority, 7–9; colonization of America, 6–13, 14; countries of origin, 7–8, 35, 40, 41, 78; in domestic service, 151–166; entry position in class system, 52–53; ethnic intermarriage among Catholics, 68; immigrant experience, 51–52; immigration statistics for 1820–1930, *table* 41, 174; immigration restrictions of 1920's, 40, 44; as labor source, 11, 13, 32, 33, 35–38, 39, 41, 162–163, 174, 176, 200, 202; literacy rates, 101–102; money owned at entry into U.S., 93; not attracted to Reconstruc-

European immigrants (*cont.*)
tion South, 25, 26, 175–176, 182–
184; sex ratios, 160–162; skilled
worker percentages, 97, *table* 98;
World War I drop in immigration, 42,
175, 202, 204. *See also* Immigrant minorities; White ethnics; *and see specific national and ethnic groups*
Exoduster movement, 174–175
Expansion, 6, 13–24; West, 17–18
Export trade, 27–29, 186, 199
Ezorsky, Gertrude, 294 *n.*

Fainstein, Norman, 289–290 and *n.*
Family, 57, 80, 85, 99 *n.*, 111, 124, 166;
effect of poverty on, 80, 107, 111,
115, 117, 119, 120–122, 124–126; fe-
male-headed, 107, 125, 126; Irish
homeland conditions, 163–164; Italian
traditions, 155
Farb, Peter, 18 *n.*
Farley, Reynolds, 208 *n.*, 278–280 and *n.*
Federal aid, urban, 216–217
Federalist Papers, 9
Female-headed households, 107, 125, 126
Feuer, Lewis S., 133 and *n.*
Fifteenth Amendment, 185
Filipinos, 273, 296
Finns, 7, 41
Fishman, Joshua, 45–46 and *n.*
Fitch, Lyle C., 111 *n.*
Florida: black migration to, 174; vagrancy
laws against blacks, 196
Fogelson, Robert M., 215 and *n.*
Foner, Nancy, 276 *n.*, 277 and *n.*
Food, ethnic, 63–65
Foreign labor exploitation, 36–38, 42; as
factor in ethnic pluralism, 5, 6, 40. *See
also* Labor
Foreign trade, 27–29, 186, 199
Foreigners, attitudes toward, 9–13, 42; prej-
udice, 55–56, 78; xenophobia, 9, 11–
12, 38–39, 225. *See also* Nativism
Forest Hills, N.Y., Jews of, 219, 259 *n.*
Fortune magazine, 90 and *n.*, 104 *n.*
Fortunate Pilgrim, The (Puzo), 257
"Forty acres and a mule" promise, 184,
192, 193
Forward (newspaper), 115
*Founders of the Republic on Immigration,
Naturalization, and Aliens, The*
(Grant), 11
Fourth-generation Americans, 44–45, 60
Francis, Alexander, 230 *n.*
Franklin, Benjamin, 11, 79
Fraternities, 231, 234
Frazier, Franklin, 207 and *n.*
Free Labor Cotton Company, 189, 191
Freedman, Marcia, 295 *n.*
Freedmen, number of, 176, 192, 199; on re-
lief, 194
Freedmen's Bureau, 191–199
French-Americans, 7, 9, 41, 155; educa-
tional level, 140; intermarriage trends,
68; prostitution, 116
Frennal, Michael, 113 *n.*
Freud, Sigmund, 131

Friedman, Melvin, 21 *n.*
Friedman, Murray, 88 *n.*
Friedman, Sharon, 52 *n.*
Friendship networks, 46, 65
Frumkin, Jacob, 95 *n.*
Fugitive Slave Laws, postbellum version of,
195
Fulmer, John Leonard, 27 *n.*
Fulton, Oliver, 145 *n.*
Future-time orientation, 144

Gambino, Richard, 49 *n.*, 84 *n.*, 154–155
and *n.*
Gannett, Lewis S., 228 *n.*
Gans, Herbert, 50 and *n.*, 61 and *n.*
Garis, Roy, 11 *n.*
Garment industry, 36, 38, 91, 99–101, 153,
154, 157, 161; in Russia, Jews in, 95,
98, 99; unions, 38–39, 157
Gaustad, Edwin Scott, 19 *n.*
Genetic determinism, 78–79
Genovese, Eugene, 186 *n.*
Georgetown University, 140
Georgia, Cherokee eviction from, 16–17
German-Americans, 8, 9, 11, 44; Catholics,
140; domestic servants, 154, 155; and
education, 135, 140, 228; intermarriage trends, 68; language loss, 45;
money owned by immigrants, 93; 19th
to 20th century immigrants, 35, 40,
41; population estimate for 1790, 7;
skilled worker percentage of immigrants, *table* 98; in South, 183; stereotype traits, 79
German Jews, 101, 135, 224–225, 226,
241; Harvard students, 223
Ghettos: black, 111, 116–117, 121, 210,
214; black, Jewish role in, 220; ethnic,
54; race "riots" in, 214–218, 220;
red, 21; unemployment in, 210
Gillette, William, 185 *n.*
Gintis, Herbert, 128 *n.*
Girls' Friendly Society, 162
Glasgow, Douglas, 284–285 and *n.*, 294
and *n.*
Glazer, Nathan, 49 *n.*, 59 and *n.*, 90 and *n.*,
92–93 and *n.*, 111 and *n.*, 112 and *n.*,
119 and *n.*, 224 and *n.*, 225 *n.*, 254
n., 259 and *n.*, 260 and *n.*, 275 and *n.*
Glenn, Norval D., 145 *n.*
Gold, Michael, 133 and *n.*
Goldenweiser, Alexis, 95 *n.*
Gordon, David, 109 *n.*
Gordon, Milton, 65–66 and *n.*, 67, 69 *n.*,
84 and *n.*, 112 and *n.*
Gorelick, Sherry, 137 *n.*
Goren, Arthur, 113 and *n.*, 114 and *n.*
Graham, Otis L., Jr., 295 and *n.*
Grant, Madison, 11 and *n.*
Graubard, Stephen, 271 and *n.*
Gray, Lewis, 25 *n.*
Great Britain: cotton trade with U.S., 28–
29; domestic service tradition, 152;
emigration agencies, 162; emigration
restrictions of 1718, 10
Greek-Americans, 41; crime among, 117
Greeley, Andrew, 66 and *n.*, 70 *n.*, 86 and

n., 105 *n.*, 116 *n.*, 140 and *n.*, 147 *n.*,
  209 *n.*
Group consciousness, 55
Gutman, Herbert, 120–121 and *n.*, 135 and
  n., 136

Hacker, Andrew, 56 and *n.*
Haley, Alex, 199
Ham, William T., 242 *n.*
Hamilton, Alexander, 12
Hammil, Pete, 281 *n.*
Hammond, M. B., 25 *n.*
Handlin, Mary F., 225 and *n.*
Handlin, Oscar, 116 *n.*, 163 *n.*, 225 and *n.*
Hanna, Elinor, 53 *n.*
Hansberry, Lorraine, 171 and *n.*
Hansen, Marcus Lee, 7 *n.*, 9 and *n.*
Hapgood, Norman, 234 *n.*, 235 *n.*
Hardy, Kenneth, 139 and *n.*
Harper's Magazine, 116
Harper's Weekly, 234
Harris, Norman Dwight, 179 *n.*, 181 *n.*
Hart-Celler Act, 267–268, 276
Harvard Business Review, 91
Harvard Center for Population Studies, 69
Harvard University, 228, 231, 232, 233,
  234, 235; color ban in freshman dor-
  mitories, 245; "Jewish problem," 172,
  222–223, 227, 232–233, 234, 238–
  246, 248–249; regional quota system,
  247–248
Hayden, Tom, 216 and *n.*
Head Start program, 109
Helper, Hinton, 176 *n.*
Hereditary determinism, 78–79
Herschel, Abraham Joshua, 63
Herzog, Elizabeth, 93 and *n.*, 101 and *n.*
Hester Street (film), 52
Higham, John, 7 *n.*, 8 and *n.*, 20 *n.*, 39 *n.*,
  59 and *n.*, 224 and *n.*, 225 and *n.*,
  254 *n.*, 255 and *n.*
Higher education, 136, 139–140, 145–150,
  227–250; affirmative action, 221,
  250–252; class character of, 147–150,
  230–236, 246; faculty makeup, 145,
  table 146, 147, *tables* 148–149, 249–
  250; genteel tradition of leisure class,
  230–233, 243; of Jews, 89, 135, 223,
  227–228, 230, 232, 249–250; "Jewish
  problem" in, 172, 222–223, 226,
  232–246, 248–249. *See also* Colleges
Hill, Robert, 208 and *n.*, 210 *n.*
Hirschman, Charles, 273
Hispanics, 268; *see also specific nationalities*
Hochbaum, Martin, 89 *n.*, 90 *n.*
Hofstadter, Richard, 139 and *n.*
Honor societies, 231, 234
Hourwich, Isaac, 39 *n.*
Housing, discrimination in, 219–220, 258,
  259 and *n.*, 260
Houston, Sam, 22
Howard, Otis, 192, 196
Howe, Irving, 53 and *n.*, 73 and *n.*, 99 *n.*,
  112 and *n.*, 114 *n.*, 121 *n.*, 133 and
  n., 135 *n.*, 261 and *n.*
Huggins, Nathan, 212 *n.*
Human capital, 266

Hungarians, 35, 41, 61–62
Hunter College, 227
Hyland, Ruth, 145 *n.*

Ideda, Kivoshi, 104 *n.*
Illegal aliens, 23
Illegitimacy, 111, 120, 124
Illinois, black migration restrictions, 181
Illiteracy, 102, 141–142, 148
"The Illusion of Black Progress" (Hill), 208
Immigrant minorities: assimilation process,
  44–48, 49, 51–59, 67–68, 71–74;
  communities of, *see* Ethnic communities; compared with racial minorities,
  41–43, 50, 117, 119, 121, 209; in
  competition or conflict with racial minorities, 40–41, 50–51, 72–73, 172,
  174–176, 177–178, 201–202, 206,
  212, 218–221; crime among, 112–
  117; cultural identity and cohesion,
  43, 49–51, 59–60; cultural identity
  crisis, 44–46, 56–59, 60–63, 73; literacy rates, 101–102; loss of native
  tongue, 45–46; mobility of, *see* Mobility of immigrants; new ethnicity, 47,
  48–51, 60, 73–74; patriotism of, 56;
  slums of, 111–117, 121; stereotyping
  of, 78, 110. *See also* Asians; European
  immigrants; White ethnics; *and see
  specific national and ethnic groups*
Immigration, 32–33, 34–40; black opposition to, 201–202; colonial period, 9–
  11; countries of origin, 7–8, 35, 40,
  41, 78; in early federal period, 9, 11,
  12–13, 33; 1840 to 1880 wave, 33,
  35; 1880 to 1930 wave, 33, 35, 44,
  82, 93; ethnic quota restrictions, based
  on crime statistics, 117; European,
  1820–1930 statistics, *table* 41; exploitation vs. opportunity view of, 36–38;
  founding fathers quoted on, 9, 11–12;
  inducements for, 10; labor needs met
  by, 11, 13, 32, 33, 35–38, 39, 41–42,
  162–163, 174, 176, 200, 202; male-
  female ratios, Irish, Italians and Jews
  compared, 160–162; nativist opposition to, 11, 13, 36, 38–39, 78, 202;
  since 1965, 267–280, 295–297; policy
  during period of industrialization, 36,
  38; policy change of 1920's, 40, 44;
  policy toward Mexicans, 23; pull factors, 10, 33, 35–36; push factors, 10–
  11, 33–35; quotas of 1924, 44, 204,
  224; Social Darwinist opposition to,
  78–79; statistics, 33, *table* 41, 161,
  162, 174, 204; World War I interrup-
  tion of, 202, 204
Immigration Acts of 1921 and 1924, 40
Immigration Commission Reports, 36 *n.*,
  93 *n.*, 97–100, 102, 116, 153 *n.*, 154
  and *n.*, 160 *n.*, 161 *n.*, 163 *n.*, 165
Import trade, 28
Income data: blacks, 205, 209–210; Jews,
  89, 100. *See also* Wages
Indentured servitude, 9, 25, 151, 159
Indian Removal Act of 1830, 17
Indian reservations, 17, 18, 20–21

Indian Territory, 16, 17
Indian treaties, 15–18, 20
Indian wars, 14, 15, 18, 21
Indians. *See* American Indians
Indians (East), 273
Industrial Commission on Immigration, 100
Industrial development, 6, 31–40, 41, 172, 173; interaction with immigration, 33–36, 174; slavery and cotton as basis of, 29 and *n.,* 30 *n.,* 36, 186
Industrialization in Europe, 33, 34, 152
Industry: job competition of blacks with immigrants, 40–41, 177–181, 202, 206; job exclusion of blacks, 172, 173–176, 181, 190, 199–200, 221, 289, 290–291; labor needs, 32, 33, 35–38, 39–40, 172, 173–174, 199–200, 203, 204, 205; lowering of color line in, 202, 204–205; slave labor in, 26 *n.*
Inequality, systematic, 172, 254–255, 256, 257–261
Inferiority, notions of: biological, 77–79, 118, 209; cultural, 79–80, 84–85, 118
Intellectualism, 129–138
Interbreeding, 47 and *n.,* 78
Intermarriage, 47 and *n.,* 68–71, 73, 260; ethnic, 68–71, 72; religious, 68–69, 70–71
Internal trade, 29, 32, 186
International Gathering of the Clans (1977), 62
Ireland, 170; socio-demographic factors in emigration, 163–164
Irish-Americans, 3, 7, 8, and *n.,* 11, 44, 209, 219; convict immigrants, 11; crime among, 116, 117; in domestic service, 81, 153–154, 155–156, 158, 159–160, 162–164, *table* 165, 166; educational level, 138, 140, 147 *n.;* intermarriage trends, 68; job competition with blacks, 177, 201; male-female balance in immigration, 161–162, 164; mobility of, 117, 164, *table* 165; money owned by immigrants, 93; 19th to 20th century immigrants, 35, 40, 41, 154, 161–164; population estimate for 1790, 7; prostitution, 116; racist attitudes of, 177, 219; skilled worker percentage of immigrants, *table* 98; slums of, 116
Iroquois Confederacy, 14
Isabella, Queen of Spain, 13
Israel, immigrants in, 103
Italian-Americans, 3, 59, 84 *n.,* 201, 219; crime among, 116–117; educational level, 140–144; illiteracy rates, 102, 141–142; intermarriage trends, 68; language loss, 45; male-female ratio of immigration, 160–161, 162; mobility of, 99 *n.,* 117, 141; money owned by immigrants, 93; 19th to 20th century immigrants, 35, 40, 41, 154, 160–161, 162; paucity in domestic service, 81, 154–156, 159–163, 164, *table* 165; skilled worker percentage of immigrants, *table* 98; in South, 184; stereotype traits, 78, 143

Italian Women in Industry (Odencrantz), 157
Italy, women as domestic servants, 155, 161
Ivy League schools, 228, 231, 234, 238, 243

Jackson, Andrew, 17
Jackson, Don, 301
Jamaicans, 276 *n.,* 279
James, Henry, 248
Japanese-Americans, 84–85, 104 *n.,* 129–130, 209, 273; educational levels, 85, 129–130, 132; superiority notions, 85
Japanese Americans (Petersen), 84
Jefferson, Thomas, 12
Jerome, Harry, 36 and *n.*
Jewish Daily Forward (newspaper), 114, 121, 226–227, 228
Jewish defense agencies, 226 and *n.,* 258
"Jewish problem," 223–225; at elite colleges, 172, 222–223, 226, 230, 232–246, 248–249
Jews, 3, 11, 55, 119, 172, 209, 266; compared to Asians, 272; assimilation of, 246; college faculty percentage, 145, *table* 146, 147, *table* 148; college faculty social background, 147, *table* 149; crime among, 112–115, 116–117; cultural accommodation during 19th century, 224; discrimination against, 225–226, 234–246, 248–249, 257; Eastern European immigrants, 91–103 (*see also* Eastern European Jews; Russian Jews); emphasis on education, 84, 88, 89, 93, 99 *n.,* 101–102, 129, 130–138, 226–229, 230, 232; ethnic intermarriage, 69; examples of cultural atrophy, 61, 62–63; exclusion from corporate business, 90–91, 252; family system strained by poverty, 115, 121; Forest Hills neighborhood fears, 219, 259 *n.;* German, 101, 135, 223, 224–225, 226, 241; income data, 89, 100; language loss, 45; learning of English by, 102; literacy rate of, 101–102, 139; male-female ratio of immigration, 161, 162; mobility of, 84, 89, 91–93, 99 *n.,* 101–103, 117, 134, 135–138, 139, 147, *table* 149; money owned by immigrants, 93; "mystery" of success of, 80, 82–84, 87–103; myth of intellectualism, 101, 132–138, 144; 19th to 20th century immigrants, 35, 40, 41, 82, 91–103, 154, 161, 162; paucity in domestic service, 156, 159–160, 161–163, 164, *table* 165; occupational advantage of immigrants, 95–101, 103, 135, 139, 222; as opponents of affirmative action, 221, 251–252; population in colonial and early federal era, 8; population before 1880, 224; population in 1924, 225; population decline projected, 225; population percentage, 145; poverty statistics, 89–90; in professions and small business, 85, 89, 90, 136–137, 147, 221, 252;

prostitution, 114, 116; relations with blacks, 219, 220–221, 259–260; religious intermarriage, 69, 70, 71; skilled-worker immigrants, 97, *table* 98, 103, 222; slums of, 112–115, 121; social class advantages over other immigrants, 93–103; stereotype traits, 79, 237; superiority notions, 85; urban background of immigrants, 94–97. *See also* Judaism

Jews Without Money (Gold), 133

Job training programs, 108, 109; summer youth jobs, 210–211

Johnson, Andrew, 192

Johnson, James Weldon, 275 *n.*

Johnson, Lyndon B., 120

Johnson, Samuel, 11

Johnson, Stanley C., 162 *n.*

Jones, Maldwyn Allen, 9 *n.*, 11 *n.*, 33–34 and *n.*

Jordan, Winthrop, 24 *n.*, 25 *n.*, 30 and *n.*

Judaism, 92–93; Conservative, 60; Reform, 71, 224, 226; "symbolic," 61; Talmudic scholarship, 132–134; traditional, 61

Kahar, Arcadius, 97 *n.*

Kallen, Horace M., 246 and *n.*, 253–254 and *n.*, 255, 260

Kansas, black migration to, 174–175

Kasarda, John D., 289 *n.*

Katzman, Daniel, 156 *n.*

Kehillah movement, 113–114, 115, 163 *n*

Kellor, Frances A., 151 *n.*, 153 *n.*

Keppel, Frederich Paul, 236 *n.*

Kerner Commission, 215

Kessner, Thomas, 99 *n.*

Kettel, Thomas, 151 *n.*

Kheyder, 101

Kim, Illsoo, 274 *n.*

Kim, Hyung-Chan, 104 *n.*

King, Martin Luther, Jr., 213, 217

Klaczynska, Barbara, 156 *n.*

Klaperman, Gilbert, 82

Kloosterboer, W., 195 *n.*, 199 *n.*

Kolko, Gabriel, 35 and *n.*, 39 *n.*

Korean-Americans, 104 *n.*, 272, 279

Kramer, Judith, 91 and *n.*

Kramer, Victor Albert, 244 and *n.*

Kuznets, Simon, 34 *n.*

Kwong, Peter, 274–275 and *n.*

Labor: black, statistics, 206–207; exploitation, 5, 23, 31, 36–38, 40–42, 156–157, 180, 190; forced servitude of ex-slaves, 185–200; foreign-born, statistics, 36; nativist backlash against immigrants, 38–39, 202; occupational segregation, 289–291; sharecropping and contract labor, 190–191, 192–200; slave vs. free, cost comparisons, 25 and *n.*, 188–189, 198; white/black North/South division, 172, 173–176, 182–184, 190, 199–200, 201; white ethnic vs. black competition, 40–41, 177–181, 201–202, 206, 212, 219; women, 151–164, *table* 165. *See also* Skilled labor; Unskilled labor; Wages

Labor needs, 6, 32 and *n.*, 39; as factor in ethnic pluralism, 5; in agriculture, 24–27, 28, 31, 35, 41, 42, 176, 182–185, 188–199, 204–205; met by black migration to North, 202–204, 205; met by importation from Europe, 11, 13, 32, 33, 35–38, 39, 41–42, 162–163, 174, 176, 200, 202; met by Mexicans in Southwest, 23, 27; met by "people of color," 40–41; met by slavery, 25–27, 28, 29–31, 32, 37; occupational match of Eastern European Jewish immigrants to, 95, 99–101, 103; post-bellum industries, 172, 173–174, 199–200; reduced in 1920's, 39–40; reduced since Depression, 204–205

Labor unions, 157; effects of cheap immigrant labor on, 38–39

Ladd, Everett, 208 *n.*

Land expropriation, 13–24; justification for, 16, 21–22; of Indians, 13–21; of Mexicans, 21–24

Land grants, 192, 199; colonial period, 14

Land rights, Indian, 14–18, 20–12, 22

Lane, James, 181

Language Loyalty in the United States (Fishman), 46

Language schools, 54

Languages: English as lingua franca, 9, 54–55; English, learning by immigrants, 102; non-English, breakdown in generational transmission, 45–46

Latham, Henry, 184 *n.*

Latin Americans, 43. *See also* Cubans

Lauber, Almon Wheeler, 24 *n.*

Lavinsky, Harry M., 251 *n.*

Leacock, Eleanor Burke, 124 *n.*

Lehman, Harvey C., 139 *n.*

Lehmann, Nicholas, 281 *n.*

Leiberstein, Harvey, 69 *n.*

Levine, Naomi, 89 *n.*, 90 *n.*

Levitan, Tina, 131 *n.*

Lewis, Oscar, 106 and *n.*, 107 and *n.*, 108, 109, 123–124, 125, 293–294 and *n.*

Liberator, The, 177 *n.*, 179 and *n.*, 180 *n.*, 181 *n.*

Lieberman, Samuel S., 69 *n.*

Liebow, Elliot, 124–127 and *n.*, 286 and *n.*

Life Is With People (Zborowski and Herzog), 93–94, 101

Light, Ivan, 104 *n.*

Lincoln, Abraham, 176, 177, 178, 180, 191

Lindstrom, Diane, 32 *n.*

Literacy, 101–102, 104 *n.*, 139, 141–142

Lithuania, Jews of, 94, 97

Lithuanians, 35

Loewen, James, W., 184 *n.*

Loewenberg, Bert James, 184 *n.*

Lofton, Williston, 179 *n.*

London Female Emigration Society, 162

Los Angeles, red ghetto of, 21

Louisiana, Chinese population, 184

Louisiana Purchase, 21

Lowell, Abbott Lawrence, 223, 236, 239–246, 248–249, 251–252

Loyola University, 140
Lyman, Stanford M., 85–86 and n., 87

McBride, Theresa M., 152 n.
McFeeley, William, 194 n., 196 and n.
McGahey, Richard, 295 and n.
Mack, Julian W., 113 and n., 241
McPherson, James, 180 n.
Magnet, Myron, 285 n.
Manetta, F., 30
Mangano, Antonio, 160 n.
"Manifest Destiny," 21
Mann, Albion P., 177 n.
Mann, Horace, 128
Manufacturing industries, 29, 37; women in, 156–157
Marcuse, Herbert, 253
Marginality, second generation, 52
Marshall, John, 17
Marshall, Louis, 113
Marx, Gary, 220 n.
Marx, Karl, 29 and n., 131, 156
Maryland, convict immigrants, 11 n.
Massarik, Fred, 69 n., 89 n.
Massachusetts crime studies, 116
Mayer, Egon, 70 and n.
Meat-packaging industry, 36
Mechanization: effect in Europe, 34; effects in U.S., 35, 40; of farming, 205–206
Meier, August, 255 n.
Meier, Matt S., 23 n.
Melting pot, 4, 72, 73; concept rejected by ethnic pluralists, 48–50, 59–60, 253; cultural pluralism as product of, 256; ethnic food symbolic of, 64; language as factor, 9, 46, 54–55; "triple," thesis of, 69
Melting Pot, The (Zangwill), 44
"Melting pot theorists," 47–48, 49, 67, 72
Mendelsohn, Ezra, 95 n., 97 n.
Merk, Frederick, 22 n.
Merton, Robert, 70 and n.
Mexican-American War, 21, 22
Mexican-Americans, 5, 21–24, 40; as cheap labor, 23, 37; crime, 117; equated with Indians, 21–22 and n., 23–24; as illegal aliens, 23; population statistics, 23
Mexicans, as illegal aliens, 299–300
Mexico, 21; Lewis study of rural poverty in, 106
Miami, Fla., black-Cuban competition, 221
Middle class: black, 207, 208–209, 211, 218; immigrant entry into, 43, 46, 53, 56, 59, 63, 91
Middle-class values, alleged role in mobility, 88, 92, 99 n.
Midstream (magazine), 69 and n.
Migration and the Business Cycle (Jerome), 36
Miller, John, 11 n., 15 n.
Mining industries, 36, 37, 184
Minneapolis, red ghetto of, 21
Mismatch hypothesis, 289–291
Mississippi, Freedmen's Bureau and vagrancy laws, 195

Mobility, sacrifice of ethnicity for, 256–257
Mobility of blacks, 207–209, 218; impaired by culture of poverty, 106–107, 117–119
Mobility of immigrants, 41, 43, 54, 56, 59, 73, 83, 86–87, 117, 119, 206; of Asians, 270–275; of Chinese-Americans, 85–86; of Cubans, 104 n.–105 n.; dysfunctional cultural values as impediment to, 106–107; ethnicity in conflict with, 53, 73, 261; of Irish-Americans, 117, 164, table 165; of Italian-Americans, 99 n., 117, 141; of Japanese-Americans, 84–85, 104 n.; of Jews, 84, 89, 91–93, 99 n., 101–103, 117, 134, 135–138, 139, 147, table 149; of Koreans, 104 n.; religious group comparisons, 147, table 149; role of ethnic cultural values alleged, 79, 80–81, 83, 86–88, 92–93, 99 n., 103, 129–132; societal factors in, 93–103, 104 n.–105 n., 131–132; of West Indians, 104 n., 275–280. See also Ethnic success
Montgomery, Ala., 213
Moquin, Wayne, 24 n.
Moral condemnation of poor, 111, 118
"Morality tale" of ethnic success, 86–87
Morison, Samuel Eliot, 223 and n.
Morris, Charles, 110 and n.
Morris, Robert, 113 n.
Mother-centered households, 107, 125, 126
Movie industry, 91
Moynihan, Daniel Patrick, 49 n., 59 and n., 119–120 and n., 121, 127, 225 n., 259 and n., 275 and n.
Moynihan Report, 120 and n., 122 and n., 124
Myrdal, Gunnar, 50 and n., 174 and n., 209 and n., 265, 287

NAACP, 260
Nader, Ralph, 250 n.
Napoleon Bonaparte, 21
Napoli, Richard, 276 n.
Nation, The (magazine), 228, 243
"Nation of nations," 254
National Advisory Commission on Civic Disorders, 215
Native Americans, 3, 5, 13, 299. See also American Indians
Nativism, 4, 13, 225; decline of, 56; opposition to immigration, 11, 13, 36, 38–39, 78; rationalization of, 78; resurgence in World War I, 236; rhetoric adopted by blacks, 202
Natural selection, 77–78
Naturalization, 12–13; founding fathers' debate on, 11–12
Naturalization Act of 1790 and revisions, 13
Needle trades, 153, 154, 156–157, 161, 164, table 165. See also Garment industry
Negroes. See Blacks
Neighborhood, ethnic and racial fears, 219–220, 258, 259 and n., 260

Nevada, acquisition of, 22
Nevins, Alan, 110 *n.*
New Darwinism, 79–80, 118
New Deal, 205
New England, early population homogeneity, 8
"New ethnicity," 47, 48–51, 60, 73–74
New Mexico, acquisition of, 23
New Republic magazine, 73 *n.*, 106, 201, 202
New York (colony), early population mix, 8
New York City: black-Irish conflicts, 177, 201; black-Jewish relations, 219, 220, 221; crime, 112–115, 116, 210; domestic service statistics, 154, 162–163; Draft Riots, 177; East Side immigrants, 53, 135–136; Forest Hills Jewish neighborhood, 219, 259 *n.;* garment industry, 99–100, 154; German population, 154; International Food Festival, 64; Irish population, 154, 162; Italian immigrants, 160; Jewish population, 89, 90, 113, 114, 225; Jews and crime, 112–115; Jews and education, 134–136 (*see also* City College); Lower East Side, 112–114, 121; prostitution, 114, 116; public school system, 134–135, 136–137; summer youth jobs, 210 and *n.*, 211 *n.;* unemployment, 210, 211 *n.*
New York Daily Tribune, 180
New York Evening Post, 22
New York Jews and the Quest for Community (Goren), 113
New York Morning News, 22 *n.*
New York Times, The, 21, 62, 64, 71 *n.*, 173, 194, 240, 241, 244, 251
New York Times Magazine, The, 20 *n.*, 50 and *n.*, 220 and *n.*
New York University, 223, 227, 234, 237, 244
Newark, N.J., race riots in, 216
Newburyport, Mass., 67
Newman, William, 70 *n.*
Nisbet, Robert, 56 and *n.*, 57, 58–59
"Noble red man," 15
North (region); benefits of black-labor-based cotton to, 27, 29, 30 *n.*, 186, 192; black migration to, 202, 203–205, 218; conditions of blacks in, 121, 177 and *n.*, 210–211; critics of slave labor system, 188–189; job competition of blacks with ethnic whites, 177–181, 201–202, 206, 212, 219; job exclusion of blacks from postbellum industry, 172, 174–176, 181, 190, 199–200, 201; labor needs of, 32, 173–174, 199–200; legacy of racism, 176–181, 185, 190–191, 199; "Negro Question" after Civil War, 176–181, 190; opposition to extension of slavery, 178; role in reconstruction of ex-slave servitude, 185–199
North, Douglass C., 27 and *n.*, 29 and *n.*, 30 *n.*, 32 *n.*, 186 and *n.*

Northeast (region): black slums of, 220; concentration of Jewish population in, 225, 226
Norwegian-Americans, 41, 102, 152
Novak, Daniel A., 195 and *n.*, 196 and *n.*
Novak, Michael, 49 *n.*
Numerus clausus, 251

"Objects culture," Jewish, 61
O'Brien, Robert H., 258 *n.*
O'Dea, Thomas, 138 and *n.*, 139, 148
Odencrantz, Louise C., 157 and *n.*
Office of Economic Opportunity, 216
Ohio, black migration restrictions, 181
Old South and the New, The (Morris), 110
Orfield, Gary, 297 *n.*
Origin of Species, The (Darwin), 77
Ortega y Gasset, José, 58
Oxnam, Robert, 271–272 and *n.*

Painter, Nell, 175 *n.*
Pale, Jews of the, 94–97
Park, Robert, 47 and *n.*, 48 and *n.*, 72 and *n.*
Parks, Rosa, 213
Parochial schools, 54
Patriotism of ethnics, 56
Pennsylvania black migration restrictions, 181; early population mix, 8, 11
Petersen, William, 84 and *n.*, 85, 104 *n.*, 129–130 and *n.*
Pierce, Bessie Louise, 177 *n.*, 181 *n.*
Piore, Michael, 296 *n.*
Piven, Frances Fox, 211 and *n.*, 213 and *n.*
Plantation system, 26, 28, 32, 186; collapse of, 190
Pluralism, 3–4, 169, 253–262. See also Cultural pluralism; Ethnic pluralism; Structural pluralism
Pogroms, anti-black, 177, 212
Polish-Americans, 3, 35, 40, 41, 52, 201; educational level, 102, 140; ethnic backlash, 219; illiteracy rate, 102; intermarriage trends, 68; language loss, 45; money owned by immigrants, 93; skilled worker percentage of immigrants, *table* 98
Polish Jews, 94, 97, 135
Polish Peasant in Poland and America, The (Thomas and Znaniecki), 52
Political motivation for emigration, 35, 161
"Popular culture," Jewish, 61
Population deficit, 6, 10, 13, 32, 40
Population statistics: American Indians, 6, 18, *table* 19; blacks, 174, 176; black employment, 206–208; black South-to-North migration, 203–205; Catholics, 145; convict immigrants, 11; ethnic shares in 1790, 7–8; farm labor, present, 206; foreigners as percentage of labor force, 36; freedmen, 192, 199; immigrant population of Chicago (1910), 47; immigrant population of New York City, 113, 154, 162; immigration, 33, 36, *table* 41, 174, 204; immigration, sex ratios, 161, 162; im-

Population statistics (*cont.*)
migration since 1965, 267–268, *table* 273; Jews, 8, 69, 90, 145, 224, 225; Mexican-Americans, 23; poverty families, 209–210; Protestants, 145; slave labor, 26 and *n.*, 27 *n.*, 28, 176
Portuguese-Americans, 35, 41
Possony, Stefan, 131 *n.*
Poverty, 38–39, 53, 172; allegation of genetic factors in, 78, 79, 118; of blacks vs. whites, statistics, 209–210 and *n.*; blame placed on victims of, 80, 88, 108–109, 110–111, 118, 211; conservative attitudes toward, 108; crime as function of, 115–117; cultural vs. social causation views, 80, 88, 106–109, 117–119, 122–127 (*see also* Culture of poverty); effect on family, 80, 107, 111, 115, 117, 119, 120–122, 124–126; federal aid programs, 109, 217; liberal answers to, 108, 109; moral-defect views of, 111, 118; 19th-century perspective (Social Darwinism), 78–79, 118; as obstacle to education, 118–119, 135–136, 138: social pathologies connected to, 78, 111–112, 117–118, 122; statistics on Jews, 89–90; stereotypes, 107, 108, 110–111; 20th-century perspective (New Darwinism), 79–80, 118; unemployment, 122, 124–127. *See also* Underclass
Powell, James Henry, 254 *n.*
Prejudice, 9, 38, 42, 85, 169; decline of, 55–56, 209; in higher education, 235–236, 238–246, 248–249; of Social Darwinism, 77–79
Present-time orientation, 107, 110, 125; vs. future-time orientation, 144
Princeton University, 231, 234, 238, 243
Prisoners of Poverty (Campbell), 151
"Problems culture," Jewish, 61
Professions: Asians in, 85, 104 *n.*; blacks in, 207, 208; Jews in, 85, 89, 90, 136–137, 221, 252; racial party as goal, 221, 251–252; teaching, 136–137
Prostitution, 114, 116
Protestants, 8 and *n.*, 10, 13, 237; class status compared with Catholics, 144–145; college faculty percentage, *table* 146, 147, *table* 148; college faculty social background, 147, *table* 149; educational status parity with Catholics, 146; elitism, 225–226, 246 (*see also* WASP elite); ethnic intermarriage, 69; mobility patterns, 147, *table* 149; population percentage, 145; protection of neighborhoods and clubs, 257–258, 259, 260; Puritan ethic, 82, 226; religious intermarriage, 70
Public school system, role in assimilation, 54–55
Puerto Ricans, 3, 106, 117
Puzo, Mario, 257 and *n.*

Quest for Community, The (Nisbet), 56

Quillin, Frank U., 181 *n.*

Rabinowitz, Dorothy, 249 *n.*
Race relations cycle (Park), 47–48
Race riots: by blacks, 212, 214–218, 220; by whites, 177, 212
Racial conflict, 172, 201, 202, 206, 211–218
Racial discrimination, 104 *n.*, 119; color ban at Harvard freshman dormitories, 245; ethnic-pluralistic apologias for, 257–260; postbellum, 172, 173–176, 185–200; reverse, 251–252. *See also* Racial segregation; Racism
Racial minorities: affirmative action for, 221, 250–252, 291, 292, 294–295; comparisons with immigrant minorities, 41–43, 50, 117, 119, 121, 209; in competition and conflict with ethnic minorities, 40–41, 50–51, 72–73, 172, 174–176, 177–181, 201–202, 206, 212, 218–221; educational handicaps of, 118–119, 250; ethnic subcultures, 43, 50–51; obstacles to progress, 80, 107–109, 117–127; poverty as source of family instability, 107, 111, 117, 119, 120–122; progress of Japanese, 85; slums of, 107, 111, 117, 121; socio-economic immobility, 41–42, 106–107, 117–119; subculture of poverty, 106–111, 118, 123–124, 127; subsocieties, 66. *See also* Asians; American Indians; Blacks
Racial polarization, 50–51, 72–73, 172
Racial segregation, 255; in employment, 206–207; waning of, 213–214
Racism, 104 *n.*, 109, 119, 120, 171, 175, 202, 211; "cycle" of, 209; of ethnics, 218–221; ideology of, 30–31, 42, 77–79, 209; institutionalized, 288; need for race-specific policies to combat, 293–297, 301; Northern legacy of, 176–181, 185, 190–191, 199; in occupations, 289, 290–291; in postbellum South, 182, 184, 190; sources of underclass, 288–293
Railroad industries, 36, 37, 181, 184
Rainwater, Lee, 120 *n.*
Ramsdell, Charles William, 193 *n.*
Ravage, Marcus, 51 and *n.*
Rebellion in Newark (Hayden), 216
Reconstruction, 190, 199; black servitude, 182, 185–200
Red ghettos, 21
Reform Judaism, 71, 224, 226
Reid, Ira, 275 *n.*
Reid, Whitelaw, 183 *n.*, 198 *n.*
Religion, decline of, 57, 73, 115
Religious intermarriage, 68–69, 70–71, 73
Religious motivation for emigration, 10, 35, 161
Removal Act of 1830, 17
Republican Party, 179, 180, 185
Reverse racism discounted, 251–252
Rhett, Robert, 187 *n.*
Rhu, Jai P., 104 *n.*

Ricketts, Erol R., 281–282 and *n.*, 283
Riesman, David, 249
Ringer, Benjamin, 300 and *n.*
Rischin, Moses, 99 *n.*, 121 *n.*
Rise of David Lavinsky, The (Cahan), 133
Rise of the Unmeltable Ethnics, The (Novak), 49
Rivera, Feliciano, 23 *n*
Road construction, 36
Rochement, Richard de, 64 and *n.*
Rockaway, Robert A., 115 *n.*
Romanians, 35, 219
Roosevelt, Franklin D., 6
Roosevelt, Theodore, 16
Root, Waverley, 64 and *n.*
Roots (Haley), 199
Rose, Peter I., 88 *n.*
Rose, Willie Lee, 189 *n.*
Rosenblum, Gerald, 36 *n.*
Rosenthal, Erich, 89 *n.*
Rubber industry, 36
Rubinow, Israel, 94 and *n.*, 95 *n.*, 97 *n.*, 101 *n.*
Rudolph, Frederick, 229 *n.*, 231 *n.*
Rudwick, Elliott, 212 and *n.*
Rudy, S. Willis, 227 *n.*, 234 *n.*
Russell, Francis, 232–233 and *n.*
Russia: economic role of Jews vs. non-Jews in, 94–95, *table* 96, 97; literacy rates, Jews vs. non-Jews, 101–102
Russian Jewish immigrants, 34, 35, 89 *n.*, 99–100, 113, 138, 226; and education, 101–102, 135, 137, 228, 230; at Harvard, 223; urban background of, 94–97. *See also* Eastern European Jews
Rutgers University, 238

St. Louis, race riots by white, 212
Salmon, Lucy Maynard, 158–159 and *n.*
San Francisco, Chinese suit against school desegregation, 259
Sandberg, Neil C., 50 *n.*
Sanders, Ronald, 226 *n.*
Sawhill, Isabel V., 281–282 and *n.*, 283
Scammon, Richard M., 208 and *n.*
Scandinavian-Americans, 7, 9, 35, 41, 44, 102; domestic servants, 152, 155; and education, 228; money owned by immigrants, 93; skilled worker percentage of immigrants, *table* 98
Schappes, Morris U., 90 and *n.*
Schmidt, Louis, 31
Schmidt, Sarah, 92 *n.*
Scholastic Aptitude Test (SAT), 250 *n.*
Schools: curricula, 55, 136; parochial and language schools, 54; public, in New York City, 134–135, 136–137; public, role in assimilation, 54–55
Schrag, Peter, 49 *n.*
Schurz, Carl, 181 and *n.*
Science magazine, 139 and *n.*
Scientific Monthly, 139 and *n.*
Scots and Scotch-Irish Americans, 7, 8; 19th-to-20th century immigrants, 41;

population estimate for 1790, 7; return trip to Scotland (1977), 62
Second-generation Americans, 44–46, 49, 54, 60, 61; educational mobility, 101; "marginality" experience of, 52; mother-tongue retention, 45; women in domestic service, ethnic comparisons, 164, *table* 165
Selznick, Gertrude Jaeger, 55 *n.*, 220 *n.*
Serbs, 35, 219
"Servant," etymology, 159. *See also* Domestic service
Settlement of America, 6–13
Seward, William, 178 and *n.*
Sex ratios of immigrants, 161–162
Shannon, Fred, 190 *n.*
Sharecropping system, 190–191, 192–200, 204
Sheatsley, Paul B., 209 *n.*
Sheingold, Carl, 70 and *n.*
Shepperson, Wilbur S., 10 *n.*
Sherrard, Thomas D., 111 *n.*
Shtetl, 94, 101, 132
Skilled labor, 35, 38, 206; differences in immigrant groups, 97, *table* 98, 99, 103, 104 *n.*, 139
Sklare, Marshall, 60 and *n.*, 69–70 and *n.*, 92 and *n.*, 93 *n.*, 112 *n.*, 130–131 and *n.*
Skolnick, Jerome, 23 *n.*, 208 *n.*
Slater, Miriam, 132–133 and *n.*
Slave trade, 26 *n.*
Slavery, 25–27, 28, 29–31, 37, 40, 188–189; abolition of, 173, 176, 178–179, 185–186; attempts to enslave Indians, 24; as factor in ethnic pluralism, 5, 40; linkage, via cotton, to industrial development, 29 and *n.*, 30 *n.*, 36, 186; Moynihan's view of lasting damage of, 119, 120–121; Northern opposition to extension of, 178; rationalizations of, 30–31, 77–78, 182, 186; statistics, 26 and *n.*, 27 *n.*, 28, 176
Slavs, 35, 140, 219
Slovaks, 31
Slum landlords, 220
Slums, 107, 220; "of despair," 111, 117; "of hope," 111, 117, 121; of immigrant minorities, 111–117, 121; of racial minorities, 107, 111, 117, 121
Small Business Administration, 105 *n.*
Smith, Abbott, 10 *n.*
Smith, James Morton, 7 *n.*, 16 *n.*
Smith, Peter, 25 *n.*
Social assimilation, 67–68, 72
Social Background of the Italo-American School Child (Covello), 128, 141
Social class. *See* Class position
Social class character of ethnic conflict, 170–171, 220, 221, 230–236, 246, 257–261
Social class theory of educational achievement, 131–132, 135–136, 137–138, 141–145, 147–150
Social Darwinism, 77–79, 80, 118

Social deprivation theories, 118
Social pathologies, 78, 111–112, 117–118, 122
Social pluralism, 65–68
Social policy deficiencies, 108, 109, 119–120, 122–123, 210–211, 216–217
Soler, Jean, 64 *n.*
Soloman, Barbara Miller, 236 *n.*
Soule, George, 99 *n.*
South (region): Black Codes, 195–196; black population of, 174, 199; cotton culture, 27–28, 175–176, 182–186, 189, 198–199, 204; early population heterogeneity, 8; exodus of blacks from, 202, 203–205; farm labor needs, 25–27, 28, 31, 32, 42, 176, 182–185, 188–199, 204–205; immigrant labor not attracted to, 25, 26, 175–176, 182–184; importation of Chinese labor attempted, 184–185; "Negro Question" after Civil War, 182–185, 190–200; plantation system, 26, 28, 32, 186, 190; postbellum economic role of, 186–187; reconstruction of black servitude, 185–200; sharecropping and contract labor system, 190–191, 192–200
South Africa, 170
South Carolina Freedmen's Bureau, 193, 196
Southern Cultivator, 182 and *n.*
Sowell, Thomas, 87 and *n.*, 104 *n.*, 112 and *n.*, 265–266 and *n.*, 268–269 and *n.*, 297 and *n.*
Spanish-Americans, 35, 155
Spear, Allan, 212 and *n.*
Srole, Leo, 67 and *n.*
Stafford, Walter W., 290 and *n.*
Starobin, Robert, 26 *n.*
Steel industry, 36
Steinberg, Stephen, 52 *n.*, 55 *n.*, 131 *n.*, 137 *n.*, 146, 148, 149, 220 *n.*, 226 *n.*, 249 *n.*, 266 *n.*
Steinfeld, Melvin, 22 *n.*
Stivers, Richard, 116 *n.*, 164 *n.*
Stormont, John W., 187 *n.*
Story of the Chinese in America (Sung), 85–86 and *n.*
Story of Yeshiva, The (Klaperman), 82
"Streetcorner men," 124–126
Strodtbeck, Fred L., 143–144 and *n.*
Structural pluralism, 66–68
Sturdivant, Frederick D., 91 *n.*
Subcultures, ethnic, 43, 50–51, *See also* Cultural pluralism; Ethnic communities
Subsocieties, ethnic, 65–68, 72, 73
Success. *See* Ethnic success
Sumner, Charles, 181 and *n.*
Sung, Betty Lee, 85–86 and *n.*, 130 and *n.*, 275 *n.*
Superiority claims, 85; biological, 77–79, 118; cultural, 79, 84–85, 118
Sweatshops, 100, 156
Swedish-Americans, 7, 9, 41, 102; domestic servants, 152; language loss, 45; population estimate for 1790, 7

Swiss-Americans, 7
Switzerland, ethnic conditions in, 170
Syracuse University, 238
Szajkowski, Zosa, 39 *n.*

Tally's Corner (Liebow), 124, 143
Talmudic scholarship, 132–134
Tenant farmers, 190, 200, 205. *See also* Sharecropping system
Tennessee Republic League, 202
Texas, 181, 189; acquisition of, 23; migration of blacks to, 174, 199
Textile industry, 29, 36, 152, 156, 157, 186; British Isles, 28, 34; women immigrants in, 153, 156–157
Third-generation Americans, 44–46, 49, 60; loss of mother tongue, 45–46
Thistlethwaite, Frank, 29 *n.*
Thomas, Brinley, 173–174 and *n.*
Thomas, W. I., 52 and *n.*
Three Centuries of Harvard (Morison), 223
Tilly, Louise A., 161 *n.*
Tobier, Emanuel, 268 *n.*
Tocqueville, Alexis de, 185 and *n.*
Tomasi, Lydio F., 151 *n.*
Tourgée, Albion Winegar, 183 *n.*
Trade. *See* Foreign trade; Internal trade
Trail of Tears, 17
Travelers' Aid Society for Girls and Women, 162
Trow, Martin, 145 *n.*
Tufts University, 236
Turner, Edward Raymond, 181 *n.*
Tuttle, William, Jr., 212 *n.*

Uhlenberg, Peter, 174 *n.*
Ulin, Richard Otis, 142–143 and *n.*
Underclass, 280–297; critique of concept, 280–284; class interpretation, 286–288; cultural interpretation, 284–286; racist sources, 288–293; race-specific public policy, 293–297; size, 282, 283 *n. See also* Blacks
Unemployment, 122, 124–127, 205, 261; black teenagers, 210–211
Unions, 157; effects of cheap immigrant labor on, 38–39
Unitarians, 139
United Hebrew Charities of New York, 121
University of California at Davis Medical School, 251
University of Chicago, 47, 52
University of Pennsylvania, 243
University of Vermont, 235
University of Virginia, 235
Unskilled labor, 35, 38, 212; black, 206, 207; immigrant, 35–36, 97–98, 141, 177, 206
Urban crisis, 216–217, 261
U.S. Congress, eligibility of naturalized citizens for, 12–13
U.S. Department of Housing and Urbran Development, 216
U.S. Department of Justice, 216
U.S. Supreme Court: and affirmative action, 251, 252; *Brown* v. *Board of Education*, 213; Indian treaties decisions of

1823 and 1831, 17; San Francisco school desegregation case, 259
Usher, John Palmer, 181
Utah, acquisition of, 23

Valentine, Charles, 107 *n.*
Value systems. *See* Cultural values
Veblen, Thorstein, 231 and *n.*, 232
Veysey, Lawrence R., 230 *n.*
Vida, La (Lewis), 106
Violence as Protest (Fogelson), 215
Viviano, Marian, 21 *n.*
Vocational education, 136, 229
Vogel, Ezra, 272 and *n.*
Vote, black, 213, 214

Wade, Richard, 27 *n.*
Wages, 38, 39 and *n.*, 156–157; black, 211; garment industry, 100; Mexican, 23; Southern contract farm labor, 192, 197
Waitresses, 154, 158
Waldinger, Roger, 291 *n.*, 296 *n.*
Walsh, Annmarie Hauck, 111 *n.*
War of 1812, 16
War of Independence, 9, 10
War-on-poverty programs, 109, 217
Ware, Nathaniel E., 25 *n.*
Warner, W. Lloyd, 67 and *n.*
Washburn, Wilcomb E., 14 and *n.*, 15 *n.*, 16 *n.*, 17 *n.*
Washington, Booker T., 88 and *n.*
Washington, George, 12
WASP elite, 4, 225–226, 257–258, 260; and "Jewish Problem" at Harvard, 172, 222, 237–246, 252
Wattenberg, Ben J., 208 and *n.*
Weaver, Robert, 218
Webster, Laura Josephine, 194 *n.*
Weinberg, Albert Katz, 22 *n.*
Weinfeld, Morton, 69 *n.*
Weiss, Richard, 264
Welfare programs, 108, 217; for freedmen, 194
Wellman, David, 109 and *n.*
Wesley, Charles W., 176 *n.*, 180 *n.*
West (region): black migration to, 174, 199, 205; economic development of, 29, 32; expansion and "manifest destiny," 21; labor needs of, 23, 32, 174, 183, 184, 199; white-Indian conflict, 17–18
West Indian immigrants, 104 *n.*, 276–277, 296; compared with African Americans, 268–269, 278–279; myth of success, 275–280; New York City and London compared, 277; selective migration, 276, 277
West Indies, 189
Weyl, Nathaniel, 131 *n.*
White ethnics, 3, 41; comparisons with racial minorities, 41–43, 50, 117,

119, 121, 209; in competition or conflict with racial minorities, 40–41, 50–51, 72–73, 172, 218–221; vs. nonwhites, in labor market, 40–41, 172, 173–176, 177–181, 182–184, 200, 201–202, 206, 212, 219; not attracted to South as laborers, 25, 26, 175–176, 182–184; race riots of, 177, 212; and racism, 177, 218–221
White Russia, Jews of, 94, 97
Whitney, Eli, 28
Willcox, Walter F., 163 *n.*
Williams, Eric, 25 and *n.*
Williamson, Harold Francis, 189 *n.*
Williamson, Joel, 193 *n.*, 195 *n.*, 196 *n.*
Wilson, William Julius, 219 and *n.*, 286–287 and *n.*, 288, 289 and *n.*, 291–292 and *n.*, 293, 295
Winchester, Mass., 142–143
Winning of the West, The (Roosevelt), 16
Witty, Paul A., 139 *n.*
Wolfe, Ann G., 90 *n.*
Women, black, 155, 206, 207–208
Women immigrants: in domestic service, 152–156, 157–164, *table* 165, 166; Irish, 160, 161–164, *table* 165, 166; Italian, 154–155, 160–161, 162, 163, 164, *table* 165; Jewish, 160, 161, 162, 163, 164, *table* 165; in needle trades, 153, 154, 156–157, 161, 164, *table* 165
Wong, Morrison G., 273
Woodward, C. Vann, 213 *n.*
Wool industry, 29, 34
Woolfolk, George Ruble, 187 *n.*
World of Our Fathers (Howe), 112, 133
World War I: cutoff of immigration and resulting black progress, 42, 175, 202, 203, 204; resurgence of nativism during, 236, 254
World War II: patriotism of ethnic minorities proven, 56; progress of black labor, 205, 207

Xenophobia, 225; colonial period, 9, 11–12; nativist labor backlash, 38–39. *See also* Nativism.

Yale University, 230, 231, 233, 234, 243
Yancy, William J., 120 *n.*
Yankee ancestry, 225
Yans-McLaughlin, Virginia, 155 and *n.*
Yekl (Cahan), 52
Yiddish language, 45
Yugoslavs, 41. *See also* Croats; Serbs

Zangwill, Israel, 44
Zborowski, Marc, 93 and *n.*, 101 and *n.*
Zeichner, Oscar, 184 *n.*, 185 *n.*, 193 *n.*, 196 *n.*
Znaniecki, Florian, 52 and *n.*

STEPHEN STEINBERG teaches in the Department of Urban Studies at Queens College and the Ph.D. Program in Sociology at the Graduate Center, City University of New York. He is the author of *The Academic Melting Pot*, and co-author of *The Tenacity of Prejudice* and *Writing and Thinking in the Social Sciences*. In addition to his contributions to scholarly journals, he has published articles in *Commentary*, *Commonweal*, *Harper's*, and *The Nation*. Educated at Brown and Berkeley, Steinberg lives in Manhattan with his wife and two children.